DRINKING

Funds for this Book were Donated by:

Chapter 15 North Bay Counties
INTERNATIONAL FOOTPRINT ASSOCIATION

I.F.A. is a social association established
in 1929 to promote respect, fellowship and
mutual understanding between law enforcement officers and civilians.

DRINKING

Alcohol in American Society—Issues and Current Research

Editors:

John A. Ewing, M.D.

Beatrice A. Rouse, M.Ed.

nh

Nelson-Hall
Chicago

Library of Congress Cataloging in Publication Data

Main entry under title:

Drinking.

Includes index.
1. Liquor problem—United States—Addresses, essays, lectures. 2. Alcoholism and employment—Addresses, essays, lectures. I. Ewing, John A. II. Rouse, Beatrice A.

| HV5292.D75 | 362.2'92'0973 | 76-47522 |

ISBN 0-88229-129-7 (Cloth)
ISBN 0-88229-569-1 (Paper)

Manufactured in the United States of America.

To Hargrove "Skipper" Bowles and Samuel H. Johnson,
two dedicated and concerned public citizens and legislators, without
whose farsightedness, help, and support the UNC Center for Alcohol
Studies would not have been established.

Contents

Preface   ix

Part I: Introduction and History
Chapter 1
Drinks, Drinkers, and Drinking   5
John A. Ewing, M.D.
Beatrice A. Rouse, M.Ed.

Chapter 2
5,000 Years of Drinking   31
Archer Tongue

Chapter 3
200 Years of Drinking in the United States:
Evolution of the Disease Concept   39
Richard W. Howland, A.B.
Joe W. Howland, Ph.D., M.D.

Part II: The Complications of Drinking
Chapter 4
Medical Complications of Excessive Drinking   63
Harold J. Fallon, M.D.
Henry R. Lesesne, M.D.

Chapter 5
The Medical Examiner Looks at Drinking   71
Page Hudson, M.D.

Chapter 6
Social and Psychiatric Considerations of Drinking   93
John A. Ewing, M.D.

Chapter 7
Drinking and Highway Safety   117
Patricia F. Waller, Ph.D.

Chapter 8
How Risky Is Drinking?   137
John A. Ewing, M.D.

Part III: Psychosocial Aspects of Drinking
Chapter 9
Formal and Informal Social Controls over Drinking   145
Ira H. Cisin, Ph.D.

Chapter 10
Prohibition Norms and Teenage Drinking   159
Gerald Globetti, Ph.D.

Chapter 11
College Drinking and Other Drug Use   171
Beatrice A. Rouse, M.Ed.
John A. Ewing, M.D.
Chapter 12
Does Your Moderate Drinking Indicate
Psychological Dependence on Alcohol?   203
Kenneth C. Mills, Ph.D.
Part IV: Social Policy and Drinking
Chapter 13
Relationship of State Law to Per Capita Drinking   219
Ben F. Loeb, Jr., J.D.
Chapter 14
Government Control Measures
to Prevent Hazardous Drinking   239
Robert Popham, M.A.
Wolfgang Schmidt, D.JUR.
Jan de Lint, M.A.
Chapter 15
Evaluating the Effect of Drinking Laws on Drinking   267
Robin Room, M.A.
Chapter 16
Drinking Laws in the Commonwealth of Virginia   291
Wayne W. Womer, D.D.
Chapter 17
Legal Controls of Drinking,
Public Drunkenness, and Alcoholism Treatment   307
Frank Grad, LL.B.
Part V: Summing Up
Chapter 18
An Overview of Drinking Behaviors and Social Policies   339
Beatrice A. Rouse, M.Ed.
John A. Ewing, M.D.
Notes   383
Index   433

Preface

BEVERAGE ALCOHOL PLAYS an important part in the lives and deaths of drinkers and nondrinkers alike in America today. Recognizing this fact, scientists have examined the pharmacological, psychological, sociocultural, and medical consequences of its use and abuse. Educators and clergy have striven to understand alcohol's role in society and to try to prepare the young to deal with it appropriately. Public officials have tried to discharge effectively their responsibilities regarding drinkers as well as alcoholics. Furthermore, both drinkers and nondrinkers have tried to evaluate and influence the drinking behavior of those around them.

These are not easy tasks. Effective action in these matters requires sound judgment and compassion based on accurate, appropriate, and timely information. Such information, even when available, is often not utilized because of the vast amount of work needed to select the relevant data, the wide dispersion of information sources, and the limited time and resources of those needing accurate facts for effective action.

Although much research effort has been expended recently on biomedical, psychosocial, and legal aspects of alcohol, the last book reviewing studies of drinking from a sociocultural perspective was published a decade ago. Since that time, not only have the social and economic conditions affecting drinking attitudes and practices changed but the science of alcohol studies has also changed.

Therefore, this book was written to provide a current review as well as a handy resource for those interested in understanding the significance of alcohol use in American society and the relationship of such drinking to the problems of intoxication and alcoholism. It includes not only a synthesis of previous relevant studies but also reports of new research.

The student and researcher new to alcohol studies will find this book provides a quick survey of the field, helps identify issues for further research, and suggests extensive references for more detailed examination.

The social scientist, health professional, student, educator, public official, and layman are all interested in the subject of drinking in general; in this book, however, they are also urged to examine the use of alcohol in their own personal lives.

A variety of viewpoints has been offered in order to stimulate the readers' thinking regarding the role of alcohol in our society and to help them clarify their attitudes toward their own drinking. Alcohol use and alcoholism are discussed by nineteen contributors from the fields of alcohol research, law, medicine, and highway safety as well as from the social sciences. While other countries are discussed, the focus is on drinking in the United States.

There is an introduction to the basic metabolic processes of alcohol in chapter 1, but no attempt has been made to delve deeply into the biochemical and biological effects. Current scientific references on these topics, however, are provided in chapter 18 for the interested reader. Indeed, no attempt has been made to cover the entire subject of drinking in encyclopedic detail. Those readers interested in such detail are encouraged to consult the references provided with each chapter.

Part I presents a history of alcoholic beverages, of social controls, and of the disease concept of alcoholism. It begins with a description of the various processes surrounding the act of drinking. Among these are the preparation, distribution, and acquisition of beverage alcohol. The properties of various alcoholic beverages are also discussed.

While Part I presents drinking in a historical context, Part II deals with the medical, social, psychiatric, and highway safety problems seen today to be associated with drinking. It not only examines the role of alcohol in sickness, injury, and death, but ends by considering the important question: "Is even moderate drinking risky?"

The personal and sociocultural aspects of alcohol use among teenagers, college students, and the general adult population are discussed in Part III. The association between drinking and illegal drug use is also considered. Further, a study is described of teenage drinking in a geographic area where drinking is socially disapproved and legally unavailable.

Part IV examines the past, present, and future attempts to control alcohol use and abuse as well as the effects of laws on drinking behavior. Here, a law expert also discusses the legal aspects of treatment for alcoholism.

Finally, Part V presents an overview of drinking behaviors and social policies. A conceptual model is offered indicating the major influences and consequences of drinking behavior. In addition, the use of alcoholic beverages is compared with nonalcoholic beverages and data on economic factors related to alcohol consumption are also examined.

We wish to thank our contributors for patiently submitting and resubmitting material and Elizabeth Hansen who, on behalf of the publisher, copy edited and provided much other useful assistance. We are also grateful to Elaine Woody, administrative secretary to the Center for Alcohol Studies, who, as usual, has efficiently and cheerfully coped with vast quantities of manuscript, and to Julia Bundy Trantham who helped type the final version for the printer.

Finally, since we anticipate future editions, we welcome criticisms and suggestions from our readers.

To your good health!

PART I

Introduction
and
History

THE CHAPTERS IN this section of the book provide a general introduction to, and a historical overview of, the subject of drinking.

The first chapter is by the editors of the book. John A. Ewing, M. D., is a medical graduate of the University of Edinburgh, Scotland, and holds the Diploma in Psychological Medicine from the University of London. He completed his psychiatric training in England before coming to the United States in 1951 where he first served as psychiatrist to the North Carolina Alcoholism Rehabilitation Center at Butner, North Carolina. At that time he did some part-time teaching. In 1954 he joined the University of North Carolina faculty on a full-time basis becoming Professor of Psychiatry in 1963. He served as chairman of the Department of Psychiatry for seven years before giving up this position in order to return to full-time teaching and research. Coincidental with this move was the establishment of the Center for Alcohol Studies at the University of North Carolina at Chapel Hill. This organization which conducts psychosocial and biomedical research studies on alcohol and alcoholism is in its sixth year of operation. Dr. Ewing is director of the center. Since completing psychiatric training in 1950, he has published over

1

one hundred scientific papers in medical and psychiatric journals. The majority of these are clinical and research reports dealing with alcohol and other drugs.

Beatrice A. Rouse is a Research Associate in the North Carolina Center for Alcohol Studies with a joint appointment in the Department of Psychiatry at the University of North Carolina. She graduated from the University of Florida where she received a M.Ed. degree in the philosophical foundations of education. She also received advanced training at the Rutgers School of Alcohol Studies, the Netherlands Universities Foundation for International Cooperation, and the Institute for Social Research at the University of Michigan. Currently, Ms. Rouse is in the Ph.D. program in Epidemiology and Social Psychology at Chapel Hill. Her previous publications in the area of alcohol and drugs have related to alcohol, marijuana, and other drug use among college students; alcohol sensitivity and ethnic background; synergistic effects of alcohol with other drugs on simulated driving behavior; and the effects of drinking practices on health.

The author of chapter 2, Archer Tongue, is the Director of the International Council on Alcoholism and Drug Dependence. With his headquarters in Lausanne, Switzerland, he has broad and intimate knowledge of his subject matter on a worldwide basis. As a scholar of alcohol problems, he is uniquely qualified to write his contribution.

The joint authors of chapter 3 are a father and son team. Dr. Howland's interest in alcohol dates back many years. His initial work was in the 1930s with Dr. George H. Whipple at Rochester, New York, studying the pathological effects of experimental liver injury in the dog. Next he studied the protective effects of alcohol on ionizing radiation (atomic bomb) injury. In cooperation with Dr. H. Bonner, he studied the effects of alcoholism on the endocrine system with particular attention to the thyroidal changes. His current interests are in the effects of alcohol on the aging and cardiovascular changes which occur, as well as possible neuroendocrine relationships and alteration in fat metabolism. Dr. Howland is Professor of Radiation Biology and Biophysics (retired), University of Rochester School of Medicine and Dentistry; and Instructor in Medicine (retired). He has recently retired as Physician at the Alcohol Rehabilitation

Center, North Carolina Department of Mental Health, at Butner, North Carolina. He is currently Clinical Assistant Professor of Medicine at the University of North Carolina School of Medicine.

Richard Howland's interest in alcoholism was stimulated by conversations with his father. As a history major, he found the story of alcoholism fascinating, and he elected to write his honor's thesis on this subject. He is currently a student at Wake Forest University Law School.

CHAPTER 1

Drinks, Drinkers, and Drinking

John A. Ewing, M.D.
Beatrice A. Rouse, M. Ed.

MAN HAS BEEN drinking for thousands of years. Obviously he likes the effect and has learned to accept any discomforts such as the hangover. In this chapter we will consider a broad mixture of historical, sociological, legal, medical, and cultural aspects of drinking.

The United States has no uniform drinking style or standard. American drinking patterns reflect a conglomeration of attitudes and customs brought to this continent by successive waves of immigrants from different geographic and ethnic backgrounds. These include a blend of Scotch-Irish drinkers of distilled spirits, German drinkers of beer, and French and Italian drinkers of wine. In some cases these influences have undergone change culminating in indigenous American drinking inventions such as the cocktail, the Mickey Finn, and brown-bagging.[1]

The lack of uniformity in American drinking practices and indeed the conflicting attitudes toward alcohol use may be attributed to this variety of cultural and historical influences as well as to the present social impact of alcoholic beverages. While "drinking" may specifically refer to the personal con-

6 PART I: INTRODUCTION AND HISTORY

duct associated with alcohol consumption, we will first survey drinking behavior in a broader scope—the making, acquisition, and distribution of alcoholic beverages.

Man Learns to Brew and Distill Alcohol

Man discovered that certain substances, such as malted grains or fruit juices, could be transformed into fermented potions before history began to be recorded. Certainly the effect of drinking these potions must have filled him with awe and wonderment. Probably he ascribed magical qualities to this liquid in much the same way as the American Indians did when first introduced to the white man's liquors. What must have started as an accidental discovery gradually became the art of brewing. Clay tablets from about 6000 B.C. discovered in the Nile Valley describe the brewing of barley and water. The fermenting of grape juice to make wine was known in Ancient Persia 3000 years B.C. and was introduced from there into Egypt soon after that time. The Bible, particularly the Old Testament, is a rich source of references to alcoholic beverages and their use and abuse. Chapter 2 covers this topic in more detail.

Although today's chemist can synthesize alcohol the beverage alcohol used by man over the millenia has been provided generously by nature. In actual fact there are many alcohols but the one which man drinks and on which this book is focused is ethyl alcohol also known as ethanol. Throughout the book we will use the terms "alcohol," "ethyl alcohol," and "ethanol" interchangeably.

Man's partner in the enterprise to produce alcoholic beverages is a simple, microscopic single-celled plant, yeast. Yeast has been around since soon after life began on earth; it must have antedated man by hundreds of millions of years. Yeasts have the property of feeding on starches and sugars and, given the right circumstances of temperature, moisture and nourishment, they multiply rapidly and their enzymes use up the sugar, a phenomenon known as fermentation. By-products from the life cycle of the yeast are ethanol and carbon dioxide. Thus, when a baker makes bread, he uses yeast to cause the dough to rise by creating millions of tiny bubbles of carbon dioxide. During the baking process the small amounts of alcohol are evaporated and the yeast is killed.

Man learned how to use yeast long before he knew anything of its biological properties, particularly that the essential individual organisms are too small for him to see with the naked eye. Not until 1837 did Theodor Schwann demonstrate that yeasts are living plants that multiply by budding and that act on sugars. Indeed, scientific brewing and wine making really only began after Louis Pasteur (1822-1895) demonstrated the microscopic nature of various organisms which could both make and destroy wine. Pasteur, while living in the town of Arbois, devoted one of his researches to understanding why, sometimes, wine turned to vinegar. Until he demonstrated that this was due to a contaminating organism growing in the wine (and living on the alcohol in the wine), there was a popular belief that life could arise spontaneously. Scientists before Pasteur were aware that a living process was involved in making both alcohol and vinegar, and since they did not know that these living cells were so minute as to float invisibly in the air, they sometimes speculated that life could arise de novo.

Pasteur demonstrated that these organisms could be destroyed by heat, that they did indeed float through the air and that wine, previously "pasteurized," could remain fresh and uncontaminated indefinitely if stored in a vessel with a narrow neck pointed downward so that no airborne organisms could float in on top of the wine.

An important offshoot of this work was the realization by Joseph Lister (1827-1912) that infection of open wounds might be similarly caused by something carried invisibly in the air. He concluded correctly that putrefaction of wine and flesh are similar processes, and he devised a plan of destroying the microorganisms by carbolic acid. Lister first used antisepsis in surgery in 1865, and he repeatedly acknowledged his debt to Pasteur's wine research.[2]

Before this scientific information was acquired, men had discovered that certain yeasts are good for certain purposes. For example, yeasts used in brewing beer or fermenting grapes and producing high alcohol content and low residual taste of the yeast itself were jealously cultured and saved for subsequent batches. Even today, the home brewer who purchases some baker's yeast in the grocery store and tries to manufacture beer or wine with this will be disappointed in the yeasty taste of the final product. What he needs, of course, is a special yeast available in home wine-making supply stores. This yeast represents a pure culture of an organism specially selected to do the best possible job and its antecedents go back hundreds of thousands of generations.

Long before man was on the scene, yeasts were busy fermenting and producing alcohol and carbon dioxide any time that nature happened to provide the appropriate combination of yeast cells, sugars, moisture, and warmth. Man merely discovered the process and, as in many other instances, adapted it for his own use. The two major approaches used to produce beverage alcohol involve starting with grains or with the juices of various fruits. In both instances there has to be an adequate supply over and above the immediate needs for food and survival. Barley which is to be brewed is permitted to germinate during which process certain enzymes change the stored starch into a form easily fermented by yeasts. Then the sprouting grain is killed by heat and the desired sugars are extracted into water with the product at this point being called brewer's wort. Other cereals may be added such as corn, wheat, rye, or rice. In addition, man has learned that he can add sugar from other sources to produce a higher final alcohol content.

Generally speaking, a 3 to 5 percent alcohol content is considered about right in beers and ales. The alcoholic content of beers vary from country to country. For example, Australian beer is much stronger than American, as many GIs found out during World War II. Recently in Canada some brewers introduced a strong beer with a 10 percent alcohol content, and Americans, used to weaker American beer, are in for a surprise if they drink that without foreknowledge. Alcohol content of beverages and taxation levels of various beverages are discussed later. However, since most beer drinkers enjoy beer for its thirst quenching qualities, its hop flavor, and its mild alcohol content, those brewers who produce an artificially "strengthened" product are doing a disservice to the social drinker.

The juices of various fruits can contain considerable quantities of sugar, and from them man has created many other varieties of alcoholic beverages. A lot depends on where he lives and what is available. Apples make cider, pears make perry, honey makes mead, and grapes make wine. Although we usually use the term "wine" exclusively for the product made from grape juice, it is possible, as most people know, to make strawberry "wine" or rice or dandelion "wine" and even the juice of a cactus can be fermented into an intoxicating brew known as pulque.

Wine

There are many different types of beers, but wine has the greatest variety. Nature supplies many different types of grapes with subtle differences in flavor. Thus there are thousands of wines. The growing of grapes today and their transformation into wine is said to give employment to at least 35 million people throughout the world.[3]

Grape seeds have been found in prehistoric caves, but whether or not prehistoric man knew how to make wine is not known. Wine making was practiced by the early Egyptians and the Persians. The discovery must have been accidental. One legend says that a king of Persia who was fond of grapes stored some away in a great jar which he had marked "Poison." Some time later one of the neglected beauties of his harem, tired of life, tried to poison herself from that very jar. The drink was so delicious and its effect so rewarding that she took some to the king who, after drinking it, accepted the lady back into favor and ordered that thereafter his grapes should be encouraged to ferment.[4]

Yeast cells that will ferment the grape sugar are found on the bloom of the grape skin itself, and thus simply crushing the grapes will begin the fermentation process. However, there is always the danger that some rogue yeasts are also present that will give unpleasant tastes. Therefore, today's scientific wine maker inhibits the growth of the wild yeasts with sulfur and relies on his own pure culture which he preserves from year to year. This yeast has been acclimatized to the presence of sulfur and is thus able to grow vigorously and establish precedence.

The juice even of most black grapes is not colored, and red wine is made by leaving the skins in the vat during fermentation. As the alcohol is formed, it dissolves the coloring pigments and the wine becomes pink if the skins are removed early or red if the skins are left in longer. Thus we have three basic types of wine—white, pink (or rose), and red. These are dry (unsweetened) if all the sugar has been fermented or sweet if the fermentation process was artificially stoppped or if there was more sugar present than the yeast could succeed in turning into alcohol. A vat of fermenting wine hisses or hums like a hive of bees as large quantities of carbon dioxide bubbles come to the surface. This heavy gas can be collected and used to put fizz into soft drinks or even pumped back into certain artificially carbonated wines.

Most wines are still (noncarbonated) since the carbon dioxide has been allowed to escape but in the case of some wines, the best known of which is Champagne, a secondary fermentation is allowed to go on in the bottle creating the well known bubbly effect. Bottle fermentation requires an extra strong bottle, a wired cork, and a lengthy process whereby the exhausted yeast is gradually brought to the neck of the bottle, frozen, and disgorged. Although some sparkling wines are still produced in this way, some vintners have resorted to faster and cheaper methods which involve putting the carbon dioxide back under pressure at the time of bottling.

Distilling

Although the distillation of sea water was known to Aristotle, it is believed that the distillation of alcohol was discovered by Arabs in the early Middle Ages, about the tenth century A.D.[5] It may have been known in China before that time. The term "alcohol" is derived from the Arabic words for "finely divided spirit." In the process of distillation the vapors arising from the heated brew are invisible until condensation occurs and the reconstitution of a liquid is apparent. The ancient alchemists must have been filled with wonder as this process occurred. Their assumption that transfer depended upon "fine division" was a reasonable one. So, today, when we drink spirits we are indulging ourselves with something that appeared out of thin air, something magical or spiritual.

Alcohol boils at a lower temperature than water; therefore, when a wine or a brew is heated the alcohol vaporizes and can be condensed in increasing concentration. Before distillation, all alcoholic beverages must have had a strength of no more than about 14 percent alcohol since the yeasts which are instrumental in converting sugars to alcohol do not survive in much higher concentration. Distillation, of course, enables a much stronger product to be prepared, thus promising more inebriation for less volume. Whether distillation was commercialized primarily as an economic maneuver or as a guarantee to more rapid drunkenness is now a moot point. Apparently the medieval English taste for French claret (Bordeaux wine) led to much trade (as well as warfare) across the English Channel so that inevitably a tax was levied on the casks being imported into England. The idea of concentrating the wine and then reconstituting it at its original strength after transportation was admirable. However, people began to develop a taste for the distilled wine which came to be known as brandy. Adding brandy to other types of wine to fortify them was a later step taken probably in the early eighteenth century.

Whiskey Is Discovered

Meanwhile, in those countries not blessed with a climate suitable for viticulture, the distillation process was applied to ale rather than to wine. This, of course, marked the discovery of whiskey. (If we are to be purists, we must follow Alexis Lichine by insisting that "whisky" is the correct spelling for the substance in Canada, England, and Scotland, and "whiskey" refers to the beverage in the United States and Ireland. Since this is an American book we will use "whiskey" generically except when discussing Scotch.)

The Scotch whisky industry as we know it today had its origins in the farm crofts and lonely cottages throughout the Scottish Islands in the fifteenth century or earlier. The discovery that any kitchen could be the manufacturing place of this fiery liquid with its promise of conviviality and its illusion of warmth must have done much to lighten the dreary, long, and cold nights of the Scottish winter. For centuries the production and consumption of this liquid was largely confined to the Highlands and the Gaelic-speaking highlanders who thus made a contribution to our language. The word "whisky" is derived, we are told, from the Gaelic words *uisge beatha*, "water of life."[6] Whether the Scots independently discovered distilling or imported the art from Ireland or from other places is unknown. It is said that distillation of spirits from fermented grain mash was well established in Ireland by the twelfth century. That Irish whiskey, however, was made from a mash of unmalted barley and other grains; the distinct difference of the Scottish whisky comes from the fact that it is distilled from malted barley only. Some indefinable quality about the Scottish water and the peat used in drying the malt creates a final product which has not been successfully replicated in any other part of the world.

The Scottish highlander's belief that he had the right to make his own whisky for drinking, selling, or bartering has important significance even today in relation to the antigovernmental attitudes still to be found in the United States, notably in the Appalachian region, where moonshining still goes on. Even after the major immigrations of Scottish people to the United States in the eighteenth century it is said that little of the Scotch whisky being produced in Scotland was under legal government supervision until 1823 when the duty was lowered significantly. By the latter half of that century, illegal manufacture was rare in Scotland and this still seems to be true today. Needless to say, successive governments have reinstated the duty time and again, so that a bottle of Scotch now costs more in Scotland than in parts of North America.

Moonshining and Bootlegging

Meanwhile in the United States the whiskey rebellion in Pennsylvania in 1794 led to a movement West. Some distillers settled in and around Bourbon County, Kentucky. Today the name "bourbon whiskey" is applied to any spirits which are distilled from a fermented mash of grain containing at least 51 percent of corn.[7] The aging process, which both colors and softens the final product, takes place in new, charred oak barrels.

Corn whiskey is often not aged to any extent. It is raw and colorless. This is the familiar "white lightning" which is said to be the preferred drink of certain Americans, particularly in the rural South. Even though this is now available legally in many areas, its illegal manufacture continues at an unknown volume. Knowledgeable experts estimate that even today between 10 and 20 percent of all whiskey consumed is illegally produced.[8] The number of illegal stills and gallons of mash seized are shown in Table 1-1.

A major incentive for moonshining is the opportunity to make a profit by not paying the customs and excise taxes. This raises an issue which will come up in future sections of this book, namely the matter of trade offs. If government increases taxes substantially, at what point will the public begin to rebel to the point of encouraging the bootlegger? The corollary is presumably true. There must be some lower point

Table 1-1
Seizures of Illegal Liquor in U. S. 1965-1974

Date	Stills (Number)	Mash (Wine gallons)
1965	7,432	3,637,881
1970	5,228	1,956,170
1973	2,589	1,121,537
1974	1,813	684,666

(U. S. Treasury Department, Internal Revenue Service, Alcohol Tobacco Summary Statistics, Fiscal Year 1965, Publication 67 (1965): p. 77; Fiscal Year 1970, p. 74; Fiscal Year 1973, p. 65; Fiscal Year 1974, p. 65.)

at which taxes, if reduced, would eliminate the incentive for bootlegging operations.

Obviously the matter is not simple since other factors, such as community respect for government and laws, must play a significant role. For example, we are told that a drastic twelve-fold price increase in Denmark for akvavit significantly changed that country's drinking patterns toward a preference for beer.[9] We have seen no reports which indicate an increase in illegal distilling in Denmark during the same period of time. Does this represent the greater scrutiny of citizens which is possible in a small country, or does it tell us something about the Danish sense of government as "we" rather than "they"? The vast forests covering the Appalachian region of the United States must contribute to making moonshining an operation more easily hidden from the revenuers. However, it is interesting to speculate how much of the attitudes toward the law enforcement agents are remnants of attitudes imported by the Scotch-Irish into the United States during the last 300 years. Both groups came from countries which suffered oppression and saw government forces as representing "these outsiders" rather than "our representatives."

Beverage Alcohol

Absolutely pure alcohol is a clear, colorless liquid with a faint characteristic smell. Nature always provides alcohol in liquid form; hence man drinks it rather than chews it or smokes it. Man has been drinking alcohol for so long that the verb "to drink" in the English language, unless otherwise qualified, means to drink alcoholic beverages. The variety of alcoholic beverage is tremendous. There are beers brewed from cereals, wines fermented from grapes and various strong spirits distilled from different substances. Whiskeys are distilled from a weaker fermentation of grains, brandy from grapes, vodka from potatoes, rum from sugar cane, and so on. Finally, there are the liqueurs which consist of various alcoholic preparations flavored with a variety of fruits, sweeteners, or bitters. From this basic stock, mankind has been having a love affair with drinks for thousands of years although, as indicated, the spirits are a relative newcomer. Most people restrict their choice of drinks to just a few varieties of beers, a handful of spirits, some dozens of wines plus a few liqueurs. In fact, however, there is an almost limitless choice when one considers the thousands of varieties of beers and wines supplied by nature and the ingenuity of man in devising ways of mixing and concocting. For the rest of this book, however, we will focus purely on drinking as a phenomenon without much reference to the types of beverage chosen.

Alcoholic beverages also differ in their strength or relative percentage of alcohol content. The beers generally tend to be around 3 to 5 percent although stronger ones are easily made. Many people detect 10 percent alcohol as slightly sweet and prefer a weaker beer with a more traditional bitter flavor. Most of the table wines drunk with meals are in the 10 to 14 percent category and the fortified wines which have had brandy added are usually around 20 percent. Whiskeys are generally in the 40 to 50 percent category and here the term "proof" is commonly used. Long before man was able to analyze alcoholic drinks and determine the exact contents, he had devised a method of determining how much alcohol was present. Spirits, such as whiskey, consist essentially of a mixture of water and alcohol (although there are many other substances known as congeners present in relatively small amounts). It was found that gunpowder dampened with a strong whiskey would burn whereas it would not do so with a weaker one which contained more water. The term "proof," then, was applied to a spirit strength which just permitted gunpowder to burn. Other spirits were labeled as overproof or underproof. Today's British definition of. proof is slightly different from that used in the United States but the latter, fortunately, as now used indicates precisely what the alcoholic content is. You simply take the given proof and divide by two and you have the percentage of alcohol. Thus 86-proof whiskey contains 43 percent of alcohol. This straight whiskey is only slightly more than twice as strong as the fortified sherry which many a housewife gulps down liberally assuming that "after all it's only a wine." When whiskey is mixed with water and ice, the final drink is usually weaker than sherry.

Alcoholic beverages are at once a food, a drug and a poison.

Alcohol as a Food

Making whiskey can be seen as a way of concentrating surplus grain and reducing it to a less bulky form which is easily stored and transported and rendering it safe from plundering and contamination by rodents. The alcohol has to be burned up in the body, and in the process it supplies calories. For every gram (1/30th ounce) of alcohol swallowed the drinker acquires seven calories to be added to his total daily

Table 1-2
Approximate Caloric Value
for Alcohol in Beverages*

Beverage	Amount	Calories (Kcal)
Beer (4 percent)	12 oz. can	94
Extra strong beer (10 percent)	12 oz. can	235
12 percent table wine	4 oz. glass	94
20 percent fortified wine, such as sherry	2 oz. glass	80
86 proof whiskey	1½ oz. jigger	126
100 proof rum, vodka, etc. or other spirits	1½ oz. jigger	147

* Beer contains carbohydrates which supply about twenty additional calories. Sweet wines supply additional calories because of the sugar content.

intake. These are often referred to as "empty calories" because, particularly when spirits are involved, there are no accompanying nourishments such as minerals or vitamins. In Table 1-2 we show the average calorie content of a variety of alcoholic drinks. This information demonstrates how it is difficult to lose weight if one drinks and continues to eat as much as before.

The Drug Alcohol

Alcohol is a drug, undoubtedly one of the earliest ones known and used by man. If, like LSD, this drug had only recently been discovered or, like marijuana, rediscovered, government agencies and legislators would likely be busy banning its production, distribution, and consumption. We make no claim that LSD and marijuana are harmless, but we must point to the enormous toll in terms of health, happiness, economics, and traffic hazards represented by excessive use or abuse of alcohol. Only the lengthy acquaintanceship of man and alcohol and the integration of alcohol into social and cultural customs prevent this substance from being placed on some dangerous drug list.

In this chapter we limit our study of the chemistry or pharmacology of alcohol to an explanation of the fact that *many people enjoy the effect that alcohol has upon them.*

Alcohol as a Poison

In sufficient quantities alcohol is a cell poison which is capable of bringing all life functions to a halt in any organism. In smaller amounts alcohol depresses the functions of living cells. In animals like ourselves the depressant effects of alcohol are most readily apparent in the case of the cells of the central nervous system. If the activity of the cells which produce blood, bone, or skin is temporarily diminished there is no way whereby the owner of these cells can subjectively identify this fact. On the other hand, the central nervous system is much occupied with the "here and now" of the individual in terms of his relationship with his environment, with his record of past relationships, and, at least in the case of *Homo sapiens,* with his consciousness of a future. Thus, if the central nervous system functions subserving sensation are impaired, a man may be unaware of the ground under his feet and may trip and fall. If the cells subserving motor functions are impaired, he will demonstrate an impaired capacity to carry out movements. If the complex mechanisms whereby man maintains upright posture are temporarily deranged, his capacity to balance may be obviously wanting. These, of course, are the gross types of sensorimotor effects of alcohol, similar, indeed, to the effects of an anesthetic or of a barbiturate or some tranquilizing medications. There is no evidence that man finds it particularly attractive to fall, stagger, or to walk a crooked line. The problem with alcohol, as with various other drugs, is to adjust the dosage in such a way as to get the desired effects without the undesired ones. Unfortunately these two levels of dosage tend to overlap to a greater or lesser degree depending upon the individual.

Our drinker may merely be seeking a respite from his worries about his mortgage or his work. But, as the parts of the brain which provide worry are anesthetized, he may overshoot the target and knock out or impair other functions such as speech, balance, sensation, movement, and memory.

Lay people have long ascribed positive stimulant properties to alcohol whereas medical experts have emphasized its depressant or negative qualities. Indeed, their explanation for the aggressive or uproarious drunk is that he has temporarily anesthetized higher control aspects of his central nervous system leading to disinhibition. Probably, however, alcohol has both stimulating and depressing effects on a complex organism like man. Some of our recent research data point to the existence of stimulating effects of alcohol on the sympathetic nervous system. This would give a sense of arousal and euphoria, in some people at least, after drinking.[10]

Being High

The desired effects of drinking are essentially a sense of euphoria accompanied by hedonistic attitudes, loss of worry and tension, and a general elevation of spirits. In today's parlance the user of alcohol is searching for a "high." While in the lower levels of alcoholic intoxication, an individual may still be aware of the environmental sources of pressure or worry which bothered him throughout the day, but now he cannot seem to care about them in the same way. Thus, this drug offers a pharmacological respite from stresses. Such drugs as alcohol and the anesthetics appear to affect the central nervous system in a hierarchical manner, first depressing functions in the evolutionary newest parts of the brain. These appear to be the structures which subserve functions such as self-awareness, concern about the future, the monitoring of social and inter-personal relationships, and the maintenance of that veneer of acquired civilization which has been provided by example from family and culture. Many people who have experienced this sense of lightening of burdens, and possibly accompany-ing exhilaration, enjoy the experience and wish to repeat it with greater or lesser frequency. Some individuals find the experience less enjoyable either because of physical discomfort, such as upset stomach, or because the feeling of beginning to lose control is too frightening or otherwise undesirable. Indeed, it may well be that some lifelong abstainers harbor similar fears. Certainly we have heard abstainers express the concern that if they ever were to try to drink they might "not be able to put it down."

For many individuals the desired effects of relaxation and social lubrication are experienced at relatively low levels of blood alcohol concentration such as .02 to .04 percent. This level is achieved in the average size man after one or two beers or mixed drinks. The issue of alcohol abuse and alcoholism will be tackled in later chapters. However, some individuals apparently do not gain the desired effects at these low levels of blood alcohol. Perhaps they were always less sensitive or, more likely, they have acquired a tolerance which requires them to imbibe more and reach higher blood alcohol levels. In this context we have heard persons suffering from alcoholism report that at last they are "beginning to feel it" when their blood alcohol levels are reaching .15 percent (a level that many social drinkers find difficult to reach and uncomfortable). For example, a man weighing 150 pounds would have to drink six beers or eight ounces of whiskey in one hour on an empty stomach to reach about .15 percent. See Table 1-3 for informa-tion regarding the approximate percent of alcohol to be found in the blood after a given number of drinks for people of dif-ferent body weights. It also shows how to calculate the change in blood alcohol levels with the passage of time.

Table 1-3
Approximate Blood Alcohol Percentage
(Illegal to drive if above .10%)

Body Weight Number of drinks (each 1½ oz. 86 proof liquor
or 3 oz. sherry or 12 oz. beer) consumed within one hour

in Pounds	1	2	3	4	5	6	7	8	9
100	.04	.09	.13	.16	.22	.26	.30	.35	.39
120	.04	.07	.11	.14	.18	.22	.25	.29	.33
140	.03	.06	.09	.12	.16	.19	.22	.25	.28
160	.03	.05	.08	.11	.14	.16	.19	.22	.25
180	.02	.05	.07	.10	.12	.14	.17	.20	.22
200	.02	.04	.06	.09	.11	.13	.15	.17	.19

Subtract .01 for each 40 minutes of drinking.

Example 1: 160 lb. man has 6 drinks
in 2 hours (120 minutes)
= .16 minus .03 = .13%

Example 2: 120 lb. woman has 3 beers
in 1 hour and 20 minutes
= .11 minus .02 = .09%

Supplied By:
The Center for Alcohol Studies
University of North Carolina
Chapel Hill, North Carolina

Physiological Factors

The central nervous system and indeed all parts of the body have mechanisms for dealing with poisonous substances. In the case of alcohol, the liver is the primary policeman which arrests and finally incapacitates the drug by rendering it harmless. The enzymes for effecting this are found in many living tissues and even in the liver of a lifelong abstainer. In his case, small amounts of alcohol produced by digestive and metabolic processes are constantly being rendered harmless if his liver is healthy. Drinking overwhelms the capacity of the liver to remove circulating alcohol immediately so that the swallowed alcohol, after absorption, circulates in the blood to all parts of the body. Small amounts are removed via the lungs and the kidneys as well as the skin, but the major job falls upon the liver which, on an average, can reduce an individual's blood alcohol concentration by about .015 percent per hour. Thus, our convivial drinker who gets to .03 percent blood alcohol, enjoys socializing with fellow drinkers and then stops drinking will have virtually no alcohol in his blood at the end of two hours. If he goes on drinking at the rate of an average drink every hour and a half, he may maintain a low blood alcohol level. If he drinks more rapidly he will gradually become more intoxicated.

A factor which is not well understood is that of actual tissue tolerance such as in the central nervous system. The actual mechanism whereby cells acquire a capacity to be less affected by a drug remains to be uncovered. However, certain changes do occur and are, in the case of alcohol, particularly prone to make themselves known when the drug is withdrawn. At such times it is as if the cells, having a capacity to withstand being bathed in a certain concentration of alcohol, now operate in a more excitable manner when the alcohol is removed. A reasonable analogy would be that of the automobile whose engine is revving hard to move it against the opposing force of a forgotten emergency brake. When the brake is released, the car will leap forward. Physiologically in the case of alcohol removal we find a "withdrawal syndrome" similar to that which appears following the administration of other central nervous system sedatives and their sudden removal. Minor degrees of the abstinence or withdrawal syndrome can occur on a "morning after" basis when an individual who drank a lot the previous night feels "out of sorts," slightly shaky, and on edge. Major degrees of the abstinence syndrome are manifested by convulsive seizures and the condition known as delirium tremens.[11]

Cultural Patterns

Complex patterns of use as well as abuse have developed in different societies and cultures. Some of these are based on the actual physiological effects of alcohol. Others are symbolic. In one place an alcoholic beverage is the representative of the holiday spirit whereas in another it is part of one's daily food intake. If the objective is to get as "high" as possible, drinking tends to be done without food and in concentrated form. Some cultures have developed "manliness" concepts whereby the capacity to hold large amounts of liquor and to get intoxicated are equated with masculine achievement. As indicated, alcohol specifically dissipates states of apprehension and overconcern. Its use to establish social relations and to promote good fellowship has thus become a significant part of man's culture and explains the integration of drinking behavior into societal patterns. Thus, the drunken debauchery of the cowboy in the frontier town for the weekend and the pious pronouncements of the wine lover as he savors the bouquet of his favorite vintage represent aspects of the same biosocial phenomenon.

Changes may occur within the same social group depending on whether or not there is drinking. For example, Roman[12] has studied the sociopsychological processes involved in student-faculty interactions and has described the changed interrelationships which are permitted temporarily when alcoholic beverages are introduced into the setting.

Patterns of controlling drinking behavior also vary. Some cultures have tended to point a finger of scorn or amusement at persons drinking excessively and apparently this has been a successful deterrent against continued alcohol abuse at a group level. This, for example, is said to be typical of Chinese cultural patterns,[13] but obviously other forces are at work including close family relations and reverence for the behavior patterns of the older generation. Quite recently, Wolff reported that some Oriental subjects when given alcohol experienced a moderately unpleasant face flushing response with associated mild discomfort in the body.[14] We have studied this phenomenon in Orientals residing in the United States and eating an American diet. Our data suggest that this a true physiologic response with the underlying mechanism presently not understood. What we demonstrated was that Oriental people, on swallowing a measured dose of alcohol, showed reactions that were significantly different from non-Orientals. Not only did they show a marked face flushing in about four out of five instances but their heart rate went up and their blood pressure fell. Subjectively they felt more discomfort such as dizziness, pounding in the head, muscle weakness, and tingling sensations. In contrast the non-Oriental subjects tended to report feeling relaxed, happy, confident, and alert.[15]

There is a slight possibility that some of these responses to alcohol by Orientals represent psychological awareness of what they have swallowed and certain feelings about alcoholic beverages. Therefore, we are in the process of repeating this work by putting the alcohol directly into the blood stream and thereby by-passing the awareness of the subject as to when alcohol has been given. However, from the studies already completed, major physiologic mechanisms seem to be at work which are beyond conscious or unconscious control. One

implication of this is that some of the cultural patterns of
drinking to be found in certain peoples may have a physiologic
foundation. Logically, if alcohol creates more discomfort than
stimulation and joy the cultural climate would encourage
modest drinking practices.

An understanding of cultural and social conditions and
customs contributes much to the understanding of an individual's drinking because they can limit, modify, or encourage his
personal inclinations toward alcohol. Often definitions of the
alcoholic or problem drinker use the society as a reference
point, e.g., repeated drinking "that exceeds customary dietary
use or ordinary compliance with the social drinking customs
of the community."[16]

As already indicated, the level of "high" sought is a
personal thing but is clearly influenced by examples demonstrated within the family and other societal units. Probably
throughout man's history the excessive users of alcohol have,
just as today, tended to gain the limelight largely by virtue of
the associated noisy or abrasive behavior. Some people argue
against all alcohol use on the grounds that it will necessarily
lead to violent and unacceptable behavior. They point to the
alleged behavioral effects of the introduction of alcohol to
ethnic groups which were previously naive. Here one of the
best known examples is the American Plains Indian who,
apparently unlike his cousins in Central America, had no
knowledge of alcoholic beverage production before the white
man arrived. A similar observation was made by Tacitus[17]
some 1,900 years ago. He reported that when the primitive
Germanic peoples, formerly only beer drinkers, came in contact with the Romans and were introduced to wine, their
moderation disappeared and they drank heavily and persist-
ently. Tacitus apparently attributed this to their having a lack
of standards for drinking wine but he also allowed for the cold
climate as an additional consideration.

The whole issue of behavior while in a drunken state is
critically examined by a psychologist and an anthropologist in
a recent book. MacAndrew and Edgerton produce evidence that
behavior with or following drinking may show no change, or
many types of change, in different cultures.[18] They see drunkenness as an excuse for "time out" behavior within the social

system and specifically produce arguments to suggest that the alleged incapacity of the North American Indian to handle alcohol was learned from the white frontiersman and provided an excuse for such behavior. These workers feel that they have demonstrated the "supremacy of social factors over physiological ones." They argue that alcohol produces incompetence which is unintentional and beyond the drinker's power to overcome. The state of drunkenness is easily discernible and the act of drinking itself has the quality of a "warning sign." Basically, then, they conclude that the state of drunkenness conveys an "increased freedom to be one's other self." Just as the Romans maintained the maxim *in vino veritas* we would agree that many clinical situations confirm that drunkenness permits the individual to bring forth the feelings which were not permitted to be overtly expressed formerly (and may not even have been permitted to be in consciousness).

In the case of the American Indian it is premature, however, to state that everything can be explained in psychological and anthropological terms. One group of Canadian workers compared Indians and Eskimos with white Canadians and reported that the former two groups became drunker (had higher blood levels) on the same intake of alcohol and stayed drunk longer.[19] In other words they metabolized, or burned up, the alcohol more slowly. One interesting aspect of this is that the original settlement of North America is believed to have occurred by the immigration of Mongolian people and therefore there may be genetic similarities among Indians, Eskimos, and Orientals that have yet to be identified. Meanwhile, reports of special reactions by Orientals, Indians, and Eskimos to alcohol or of differing metabolic rates must be taken with caution. Replication in other studies is required and the biochemical or physiological mechanisms need to be identified as does the significance of these differences. For now, it is sufficient to emphasize that only a multidimensional theory which considers inherited constitutional factors, the culture to which an individual is exposed, and the individual psychological makeup of that person is sufficient to account for drinking in its multitude of patterns and degrees. In other words alcohol use, alcohol abuse, and alcoholism must be looked at as biopsychosocial phenomena.

A few more words need to be said about societal pressures. Obviously one's feelings about alcohol use will depend
upon the exposures during childhood, particularly within the
family. Some communities are patently wet while others are
dry. Religions have adopted specific attitudes about "time out"
behavior in some instances, and all use of alcohol in others.
Specific types of culture patterns appear to exist. The classic
Jewish pattern[20] is one of moderation and assimilation of
alcohol use with religious practice. Again it may be oversimplification, however, to assume that cultural factors alone are
at play here since the Jew's relative freedom from alcoholism
may be balanced by his vulnerability to obesity and diabetes.
We cannot dismiss the possibility of genetically determined
biochemical factors which have yet to be demonstrated.
Changes in cultural values are particularly visible when
cultural assimilation is in progress. Here, studies of consecutive Italian generations under Americanization have shown the
trend to abandon traditional "wine with food" patterns and to
adopt "American" drinking patterns running parallel with the
acquisition of problems with drinking.[21]

Laws Controlling Drinking

Alcohol use has such a lengthy history and is so thoroughly an integrated part of many cultures that it should not
be surprising that ancient laws also dealt with the regulation
of alcoholic beverages, drunkenness, and crimes associated with
drinking.[22] Indeed, legal approaches to regulating drinking
appear in man's earliest historical records. The oldest known
system of codified law, set up by Hammurabi, King of Babylon
around 2225 B.C., contains several references to alcohol. It
regulated the measure and price at which alcoholic beverages
could be sold and who could patronize taverns and prohibited
priestesses from selling liquor. Plutarch reported that early rul-
ers destroyed vineyards and forbade further planting without
imperial license in order to curb intemperance. In England,
regulations for ale houses existed before Parliament; for example, the owner was enjoined to "serve such as be of good disposition and conversation."[23] Even today there are laws and
practices which discourage serving more alcohol to the obviously intoxicated customer.

Discriminatory legislation, therefore, is not a modern phenomenon, although the groups prohibited from the purchasing of alcoholic beverages may in some cases differ. Neither are laws regarding beverage quality and manufacture, price fixing, licensing, and revenue solely a modern phenomenon. Over many centuries various attempts have been made to limit the number of outlets where alcohol may be obtained. Attempts to encourage drinking of one type of beverage over another are familiar as in the Danish example cited. In seventeenth century England anyone was allowed to distill spirits; this resulted in a gross overproduction of gin and some of the behavior which Hogarth portrayed so vividly. The problems which developed led to attempts to encourage the drinking of beer instead to spirits; these attempts may be considered relatively successful since England is still primarily a beer-drinking nation.

The model for the American colonial legislation regarding drunkenness was a 1606 Parliamentary statute, which was the first to authorize secular courts to fine persons found guilty of drunkenness. Habitual, excessive drinking, which in those days was called tippling, and the practice of lingering over one's drink were both considered crimes. The moral justification for punishment of drunkenness as a crime is clear in the preamble of this statute:

> Whereas the loathsom and odious Sin of Drunkenness is of late grown into common Use within this Realm, being the Root and Foundation of many other enormous Sins, as Bloodshed, Stabbing, Murder, Swearing, Fornification, Adultery, and such like, to the great Dishonour of God, and of our Nation, the Overthrow of many good Arts and manual Trades, the Disabling of Divers Workmen, and the general Impoverishing of many good Subjects, abusively wasting the good Creatures of God: Be it therefore enacted. . . .[24]

The language of sin and evil was removed from later statutes; those acts designated as sinful and immoral, however, still remained as punishable offenses.

While current moralistic attitudes about *drunkenness* may be traced to ancient times when the ecclesiastical dominated the secular law, there is less foundation in the ancient canons for such attitudes toward *drinking*. After reviewing attitudes toward drinking and drunkenness recorded in the history of the early Christian church, Baird concluded that drinking *per se* was not considered sinful and that

> simple drunkenness (due to) exuberance or a holiday spirit, or from ignorance, or even negligence, was excusable under the canon law. . . . Even periodic drunkenness may not have been more than a minor "peccatum," a small sin . . . and not regarded as gross or cardinal until it had become frequent, and the communicant so disregardful of repeated admonitions and so contumacious to summons as to be thought guilty of gluttony or luxury.[25]

After the Reformation, however, religious leaders turned their attentions and moral indignation toward drinking itself. Calvin and Luther urged the adoption of temperance in general; Wesley, on the other hand, advocated abstinence from spirituous liquor. Baird credits the Methodism founded by Wesley as a dominant influence in spreading the doctrine that it is sinful to drink alcoholic beverages of any variety. The doctrine was successfully transplanted in America where it blossomed into a reform movement culminating in the enactment of Prohibition. The development of the American Temperance movement is discussed further in chapter 3.

Religious convictions, whatever the denomination, which put a premium on deprivation and suffering with a promise of later rewards have condemned carefree, pleasure-seeking behavior such as alcohol permits. Perhaps some of today's ambivalent attitudes toward alcohol reflect at once the desire for relief of tension and at the same time a guilty feeling which says, in effect, "I shouldn't be enjoying myself in this way."

The morality of drinking itself became an issue in nineteenth century America even among the clergy. Scripture was cited recommending the moderate use of wine, "for thy stomach's sake and thine often infirmities" (I Timothy 5:23) and "Go thy way, eat thy bread with joy, and drink thy wine with a merry heart for God now accepteth thy works" (Ecclesiastes 9:7). The opponents' counterargument was that the wine referred to was unfermented grape juice. While acknowledging the fact that not all religious groups agreed on whether drinking itself was sinful, the Reverend O. T. Binkley summarized the arguments upon which were based the criticism of moderation and the plea for abstinence:

(1) moderate drinking makes men careless of their social responsibilities and engenders hazards in our complex culture, (2) popular consumption of alcoholic beverages is a factor in producing the disease of alcoholism and (3) moderate drinking increases the social pressure toward drink upon youth and has a detrimental influence on spiritual development and religious achievement.[26]

The great experiment in legislating behavior on a national scale was prohibition. It has been suggested that its failure was inevitable because it dealt with customs embedded in the culture that "serve societal functions which cannot be eliminated by mere legislation."[27] This was beautifully demonstrated by Will Rogers when he said that prohibition's only virtue was that it was better than no whiskey at all!

National prohibition has been well discussed and documented.[28] It should be mentioned that other countries such as Iceland (1915-1922), Russia (1916-1917), and Finland (1919-1932) also experimented with national prohibition so this legal approach in the United States (1920-1933) was not without precedent.

In evaluating national prohibition as a viable means of controlling drinking behavior, we return again to the issue of trade-offs. On the one hand, prohibition was associated with a temporary decline in deaths from liver diseases and delirium tremens. On the other hand, there were the negative effects of increasing crime and disrespect for the law with repercussions reaching into our lives today.

At the time of national prohibition, thirty-three of the forty-eight American states, beginning with the Maine Law of 1851, had already enacted statewide prohibition. Monopoly or license systems were later developed to regulate alcohol consumption after the repeal of the Eighteenth Amendment. The underlying aim was temperance and the protection of public health and morals.

Many motivations exist for regulating drinking behavior. An early need developed, it has been suggested, when primitive man took the risk of being at the mercy of his enemies while intoxicated.[29] In today's complex society the need to prevent abusive use remains. Legislators have attempted to control or reduce the problems associated with drinking and to diminish the consumption of alcohol in general by limiting its availability, placing restrictions on its use, and punishing its abusers.

Opponents of legislative control include members of the liquor industry, drinkers who resent interference with their drinking activities, and citizens who feel that this is not a legitimate area for legislation.

Trends for Change

At the present time as we look at the relationship of laws and drinking we are at a turning point in the United States and in many other parts of the world. In the first place, alcoholism is now largely regarded as a health problem rather than a moral problem; consequently, there are trends toward recommending treatment programs rather than punishment or incarceration. Secondly, a new sense of "freedom" is pervading society. The "legislation of morality" is generally beginning to be seen as ineffectual and possibly unethical. Thus we have the "sexual revolution," the "drug revolution," the "women's liberation movement," and we even hear some voices crying that man has a "right" to use drugs or commit suicide. In this country there is an obvious trend toward taking a more lenient view of public drunkenness. Many people believe that eventually chronic alcoholism will become a valid plea as a defense of some legal charges. There are a few dry countries in the world and no totally dry states in the United States. We still have local options and still see the paradox of the religious proponents and the bootleggers combining to keep certain territories dry. It is unlikely that anyone at this time in our history will question another's right to drink unless he is propounding a minority religious or moralistic position.

It is possible that we will soon see an attempt to introduce prohibition in India. Former Prime Minister Indira Gandhi indicated this to be a national goal. The sole Indian state of Gujarat already has prohibition of twenty-five years' standing and claims are made for this as an enormously successful experiment.[30] Clearly prohibition had popular support there when initiated and whether Gujarat can lead the way for the rest of India remains to be seen.

We are still faced with the question of the right to be drunk under certain circumstances. Does the individual have the right to drink toxic quantities of alcohol which will eventually give him liver disease, break up his family, prevent his holding a remunerative position (and paying taxes), and shorten his life? No one would claim the "right" of the impaired and intoxicated driver to mow down pedestrians or otherwise create a hazard to others. Likewise we find it objectionable if he falls down dead drunk on our paved highways. We are less disturbed if he stays on the sidewalk or in the gutter. Obviously if our neighbors give loud drunken parties we might find this socially abrasive and wish to object. However, there are other laws (e.g., disturbing the peace) to take care of most conceivable circumstances. The question of whether or not people are intoxicated, and to what level, in their own homes has not yet become a matter for the courts.

What, then, are reasonable objectives of laws pertinent to drinking? It is plainly unreasonable for a minority to decide to prevent a majority from drinking. In the United States the majority does drink (68 percent of adults),[31] and we can conclude that drinking will continue in the foreseeable future. If future research should show that even light or moderate alcohol use is a significant health hazard, some people would likely find it possible and desirable to exercise their choice not to drink. Others might find this difficult or impossible to accomplish, just as some smokers find they cannot quit. Under such circumstances, legislative steps would be taken to discourage alcohol use and to educate the public just as is presently the case with cigarette smoking. Socially abrasive behavior can reasonably be controlled within the framework of laws which do not question the sobriety of the offender.

Governments traditionally see alcoholic beverages as a lucrative source of tax money, much to the unhappiness of the industry and their lobbyists. Legislators, as well as those who execute and enforce laws, like to maintain a state of order and quite reasonably wish to collect all the taxes which are their due as well as to discourage criminal behavior. Clearly, though, the laws they create must be acceptable to the majority of the population and must not call for excessive or unreasonable sacrifices.

Laws for What?

The more we look at this issue the more we see it as a matter of survival. We want to keep alcoholic and drunken drivers off our roads as a simple matter of self-protection. (See chapter 7.) Likewise, many people do not care to see socially abrasive and unacceptable drunken behavior (even if not patently dangerous). Here, though, if we are dealing (as we probably are) with sufferers from alcoholism, the public trend seems to be toward advocating treatment rather than punishment. Then, many of us are wondering how we can maintain the production, distribution, and consumption of alcoholic beverages while *not* promoting excessive use or abuse of these substances.

Chapter 6 on alcoholism explores the issue of prevention of drinking problems, and here laws may have a part to play. However, many of the laws with which we live are sumptuary and of little proven significance. In one location an individual can freely purchase what he wants whereas in another he has to provide his name and address or own a permit. In some states, he can purchase five bottles but not six. Sometimes he can buy a bottle of whiskey but not a single drink. In some places a youth can drink all he wants at eighteen whereas in others he has to wait three more years to do it legally. The more we examine the present situation the more it looks as if we are dealing with a cloak of laws so covered in patches that the original garment is no longer visible.

This leads to a significant question: Should we do away with all drinking laws or some, or should we make new laws concerning drinking behavior? The various contributors to this book will present information that will assist the reader in considering this question.[32]

CHAPTER 2

5,000 Years of Drinking

Archer Tongue

FROM THE EARLIEST periods of recorded history, alcoholic beverages have been produced and consumed. There is evidence of the use of alcohol as a beverage in Stone Age cultures, and strong claims are made for honey as the oldest agent of fermentation. It is even possible that mead, or honey-wine, was the first alcoholic beverage distilled by man. Evidence of its use in sixth century Ireland predates by two centuries the Arab claim to invention. This ingenious process may also have been known to the Ancient Greeks and Chinese.[1] Whatever the facts are, it is undisputed that alcoholic beverages produced from an astonishing variety of substances found an established place in most human societies which they never relinquished.

The Dilemma

Accompanying this age-old use has been the inescapable dilemma in which societies and individuals have found themselves with regard to beverage alcohol. The problem has been that of reconciling the positive and negative aspects of its use: On the one hand, alcohol's qualities as a social lubricant and relaxer of tension must be set against the abuse and grosser manifestations of drunkenness and the harmful effects of

abuse. The ambivalent popular reaction to alcohol characterized by amusement at one time and disgust at another crystal-
lizes the century-old dilemma. Formulated in another way, the
history of drinking cannot avoid being the history of excessive
drinking.

Reaction to the unpleasant phenomenon of excess led to
a search for means of protecting the drinkers themselves and
society from their intemperance. Legislation and other restrictions against drinking or drunkenness appear throughout history in many lands. Alcoholic beverages and the places where
they were purveyed also became the target to regulation sometimes but not always on purely economic grounds. This diversity of motivation to regulate alcohol production, distribution, and consumption has continued to the present time.

It is in the study of measures enacted by civil and
religious authorities that one learns much of the drinking
habits going on in their area of influence. What the law forbad
was undoubtedly what had been going on or what was experienced in an acute form.

Early Drinking Restrictions

Some of what must be the earliest legislation on alcohol
contained in the Code of King Hammurabi of Babylon concerns the regulations of sale, the entering or opening of taverns
by temple priestesses, and the use of tavern premises by
criminals or conspirators. Infringements were to be severely
punished, the death penalty being invoked.[2]

Legislation and regulation of the drink-selling establishment can be summarized under three main heads:
(1) attempts to limit the number of such establishments;
(2) attempts to influence the manner of drinking; (3) attempts
to restrict the entry or serving of certain categories of people.
Such aims were pursued in early periods of history.

In 781 A.D. in China the Emperor Tci-Tsung is reported
to have decreed that in all districts of the empire the number of
persons and places allowed to sell alcoholic beverages should
be fixed with grading of liquor outlets.

In Anglo-Saxon England the early beginnings of a
rudimentary licensing system became apparent. Ine, King of
Wessex in the eighth century, regulated ale-booths and ale-

stands. Under Edgar, King of England (959-975), acting on the advice of Dunstan. Archbishop of Canterbury, regulations were issued which have come down to us in more detail. Two provisions standout. The first concerned the distribution of ale houses, only one being allowed for each village. The other concerned the mode of consumption. Drinking horns had to have pins fixed at stated distances to control the amount drunk. This stipulation was not as effective in controlling drunkenness as was hoped.[3]

The restriction of drink-selling licences has been resorted to in many countries throughout the ages. The ordinance of the Russian Tsar Alexei (1652) that there should be one liquor outlet in the larger villages and only one cup of vodka sold to any one customer bears a striking resemblance to controls proposed in recent years to reduce drunkenness.[4]

Restrictions to prevent certain classes of persons from entering drink establishments were often concerned with clergy. This has already been alluded to in connection with Hammurabi's Code. While in Jewish and Christian tradition wine has always figured as a part of religious rites or ceremonies, people have frowned upon the clergy frequenting drink-selling establishments. For example, in the Canons of Aelfric, Archbishop of Canterbury (995-1005), it is laid down that no priest should drink at taverns as do secular men. The Emperor Charlemagne likewise forbad monks to resort to taverns.

The appearance of clubs which were often closely associated with drinking excesses dates from the eleventh century if not earlier. In Norway during the time of King Olaf Kyrre (The Tranquil), the guilds had their own club houses. Drinking rules were introduced, one of the more curious being that if a member allowed more drink to spill on the table than he could cover with his hand he was subject to a fine.

The Middle Ages

During the Middle Ages, in many countries regulations concerning the inns and taverns proliferated. In England in 1285 taverns in London were not allowed to stay open after curfew[5] and the Act of 1436 in Scotland ordered the closing of taverns, wine shops, and ale houses at 9 P.M. with penalty of imprisonment for those found in them after that time.

In Switzerland a whole series of enactments concerning closing hours were introduced in the different cantons of the country. From 1226 onwards no landlord was supposed to dispense liquor after the "night-bell, fire-bell or wine-bell." In 1580 in St. Gall anyone who remained in the tavern after closing time (door closing) had to stay the night there.[6]

On Sundays and Holy Days landlords could not serve local inhabitants before the end of Mass or service. To this and many other restrictions there was the exception of the bona fide traveler, the special case which has survived into our own times.

Although complete Sunday closing of taverns seems to be a device of more recent times, Sunday prohibition of the retail of spirits was not unknown in earlier times. For example, the sale of distilled wine on Sundays and festival days was prohibited by the Nuremburg Council in Germany in 1496. In general, however, it would seem that a restriction, such as that applied in Norway in 1586 forbidding the sale of spirits during the hours of divine service, was more usual.

In the Middle Ages in England the main thrust of legislation was toward securing good quality and a fair price for alcoholic beverages. In most countries this was of prime importance in view of the undrinkable nature of water generally. Misrepresentation of wine was also condemned. The landlord was responsible for not making false claims. In Lucerne, Switzerland, in 1315 we find that it was an offense for landlords to pass off local wine as wine from Alsace.[7] The importation or sale of corrupted or mixed wines or any adulteration was forbidden under penalty of death in Scotland in 1492.

In Tudor England, the powers given to the Justices of the Peace to select those who were to have the right to operate the liquor-selling establishments[8] marked the foundation of that licensing system which continues to the present day, spreading to North America, Africa, Australia, New Zealand, and elsewhere.

Some consideration should be given to what appeared at first to be the simplest regulation possible, namely, total or partial prohibition of the provision and use of intoxicating beverages. Two world religions, Islam and Buddhism, have required abstinence from alcohol by their adherents. Apparently, there has been no period of history including the present when prohibition has not been in force somewhere.

Prohibition in the Early Ages

The types of prohibition have varied considerably. In Ancient China Emperor King Ti (147 B.C.) prohibited the preparation of certain alcoholic beverages; the Roman Emperor Domitian, in 81 A.D. ordered the destruction of half the vineyards and prohibited new plantings of vine. This edict was not revoked until 276. In Egypt in 996 during the reign of Hakim there was prohibition of liquor producing and of the importation of alcoholic drinks. In 1279 in Asia, Kublai Khan required the banishment of all liquor producers, confiscation of their property, and their children made wards of the government. Complete and total prohibition does not seem to have been regarded as attainable except in those countries where by far the large majority practised a religion prohibiting the use of alcohol.

Accompanying the various attempts to control the sources of alcohol and restrict its use were the legislative and regulative attempts to curb the individual's alcoholic excesses. Sometimes this was aimed at reforming him, at other times at sparing and protecting society from the results of his overindulgence.

This can be seen in Greece and Rome and elsewhere. The regulation of the symposia in Ancient Greece which controlled such matters as the mixing of drinks, the regulation of the size of the drinking vessels and the distribution of food and drink were elaborated into a system.[9]

Groups with Special Drinking Restrictions

Ideas as to who could not drink at all appear early in history. In early Rome, women were forbidden wine[10] and a woman's drunkenness without her husband's knowledge could be grounds for divorce. Among the Aztecs, young men drinking were clubbed to death and young women were stoned. Unless one were advanced in age, it was apparently necessary to have the permission of a judge to drink at all.[11]

As mentioned earlier, the clergy were one group among whom intemperance was felt to be particularly unseemly.

Although those religious orders insisting on total abstinence may not have been in the majority, the general appeal was made again and again to avoid excess in the use of alcohol. In fact, there were always some groups in those religions which did not forbid alcohol who took upon themselves the rule of abstinence in view of the spiritual and bodily harm which they believed was inevitable from abuse. Such were the Rechabites, among the ancient Jews, and the orders of St. Pachomius of Egypt (third century), the Canons Regular of St. Gilbert (England; twelfth century) and Irish monasteries founded by St. Boniface, among the Christians.

Clearly recognized at an early stage of human history was the fact that alcohol could impair job performance. In those periods when life was not mechanized, intellectual impairment due to alcohol did not go unnoticed.

One of the earliest recorded instances of the results of drinking on the job was in Ancient China in the reign of Emperor Chung K'iang (2159-2147 B.C.). His two court astronomers failed to predict an eclipse because they were drunk. They were executed because of their inattention to duty. Plato admired the Carthaginians for requiring abstention from wine by magistrates and judges in office and those going to deliberate upon weighty matters in the senate.

The Emperor Charlemagne forbad counts to sit in judgment when not sober and had strict rules regarding the treatment of soldiers who became drunkards. Soldiers indeed followed a profession where the disadvantages of alcohol abuse were often reckoned. In the seventeenth century Gustavus Adolphus of Sweden prohibited spirits to his soldiers but could only maintain the interdiction for ten years.

In some primitive societies taboos on drinking existed for a variety of reasons. An example is the prohibition of use by the father during the six days after the birth of his child among the Ainu in Hokkaido, Japan.[12] Anthropologists have drawn attention to the controls exercised by the heads of tribes who determine the periods for which drinking may be indulged in by the whole group, as for example after the harvest has been gathered.

Health Concerns

Regulations directly to improve the health of the

drinker are not so easy to disengage from the mass of legislation which emerges in an historical study. Certainly the general tenor of the legislation throughout the Middle Ages, when not specifically economic in motivation, could be considered as being directed against drunkenness. The Athenian fashion of mixing wine with water and indeed, according to Plato, the regarding of undiluted wine as barbaric could be seen as being followed in the interests of health. Such regulations as that in sixteenth century Bavaria which stipulated that no one should drink more than two pennyworth of brandy daily might similarly be regarded.

Credit for being early proponents of the medical concept of alcoholism goes to the third century Roman jurist Domitius Ulpinus whose commentaries on imperial law contain a suggestion that drunkenness be considered a medical rather than a legal problem and King James I of Aragon (1213 to 1276) whose numerous edicts include one for the hospitalization of those persons subject to recurring drunkenness.[13] Not until the Age of Enlightenment in the eighteenth century did pronouncements by physicians themselves come to prominence. In this epoch the Philadelphia physician Dr. Benjamin Rush refers to alcohol addiction as an illness at the same time as Dr. Zacharius T. Huszty, Town Physician in Bratislava, Slovakia, was petitioning for state action against alcoholism (1786).

Pre-Modern Temperance Societies

The formation of specific societies to combat drunkenness or alcoholic excesses is, however, of earlier date. Toward the end of the sixteenth and the beginning of the seventeenth century, Shakespeare wrote his great tragedies in which realistic conception of alcohol addiction is in striking contrast to the levity with which drunkenness is treated in his earlier comedies. Another poet, who was also politician, headmaster, and judge in Kosice, Slovakia, Johannes Brocatius (1549-1621), was founding the first movement against alcoholism in Slovakia. He stated that one of the reasons he decided to avoid drunkenness was that "illustrious physicians demanded it."[14]

Actually Brocatius was preceded in Germany by Frederik III who founded an order of temperance. In 1517 Sigismund of Dietrichstein organized the Order of St. Christopher among nobles which attacked the drinking of healths, and in 1524 a temperance brotherhood was founded among high dignitaries in Heidelberg. Needless to say these bodies were not abstinence organizations, but they were dedicated to mitigating the results of the excessive drinking practices of the epoch.

These early precursors of organized movements to deal with the alcohol problem reveal the inability of society to cope with the results of drinking and drunkenness through regulation alone. They give credence to the point of view that legislation can at best be a palliative and that the nature of alcohol addiction itself is such that it can never be effectively controlled by restrictive measures alone. In any epoch once the social drinker has crossed over the line from social drinking to compulsive consumption he is impervious to the repressive measure even if it were the death penalty itself.

This characteristic of the alcohol problem is vital when we ask whether or not any of these control measures were really effective. At least one might conclude that regulation of drinking practices and taverns acted as a brake on excess. Such legislation would of necessity be limited by the nature of alcoholism itself. It might be expected to protect those who are not yet dependent on alcohol by setting some limits to their drinking patterns. Taxation and pricing would here have a significant role. The person who had become alcoholic in the strict sense of the word would be virtually untouched because of his compulsion to consume. The attempts at legislation throughout history probably have had their greatest value in redressing situations in which consumption is out of hand.

Perhaps the main lesson to be drawn from the history of man's preoccupation with control of alcoholic excess is that there must be a harmony between the controls exercised, the recognition of the alcoholic as a sick person, and the need to protect him as well as the society of which he is a member. Clearly alcohol will continue to be the principal social drug used by man in a majority of countries. The lesson from 5,000 or more years of drinking is to accept that fact and to plan constructively to limit and mitigate the undesirable effects which arise.[15]

CHAPTER 3

200 Years of Drinking in the United States: Evolution of the Disease Concept

Richard W. Howland, A.B.

Joe W. Howland, Ph.D., M.D.

THE BICENTENNIAL OF the United States of America seems an appropriate time to consider the history of drinking during the past 200 years. With a focus in particular upon changing attitudes toward drinking and drinkers in America, this chapter covers the rise of the temperance and prohibition movements and the gradual evolution of the disease concept of alcoholism.

The Disease Concept

Dr. Benjamin Rush was a famed Philadelphia physician who left his name and influence on many revolutionary aspects of medicine.[1] In the year 1785, both Rush and Thomas Trotter, a British physician, independently and accurately described the disease syndrome of alcoholism in its complexity.[2] These descriptions paralleled in detail those of many other disease complexes whose definitive nature ultimately led to active therapy and correction. But the pathophysiologic process of alcoholism was apparently ignored by the physicians of that time. The fate of the alcoholic fell to a myriad of public devices. At that time and continuing to the present, the alcoholic has been looked upon as a drunkard, a social misfit, a moral degenerate, a sinner without shame. In a way, the stigma of alcoholism parallels that of the much better known disease of leprosy (Hansen's disease) or, in recent memory, the horror of alcoholism equals the horror of cancer. Just as mental disease in its various disguises is accepted today in a guarded fashion, so is alcoholism. To be an alcoholic is to be shamed, not pitied; to admit the presence of alcoholism is to invite a curse upon one's social, occupational, and personal status. Who is to know to what degree the success of Alcoholics Anonymous rests on the anonymity of its members?

As one reviews the history of alcoholism through these significant years, he is amazed at the chimeralike nature of the disease concept. It appears and disappears like a will-of-the-wisp, leaving no lasting impression and making little if any contribution to the understanding or control of the problem. The moralists, the theologians, the sociologists, the demographers, the psychologists, and the psychiatrists have all had their turn in attacking it. While for more than 150 years substantial proof and knowledge attest to the fact that the alcoholic is a diseased person, until the 1940s the disease concept was not officially recognized.[3] Prior to that time, a lack of morals was considered to be the major, if not the only, cause.

Even today the understanding of alcoholism by the public and some of the medical profession is quite shallow. Lack of information, genuine disinterest, or even complete apathy contribute to the entire problem. The protean nature of this complex disease certainly discourages all but the expert from exploring the problem. A more complete interdisciplinary approach is necessary if advances are to be made.

Definitions

Perspective may be gained by reviewing certain definitions of alcoholism which have been proposed. The Committee of Experts of the World Health Organization define alcoholics as those excessive drinkers whose dependence upon alcohol has attained such a degree that it results in noticeable mental disturbance, or an interference with their bodily and mental health, their interpersonal relations, their smooth social and economic functioning or those who show the prodromal signs of such development.[4] Another description is by Mann:

Alcoholism is a disease which manifests itself chiefly by the uncontrollable drinking of the victim. . . . It is a progressive disease, which if left untreated, grows more and more virulent year by year driving its victims further and further from the normal world, and deeper and deeper into an abyss which has only two outlets: insanity or death.[5]

In turn, Jellinek divided alcoholism into definitive stages: early, middle, and late.[6] His classification bears a strong resemblance to the first definition of Rush in that the symptomatology of each of these stages is specifically described and is of primary value for diagnostic purposes.

In all instances, the parallelism between alcoholism and drug addiction is striking. In both, mental and psychologic aberrations exist, accompanied by pathophysiologic changes of reversible and nonreversible nature. The final result depends on the vigor of combined medical and psychologic therapy.

The continuing argument as to whether alcoholism is a mental or medical illness has done much to hinder progress in the development of adequate means of therapy. Both psychiatry and medicine are essential; it is only in the marriage of these disciplines that progressive and successful therapy can result. Seeley implies that the idea of the disease concept could have negative results by fostering a public expectation that doctors and scientists will discover the absolute cause. [7]

While the causes of cancer, diabetes, and heart disease are unknown, disciplined advances in their therapy have been made through tremendous worldwide effort and the expenditure of vast sums of money. This the public accepts unconditionally—the war will eventually be won. While scientific advances into the causal relationship of alcohol and alcoholism have been made, the moneys spent and the caliber of the investigational effort made are minimal. The alarming increase in the disease places alcoholism in the forefront of unsolved disease processes.

The importance of the disease concept is to stimulate increased activity in all areas of this field. While the public generally accepts the disease concept, the medical critics demand definitive proof. In the meantime the alcoholic is often a forgotten individual. Many professionals are almost completely ignorant of the total picture and, benumbed by lack of success in treating alcoholism, they pass the alcoholic from one situation to another without significant progress.

The history of alcoholism in this country has evolved within this context of battles between various groups. The lack of a specific pathophysiologic process has baffled the physician; the relegation of the alcoholic to moral, religious, and eventually to psychologic and psychiatric disciplines is characteristic of the medical procedure. Psychosomatic medicine, which relates the effect of the brain on bodily ills, had its origins about the time that the disease concept of alcoholism became generally accepted. To it was relegated all of the unknown or unconquerable disease states such as ulcerative colitis, regional ileitis, peptic ulcer, and allied states—but not alcoholism. Evolution of medical knowledge can also be partly blamed for the tremendous ultraspecialization, paralleled with the disappearance of the family practitioner. His common-sense approach was often more successful with alcoholism than treatment based on the advanced knowledge of the research laboratories and specialty groups. This in no way indicates that experts in the field of alcoholism, too, are limited in number, but it emphasizes that a general overall interest of the entire medical profession must be developed using all methods of education, training, and experience.

Alcoholism in America

The difficulties encountered by developing medical science show why the baffling nature of alcoholism has had such a disturbing history. The story of alcoholism in the United States starts with the colonial period to the 1900s; the disease concept begins in the period 1900 to 1930; and this concept comes of age in the period 1930 to the present.

At the time of the discovery and colonization of America, alcohol was firmly entrenched in the society of the Old World. The drunkard was common particularly in the urban areas. He was treated poorly and often imprisoned. But for the most part, he was ignored.[8] During the colonial period, drinking was an accepted and commonly practiced social function. The first spirituous liquor manufactured in America was made on Staten Island by William Kieft around 1640. In New England, rum making became the most profitable of businesses encouraged by the poor agricultural environment and the large demand. Woodrow Wilson once remarked: "Out of the cheap molasses of the French Islands, New England made the rum which was the chief source of her wealth."[9] Liquor was no problem to the colonists. Drinking laws were in effect, and, while drunkenness occurred and was punished, it was not frequent.[10] The drunk was a social misfit and a source for pity, but he rarely appeared, and caused little if any alarm or concern to the other colonists when he did.

Alcohol became a problem during the Revolutionary War. "The first serious and effective efforts against the use of distilled liquor as a beverage began with the movement for American Independence."[11] The Continental Congress realized the dangers of their troops using intoxicants and recommended that the states cut back on alcohol quotas issued to their soldiers. Gusfield explains this shift to a liquor problem by stating that prior to the revolution, the American society was rigidly divided into distinct classes and status levels which developed strict codes of conduct. During and following the revolution this old order was broken apart, and the old codes no longer governed society and its actions. The Calvinistic ideals of the colonial period lost their relevance, and society tolerated excessive drinking.[12] Whatever the reason, following the revolution, drinking—especially to excess—became more of a social phenomenon.

During this period, Dr. Rush wrote a detailed investigation of alcohol and its effects. In 1785, he published a number of clinical observations which even today are considered reasonably accurate. He made the first documented statement that alcoholism is a disease: "This odious disease (for by this name it should be called) appears with more or less of the following symptoms. . . ."[13] However, he did not expand upon the disease concept or the social implications that might have evolved.

A strong supporter of temperance, Dr. Rush dealt mainly with the devious effects of alcoholism (or drunkenness as it was referred to at the time). Dr. Rush believed equally in the moral concept, and the growing temperance organizations used his work as a reference for many years.[14] The moral concept of alcoholism saw the drunkard as a sinner, a weak individual, a degenerate who did not possess the inner strength to abstain from intoxicating beverages. In short, the fault existed in the drinker but never in the drink. Abstinence was a virtue; drinking a sin. This concept existed for several centuries in Great Britain and migrated with the colonization of the United States.

At the same time, Thomas Trotter, a British physician, in his "Essay, Medical, Philosophical and Chemical on Drunkenness," defined drunkenness (alcoholism) in a more modern light. He stated: "In medical language, I consider drunkenness strictly speaking to be a disease; produced by a remote cause, and giving birth to actions and movements in the living body that disorder the functions of health."[15] This work was also widely acclaimed by physicians and some governmental officials. However, the disease concept was largely overlooked by specialists and public alike.

Drunkenness was much more frequent following the revolution. For the most part, however, the problem was either ignored, tolerated, or even condoned. In fact, no one drank harder than the clergy.[16] Records indicate the economic importance of whiskey around 1800,[17] and drunkenness became more evident. But the public showed little concern about this developing problem.

Temperance

Before 1810, the moral concept was not popular. Temperance thought and related organized societies existed in only a few communities. Likewise, the disease concept achieved little interest or concern.

To trace the trends of public opinion toward alcohol and the alcoholic during this period is to follow the history of the temperance groups and their religious affiliations; these were apparently responsible for the birth and spread of the moral (and social) concepts toward alcoholism. Stimulated by the teachings of these organizations, the moral concept gained increasing popularity. The first temperance organization in America was founded in 1789 by residents of Litchfield, Connecticut, who pledged never to drink. Following this lead, a number of similar groups began to operate on a local scale.

The first wide scale move was taken by the Presbyterian

and Methodist churches. In 1812, the General Assembly of the Presbyterian Church and the General Conference of the Methodist Episcopal Church began to take a temperance position. The Presbyterian Assembly urged its ministers "to deliver public discourses on the sin and mischief of intemperate drinking."[18] Following this proclamation, the temperance idea gained greater appeal particularly among the rural masses.

The first national organization, the American Temperance Society, was not formed until 1826. With the renewed interest in morality and religion of this period, this organization found support particularly in rural areas, the stronghold of the moralist movement. By 1827, the American Temperance Society numbered 222 local groups and had been able to close a few rural distilleries and taverns. By 1830 more than 1,000 temperance societies existed, and churches were opposing liquor. With the increase in temperance thought, various state and federal governments discussed alcohol control. The War Department eliminated the regular spirit ration to their soldiers and also limited that amount available to soldiers by public sale.

The Connecticut State Medical Society appointed a committee to report on possible need for sending inebriates to a special asylum rather than to jail, workhouse, or poorhouse. In its formal report, the committee states: "Before attempting to eradicate any disease, we should endeavor to investigate its character, to inquire into its nature and tendency, and ascertain as far as practicable the impediments which exist to its removal."[19] This recognition of alcoholism as a disease and of the necessity of additional research was apparently ignored by all concerned.

During the thirty years from 1830 to 1860, temperance organizations were gaining great strength and popularity in the rural communities. More importantly, they were beginning to initiate statewide prohibitory measures in Oregon, Michigan, Maine, New Jersey, Vermont, Wisconsin, Massachusetts, Minnesota, Indiana, Ohio, Rhode Island, and Connecticut, all of which adopted prohibition measures of varying restrictive nature ranging from licensing to complete prohibition. Being premature, most of these measures were soon repealed. Such actions, however, showed the strength and appeal of the temperance organizations and the growing popularity of antialcohol sentiment.[20] They certainly predicted events which were soon to follow.

About this time a change took place in the basic philosophy of the temperance organizations. The earlier groups were concerned with the plight of the drunkard. This is shown in a quotation by Palmer:

> The earliest teaching of the Temperance reformer was that . . . multitudes of persons are so susceptible to the narcotic influence of alcohol that whatever their accomplishments or station, if they drink at all, they drink to drunkenness; and that the confirmed inebriate is a diseased individual undergoing the tortures of a living death.[21]

Many of these earlier societies (1825-40) dealt primarily with the problem of sobering up the drunks; many used reformed drunkards to help other inebriates and to preach the gospel of prohibition (personal sobriety as used later in Alcoholics Anonymous was not dealt with). To their credit they did not write off the drinker or the drunk as a moral sinner, but rather they offered understanding and help.

Between 1830 and 1840, however, the majority of the temperance societies took on a national status and began to stress that the drunk was a moral sinner who could stop drinking if he so desired. The goal of these groups changed drastically. Instead of helping the drunkard, they became involved in the issue that the best and perhaps the only way to prevent drunkenness was by removing the cause, alcohol. Thus the idea of universal prohibition was born. The doors of these groups were not entirely closed to drunks needing help. However, the development of an insidious obsession with prohibition was accompanied by a diminishing interest in the sinner. The Temperance Manual, published in 1836, declared: "The Holy Spirit will not visit, much less will he dwell with him who is under the polluting, debasing effects of intoxicating drink. The state of heart and mind which this occasions is to Him loathesome and an utter abomination."[22]

The ultimate goal of the reformers was not to waste time with the sinner but to take his "devil rum" away. They attacked all who drank as moral degenerates. Not surprisingly, as is the way with emotional ideas, this moral concept developed quickly. The passage of laws toward prohibition indicates the acceptance and support of this attitude. Much more surprising, this popularity was accomplished without the aid of mass media.

Two distinct factors stimulated the acceptance of the moral concept. First, the alcohol problem was relatively new with no previous theories or concepts to be challenged; second, the churches were closely aligned with the temperance organizations and joined forces in mutual support. A geographic conflict also existed. The temperance groups held great strength in the rural communities with strong religious and moral backgrounds. They consisted of native, Protestant, middle-class professionals and farmers with a high religious orientation as their major social outlet. These people united in alarm against the urban plight, the rise in crime, and above all the destruction of traditional moralities. The battle cry of the temperance groups was for the symbolized "return of morality," which meant a return to the status levels of the pre-Revolutionary period as well.

For the most part the general population showed little concern with temperance thought during the nineteenth century to the Civil War period as indicated by the short life of prohibitionary measures. Strong islands of temperance thought continued to exist in the rural areas with the chief concern being the steady increase in alcohol consumption and drunkenness. Their actions on the moral front were so strong that they brought about a condemning attitude toward the drunkard and alcohol. Coordinated activity between these groups established as their main goal National Prohibition, for which they strived the next seventy years.

The Civil War divided the early and the late temperance movements. This conflict brought an increased awareness of the harmful effects of alcohol to the general public. There was a sharp breakdown in morality. The pressures of the war resulted in increased drunkenness among soldiers, alarming commanding officers as well as the government. Strict anti-drinking regulations for troops were ordered in 1862. Sale to soldiers by private citizens was forbidden, and another law prohibited sale to Indians (who were known to be sensitive to alcohol).[23] An asylum for the inebriate opened in Binghamton, New York, but this reverted into an insane asylum within the short period of three years.

With the lessons learned during the Civil War, temperance thought became increasingly popular. As is characteristic of so many reform groups, temperance societies were also caught up in a variety of other ideas including Populism (which espoused a complete order of socioeconomic reform). Most of these groups were short lived, but they did definitely dilute the total effort. After the war, the characteristic rebound, so often seen in history, occurred and alcohol consumption and the "plague of alcohol" decreased sharply in the decade following the conclusion of the Civil War. This decline was interpreted by the moralists as a partial victory. Hence, they preached that moral virtues (the most concrete being abstinence from alcohol) were keys to economic and social growth.

Because of this moral upswing, more churches became directly involved in the temperance movement. The Catholics formed their Total Abstination Union in 1872.[24] The Methodist, Baptist, and Presbyterian sects, already deeply involved, set up similar groups and their respective publishing houses printed extensively on the subject of alcohol and abstinence. The entire movement following the Civil War became embroiled with all of the problems of society and were seemingly convinced that alcohol was a main causative factor. This movement definitely dominated rural, Protestant, and middle-class society.

Any mention of the temperance movement should include a brief review of the actions of the Women's Christian Temperance Union (WCTU), as this group was much in the public eye during the preprohibition era. Initially conceived to promote moralism and convert man from the "evils of alcohol," the WCTU, too, became caught up with other problems of society, particularly when Frances Willard assumed the presidency of the group. The previous "singleness of purpose" policy was changed to a "do everything activity." Members were extremely vocal concerning women's rights, civil reforms, morals of society, and related issues. Such dilution temporarily paralyzed the effectiveness of the attack on alcohol. Even though temperance continued to be talked and written about, it lost a great deal of its public acceptance — except for the continued and loyal support of the rural, middle-class American who with his traditional moralities was the backbone of the program.

Prohibition

With the fading of the populist movement in the 1890s, attention of the WCTU and the other temperance groups was once more focused on alcohol, particularly at the local level. Attacks on local saloons and taverns were initiated. The "free will" attitude of the preceding era had shown little profit in any attempt to reform society. And society itself was considered as much to blame for the condition of alcoholism as was the alcoholic himself. Do not assume that the alcoholic gained any social or moral acceptance, or that much curiosity existed concerning any medical aids which might benefit him. The one and only solution would be the enactment of National Prohibition which would remove the alcohol from the alcoholic and alleviate his moral weakness. For this period and that which was to follow, a clear and concise view of the status of the problem is now difficult to form. All of the writings were biased — either for or against prohibition. The moral concept was at its zenith.

The twentieth century found the antisaloon and anti-alcohol forces gaining increased power and support. As a political issue, many seats in legislatures were won and lost on the prohibition front. This was particularly true of the rural communities. By 1912 seven states had adopted complete prohibitionary measures; in a number of others prohibition lost by a small margin. In 1913, the federal government contained a majority of members favorable to the issue as shown by state, county, municipal, and township opinion polls. At the same time, the Anti-Saloon League had developed into a strong lobby; the proposal of National Prohibition soon became their central theme. The contrast is well shown by the following example: In 1880 the Prohibition Act was soundly defeated by Congress; in 1914 the Hobson Joint Resolution for a prohibition amendment to the Constitution showed a slight majority but less than the two-thirds required in the House. The next three years showed a marked increase in popularity, and on December 18, 1917, the measure was solidly adopted by both houses. Congress firmly believed that this would terminate the liquor problem. Analysis of the voting shows that the votes of more than three-fourths of each congressional delegation in thirty states were in favor of the measure; a majority existed in an additional six states and only two states voted solidly against it.

As is so common in legislation, the War Prohibition Law went into effect on July 1, 1919, after peace had been declared. Even so, the usual cumbersome political machinery followed its usual policy with the official date of the Eighteenth Amendment as law occurring on January 17, 1920.

Three-fourths of the states had ratified the amendment by January 16, 1919. However, before the one year grace period expired after which the Eighteenth Amendment would become law, a War Time Prohibition Law was passed, effective July 1, 1919. The economic repercussion was staggering; 236 distilleries, 1,090 breweries, and 177,790 saloons were put out of business. On January 17, 1920, the Eighteenth Amendment became law; the forces against alcohol had won—politically.

The moral concept reached its height of popularity during this period. Drunkenness was "nothing but a wanton immorality, a willful sin."[25] "The fault existed in the drinker and never in the drink."[26] The Committee of Fifty, a group of government-appointed researchers to study the effects of alcohol on society, concluded that "Intoxication is not the wine's fault but the man's."[23] Society had no sympathy, no place for him. To summarize the general attitude, the individual drunkard was a moral degenerate, an object of shame. No mention of concern, of pity, and no offer of professional help were forthcoming. The Committee of Fifty, which published its findings in 1905, continued to be quoted for the next twenty years or more. Little original thought or modification of their recommendations was made.

As is the case today, more space was given to the topic in the popular literature of the period than in the scientific journals. Most of the articles were biased, either supporting the liquor industry or taking the completely opposite view. Both were intensely emotional in character. However, the moral concept continued to prevail, reaching its maximum about

1920. Thereafter it gradually lost appeal. However, the word "alcoholism" rather than "drunkenness," was first used during this period. Its definition, however, did not specify that it was a disease in itself but that alcohol had an effect on the occurrence of other diseases. The Committee of Fifty used this "association that alcohol has on other diseases" statement in their definition. [28] Temperance books adopted the term—always in the moral sense. Pickett accepted the fact that alcohol was a narcotic drug and that alcoholism was a condition, not a disease (using the parallelism with morphine as an example). He continued, however, to look upon the user as a sinner and moral degenerate, and his position must be included as that of a temperance advocate. He realized that alcohol shortened the life, threatened the kidneys and liver, and was a narcotic drug. However, these were only side effects which served to remove the finer edge of one's morals, permit an escape from society, and then lead to poverty and other morally related actions.[29] Cherrington defined alcoholism as the relation of the condition caused by the inordinate use of alcohol to the commission of criminal acts.[30] He mentioned effects of alcohol on the body but did not describe alcoholism as a disease or sickness.

The first description of alcoholism as a treatable disease is by Palmer who stated that inebriety or alcoholism is a disease that may be inherited or acquired. Significantly, he said:

> Chronic inebriates are rarely, if ever, wicked; they are weak, diseased, and imperfectly developed. If they were wicked they would not remain drunkards, for uniform wickedness implies a certain amount of will force which is all that the inebriate ordinarily requires for a cue . . . he cannot stop drinking and the power is not within him to stop on his own accord . . . it remains for his solicitous friends to step in and through persuasion and argument to seek professional help.[31]

In addition he rejected the idea of moral treatment by stating that it was in many cases a detriment.

Strangely, the disease concept continued to be overlooked. The moralists extracted those portions which suited their use; the medical journals gave it little emphasis (although most were in agreement with Palmer's general thesis). The lack of acceptance may lie in the tremendous enthusiasm concerning the early success of prohibition; also Palmer and others of this period who recognized alcoholism as a disease did not stress it sufficiently or make the necessary effort to inform or educate the public. Hence this favorable beginning of the disease concept met with an early death. The absorption of public interest was primarily on developments which occurred during prohibition.

Prohibition is a fascinating era in American history. Equally important in the story of alcohol and the evolution of the disease concept, it was initially a colossal success and then a stunning failure. During this short period of thirteen years, the whole moral tone of America changed. Drinking attitudes of the middle class were no longer that of scorn but acceptance of alcohol as a social necessity. Crime flourished; in fact, this period gave birth to the organized crime which has continued to the present. A flagrant disrespect for the law also developed. The moral concept was endangered.[32]

For the first few years, prohibition was successful as indicated by a sharp decrease in alcohol consumption. Hospital admissions dropped; people accepted the fact that alcohol was illegal and only the heavy drinkers continued their drinking pattern while moderate drinkers abstained.[33] In urban society prior to prohibition, an opportunity to escape from the drudgeries of everyday life in an industrial environment was provided by the saloons. A survey of the population of Chicago made in 1898 showed that more than 50 percent visited saloons daily.[34] Nothing replaced this important part of life; so the absence of that gaiety, excitement, and social escape in 1920 left a void. A solution was soon found in the appearance of speakeasies and illegal alcohol. It is difficult to assay the amount which was consumed but the size of the organized bootlegging, the associated growth in organized crime, the corruption of law enforcement, and related factors attest to the flagrant illegal production and consumption of alcohol by millions of Americans.[35]

During this period the drys initially appeared satisfied and did little to maintain their victory. Although studies were made by expert groups which recommended increased enforcement, their effect was lost. By 1933, abstinence was no longer the norm of society. Also the severity of the depression caused a demand for the return of the liquor industry for economic reasons. Opponents pointed out the evils of the Eighteenth Amendment—its violation of personal liberties, its cost of enforcement, its failure, its causing of a growth in crime as well as an economic hardship. An additional argument was the freedom of choice, i.e., people did not like to be told that they could not do something, particularly when that something had been allowed for years and was a part of their normal lives. Coupled with this was the backing of the former liquor industry and many millionaires (such as Irenée DuPont) who supplied substantial funds for support of repeal.

Studies of Alcoholism

Perhaps the most important contribution of prohibition to the disease concept was that it happened. The moralists forced the prohibition amendment through, and it did not work. Thus the argument of the temperance cause was severely weakened. The increased popularity of drinking and its social acceptance were evident. The concept that the alcoholic was a sinner gradually disappeared. The moral concept did not disappear but its failures left the American public and researchers more receptive to newer approaches toward alcohol and alcoholism. These new approaches invited a serious study of the complex problem in a much more open fashion. Researchers and students of all types were attracted by this frustrating problem. Those who were researching the problem adopted the policy that the only way to treat alcoholism successfully was as a disease. The public had to be made aware that the moral concept, as such, was a hindrance rather than a solution.[36] Studies of the prevalence of alcoholism (although only approximate) showed changes from 671 per 100,000 adult population in 1930 to 857 per 100,000 in 1945. This was an increase of 32.3 percent in urban areas and a decline of 8.5 percent in rural areas. This rapid growth stimulated a significant amount of investigation during the period of the late 1930s to 1950. First, psychological research eventually came to the almost unanimous acceptance that alcoholism was a mental disease with possible medical complications. This led to the popular acceptance of the disease idea. Until the early

1940s, however, the medical aspects considered were almost solely the relation of alcoholism to other disease states.

This sudden acceptance of alcoholism as a mental disease is surprising inasmuch as the mental idea had been presented in the early 1900s. The Committee of Fifty had recognized it, but their findings were apparently ignored. A general survey of papers published in *Psychological Abstracts* between 1928 and 1940 shows a gradual increase in such articles toward the end of the decade. Not until 1938 did the disease concept become a major topic. Lee, presenting the viewpoint of many psychiatrists, acknowledged the need for social recognition and education of the public into this problem.[37] Durfee stressed that alcoholism was a sickness and not a sin. He also clearly stated that society must accept the fact that alcoholism was a disease, "not of sin, but of sickness . . . not a sign of moral degradation but pathological expression of an inner need . . . which requires professional treatment like any physical disorder."[38]

By 1939 the number of studies on alcoholism increased significantly. A summary of their conclusions indicates that most classed it as a mental disease with medical implications.

The year 1940 marks the turning point with the creation of the Center of Alcohol Studies at Yale University for the sole purpose of research and reporting on alcoholism, alcohol, and directly related topics. The *Quarterly Journal of Studies on Alcohol* became the periodical voice of this unit. While Jellinek, the first director, described alcoholism as a mental disease, studies made by Yale researchers and others showed the success of medical techniques, thereby implying that alcoholism was not only a mental disease but a physiopathologic disease as well, requiring both medical and psychiatric attention.

Despite the damning information published by the Yale group and others, a steady increase in alcohol consumption was paralleled by an increase in alcoholism. The public ignored this fact and continued to hold a dangerous, naive, or apathetic view. Hence the experts recognized that the public must become more aware of, as well as better informed on, the subject. Numerous articles stressed this point. In the first issue of the *Quarterly Journal,* Myerson expressed the opinion that society needed to understand the problem and that people should learn to control their drinking.[39] Hall criticized the Supreme Court's views and decisions toward the alcoholic and those laws which showed no understanding of alcoholism as a disease.[40] Kolb summarized the attitude of the Public Health Bureau advising extensive revision of its policies.[41]

Perhaps the most relevant article of the period was written by Anderson. He summarized present attitudes toward alcohol and alcoholism as well as giving a short history of the disease concept.[42] His sensible and forthright paper is recommended to those desiring a clear view of professional and public attitudes of the year of publication, 1942.

Although the researchers of the Yale group and others recognized the need for greater public acceptance, they viewed their responsibilities as primarily to be directed toward research, collecting data plus other material which could be presented to others working in the field. The mass media, churches, and schools reacted extremely slowly to the task of informing the public although numerous articles aimed at the public interest were published in popular magazines and books. Almost the opposite is true today when the public is almost deluged with newspaper articles, features in periodicals, and television coverage. It is almost impossible for the professional to keep pace with advances in this complex field.

In the direct education field, little was accomplished. As indicated above, the mass media exercised the most influence. Linsky surveyed the *Reader's Guide to Periodic Literature* from 1900 to 1966 and made an exhaustive analysis by decades. He reported "Mass media have undoubtedly played a part in changing public opinion on alcoholism." His community survey found "evidence that exposure to mass media was directly related to enlightened attitudes on alcoholism among the public." He also found that by 1966, 54 percent of those favored a psychologic and biologic explanation while only 32.7 percent held for a sociologic position; the remainder were moralistic or for social criticism.[43] An independent study by Howland using Linsky's source *(Reader's Guide)* showed that two important defects existed in his analysis. First, during the period prior to 1947, most of the magazines in which the articles appeared were those of limited circulation such as *Hygeia, Science* and the *Literary Digest* which were subscribed to by the intellectual population. It must be assumed that little of this information reached the masses. Second, after World War II, by 1947, material on all aspects of alcoholism was widely circulated in popular magazines. This shows a trend or at least an attempt to reach the public with vital information.

Pfautz did a survey of the novels of two periods 1900-04 and 1946-50. The popular novels of the later period dealt much more freely with the subject of alcohol and alcoholism. Apparently public acceptance had followed the rejection of the moral concept.[44]

Also aiding the promotion of the disease concept was the role of the churches which had long been plagued with the problem. The Catholic Church was in the forefront of this movement and, in 1949, formed the National Clergy Conference on Alcoholism (N.C.C.A.).[45] Initially the main concern of the group was the alarming increase in alcoholism in the priesthood. This conference recognized that alcoholism was more than a moral failing, accepting the disease concept in part but agreeing that moral rejuvenation was also needed. The recommendations agreed upon were:

1. Education of the Catholic clergy through an annual Pastoral Institute on Alcohol Problems.

2. Prevention of alcoholism, through the dissemination of information and through an education program, especially in seminaries.

3. Recovery of alcoholics, through the Sacraments of the Church and the program of Alcoholics Anonymous.

4. Cooperation with all the ordinaries, and with all organizations working effectively in the field of alcoholism for the promotion of the above purposes.

Thus the priests became better educated about the problem. Probably many were much better informed than most physicians. From this time, the Catholic Church has been a leader in the field. Other denominations followed it. A widely recognized priest, J.C. Ford, wrote *Man Takes a Drink*, a text aimed at promoting public awareness of the problem.[46]

As the fifties progressed, the trend changed from merely accepting the disease concept to one of educating the public to the causes, symptoms, and other problems connected with alcoholism. By this time the public seemed to have shallowly accepted the fact that alcoholism was a disease. Magazines, newspapers, journals, alcoholism councils, health officials, and churches continued to stress this concept well into the 1950s and 1960s. Researchers explored the complexity of the disease ranging from proposed medical cures to sociological surveys. The attitudes of most researchers were that the public had accepted the disease idea, but knew little about it, and more importantly had difficulty in associating alcoholism with their conception of "disease." Although no public opinion polls on attitudes toward alcoholism were taken during the early fifties, in general the disease concept seemed to be accepted, but in turn serious moral doubts existed concerning the alcoholic. Certainly little knowledge about the disease existed in the public mind. It would be difficult to prove this assumption, but attitudes and trends indicated by the literature, actions of the churches, and opinions of experts in the field of alcoholism support this opinion for this period.

Alcoholics Anonymous

In the midst of this mass confusion concerning the problems of alcohol and alcoholism was the quiet founding in 1934 of Alcoholics Anonymous. With an approach similar to a religion, they also promoted personal and medical as well as psychological and moral therapy. An alcoholic had a weakness which he could conquer only by the reorganization of his lifestyle. The AA approach was quite practical, substituting the informal meetings and clubrooms for bars and cocktail parties. The need for professional help was stressed and that every alcoholic must establish a purpose in life even if that purpose was only to help others with similar problems. Thus, many members became among the best trained "professionals" in this field. Outside financial support was refused, the leaders insisting that in order to maintain complete control any activities should be self-supporting. The program grew slowly from its founding place in Akron, Ohio, to surrounding cities and eventually to all portions of the United States and Canada. AA meetings are now held throughout the world. The fact that AA was the first effective mass therapy for the alcoholic as well as the dedication of its members attracted the attention of the mass media which published extensively on various aspects of the movement during the forties and fifties. The acceptance that the alcoholic was "different" stabilized the disease concept; moral issues were considered secondary. The widely proclaimed membership of more than 650,000 (official figures have never been obtained) attests to the power and success of this group.

However, always conservative, the American Medical Association did not officially recognize alcoholism as a disease until 1958. In turn, the American College of Physicians, representing the peer group of experts in the diagnosis and treatment of human disease, did not issue a formal recognition until 1969, perhaps demanding more concise scientific information. It must be noted, however, that these groups' acceptance that alcoholism is a disease did grant its victims the privileges of insurance protection, treatment programs, and followup by industry, and the increase in public health funds both for direct care as well as inquiry into the scientific aspects of the problem which would provide improved methods for diagnosis and therapy.

In review, most changes in public attitude follow distinct periods of change associated with public unrest. The Revolutionary War created a definite change in lifestyle. The Civil War and its aftermath provoked tremendous alteration in the public way of life, producing many reform movements, prominent among which was the temperance group and others concerned with moral issues. World War I ended with National Prohibition, followed by changes in socioeconomic problems leading to the Great Depression of the 1930s, and with it the repeal of the Eighteenth Amendment.

The gradual international events which led into World War II in the latter portion of that decade ended in actual military participation when the United States entered the war on two fronts. While the Germans capitulated, the Japanese war ended abruptly with the detonation of two atomic bombs. This ushered in the atomic age with all its attendant moral, political, and social issues. The unpopular Korean and Vietnam undeclared wars produced great social chaos particularly among the young, and certainly became a major factor in the appearance of the drug culture. As time progressed, the drug and alcohol cultures have become inseparably intermixed leading to a tremendous increase in alcoholism, drug usage, or both. These periods have also been accompanied by increases in the most sophisticated of technologies with increasing complication of sociopolitical-economic issues. The young are resisting formal restraints in search of a more meaningful life; at the same time industry and government are forcing individuals into retirement at earlier ages. In the latter case, few are prepared to face the drastic changes of their new life and leisure living, and seek alcohol among other means to relieve the resultant boredom. Accordingly, it is definite that alcoholism is increasing in these two particular classes. Among the working group, the uncertainty of the future, political chaos, and the like have provided tensions not so prominent in previous times. Alcohol is the tranquilizer of choice in the relief of their anxieties, and continued use is certain to result in a definite number of these individuals becoming sensitive to the drug, alcohol, with resultant development of alcoholism.

The Future

A study of history enables one to gain insight into the present nature of any problem. The purpose of this review has been to analyze past and present thinking and develop from them specific recommendations as guides to future activity. Three specific programs are necessary:

1. More education of the medical profession, other workers in the alcoholism field, and the public about the problems of alcoholism and its control. The mass media have already taken advanced steps in this direction.

2. Provision of facilities in the form of treatment centers, half-way houses, club rooms, and counseling services for the continuing treatment of the alcoholic who has not progressed into the irreversible stage. Also provision of installations to care for the individual who has progressed beyond medical help and requires institutionalization on a long-term basis.

3. Stimulation of research activities into all aspects of the medical, psychological, and sociological aspects of alcoholism. These should be directed toward determining the etiology and pathophysiological underlying processes, the associated psychologic aspects and accompanying sociologic

patterns. Particular attention should be directed toward racial, familial, and genetic aspects of the problem and its relation to other diseases.

The evolution continues. It remains for the public, the medical profession, the clergy, the social worker, and all others directly connected with the health field to organize their resources and apply them intelligently to the problem. Progress has been gradual but evident. However, the alcoholic continues to be much the same rejected individual he has always been. Only when a proven cure or arrest of this disease state is discovered, one which can permanently alleviate this mysterious defect which makes the alcoholic different from other men, can the battle be considered as won.

PART II

The Complications of Drinking

THE FIRST FOUR chapters in this section review medical, medico-legal, psychiatric, and highway safety complications of drinking, and the final chapter considers the question, is moderate drinking risky?

Drs. Fallon and Lesesne, both distinguished contributors to the literature on liver damage, are well qualified to discuss the overall medical complications in alcoholism. Dr. Fallon is now professor and chairman of the Department of Medicine at Virginia Commonwealth University in Richmond and Dr. Henry Lesesne serves as Assistant Professor of Medicine, Division of Gastroenterology-Hepatology, University of North Carolina at Chapel Hill.

Dr. Page Hudson is a pathologist who is involved in the academic as well as the many practical applications of his science. An expert in forensic medicine, he serves as Chief Medical Examiner for the entire state of North Carolina, and he has been responsible for upgrading local medical examiner programs and for instituting major scientific advances in the study of deaths, particularly those not attributed to natural causes.

Dr. Ewing as a psychiatrist and alcohol specialist has already been introduced as editor and is author of the chapter on psychiatric complications and the chapter on the risks of moderate drinking.

Dr. Patricia Waller is a clinical psychologist with major interest in injury control and emergency medical services administration in the Department of Health Administration at UNC Chapel Hill. At the UNC Highway Safety Research Center, she has been responsible for a major project concerning the evaluation and upgrading of driver licensing and driver improvement programs. She is currently chairing a national task force concerned with driver regulation.

Of course, we cannot exhaust this subject fully in these four chapters. Alcohol has destroyed many a marriage, has precipitated accidents in many situations other than on the highway and its relationship to criminal activities of various types is only too well known. However, these four chapters will convincingly demonstrate to the reader why we should be concerned about the drinker who drinks too much, who loses control, and for whom alcohol has become the tyrannical master.

CHAPTER 4

Medical Complications of Excessive Drinking

Harold J. Fallon, M.D.
Henry R. Lesesne, M.D.

SINCE ANTIQUITY CHRONIC alcoholism has been recognized to
have medical complications. The ancient Greeks associated
cirrhosis with wine drinking. The neurological manifestations
of delirium tremens, psychosis, seizures, and neuropathies
have been well described for many years. However, only recently has the full range of adverse effects of alcohol ingestion
been recognized. Many organ systems are affected by alcohol
ingestion, either directly or by an indirect metabolic mechanism. In some cases, the incidence, pathology, and physiological consequences of alcoholism are well described. In
others, there is only fragmentary information.

Table 4-1 lists some of the more commonly recognized
disease states related to alcoholism. The incidence of these
complications is variable, but none are rare. This variability
may be attributed in part to differences in the quantity of
alcohol consumed. However, little or no information exists
regarding the minimum amount of alcohol consumption
necessary to produce these disorders. There may be a threshold
effect in which a given complication becomes manifest when a
critical level of alcohol consumption is reached. Alternatively,
there may be a continuous spectrum of increasing pathology,

from clinically undetectable change in mild or moderate users of alcohol, to a more severe abnormality in those who regularly consume large quantities of alcohol.

Table 4-1
Major Medical Complications of Excessive Drinking

Neurological syndromes
Myopathy
Cardiomyopathy
Pancreatitis
Gastritis
Bone marrow suppression
Hypoglycemia
Hypertriglyceridemia
Liver disease

Neurological Disorders

Perhaps the most commonly recognized complications of regular alcohol ingestion are the various neurological disorders. The intoxication syndrome is well known in all drinking societies. The more dramatic effects of alcohol withdrawal after prolonged ingestion are also well described. Delirium tremens (the DT's) is the most severe syndrome in this category. It is marked by tremulousness, hallucinations, and localized or grand mal seizures. A substantial mortality rate is associated with delirium tremens. Usually in such cases, there is profuse sweating, rapid heart beat, dilatation of the pupils, and fever. With patients manifesting this constellation of findings, a mortality as high as 15 percent has been recorded. More unusual neurological complications of alcoholism include the so-called Wernicke's syndrome (manifest by ophthalmoplegia, ataxic gait with cerebellar signs, mental confusion, and apathy) and Korsakoff's psychosis (manifest by inability to learn, poor concentration, and defective memory).[1]

Myopathies

Another common complication is alcoholic myopathy. Muscle injury and weakness in chronic alcoholics were first recognized in Europe, and later studied in this country by Perkoff and associates. This syndrome is usually manifest by muscle aching and tenderness and the development of weakness which may become profound. Muscle cramping and

edema are also common. Laboratory findings include eleva-
tions in the serum glutamic oxaloacetic transaminase and
creatine phosphokinase. Myoglobinuria of an occult type also
occurs. The chemical abnormalities of this syndrome may
occur in the absence of obvious muscle symptoms. Therefore,
the incidence of alcoholic myopathy is conjectural, although it
is apparently common. The studies of Perkoff et al. have
shown an interference in muscle metabolism with impaired
conversion of glycogen or glucose to lactic acid. This abnormality seems to be reversible, and, in most patients, the
symptoms disappear after withdrawal of alcohol. However, in
a severe form of the disease, muscle necrosis may occur, and the
patient is left with permanent muscle weakness. Abstinence
from alcohol is the only recognized therapy.[2]

Alcoholic cardiomyopathy may be closely related in
etiology to the skeletal-muscle disease.[3] Some investigators in
England and the United States have proposed that unexplained heart failure in young and middle-aged adults is most
frequently related to chronic ingestion of alcohol. Moreover,
these investigators have suggested that mild abnormalities in
heart function may occur much more commonly in the drinking population and be unassociated with obvious congestive
failure. This cardiomyopathy is not related to the classical
beriberi syndrome recognized many years ago in alcoholics.
Beriberi is clearly caused by dietary thiamine deficiency and is
reversible. Over the past fifteen years, the view that alcohol is a
direct myocardial toxin has been supported by several studies
in animals and man.[4]

These patients often present with mild fatigue, short-
ness of breath on exertion, palpitation, or chest pain without
changes on chest x-ray or electrocardiogram. As alcohol consumption continues, the cardiomyopathy worsens with development of severe congestive heart failure. Unfortunately, the
depressed cardiac output and the poor cardiac response to
exercise do not seem to be reversible in the extreme forms of
this cardiomyopathy if not recognized early. Therapy is
directed at bed rest and complete abstinence from alcohol.

Gastrointestinal Complications

Gastrointestinal complications of prolonged or acute
alcohol ingestion are common. These include mild nausea,

vomiting, diarrhea, and anorexia. Of much greater medical importance are the problems of pancreatitis[5] and gastritis. It is estimated that 20 to 40 percent of all patients with acute pancreatitis in this country are alcoholics or heavy drinkers. Acute pancreatitis is associated with a substantial mortality, and the long-term complications of malabsorption, malnutrition, development of glucose intolerance, and the eventual addiction to narcotics because of persistent pain are well known. Studies have shown that prolonged ingestion of alcohol in animals may produce pancreatic fibrosis, and also changes in pancreatic lipid and protein metabolism. Therefore, alcohol seems directly toxic to the pancreas, although the mechanism remains unexplained. Alcohol may increase gastric acid secretion and directly damage stomach mucosa leading to a diffuse gastritis. In many patients, this produces only upper gastrointestinal pain. However, in others, massive bleeding from the stomach occurs with its associated complications.

Bone Marrow Function

Alcohol interferes with bone marrow function in several ways. For example, alcohol ingestion in man is frequently associated with anemia and depression in platelets and polymorphonuclear leukocytes.[6] Various animal studies have shown that alcohol interferes with folate absorption and also with the conversion of vitamin B-6 to its active form, pyridoxyal phosphate. These latter effects may account in part for the anemia so frequently seen in chronic alcoholics, even in the absence of gastrointestinal bleeding. Toxic effects on bone marrow have been recognized by histological studies. These may account for the suppression in platelet and leukocyte production. Shortly after alcohol is removed from the diet, the platelet count and white count return toward normal and frequently rebound to exceedingly high levels. The overwhelming majority of alcoholic patients manifest a partially suppressed bone marrow function.

Metabolic Changes

Metabolic changes are common in alcoholics. Perhaps the most serious is the syndrome of alcoholic hypoglycemia. A profound fall in the blood sugar of fasting alcoholics was reported several years ago.[7] The mechanism of this effect appears to be an interference by alcohol metabolism with gluconeogenesis by the liver. Since the latter sustains blood sugar levels in the fasting state, alcoholics are most sensitive to a lack of food intake. Alcoholic hypoglycemia probably accounts for many of the acute and sudden deaths in the alcoholic population. Other factors also may be involved, but hypoglycemia is a frequent contributing factor in sudden death. Elevated alcohol concentrations in the blood will increase the osmolality of serum. Thus, a "hyperosmolar syndrome," similar to that seen in diabetics with high blood sugar, has been observed. This syndrome is marked by mental confusion and coma, and it may also account for some of the sudden deaths in alcoholics. Ketoacidosis without significant hyperglycemia has also been encountered in alcoholics and can be difficult to recognize.[8]

Alcohol stimulates the hepatic formation of triglycerides and is a well known cause of hypertriglyceridemia. This response of blood fat levels to high alcohol intake may be exaggerated in patients with inborn errors of lipid metabolism. The significance of this type of abnormality to the development of atherosclerosis is unknown.

Effects on Pregnancy

Excessive drinking during pregnancy can result in altered growth and morphogenesis of the infant. This has been termed the "fetal alcohol syndrome" and is manifest primarily by increased perinatal mortality, and in those surviving, growth deficiency and deficient intellectual performances. The long-term effect of this adverse situation for the fetus has yet to be fully elucidated.[9]

Liver Disease

Probably the most commonly recognized complication of chronic alcoholism among the lay public is liver disease. There are various forms of alcoholic liver disease, and these include fatty infiltration of the liver, alcoholic hepatitis, and Laennec's cirrhosis.[10]

Studies of the effect of alcohol ingestion on the appearance of fat in the liver have been conducted in human volunteers. As little as 70-270 gm of ethanol per day in normal volunteer subjects will produce detectable fat in the liver, as measured by histological and chemical means. This effect appears in two to three days and is maintained for as long as two weeks. These studies were conducted by Lieber and Rubin and strongly suggest that all alcoholics and most heavy drinkers will manifest fatty infiltration of the liver. In addition to the increase in liver fat, there are changes in the appearance of mitochondria and endoplasmic reticulum by electron microscopic study.[11] The meaning of these changes is as yet unclear. In most studies, alcoholic fatty liver appears freely reversible, and the contribution of fatty infiltration of the liver to the development of more serious liver disease is uncertain.

Laennec's cirrhosis is one of the most dreaded complications of chronic alcoholism. In the United States, this disease is recognized in some 8 to 10 percent of chronic alcoholics. There are a variety of studies from Europe and South America which suggest that Laennec's cirrhosis occurs in only a minority of alcoholics. In a German series, it was noted that cirrhosis appeared in highest incidence when patients ingested the equivalent of eight to ten ounces of whiskey per day for greater than fifteen years. However, even at this high rate of consumption, cirrhosis occurred in less than a third of such patients. This relatively low incidence suggests that factors other than alcohol ingestion must be important in determining which patients develop cirrhosis. Whether this is a genetic predisposition or related to dietary or other environmental factors is a matter of great importance.

Laennec's cirrhosis is frequently complicated by ascites, splenomegaly, bleeding esophageal varices, and ultimately death. However, in those patients with cirrhosis who discontinue alcohol ingestion, the prognosis is often excellent. For example, in a detailed study of a large number of alcoholics, Powell and Klatskin observed that the survival rate for patients with uncomplicated Laennec's cirrhosis who had discontinued alcohol ingestion was nearly normal after the first twelve to eighteen months.[12] Thus, a good outlook in such patients should encourage physicians and other health personnel to make especially strenuous efforts at removing alcohol from the diet of such patients.

A much more recently recognized syndrome associated with alcohol ingestion is alcoholic hepatitis. This syndrome also occurs in a minority of alcoholics, estimated at 10 to 20 percent. The lesion is characterized by an acute necrotic and inflammatory response in the liver which is often associated with severe abdominal pain, fever, jaundice, and an elevation in white count. However, it may occur in a totally asymptomatic patient. A recent study conducted at the University of North Carolina School of Medicine showed that patients with alcoholic hepatitis may develop cirrhosis as their acute lesion heals.[13] It is postulated on the basis of these studies and those of others that alcoholic hepatitis is the initial pathological event which may result in Laennec's cirrhosis. Therefore, an understanding of the mechanisms by which alcohol causes liver necrosis in humans will be of critical importance in preventing serious liver disease in the drinking population.

Death occurs in approximately one-third to one-half of seriously ill patients with alcoholic hepatitis. In some studies, treatment of such patients with corticosteroids has markedly improved the survival rate. Other investigators have reported that corticosteroid therapy is not effective in this group and therefore such treatment remains experimental.

Needed Research

Alcohol ingestion in man is obviously associated with multisystem organ damage. The mechanisms of this damage, its incidence, and serious consequences have not been sufficiently studied. Although severe alcoholics have a high mortality rate in relationship to these complications, it is not clear whether such complications contribute to death or serious illness in mild or moderate social drinkers. Much more information about these clinical syndromes will be required before we can attempt to prevent or more properly treat these manifestations of alcohol ingestion.

CHAPTER 5

The Medical Examiner Looks at Drinking

Page Hudson, M.D.

MORTUI VIVOS DOCENT, "The dead instruct the living," is inscribed over the door of the first pathology laboratory I ever entered. The inscription encourages the attending physician to seek information and insight from autopsy studies that should enable him to better counsel the deceased's family and to better treat his other patients. The same phrase also applies to the medical examiner who examines one quarter of all deaths. He is concerned not only with answering questions about each specific death but in deriving both hard data and philosophy from all his investigations that can enhance the quality of life for others.

Even the more sophisticated, nonmedical public has certain misconceptions about what can be learned from the dead. The public has a vague awareness that postmortem studies are made in some natural disease deaths, the frequency of the studies varying with the community. The popular assumption is that natural deaths are clearly distinguished from all others and that the latter receive close scrutiny. This assumption is frequently not well founded, particularly in the United States. Many states have grossly inadequate statutes, personnel, and systems for investigation of suspicious, unnatural, or unattended deaths. One measure of the degree of civilization of a human society is the attention paid to the circumstances pertaining to unnatural deaths. This refers not to complicated funeral rites, for these reach their zenith among the more primitive societies, but to the public health, law, and science oriented matters of the cause and the manner of death. Throughout the world about one quarter of all deaths do not follow a physician-attended natural disease process. These instead fall into one or more of the following categories: sudden, unexpected while in "good health"; without medical care; violent or traumatic; suspicious (homicide, suicide, or accident); unusual or unnatural. The stories that are to be told from these deaths are commonly quite different in many regards from those 75 percent of deaths that occur following a documented and medically attended natural illness.

The 25 percent that are referred to as "medical examiner cases" have by the very nature of their occurrence or circumstances more legal significance than the others. A variety of civil and criminal issues are involved. The medical aspects of the investigation of these deaths require training and orientation beyond the usual fields or specialties of medicine. In most parts of the world and in many areas of the United States there are systems with physicians involved part-time or full-time in the investigation of these deaths. Physicians so oriented and engaged are generally called "medical examiners" in the United States.

An equally high level of investigation is also carried on in other parts of the world, particularly in the English speaking nations and a few communities in the United States, under the term "Office of the Coroner." In most of the United States, the coroner, however personally well-intentioned, is an elected political figure and has no medical or legal training or experience. Too often he is the local funeral director for reasons of expediency. Still other nations have advanced investigational systems comparable to the medical examiner system under a variety of terms.

The medical examiner is charged by law with examining the deceased, investigating the circumstances in situations referred to above and rendering in his best judgment opinions as to the cause and as to the manner of death. He may visit the scene of death, collect such information as he can from the family and associates of the deceased, communicate closely with any law enforcement agency involved, draw blood or other body fluid for chemical studies, and have an autopsy conducted when he believes this is in the public interest. The official death certificate in these cases is certified and filed by the medical examiner. If he is a full-time, career medical examiner, he is generally a forensic pathologist and conducts autopsies himself. Information pertaining to the cause and to the manner of death is made available to appropriate parties such as the family of the deceased or their legal representative, insurance companies, public health or welfare agencies, law enforcement agencies, or the prosecuting attorney's office. The medical examiner system also looks beyond individual cases and helps to identify problems, trends, new hazards, social phenomena, medical care deficiencies, and research needs that relate to improvement of the quality of man's existence. This is done in a state medical examiner system at the office of the chief medical examiner where, among other functions, all medical examiner, autopsy, and toxicology reports are collected and analyzed. A major flow of the system's output to other agencies and services is through the office of the chief medical examiner.

The medical examiner seeks not only the direct cause of death such as a heart attack or poisoning, gunshot wound or fractured skull, but also other circumstances, injury or chemical that might have been a contributing, aggravating, or otherwise relevant factor. One is not a member of the medical examiner team long before he realizes that alcohol is either a highly significant factor in a vast proportion of the deaths or that at any given time a great percentage of the population has been imbibing. Either of the two possibilities would be an important lesson to be learned from the dead. All career medical examiners would contend that alcohol is one of the most significant and frequent factors in the death cases we investigate. Some of us believe that alcohol is currently the most significant single public health problem in the United States today—automobile crashes, environmental pollution, malnutrition including obesity, lung cancer, and heart diseases notwithstanding.

Many natural and unnatural deaths represent weaknesses in our medical and social systems. Analysis, with the view of determining and correcting those weaknesses, must be made of groups and classes of cases rather than of isolated deaths. The narrow viewpoint or perspective in this chapter then is that of the medical examiner, involved almost exclusively with death cases, concerned with a prevalent factor in these deaths. From this perspective there is much information pertaining to frequency of the use and abuse of the drug alcohol, and information pertaining to deaths contributed to or caused by alcohol.

Death Associated with Alcohol

The presence of a high blood level of alcohol is one of the most common factors among medical examiner death cases. Rivaling this and not necessarily related are the presence of microscopically or grossly visible fat in the liver, low socioeconomic status, previously unappreciated coronary artery disease, and lack of previous medical attention. These observations are based primarily on evaluation of predeath circumstances, scene of death, autopsy studies, toxicology, and other environmental and personal information. Since the exogenous substance alcohol is present so frequently in the 25 percent of all deaths that constitute medical examiner cases, an attempt will be made to categorize these alcohol-related deaths. The following outline will be used:

1. Coincidental (death and alcohol)
2. Aggravation of existing disease
3. Alcohol obscuring disease or injury
4. Increased susceptibility to all manners of death (natural, accident, suicide, homicide)
5. Acute alcoholism and acute alcohol poisoning
6. Chronic alcoholism
7. Sudden, unexpected-death-with-fatty-liver syndrome

1. Coincidental: The drinking man is subject to all of the same afflictions as everyone else. His drinking, however, makes him subject to some additional ones. That he had alcohol in his system at the time of death is not necessarily of real significance. The degree, when there is significance, correlates with the alcohol level. For example, in over 10 percent of unattended but "natural" deaths and in more than 10 percent of fatal industrial accidents there is detectable alcohol in the blood. In the latter the average blood alcohol level among the positive cases is about three times that seen in the "natural" deaths. The average blood alcohol level is .15 percent or 150 mg. per 100 ml blood in positive industrial accident cases and .05 percent or 50 mg. per 100 ml blood in the "natural" deaths. The inexperienced medical examiner or coroner may occasionally attempt to ascribe death to low levels of alcohol or to attribute precipitation of an accident or other violent death upon low levels. The experience of those of us in forensic medicine is generally that when alcohol is present in cases of violent death it is present not in low but in remarkably high levels.

2. *Aggravation of existing disease:* To present anything approaching valid numbers or statistics in this category is extremely difficult. One must communicate from experience and subjective impressions. It is not an uncommon circumstance during the careful investigation and autopsy of a medical-legal death to find a moderately high level of alcohol in the person who died with a relatively severe natural disease but a disease with which he had existed for months or years. In the face of the circumstances and history of some of the cases, it is tempting and seems reasonable to believe that alcohol may have been significant in aggravating or causing decompensation in an existing natural disease process. Certainly some medical examiners are impressed with those cases that have a significant history of alcohol overindulgence only in the immediate past and in whom they find at autopsy an intestinal tract full of blood from a bleeding peptic ulcer, decompensated valvular heart disease, or profound pulmonary emphysema and fibrosis. The toxic effect of large quantities of alcohol stresses the individual; the diseased organisms can withstand less new stress than the healthy one. When in the judgment of the medical examiner the natural disease was the basic cause of death with alcohol contributing to the natural process, he should so indicate appropriately on the death certificate rather than shying away from the mention of alcohol because of concern for real or imagined social stigma. Physicians attending people dying in hospitals with recognized "natural"

complications of chronic alcoholism characteristically certify the cause with euphemistic terms or phrases that becloud the real issue.

3. Alcohol obscuring disease or injury: Those of us daily involved with obscure or violent deaths find it common that a treatable or curable disease or injury had a fatal outcome because the patient was unaware of his disability or discomfort because of his state of intoxication. Abdominal pain from a blood-leaking injury to the liver, mesentery, intestine, or spleen may be masked by high levels of alcohol.[1] Some of these victims have been aware of discomfort, but in their befuddled judgment they have not related the discomfort to trauma or are unwilling or unable to seek medical care. The other side of the coin is that the law enforcement officer or physician may wrongly attribute the disease or injury symptoms to the effect of alcohol with the result that the victim soon dies of his injury in jail, at home, or on the street.

The effect of shock and internal hemorrhage, disability from head injury such as subdural hematoma, and symptoms from uncontrolled diabetes mellitus or abdominal injury are all too often attributed to the central nervous system effect of alcohol or to one of the complications of overindulgence such as gastritis. A basic assumption too commonly made is that the complaints of the "drunk" or the causes of his health problems are due to alcohol and that any other possibility would have to be proven. The opposite should prevail in that the assumption must be that there is treatable organic or metabolic disease until proven otherwise. The attending physician must proceed with his best diagnostic and therapeutic efforts. The medical, moral, and legal pitfalls here are vast.

4. Increased susceptibility to all manners of death: With perhaps no more or less of the arbitrariness and inflexibility that generally go with classification procedures, most states classify deaths into the categories of natural, accident, suicide, or homicide (or unknown or pending). The chronic or acute abuse of alcohol tends to bring a person to one of these four "before his time." This is not even to mention death due to the most direct complications of chronic alcoholism or to acute alcohol poisoning as these will be discussed later.

The chronic alcoholic is more likely to incur sudden

infectious disease than those who consume little or no alcohol. Tuberculosis and hepatitis, among others, are more frequent in the alcoholic. This may be due to exposure because of his way or place of life. There are certainly nutritional factors as well. The alcohol addict has an increased susceptibility to pneumonia particularly that caused by the pneumococcal and the Friedlander's bacteria. There is evidence that this is due in part to alcohol's reducing leukocyte mobilization, phagocytosis, and intracellular bacterial killing.[2] Aspiration of oral secretions or gastric content into the respiratory tract in the unconscious alcoholic is another factor. There are good data suggesting that alcoholics are more susceptible to cancer of the pancreas than is the general population although this is a relatively rare disease under any circumstances.[3]

Accidental death is the fate of tens of thousands of alcohol abusers annually. Effects of alcohol (reduced coordination, mental alertness, and visual acuity) precipitate or otherwise contribute to most fatal automobile crashes, falls, fires, drownings, and other violent deaths.[4] Another distinct effect is reduction of judgment leading a person to undertake action he would not in a more sober state. The best recognized example of violent deaths related to alcohol are those resulting from auto crashes. Data from many areas of the United States indicate that about 50 percent of drivers killed in automobile crashes are considered legally under the influence of alcohol (that is, have a blood alcohol level of .10 percent or higher in North Carolina and many states; .15 percent minimum in others). The same national data indicate that about 60 percent of the drivers killed in single car crashes had been drinking. In North Carolina, our 1970-74 data show 60 percent of the drivers killed in single car crashes were legally under the influence and another 10 percent had been drinking. The average blood level of those drivers killed having some alcohol in their blood was .18 percent. Minimum consumption required for an average sized man to reach .18 percent would be nine standard drinks in an hour. See Table 5-1 for guidelines for estimating blood alcohol levels. Liver examination on these drivers in our autopsy studies suggest that the majority are chronic alcoholics. Relatively few of those killed had low levels (.05 percent or less).

Table 5-1
Guidelines for Estimating Blood Alcohol Levels

Amount and Time	Breathalyzer Reading
1 drink in 1 hour	.02 percent
4 drinks in 3 hours ("party glow")	.05 percent
5 drinks in 2 hours	.10 percent
10 drinks in 2 hours	.20 percent
1 pint whiskey in 2 hours	.35 percent

The approximations above assume a body weight of 155 pounds and light eating. One drink is assumed to be about 1 ounce of 100 proof whiskey or a 12 ounce beer or 5 ounces of table wine. Greater body weight would require more alcohol to reach a given level. A full stomach slows absorption of alcohol.

In North Carolina, approximately 3,300 drivers are arrested each month for driving under the influence of intoxicating liquors. The average and indeed the typical blood level among these drivers as determined by the Breathalyzer is .17 percent. Those arrested and on testing found to have less than .05 percent constituted less than 1 percent of the total tested. The arrested drivers were only those observed to be driving erratically or to have had a crash and who demonstrated a subjective impression of intoxication to the investigating officer.

The driver involved in a death-related crash is finally becoming fair game for suspicion of alcoholism with good reason. However, when the crash victim is an adult pedestrian, the driver is commonly innocent relative to alcohol. Table 5-2 shows average blood alcohol levels for victims of violent death in North Carolina. From our 1971 records, of 159 pedestrians killed who were at least age fifteen years and from whom a blood sample was taken, ninety-nine (63 percent) were found to have been drinking alcohol. The average blood level of those drinking was .27 percent. To ascribe direct correlation is impossible but alcohol is at least a major factor in over half of the nearly 60,000 deaths a year attributed to motor vehicle "accidents."

Drownings cause about 7,500 deaths a year in the United States, perhaps a third of these being young children.

Table 5-2
Frequency Rate for Blood Alcohol and Average Levels in Violent Death Victims (Over Age 15) in North Carolina

Means of Death	Number of Cases in Study	% Alcohol Positive	Average Blood Alcohol Level
Pedestrians	159	63%	.27%
Fire	100	75%	.26%
Homicide (Knife)	50	85%	.21%
Homicide (Gun)	500	71%	.20%
Drowning	100	58%	.19%
Auto driver (Single car crash)	1000	70%	.18%
Suicide (Gun)	150	34%	.16%

The data are from several studies involving presence and levels of alcohol, conducted variously between 1970 and 1974 (Office of the Chief Medical Examiner, North Carolina).

The adult drowning victim commonly has a high level of alcohol. In an examination of the records of one hundred consecutive investigations in North Carolina of drownings of persons sixteen years of age or older, 58 percent were found to have been drinking alcohol. Only nine had been drinking relatively small quantities and had levels below .10 percent. Using the same criteria for people dead after fires, as opposed to those who survived fires by hours or days, examination of one hundred consecutive cases revealed alcohol in 45 percent. Only seven had levels of less than .10 percent; the average was .26 percent. In seventy-nine of these the liver was fatty, highly indicative of chronic alcoholism. The Office of the Chief Medical Examiner of the Commonwealth of Virginia reports the presence of alcohol in over 50 percent of their tested accidental deaths, this figure being uncorrected for age. Obviously the percentage would be much higher were the young victims not included.

Suicide and alcohol also appear to the medical examiner to be related. The nature of the relationship is speculative, but there would seem to be two associations. One is that alcohol may precipitate depression leading to suicide in some people. The other is that a considerable proportion of people contemplating suicide fortify themselves with alcohol. In recent data from the North Carolina medical examiner system, samples from 150 "successful" victims of suicide using firearms as the fatal agent revealed that 34 percent had been drinking. The average blood level was .16 percent.

Homicide is the product of so many factors known and unknown that to blame this manner of death on alcohol would be absurd. However, when any factor is present in 70 percent of homicide situations the factor appears significant, whether or not it was a "cause." The medical examiner obtains more information about the homicide victim than about the person who does the killing. This is due primarily to the fact that in our jurisdiction all homicide victims are subjected to autopsy and toxicological examination. In our most recent study, of 500 homicides due to firearms, 71 percent had been drinking. Levels below .10 percent were rare; the average was .20 percent. Of fifty recent victims of homicide due to stabbing or incised wounds, 85 percent had been drinking, and the average level was .21 percent. The presence of high levels of alcohol in homicide victims is consistent among our cases whether the death results from an altercation, sexual assault, or some other crime or some other circumstance.

The alcohol level in the homicide victim has on occasion been so high (over .35 percent) as to bring out the possibility that the death was due to alcohol poisoning rather than the shooting or stabbing which theoretically could have occurred after death. This contention is occasionally employed in court by the defense attorney; the medical examiner must be precise and knowledgeable about his evidence that the deceased was alive and perhaps even involved in an altercation at the time he suffered his fatal wound. Frequently the defense contends that the deceased was the aggressor and presents evidence that he was belligerently aggressive when intoxicated. The law in theory makes a man responsible for his actions irrespective of his having been intoxicated by alcohol. In practice, however, society does tend to mitigate the circumstances if the perpetrator was "under the influence," to the extent of allowing a plea of second degree murder in an obvious first degree situation or of minimizing the sentence.

5. *Alcohol as a poison:* Ethyl alcohol is a central nervous system depressant, having an inhibitory effect on the respira-

tory center in the brain stem. It can and does kill in a similar manner to barbiturates or other sedative drugs. That this occurs rather commonly surprises many in the medical profession as well as the laity. Most of the nonheavy drinking population is under the impression that a person consuming alcohol in the quantity of a fifth within a few hours would vomit or pass out before he could down that much. Many who only rarely overindulge have had one or both of these experiences and assume that they are common to all. People accustomed to frequent use of large quantities of alcohol, and some who are not, have the ability to keep down this volume. There is no established "LD-50" for beverage alcohol, but attributing the death directly to the depressant effect should be considered with a level of .35 percent and greater. "LD-50" stands for "lethal dose, 50 percent" meaning the dose at which one half of the subjects survive and one half die. Some people succumb with lower levels in their blood at the time of death either because of their greater individual susceptibility or because they have survived in coma long enough to have metabolized much alcohol, lowering their original alcohol level. We find people occasionally who can still get about in more or less successful fashion with levels of .40 percent or more. There is no one level below which all survive and above which all die.

The acute toxic deaths are almost invariably accidental. Suicide among these people must occur, but it is very rare. This phenomenon of acute alcohol poisoning is relatively infrequent in many parts of the nation. It is too often unsuspected and unsought, even among career medical examiners. When one has an otherwise negative autopsy and toxicology appropriate history or circumstances, and a blood level of .35 percent or higher, acute alcohol poisoning is the appropriate term. Even when this phenomenon is recognized there is strangely a tendency among medical examiners in systems in some other states to certify the death as "natural." Reasons given me in a survey included: (1) "The insurance companies want it that way"; (2) "They are accidents but the boss says call them natural"; (3) "The International Classification Code requires it" (incorrect); (4) "I can't see giving those alcoholics a break"; (5) "You're correct. I just never thought of acute *alcohol* poisoning as an accident."

It would seem important for a variety of reasons, insurance settlement not the least, to consistently determine with accuracy the manner of death. The reader may be considerably surprised to realize that the vital statistics offices of state health departments throughout the nation frequently do not even code this form of death as "accident" even though the medical examiner may have so indicated on the death certificate. If on the certificate he has certified the cause of death as acute alcoholism, acute alcohol intoxication, or acute ethylism or other similar terms rather than as acute alcohol poisoning, the cause is coded with chronic fatal complications of alcoholism such as cirrhosis, fatty liver, or Wernicke's disease. If the cause of death is classified among these "natural" phenomena, the manner is then pigeonholed as natural rather than accident in disregard of the certifying officer's determination. This is one more bit of evidence that our state and national statistics from death certificates are worse than valueless in terms of valid data about acute and about chronic alcoholism. The reader is reminded that these deaths under discussion are due to ethyl alcohol ("grain alcohol") and not other alcohols or the contaminants sometimes found in alcohol, particularly in moonshine or white whiskey.

In 1971, I collected information about alcohol testing and acute poisoning from established medical examiner systems and some of the more sophisticated coroner offices about the nation. Table 5-3 summarizes some of the more important results. The study was concerned primarily with acute alcohol poisoning cases where there was a blood (or equivalent) level (BAC) of .40 percent or more. Though inconsistencies in the frequency or incidence of this phenomenon and in terminology exist, there was uniform consistency in alcohol-testing capability and in definition of "acute alcohol poisoning." The criteria in these death cases were blood (or equivalent) level of .35 percent alcohol or greater; absence of other anatomical or chemical cause of death; compatible history, situations, or circumstances; evaluation of each case on its merits. The other important factor was the availability of standard methods of analysis (usually gas chromatography) in an adequate laboratory performed by trained and experienced toxicological chemists. All of the laboratories whose data were used apparently included internal controls in their testing as well as daily alcohol standard check. Both the data included on Table 5-3 and some lesser data not included point toward a much higher incidence of acute alcohol poisoning in the southeastern states than in other parts of the nation.

Acute alcohol poisoning deaths were recorded by the statistics section of the State Board of Health rarely in North Carolina before the advent of the medical examiner system in 1969. This system encompassed approximately 80 percent of the population and land area of the state in July 1971. Using the above criteria and eliminating those cases in which there are other factors such as severe coronary disease, aspiration of vomitus, exposure to cold, and other likely causes of death, the medical examiner is discovering and certifying nearly 200 accidental acute alcohol poisonings each year. The number has increased as the system embraced the remainder of the state and as the practicing physician county medical examiners acquired more experience and became more consistent in submitting blood samples from each investigated death. Their sampling frequency has risen to a current level of about 55 percent and should ascend to at least 80 percent. Some of the cases, because of their hospital stay, or advanced postmortem change (e.g., skeletonization) cannot be tested. All of the medical examiner reports as well as the autopsy reports are reviewed in the central Office of the Chief Medical Examiner where also all the toxicological determinations are made.

In addition to those deaths from ethyl alcohol, there are approximately a dozen deaths (of about 10,000 deaths investigated annually) certified as due to isopropyl alcohol poisoning. This substance is best known and available as "rubbing alcohol." Circumstances generally indicate these are accidental deaths, such as those caused by occasional methyl or wood alcohol poisoning.

Despite North Carolina's being among the nation's leaders in the production of illicit whiskey, lead poisoning from the consumption of this material is extremely rare. In the seven years of the existence of the state's medical examiner system, there has been a continual search for lead both in white whiskey specimens and in liver of autopsy subjects known to habitually consume this beverage. Significantly elevated levels

Table 5-3
Acute Ethanol Poisoning Deaths (A.E.P.)
Solicited Data From County and State Medical Examiner Systems*

AREA	Certified Deaths	Percent Tested for Ethanol	Acute Ethanol Deaths (BAC ≥ .35%)	Number of A.E.P. Deaths with .40 Percent or More B.A.C.	Percent of all Certified Deaths with .40 Percent Blood Alcohol or More
Sedgwick Co. (Witchita)	450	—	1	0	.00
Clark Co. (Las Vegas)	796	65%	1	0	.00
Nassau Co. (N.Y.)	2600	98%	24	1	.04
Hennepin Co. (Minneapolis)	3006 (2 yr.)	31%	10 (2 yr.)	5 (2 yr.)	.04
Hamilton Co. (Cincinnati)	3058	15%	6	2	.06
Dallas Co. (Dallas)	2720	97%	11	2	.08
New York	25000	7%	300	20	.08
Delaware	1120	50%	9	1	.10
Cook Co. (Chicago)	11108	22%	16	12	.10
Utah	848	63%	4	1	.12
Monroe Co. (Rochester)	1655	33%	7	2	.12

Dade Co. (Miami)	4547	34%	10	6	.13
Maryland	7052	33%	33	9	.13
Cuyahoga Co. (Cleveland)	11104 (2 yr.)	57%	17 (2 yr.)	15 (2 yr.)	.13
Oklahoma	6134 (2 yr.)	40%	14 (2 yr.)	10 (2 yr.)	.16
Philadelphia	4059	73%	7	7	.17
Wayne Co. (Detroit)	11000	27%	27	20?	.22
Alameda Co. (Oakland)	2798	21%	10	7	.25
Los Angeles Co.	13781	41%	50	40	.29
Shelby Co. (Memphis)	1750	25%	9	4	.30
Virginia	15742 (2 yr.)	32%	200 (2 yr.)	48 (2 yr.)	.30
San Francisco Co.	2501	97%	15	10	.30
Harris Co. (Houston)	4500	—	25?	20?	.40?
Alleghany Co. (Pittsburg)	3500	100%	21	20	.57
North Carolina	4570	42%	87	63	1.38
Georgia	2040	98%	72	70	3.43

*The North Carolina data are from the approximately one-half of the state under the medical examiner system at the time of the study (July 1, 1969-June 30, 1970). Data from Sedgwick Co., Kansas; Clark Co., Nevada; Cook Co., Illinois; Cuyahoga Co., Ohio; Alameda Co., California; San Francisco Co., California; and Alleghany Co., Pennsylvania are from the respective Coroner's Systems (Data reported for various years from 1967 to 1970).

of lead have been detected less than once per year. The majority of reports of lead contamination from whiskey have come from Alabama and Georgia which more than rival North Carolina in the production of nontaxed whiskey.

Alcohol is a co-cause in many deaths investigated by the medical examiner in which other central nervous system depressants are found. It is a common experience to detect a moderate level of alcohol in a person who also has a moderate level of propoxyphene (Darvon), barbiturate and/ or other analgesic, sedative or antidepressant drugs. These drugs certainly do not ameliorate the effect of each other. Some act synergistically, particularly alchol and barbiturate. Most are at least additive in effect. For example, alcohol at the level of .25 percent can rarely be indicated by itself as a cause of death. However, when present with the usually sublethal level of 0.5 mg per 100 ml of a rapid-acting barbiturate, one has ample explanation of the cause of death from the respiratory depressant effect of the two together.

Determination of the manner of death is often difficult in these cases. The possibilities are often excellent for accident as well as for suicide, not to mention the rare cases in which these levels plus other information has one suspecting homicide. A subtle cause of death and hopefully a rare one is the fatal complication of alcohol plus disulfiram (Antabuse). Here blood levels of alcohol and of disulfiram are relatively meaningless; death has been witnessed where both levels are low and survival is common with high levels of the two together. In addition, disulfiram is difficult to detect by standard methods even when suspected. Blood acetaldehyde levels build up when disulfiram blocks alcohol metabolism, thus determination of the acetaldehyde levels by gas chromatography is of limited value in defining this complication. The interaction is almost impossible to certify as a cause of death unless the circumstances were witnessed, and autopsy and complete toxicology rule out other possibilities.

6. *Chronic alcoholism (usually associated with poor nutrition):* Many of the alcohol-related deaths mentioned in previous paragraphs are unknown or rare in the hospitals. On the other hand, deaths that are attributable to chronic alcoholism and concomitant poor nutrition are frequently cared for

and documented medically in appropriate medical environments. Hence they may not fall among medical examiner cases.
Even so, these complications still represent a relatively large
and important proportion of those sudden, unsuspected, violent, and unnatural deaths reported to the medical examiner.
He generally sees these cases because the victims are found
under peculiar or suspicious circumstances, because their
previous degree of alcoholism had not been appreciated, or
because as known alcoholics they were suspected of being
victims of assault, accident, or suicide. One of the several
classifications of these deaths is that by organ system as will be
used in giving examples.

Occasionally, a central nervous system degeneration
such as Wernicke's disease is found in the absence of another
explanation of death. The central nervous system and the heart
are suspect in that large number of alcoholics who are found
dead or who are witnessed to die, but in whom the most careful and extensive of available studies are unrevealing save for
evidence of nutritional deficiencies, fatty liver, and some water
logging of tissues. With the exception of occasional food fad-
dists, most occurrence of beriberi in the United States is among
alcoholics. The lesions at autopsy are not specific. Available
techniques do not yet reveal the pathology of many conditions. In recent years, an entity given the intriguing label of
"Quebec beer drinkers heart" has been recognized by forensic
pathologists. Various investigators eventually determined that
the phenomenon was due to a block in any enzyme system
caused by an elevated cobalt level. The cobalt was ingested
with vast quantities of beer (typically twenty for forty bottles of
beer per day) to which it had been added by the manufacturers
to maintain the foam or the "head." Sometimes the medical examiner may use the clinical term "alcoholic cardiomyopathy"
or "alcoholic heart disease" to explain sudden, unexpected, or
unattended death in an alcoholic who shows no good evidence
of other cause of death. Vague as these terms are to any attending physician, they may be even less satisfying to pathologists including forensic pathologists, for there are no consistent lesions or specific stigmata. Much clinical research and
experimental laboratory work are yet to be done.

Alcohol precipitated disease of the respiratory tract was

briefly referred to earlier in mentioning the alcoholic's increased susceptibility to pneumonia. There are several other
respiratory tract related deaths in the alcohol abuser. The
victim of oversedation or coma from alcohol may collapse with
his head so flexed upon his chest that his airway is fatally
compressed. He may collapse with his neck across the back
edge of a chair or across some other relatively sharp-edged
object. This pressure also can block his airway and the major
blood vessels in the neck. These plus the face in the mud or
other obstructing substance are rather common examples of so-
called "positional asphyxia" in the comatose alcoholic. The
intoxicated individual is prone to aspirate vomitus into the air
passages because of the alcohol's effect on the central nervous
system altering the gag and swallowing reflexes. This in small
quantities can lead to pneumonia and in large quantities to
asphyxiation from tracheo-bronchial obstruction. The ob-
tunded victim of alcohol may also die of asphyxia from blood
in his airway from a facial injury. Despite publicity given the
"cafe coronary," many accidents due to aspiration of food
plugs lodged in the glottis or larynx are certified as natural
deaths due to coronary thrombosis because of the lack of
knowledge of the entity or lack of diligence in pursuing this
accidental manner of death. The presence of moderately high
blood alcohol levels in the adults to whom this happens is
characteristic.

Every medical examiner can recall many scenes of apparent violence in which suspicions of "foul play" were
resolved by the discovery at autopsy of a natural source of
bleeding. The ruptured esophageal varices or hemorrhaging
gastric ulcer that was a result of cirrhosis or other manifestation of alcoholism was the source of the blood about the
discovered body rather than external injury. Hemorrhagic
pancreatitis, a related complication, also accounts for some of
the sudden unexpected deaths that we see.

7. *Sudden, unexpected-death-with-fatty-liver syndrome:*
One of the more mystifying complications of the abuse of
alcohol is an entity so poorly understood that it does not even
bear a generally accepted label or name. However, experienced
medical examiners and forensic pathologists know the term
"sudden, unexpected-death-with-fatty-liver syndrome." This

death situation is one of the more frequent among medical examiner cases. This situation is typically that of a body found dead with no apparent cause. Complete autopsy workup reveals an enlarged, fatty liver plus often other more subtle stigmata of chronic alcoholism. Toxicological analyses reveal little or no alcohol and no other drugs, poisons, or unnatural chemicals. Clinical history is that of a consistently heavy drinker who has not had a drink in the previous twelve to thirty-six hours. Occasionally these deaths are witnessed; on these occasions the clinical picture is one of lack of coherence, chills or minor tremors, pallor, sweating, and collapse. Although the logic is somewhat difficult to defend, it has been traditional to certify these deaths as "fatty liver," "hepatic failure," or simply "chronic alcoholism." The manner of death is ordinarily certified as natural. The circumstances and findings or lack of same suggest to many a close relationship to delirium tremens (DT's). This possible relationship is of little satisfaction as the mechanism and pathogenesis of delirium tremens are unknown. Various explanations have been offered and there are some data to support each of these.[5] These are generally in the area of metabolic derangements such as hypoglycemia, hypocalemia, magnesium deficiency, alkalosis, or alcoholic ketoacidosis. The once-held theory of massive fat embolization to the lung from the fatty liver as a cause of the sudden unexpected death is not substantiated by autopsy findings.

Conclusion

One's personal philosophy might be either that alcoholism is the cause of many ills or that it is a symptom or manifestation of other problems. In any event, the abuse of alcohol is in itself a monumental problem in this country. Perhaps this chapter has provided the reader with some insight into the size and the scope of the problem. It is apparent not only that do we not know all of the answers about alcoholism, but that we do not even know all of the questions. A great and frequently overlooked source of material pertinent to both questions and answers should be available through medical examiner investigations. Fortunately, there are more states adopting such a system of investigation of nonnatural deaths.

Too, there is an increasing sensitivity on the part of medical examiner offices to the need of more refined analysis and greater output from their systems into other agencies. There are many actions to be taken and many changes to be made. These depend upon the cooperative effort of many organizations and agencies—private, governmental, academic, and others. Specific contributions from the medical examiner system include: 1) Identification of chronic alcoholics among the population he investigates that would not otherwise be so identified. 2) Identification of the old and the new complications of alcohol abuse. 3) Making available for students of alcohol problems information determined from those cases found to have alcohol in the blood at the time of death and the level thereof. The alcohol level information would also be available to other appropriate agencies such as courts, law enforcement, insurance companies, Department of Motor Vehicles, and attorneys in civil and criminal suits. 4) Contribution to epidemiological data on alcohol abusers. 5) Identification of specific problems such as the vast numbers of acute alcohol poison deaths in certain geographic areas; places where nonbeverage alcohol is imbibed. 6) Data and tissue for research efforts. 7) Encouragement of insurance companies to apply economic leverage on their insured through alcohol oriented limitations in types of insurance coverage.

As part of the total effort to which the medical examiner system can make some contribution, there must come a change in our cultural pattern relative to use, knowledge and acceptance of alcohol. Future generations must not grow up with attitudes that it is necessary at social gatherings to consume alcohol, that one cannot be a real he-man without drinking whiskey, that intoxicated people are a source of humor, and the rationalizing attitude that "after all, a drink or two is really good for me and relaxes me." The latter may well be true for most people, but as part of our social culture it helps provide a base for those who become addicted to alcohol or abuse it to solace the pain of attempting to cope with problems in their daily life. Why have the schools so long neglected an opportunity to educate children about alcohol? A sense of values seems strangely misplaced when a school spends an hour a day for twenty days teaching children about drugs without a discussion about the most commonly abused drug, ethyl alcohol. Should it be necessary for the legislature to dictate this part of the curriculum to the Department of Public Instruction?

In the part of the nation, the Dixie States, in which acute alcohol poisoning is ten to twenty times more common than in other parts of the country and where that type of poisoning is more frequent than all accidental, suicidal, and homicidal drug and chemical poison deaths combined, we have a more specific problem. There are so many things different about the social and cultural heritage and mores of this part of the nation that we shall perhaps never know why consumption of large amounts of straight whiskey is so prevalent (or why North Carolina leads the nation in soft drink consumption for that matter). One of the many factors that might be suggested is that these states generally have brown-bag laws and do not have liquor legally available by the drink. People tend to buy whatever they buy in the most conveniently available form. If whiskey in small quantities appeared more conveniently available than in fifths, it is conceivable one might see diminished numbers of fatal acute alcohol poisonings. Perhaps this would serve as some deterrence to selling and buying whiskey in fatal quantities, perhaps not.

The subject of driving and drinking easily warrants a separate volume in itself. It is beyond the scope of this chapter to discuss this in depth. Surely it must be possible in the United States as in other countries to so alter by legislation or by education the cultural pattern and customs that people driving do not drink and those drinking do not drive. For the habitual alcoholic, what solution is there but to keep him from driving? Whether he should be restrained in a treatment or rehabilitation facility on one hand or prison on the other is not the point. He should not and cannot be allowed to continue to impart the risk upon his passengers and other users of the highway that he does. I can not resist at this point interjecting my opinion that the driver that causes death on the highway is more likely than not to be a chronic alcoholic. One hopeful reflection of concern and change of attitude in this nation is in those federal and state laws and judicial rulings that would have the chronic alcohol abuser directed to medical care or to rehabilitation centers rather than to jail or back to the alleys. Will we ever be able to identify well the potential alcoholic and take appropriate measures?

The abuse of alcohol is a problem or series of problems that potentially lends itself to the many well-established problem-solving techniques. A coordinated effort is needed to collect relevant data and to translate that data into action programs designed to better equip out society to deal with the alcohol problem. The medical examiner system can provide a portion of the required information, and support efforts to attack the problem.

CHAPTER 6

Social and Psychiatric Considerations of Drinking

John A. Ewing, M.D.

I WILL MAKE no attempt here to delve deeply into psychiatric syndromes associated with alcohol abuse or to discuss comprehensively the psychiatrist's specific interest in the area or his therapeutic maneuvers. However, certain special psychiatric considerations of drinking are necessary since the term "psychiatric" generally covers disorders of behavior, emotions, and thinking. Other factors stem from medicine, pharmacology, biochemistry, physiology, anthropology, sociology, psychology, and epidemiology.

The "good" or desirable effects of alcohol have been mentioned (chapter 1) and from medical and psychiatric viewpoints, some drinking represents self-medication with alcohol. The average drinker may not see himself as "treating" his tension, anxiety, depression, or social relationships with a drug when he orders a drink. However, there is no question that the alcohol in that drink produces effects upon these aspects of his life.

As Cisin points out in chapter 9, moderate and controlled drinking is typical of our present society. If this were the only kind of drinking, our culture probably would not have produced laws about drinking. Obviously the existence of abrasive drinking behavior and the destructiveness of heavy excessive drinking are the precipitants, and on-going justification, for both psychiatric concerns and legal attempts to achieve control.

Safe Versus Dangerous Drinking

In the other chapters we discuss present knowledge about the risks of moderate and excessive drinking. One question of interest to the majority of readers is what can be said to represent "moderate" as opposed to "immoderate" drinking? Granted that there are individuals who believe that even one drop of whiskey represents an unacceptable amount, we still would like to know what is "reasonable" or "acceptable" in medical, physiological, and psychiatric terms. Unfortunately our present state of knowledge does not permit a simple direct answer. Instead one has to hedge with comments about "individual susceptibility."

If medical authorities are pushed to express opinions, they generally seem to agree that 80 grams (100 ml or 3 1/3 fluid ounces) of absolute alcohol per day represent approximately the level above which hazardous effects will eventually begin to be significant in terms of general health. In approximate terms, this is achieved by the regular consumption of four martinis or mixed drinks (each containing two ounces of spirits), seven or eight glasses of sherry (each two ounces), about eight glasses of wine (each three ounces), or five to six small cans of beer (each twelve ounces) in a twenty-four hour period. However, it is conceivable that there are individuals who can safely drink larger amounts per day just as there are certainly others who cannot even consume the amount specified here.

At the present state of research, there is no uniform agreement as to what amounts represent light, moderate, heavy, or excessive drinking. Nor is it certain if there are different effects depending upon whether the alcohol is taken over long periods of time (so as to maintain low blood alcohol levels for long periods) or in binges (so as to give high blood levels for short periods). These issues can be studied in a variety of researches, and we can anticipate an improvement in our overall knowledge and understanding. The National Survey of

Drinking Practices conducted by Cahalan, Cisin, and Crossley involved developing a Quantity, Frequency, and Variability Index with respondents being divided into five groups. Abstainers (32 percent) reported no drinking during the last year. Infrequent drinkers (15 percent) drink at least once a year but less than once a month. Light drinkers (28 percent) drink at least once a month but with a low quantity-variability rating. Typically this means only one or two drinks on a single occasion. Moderate drinkers (13 percent) drink at least once a month with a medium quantity-variability rating; this means typically that they drink several times a month but usually with no more than three or four drinks per occasion. Heavy drinkers (12 percent) drink at least once a month with a high quantity-variability rating (typical would be a drinker who has five or more drinks on occasion and drinks nearly every day, or drinks at least weekly with five or more drinks on each occasion).[1]

In an attempt to overcome the problem of lumping together those who drink relatively small amounts frequently and those who drink relatively large amounts these workers developed another approach known as Volume-variability Index. To develop this each respondent is classified according to his average daily volume, and daily volume groups are subdivided according to how variable the person is in his intake from day to day. Such an approach does seem to be more useful in attempting to classify drinkers, and we might anticipate that improvements will follow.

I have devised and described a concept of an Alcohol Quotient (AQ) which can be calculated for any drinker on the basis of his drinking during the past year.[2] Provided the necessary information is available as to weight, the number of drinks consumed at a time, the number of times, the nature of the drinks, and the size of the drinks, AQ gives us a figure which, relative to other AQs, indicates a greater or lesser consumption. The figure, in fact, reflects the calculated blood levels of alcohol achieved and allows for the number of hours that alcohol was present in the blood in the year. One advantage of the AQ approach is that it assigns a numerical value only, rather than labeling people with words such as "heavy frequent drinker" or "moderate intermittent drinker."

Whether or not the AQ approach will be adopted by research workers is not yet clear, and undoubtedly the present formula on which it is based can be refined. However, this technique, like the others, remains essentially a research tool.

Alternative methods include arbitrarily selecting an amount above which it is concluded that a certain category of drinkers is unlikely to go. Beaubrun established a system of units of drinking per annum and in a similar study my colleagues and I have classified student drinking according to total milliliters of absolute alcohol consumed in the one year preceding.[3] In chapter 14 Popham, Schmidt, and de Lint label absolute alcohol consumption of 10 centiliters [100 ml (3 1/3 fluid ounces) or 80 grams (2.8 ounces) approximately] as "hazardous" and define the consumption of alcoholics as 15 cl [150 ml (5 fluid ounces) or 120 grams (4.2 ounces) daily]. Remember that these figures are in terms of pure alcohol (200-proof) so that, for example, you would need to double the figures to get the equivalent in 100-proof whiskey. If these criteria are used, a hazardous drinking level in one year implies the consumption of at least 36,500 ml and the consumption of a typical alcoholic would be 54,750 ml of pure alcohol.

For the reader who is anxious to know whether his own personal drinking falls into a hazardous or "alcoholic" category, the above figures place a daily consumption of seven ounces of 100-proof whiskey into the hazardous classification. Similarly, based on Popham's figures, the average alcoholic is consuming the equivalent of about ten ounces of 100-proof whiskey per day on a yearly basis. However, these are arbitrary and averaged figures. No one should feel that his drinking is guaranteed "safe" if it remains below seven ounces of whiskey per day any more than an eleven ounce daily consumption should necessarily be taken to mean that the consumer is alcoholic. "Alcoholism" is an operational term and cannot, and should not, be reached solely on the basis of alcohol consumption figures.

The concept of Anstie's Limit has recently been resurrected by the National Institute on Alcohol Abuse and Alcoholism.[4] Anstie was a British physician in the nineteenth century whose findings influenced the Committee of Fifty (which was discussed in chapter 3). He believed that a safe level of drinking which would not cause disease was the equivalent of 1.5 ounces of absolute alcohol per day, for example, 3 ounces of whiskey (100-proof) or half a bottle of wine or four glasses of beer. He emphasized that this should be taken with meals and whiskey was to be well diluted.

Some "typical" alcoholics show binge drinking with considerable gaps of weeks or months between. Such people consume immoderate amounts of alcohol for days or weeks but may not necessarily do so long enough to reach the annual consumption figures given above. Indeed, I have surprised classes of medical students by claiming that I personally drink more than some of my patients who are chronic alcoholics. The secret is, or course, that some such patients spend significant periods of time in jail or hospitals or rehabilitation centers in an average year and also many chronic alcoholics are binge drinkers who have a "lost weekend" or "lost week" occasionally during which all sorts of medical and social complications of their drinking arise. On a total yearly basis such a patient may only consume a few gallons of spirits and/or beer. Compare the intake of your moderate but frequent drinker who has a single two ounce cocktail before dinner every night of the year. That alone adds up to almost six gallons of spirits annually. Let's say that he drinks two cans of beer most nights and perhaps three on Saturdays and Sundays. That adds up to two gallons a week or over 100 gallons a year. Remember that this is the consumption of a moderate drinker who never gets intoxicated to any significant degree. In North Carolina for example, we buy enough beer for every man, woman, child, and infant to drink thirty-five gallons each year! Some people, of course, drink none at all and others consume hundreds of gallons annually.

Table 6-1 offers suggestions on how best to drink safely.[5]

Alcoholism

Many attempts have been made to come up with a satisfactory and universal definition of "alcoholism" but none has yet been achieved. Some people avoid the issue by using a variety of other terms including "problem drinking" or "alcohol problems." Chafetz defines alcoholism as "a chronic

Table 6-1
Tips for Safe Drinking

When taking a drink, remember you are taking "a fix" of your favorite drug.

Determine in advance how much you are going to drink and never exceed that.

In regard to your drinking, always think of moderation and keeping watch on how much you have had.

Use a jigger to measure spirits (the heavy-handed host who pours generously for his guests or himself is doing no one a favor).

Spirits should be diluted with a mix.

A beer with lunch may be all right, but the two or three martini lunch spells danger.

Avoid mixing two different alcoholic beverages such as in martinis and Manhattans.

Sip and savor your drinks—don't gulp them down.

Eat something when drinking (the one possible exception would be when you are having no more than two small drinks in the twenty to thirty minutes before dinner).

Limit the length of time of your drinking. Stop after an hour or two.

Perceive getting drunk as something to be guilty and worried about.

Do something else when you are drinking—like having a conversation or reading.

See drinking as something to enhance life, not as a remedy for boredom or "having nothing to do."

Always have soft drinks and food available for your guests.

Remember that the host who pushes drinks is a drug pusher.

See a hangover as a definite warning that you were drinking too much the night before. Remember, though, that some people *can* drink too much and never suffer a hangover.

The worst time to drink is when you feel "I need a drink."

At a party, sip the first drink over thirty minutes and take the same time for the second; stretch the third drink out until you leave. Never take a fourth.

Surprise yourself occasionally by doing something else when you otherwise would have had a drink—take some exercise, or a hot bath, or some fruit juice.

Never use alcohol in the morning to get you going or to fight a hangover.

behavioral disorder manifested by an undue preoccupation with alcohol and its use to the detriment of physical and mental health, by loss of control when drinking is begun, and by a self-destructive attitude in dealing with personal relationships and life situations."[6] Important assets of this definition include the focus on preoccupation rather than amount, the fact that a degree of intoxication is not required in the definition, and the emphasis on destructive attitudes. Also the use of the word "chronic" eliminates the occasional excessive use of alcohol and the focus on personal relationships emphasizes the importance of looking at the individual in his social context. Recent workers, including Cahalan et al., have emphasized the concept of "escape" drinking and this is another way of looking at problem drinking or alcoholic drinking.[7] Such individuals typically do not use alcohol for simple dietary, hedonistic, recreational, or social purposes but as a means of seemingly turning away from life's problems. I cannot overemphasize the negativistic aspects of such behavior which, instead of coping or resolving, resorts to flight. The problem for the alcoholic is, of course, that his living and interpersonal difficulties are likely to be unchanged or even worsened when his alcoholic flight is eventually temporarily abandoned. Thus, it is no surprise when we see him repeatedly utilizing his acquired escape mechanism. It is this lack of acceptance of opportunity for emotional growth which underlies the self-destructive component of alcoholism.

Of course, the destructiveness of alcoholism also reaches other people, particularly the spouse, and alcohol abuse is a potent marriage breaker. One major health aspect of alcohol abuse which does not display itself as immediately as disruption of the marriage is the overall effect upon the development and mental health of children. Exposure to alcoholic drinking patterns in the home does involve demonstrating to a child inefficient and unhealthy escape patterns from life's problems. The tendency for such patterns to be imitated in subsequent generations has been noticed by many clinicians. Interestingly enough, in one of our studies we found that certain abstaining students were more likely to report having had an alcoholic father, so that apparently under some circumstances the parent's drunkenness may be taken more as an awful warning than an example.

Other deleterious effects upon the child raised in an alcoholic home are familiar to those who work in psychiatric clinics and include the whole gamut of emotional psycho-pathology. In addition to this there is a tendency for such children to feel guilty, to be social misfits, to drop out of educational programs, and to be involved in delinquent behavior. Fortunately, the Alateen movement has helped some children to overcome these environmental hazards.[8]

Even though various medical authorities and organizations have officially acknowledged alcoholism as a disease, it is an oversimplification to assume that such useful moves (designed to encourage professional concern and attention) imply that there is an entity known as "alcoholism." Indeed, it is quite possible that we should be talking about "the alcoholisms," and the majority of psychiatrists actually prefer to think of alcoholism as a *symptom* of underlying disorders. While it is true that there are certain typical patterns for the history of alcoholics, a working definition which focuses upon the excessive use of alcohol for "escape" purposes and with deleterious effects upon health, economics, marital, familial, and interpersonal relations will reveal some cases which are atypical.

A good example is the man or woman beyond middle age with a history of controlled social drinking for many years and the relatively sudden development of loss of control in recent months. In my experience many such people are suffering from typical states of psychic depression and have begun to "treat" themselves by greater and greater use of alcohol. Pharmacological studies of alcohol suggest that it may have antidepressant effects within such people. I have seen a few such patients return successfully to social drinking after being appropriately treated for their depression. Some years ago, when Davies described the return to social drinking by some "alcoholics," some of his critics responded by saying that successful returning to social drinking proved that they were not "alcoholic" in the first place![9] Of course if one chooses to define alcoholism as a condition which precludes the individual from ever drinking normally again, the symptomatic excessive drinker of middle life who is suffering from depression will simply not be included among "the alcoholisms." Most of us who are clinicians, however, find it more rewarding to concentrate upon diagnosis and treatment rather than to argue about the definition.

A Biopsychosocial Disease

Much has been said and written about the cause or causes of alcoholism and here it is necessary to say first that it is at present a condition of unknown etiology. Of course the drys do sometimes claim that alcohol is the cause of alcoholism, thereby ignoring the more than 90 percent of alcohol users who succeed in drinking rationally and moderately for a lifetime. Such a concept is as simplistic as saying that gasoline is the cause of highway accidents. The truth is that we do not know "the cause" of alcoholism although we have plenty of theories available to us. These come from a variety of sources including genetics, biochemistry, physiology, psychology, psychiatry, psychoanalysis, sociology, and anthropology.

I believe that the present state of our knowledge permits us to make a reasonable assumption that we may never find a single cause for alcoholism—in the sense of explaining the appearance of excessive drinking in all cases. Instead, I think we will gradually acquire a greater understanding of the factors at play within the basic biological and sociological milieu of the individual. Presumably such factors are significant in individual cases in different proportions. Thus, we can conceive of an individual who has a biological propensity to develop alcoholism which he has inherited. Yet, this alone might not be enough to determine his destiny even if he were to start using alcohol. Other factors such as early emotional development, exposure to role models for drinking, personality features, and sociocultural pressures might have to be considered. In a similar way it does appear that certain cultures contain practices and attitudes about alcohol use which predispose toward the development of alcoholism. Here we could be thinking of the differences between Scandinavians and Italians or Irish and Jews.[10] Yet, future studies may show that, in the case of any individual, the other factors alluded to already (of a biomedical and psychological nature) must be taken into account in order to understand the development of alcoholism even in someone exposed to a predisposing culture.

Is Alcoholism Inherited?

A "familial tendency" to alcoholism does not necessarily mean that it is inherited by transmission from the parents. Most people are raised by their real parents who obviously provide major environmental factors throughout childhood which might create a psychological and sociological predisposition toward alcoholism. This indeed is the familiar nature versus nurture controversy which argues on the one hand that the main factors are those acquired by direct inheritance and on the other hand that those of the environment have the greater influence.

Alcoholism is by no means the only condition in which scientists are concerned with these issues. Some workers have been able to breed mice and rats so that one strain now shows a greater preference to drink alcoholic solutions and another strain avoids alcohol.[11] Scientists in Chile have presented evidence suggesting that there is an association between color blindness and alcoholism.[12] Others have found that the color blindness improves after the excessive drinking is stopped,[13] but now the workers in Chile have reported that this trait is more prevalent among the nonalcoholic blood relatives of alcoholics.[14] The last word on this topic has not yet been written, but if a "genetic marker," such as color blindness, could be shown to be associated with alcoholism, we might be able to test people for their degree of predisposition toward the illness.

Some ingenious studies have been devised to explore the issue of nature versus nurture in humans. One approach is to look at the rates of alcoholism (or any other disease being studied) in twins, recognizing that some twins are genetically identical (monozygotic) while others are much less similar (dizygotic) since they are the product of two fertilized eggs rather than a single ovum. The assumption is that the condition will show concordance more frequently in identical twins than in dissimilar twins if it has significant genetic origins. In one study of 174 twin pairs with at least one suffering from alcoholism, it was found that the disease also existed in 54 percent of monozygotic twins and only 28 percent in dizygotic twins.[15] Another study showed that the frequency and amount of drinking were more similar in identical twins as was the tendency for abstinence. However, there was no difference between one type of twins and the other for the consequences of excessive drinking.[16]

Recently an American group of workers has compared alcoholism rates occurring in half siblings.[17] The subjects were individuals who were reared apart from a biological parent where either that parent or the adoptive parent had a drinking problem. It turned out that the subjects were much more likely to have drinking problems themselves if the parent from whom they inherited half of their genes was considered alcoholic than if the parent raising them (but not their biological parent) was alcoholic. Thus, 62 percent of thirty-two alcoholics had an alcoholic biological parent as compared to only 20 percent of 132 nonalcoholics. This finding appeared whether or not there was personal contact between the child and the alcoholic biological parent. Simply living in the home with an alcoholic surrogate parent appeared not to relate to the development of alcoholism.

Carrying out studies of people who were adopted is extremely difficult, and probably impossible in this country where such records are considered highly confidential. However, recently Goodwin and a group of colleagues have reported an excellent study which they carried out in Denmark.[18] That country maintains registries about adoptions, psychiatric hospitalizations, and criminal histories which are made available when reputable scientists need access to them. In this study 133 men were interviewed in depth by a Danish psychiatrist who had no knowledge of the biological parent, nor did the subjects themselves. They had been picked from several thousand adoptees because it was known that fifty-five of them had had a biological parent who had been hospitalized primarily for alcoholism (in 85 percent the alcoholic parent was the father). All of these men had been separated from their biological parents within six weeks of birth and then adopted by nonrelatives and had no known subsequent contact with their original parents. The other seventy-eight were the control group who had been adopted under similar circumstances with the only known difference being that they had no alcoholic parent. Since 60 percent of those interviewed were still under the age of thirty, possibly some will still develop alcohol problems in the next decade or two. However, already some significant differences exist. Those who had a parent who was alcoholic are more likely to have had a divorce, to have had psychiatric treatment, to have been hospitalized for psychiatric illness, to have had more drinking problems, and to have been hospitalized for drinking. They show nearly four times the alcoholism rate. This important study suggests that humans may indeed inherit a predisposition for alcoholism.

In a further report of the same project Goodwin has recently announced that the brothers of the adoptees from alcoholic families, who were raised by the alcoholic parent without being adopted, show no significant difference in their rate of alcoholism. Goodwin concludes that environmental factors contributed little to the development of alcoholism in sons of severe alcoholics in the sample under consideration and that genetic factors influence the development of at least some forms of alcoholism.[19]

Although I have indicated that alcoholism is more frequent in the relatives of alcoholics, other conditions also appear in significant association. Studies by various workers have shown excessive rates of depression, criminality, sociopathy, and "abnormal personality" in families of alcoholics. Particularly the family studies of Winokur and others in the St. Louis, Missouri, area have shown a tendency for depression to occur in the female relatives and alcoholism and/or sociopathy to appear in the male relatives.[20]

Some recent research has looked at the drinking alcoholic in experimental clinical settings and has shown that significant changes do occur in terms of his physiology, his emotional status, including his general sense of well being, and his interpersonal relationships.[21] Far from being the delightful experience which they may recall in retrospect (or may anticipate in advance) a drinking binge involves much discomfort, feelings of depression, and defects of memory for most alcoholics. Indeed, some research has shown that suicidal tendencies increase as a drinking binge progresses, and the major association between drinking and violent death including suicide is well known.[22]

An enormous amount of work has been done, but even greater amounts lie ahead. Anyone who thinks that it is legitimate to focus upon discovering "a chemical pill" to banish the problem of alcoholism is unduly naive, just as is someone who feels that the problem can be resolved by better psychological experiences in childhood, or by changing social attitudes. There is no question that major endeavors are required of medical, behavioral, and social scientists in order to give us adequate understanding of these complex issues.

Other Psychiatric Concerns

A focus on alcoholism does not by any means comprise the entire gamut of psychiatric concerns regarding alcohol use. In addition we would have to include the effects upon memory processes of heavy alcohol use, the existence of alcoholic psychoses, hallucinosis, delirium tremens, and some conditions involving neurological damage due to extensive alcohol use. Whether alcohol exclusively damages by direct effect, or in indirect ways (e.g., by leading to nutritional deficiencies or cerebral trauma), there are certainly many such complications.

Treatment

This is not the place to discuss in detail the treatment of the alcoholic or what can or should be done for the alcoholic marriage or family.[23] The interested reader should look elsewhere for details, but a few general comments are justified here. In the first place it is by no means certain that the medical profession is, or ever will be, the major source of help for the alcoholic. Community surveys have suggested that no more than 5 or 10 percent of active alcoholics are known to the medical profession and this is corroborated by a recent national physician survey.[24] Obviously some alcoholics go for long periods of time getting no treatment or help of any kind. Others obtain what they need from recovering alcoholics notably through Alcoholics Anonymous. Still others shop around in a variety of ways.

In one of my own studies the analysis of our data made it clear that typical alcoholics who are not socially deteriorated may see a physician as often as three times a year for a variety of complaints.[25] Unfortunately, physicians are notoriously slow at suspecting alcoholism particularly when it occurs in someone of their own social and economic class. I have said with some justification that doctors have trouble diagnosing alcoholism unless the patient clearly drinks more than they do! Training the physician to identify the hidden alcoholic is a task confronting us in our medical schools, and significant efforts are also being made by the National Council on Alcoholism and the American Medical Society on Alcoholism.[26] The difficulty is of course compounded by the patient, since he rarely comes in directly complaining of his alcohol problem. Typically he tends to deny the nature of his problem to his physician and others. Denying it to himself, however, is the biggest problem of all. This leads to projection maneuvers such as concluding that his difficulty is whiskey and therefore he should switch to gin. Alternatively he may conclude that his problem lies exclusively in his work, his mother-in-law, or his wife. The social history often includes evidence for maneuvers based upon such thinking. A vast variety of medical conditions (and sometimes the results of injury) do periodically bring the alcoholic into contact with the medical profession. Frequently the patient is treated for his complaints and sent on his way without any inquiry as to his drinking habits. Many physicians have not yet learned that the average alcoholic is a middle class individual who is still employed, often still married, and far from the traditional skid-row inhabitant who represents a minute percentage of the overall problem. Likewise the belief that there were ten alcoholic males to every one female has gradually succumbed to a changing proportion of five to one or four to one, and many of us believe that eventually the true proportion will be found to be actually even lower.

The facts are that, for unknown reasons, about one in every twelve drinkers will eventually fit the operational definition of "alcoholic." Whether these people are seen as allergic or chemically oversensitive to alcohol (a popular Alcoholics Anonymous posture) or as having developed the condition because of cultural or psychological factors makes no difference at the present time. They need to be informed that they are different from the majority of drinkers and that, for them, alcohol constitutes a problem. The analogy of the diabetic who can usefully and safely live with dietary restrictions is a good one for doctors to make. This approach makes no moral judgment of the alcoholic nor does it anticipate future discoveries as to causation.

In developing treatment programs for the alcoholic, one should conceive of a wide spectrum which incorporates medical and community agencies ranging all the way from the Salvation Army Shelter to the Park Avenue psychoanalyst. These two examples are at opposite ends of the spectrum, and each will be applicable to extreme minorites of the alcoholic population. For the majority, the primary hurdle is the acceptance of a drinking problem, and here members of the medical profession have an obligation to perform. Beyond that the physician can guide his patients toward Alcoholics Anonymous, assist in correcting nutritional deficiencies, perform alcoholic detoxication (in or out of the hospital) if necessary, prescribe disulfiram (Antabuse) when appropriate, and give general counseling to the individual as well as to his wife and family.

Many physicians feel that alcoholism with its obvious emotional concomitants is the natural territory of the psychiatrist. However, the psychiatrist does not have any specific answers at the present time. It is true that the psychiatrist can and should offer assistance whenever possible and that this may involve medication, simple counseling, marriage counseling, or individual or group psychotherapy. However, the sheer number of alcoholics (8 to 10 million in the United States at the present time) means that we will have to offer comprehensive and flexible programs designed to catch the attention and interest of the alcoholic whenever he comes within range. Such programs call for knowledge, interest, and involvement on the part of clergy, nurses, psychologists, psychiatrists, social workers, and others in the general population. Programs need to be developed which utilize a variety of health and mental health resources within communities. Any comprehensive program must include many components such as general acceptance and support by staff and other patients, a medication program, Alcoholics Anonymous, family therapy, insight therapies, behavior therapies, patients' clubs, encounter therapy, occupational and recreational therapies, vocational rehabilitation programs and some system of followup which involves an outreach program for those patients who inevitably lose contact with the alcoholism services whether developed in a community center or through a hospital.

The results of treatment programs such as these depend upon many variables so that comparing approaches can be misleading unless careful plans are made in advance. However, as in other psychiatric areas, the rule of thirds often seems to apply — one-third of the patients are much improved, one third show little or no change, and the rest continue to deteriorate. In dealing with a complex condition like alcoholism, one should realize that stopping drinking by itself is by no means the sole criterion to be measured. Other aspects such as the patient's general and emotional health, his productive capacity, and his interpersonal relations need to be taken into account. Alcoholics Anonymous can offer an individual enormous help in becoming a recovering alcoholic when such a person can fully involve himself in their program.

Although statistics in the total sense are not kept by Alcoholics Anonymous, there have been surveys in recent years, the latest of which was reported in late 1974.[27] This was based on 13,467 questionnaires filled out by AA members in the summer of 1974 at meetings throughout the United States and Canada. The percentage of women members has gradually crept up to the present figure of 28 percent. The number of AA groups in the world is about 22,000 with 800,000 members, 595,000 of whom reside in the United States and Canada. In terms of age of members, 7.6 percent are under thirty years of age, 55 percent are thirty-one to fifty, and 36.5 percent are fifty-one or above. The average is 46.9 years and the longest period of continuous sobriety, thirty-four years, was claimed by a seventy-seven-year-old man. Based on results from surveys carried out from 1968 to 1974, it is estimated that 35 percent of those sober less than a year in the fellowship of AA will not drink again and will remain in AA during the succeeding year. Of those sober from one to five years, about 79 percent will stay sober in the fellowship. Of those sober more than five years, 91 percent will not drink again and will remain in AA. Average length of sobriety for all respondents was four years.

Almost all of those in the survey reported an improvement in the quality of their lives in the areas of family, health, work, and community since their membership in AA. Over a third of the members are in the executive, professional, or technical categories of occupation and about a third are blue collar and office workers. About one in ten reports have been referred to Alcoholics Anonymous by a counseling agency with one in three believing that medical, psychological, or spiritual counseling (other than AA) was important in their coming into the fellowship. This finding correlates with other evidence that physicians feel positively about referring alcoholic patients to Alcoholics Anonymous.[28]

Whatever the shortcoming of all or any treatment programs at the moment, they do offer much constructive help to many sufferers from alcoholism. Thus, referral to such programs (even under the duress of a court order or an employer's threat) is a much more constructive and promising maneuver than a jail sentence or a summary dismissal.

A relatively new approach to "alcoholic type drinking behavior" is based on learning theory and studies the behavior itself, attempting to change it without regard to its possible origin. Behavior therapy concerns itself with the actual performance of the individual and not with speculations as to why the performance is occurring. Thus, the alcoholic can be seen as having acquired alcoholic drinking patterns and as needing to learn nonalcoholic drinking patterns. There is no question that those who abuse alcohol use it in a different way from those who drink socially. For example, many tend to order drinks in undiluted form and to gulp them down.[29] Research workers in different places are exploring behavior therapy methods to "teach" alcoholics to drink like social drinkers again.[30]

Beatrice Rouse and I attempted such a plan with thirty-five alcoholics from 1970 to 1973. Patients were unselected except that they refused Alcoholics Anonymous and total abstinence. Weekly four hour training sessions called for active and enthusiastic participation on the part of patients. Ten people came one time only and decided that they did not want to participate. Eleven others came less than six times, some of them saying they felt that too much effort was required of them and that it would be easier to quit drinking altogether. A total of fourteen people came six or more times with nine having treatments on from twelve to twenty-four occasions. All of the latter appeared to acquire good habits of controlling their drinking during and between these sessions, as corroborated by drinking diaries and reports of family. At the conclusion of treatment no attempt was made to invoke regular followup contacts (since these may have therapeutic effects in themselves) but patients were invited to return for "refresher sessions" as they wished. Information about the fate of these patients was gradually acquired during subsequent months and years. In some cases they contacted me for needed hospitalization or to be placed on Antabuse so that they could be totally abstinent. We did not hear from others until a followup survey was conducted in mid-1975. By then, patients had had from twenty-seven to fifty-five months in which to test their capacity to maintain controlled drinking. All fourteen of the patients who had spent at least twenty-four hours in the treatment program had failed to maintain controlled drinking patterns such as are typical of social drinkers. Thus, this technique, at least in our hands, does not seem to be a promising one. Ours is the longest such followup study as yet reported and we await similar studies from other workers with interest.

The treatment of alcoholism is by no means an area in which the medical profession, or any other group, has acquired great skill. Certainly the self-help concept of Alcoholics Anonymous has proven of immeasurable value to many of those who have affiliated themselves. Nevertheless, when faced with a new case of alcoholism we are hard put to determine what is the best course to be taken. In general, we find ourselves trying one thing and then another. There is no question that future research must assist us in identifying better the factors which determine the probability of success of one approach with one patient but not another. Matching of the patient's "treatment needs" with the available treatment should greatly improve our success averages.[31]

All of these treatment approaches are dealing with the patient whose alcoholism has already made itself manifest in terms of health, occupational, economic, social, or familial complications. Dealing exclusively with "downstream" late cases of any condition is inevitably frustrating to the therapist who realizes that getting access to earlier cases and being involved in preventive programs might give a better payoff. In this regard we have barely begun to do anything when it comes to alcoholism. Even if, some day, therapists can identify and treat incipient cases of alcoholism and develop measures which can, in some instances, prevent the downward progress of the individual, we still must consider the overall question of prevention of alcoholism in the population as a whole.

Prevention

In 1967 a report to the nation was published by the Co-operative Commission on the Study of Alcoholism entitled "Alcohol Problems," sometimes called "The Plaut Report."[32] This is an important book with specific recommendations, in the history of alcohol problems. The commission recognized that it is reasonable to presume that general mental health improvement as well as better social conditions would have beneficial effects on alcohol problems. However, they also specified preventive measures which might be aimed at problem drinking. They postulated that a basic requirement would be the changing of drinking practices and attitudes within the general population. This, they wrote, could be accomplished by education and public discussion about American patterns of alcohol use and by introducing certain legal changes. Specifically they called for an attempt to reduce the emotionalism associated with alcoholic beverages. They recommended devices such as creating a better atmosphere in which there is more of a neutral "take it or leave it" feeling about drinking, with advertisers showing drinking as an activity that can add to enjoyment of other situations without altering them. Advertising of drinking within a family context would be permitted. Next, they felt that it was important to clarify and emphasize the distinctions between acceptable and unacceptable drinking. This would include such things as encouraging the use of beverages of lower alcohol content (some legal changes would be called for here), better education as to the nature of the impaired functioning which adversely affects driving, and trying to develop a national consensus regarding approved drinking behavior.

Another principle is listed under the heading of discouraging drinking for its own sake and encouraging the integration of drinking with other activities. This would be, for example, to emphasize the other activities rather than the drinking and potential drunkenness. Drinking in sports settings, with meals and de-emphasizing drinking as an escape mechanism are suggested here. The fourth proposal is to assist young people to adapt themselves realistically to a predominantly drinking society. This might call for such things as national policies regarding age for drinking, encouraging colleges to permit the serving of beer and wine in student social centers and cafeterias, establishing models for acceptable drinking, and respecting abstinence wishes which others possess.

The report also discusses the possibility of altering drinking practices through education in schools and in particular for integrating this in driver education courses. The need to develop alcohol education consultants and experts is plain. Finally, the commission recommends the development of a coordinated national approach to alcohol problems by the creation of certain types of organizations including a "Committee for a National Alcohol Policy," interdepartmental committees within the federal government, and the development of a National Center on Alcoholism. The latter has now been accomplished and indeed has reached institute status. Additional governmental activities at a state and local level are called for, and the role of nongovernmental agencies must not be ignored.

A more recent publication which tackles some of these issues in more detail is that by Wilkinson in 1970.[33] In the first part of his book he explores drinking patterns, discusses the prevention of drinking problems, and reviews certain historical events. Next he discusses the industry and its regulation under the present system, and finally he develops proposals based on the identified concepts. This volume, too, emphasizes the importance of giving youth an opportunity to learn moderate drinking in controlled circumstances. School education is discussed as are advertising policies including certain restrictions which stigmatize alcohol. It is suggested again that alcohol should be moved away from a "drinking only" setting into activities which can often be enjoyed by the whole family together, while other things than drinking are emphasized. Inducements to change taverns from "dark and furtive haunts to well lit, cheerful places where people can get food as well as drinks" are discussed.

Finally, the need for tax changes and new agencies, both public and private, to bring these about are defined in some detail. The reader who has a special interest in prevention of drinking problems should consult these publications. Here it will be sufficient to outline some of the legal approaches which are suggested. In terms of taxation there is a proposal that this should be progressive in relation to alcohol strength. Present federal alcohol regulations do not permit the use of the words "whiskey" and "gin" unless the liquor is at least 80-proof strength. The possibility of changing this should be explored. Some of the regulations regarding the retail sale of alcohol appear to be unnecessarily restrictive and thus difficult to justify. The concept of making situations for drinking more conform to problem-free drinking patterns can be promoted by encouraging certain changes in commercial drinking places. This would include, for example, there being other points of interest besides alcohol in the tavern such as billiards, juke-boxes, and television. In new residential areas, model neighborhood taverns can be developed providing a range of leisure activities. New licenses for such drinking places could emphasize the importance of integrating drinking with other leisure activities. Wilkinson also considers types of arrangement which would promote healthier drinking patterns and which involve grocery stores, license issuance and retailing standards. He devotes some attention to public policy regarding the drinking driver; then he discusses how such actions might be sought and promoted using federal and state agencies. The main body of the book ends by discussing the price of such a public policy and the responsibility of the trade. Wilkinson specifically addresses himself to the prevention of "drinking problems" and does not claim that this would prevent alcoholism. However, if social changes can influence the overall milieu in which drinking occurs there is reason to hope that the prevalence of alcoholism might be affected for the better.

It undoubtedly is an oversimplification to assume that if we in America could adopt Jewish, Italian, or Chinese attitudes toward drinking we would then find ourselves enjoying the relatively low rates of alcoholism of such cultures. Nevertheless these volumes do present positive approaches to a public health problem of enormous size and the proposals listed are worthy of consideration in every case and of implementation in many. A serious possibility to be entertained would be the support of a series of research studies which would test, under controlled conditions, the effectiveness of a variety of such legal approaches. Some research endeavors could be established at a local or state level while others would benefit most from federal sponsorship. Here, I must plead for building evaluation studies into any legislative or administrative change which involves alcohol manufacture, distribution, or consumption. Scientific scrutiny of such changes could gradually supply us with the necessary information on which to build further developments of public policy.

As an example of what I have in mind, there was a time in North Carolina when it was illegal to transport in one's automobile any liquor bottle with the seal broken. Obviously the objective was to discourage drinking while driving. Finally the legislature altered this to permit an opened bottle to be carried, provided it is not in the passenger compartment of the car. There is anecdotal evidence to suggest that such a simple measure has had significant effects upon some drinking behavior. The owners of some supper clubs have been quoted as saying that there is less drunkenness among people leaving these now that they no longer have to finish the bottle or leave it behind half empty to comply with the law. It should be kept in mind that at present North Carolina has no liquor-by-the-drink law and therefore the drinker has to take his own bottle with him to the supper club.[34] Unfortunately, this legal change occurred without any scientific scrutiny of its effects and therefore we are limited to anecdotal evidence as to its usefulness.

Conceivably in some parts of the United States local beverage control agencies might promote some of the types of drinking establishments such as are suggested by the Cooperative Commission. When this is being contemplated I hope that before-and-after studies can be conducted and perhaps similar legislative areas which have not introduced such changes might also be compared.

Conclusion

My final point is that we are now beginning to think of moving upstream to try to get at the sources of alcoholism. At the present moment we have no reason to believe that social and cultural factors *alone* are operating, but we can believe that these are significant powerful influences in the development of alcoholism. Thus as proposals for "social engineering" are made, it is my plea that these changes should be introduced under circumstances which permit adequate evaluation after an appropriate period of time. Too often in the past we have seen public money and public energy being devoted to well-meaning attempts to reach some vague goal without any means of telling whether or not anything was actually accomplished. As attempts are made to evaluate the effects of social policy changes, other efforts must be directed toward greater understanding of the psychological and biomedical aspects of excessive drinking and alcoholism. Thus I foresee the eventual arrival of a time when those who choose to drink can do so moderately and without today's fear that they will damage their health or prove to be the one out of twelve drinkers who becomes an alcoholic casualty.

CHAPTER 7

Drinking and Highway Safety

Patricia F. Waller, Ph.D.

WHILE THIS CHAPTER is not an exhaustive review of the role of alcohol in highway crashes, it does provide a brief overview of the subject. The references listed at the end of the chapter will introduce the serious student to the voluminous literature in this area.

Alcohol and Highway Crashes

Alcohol is the single most important factor yet identified in traffic fatalities. The association between the use of alcohol and highway deaths was noted as early as 1904 in the *Quarterly Journal of Inebriety* which carried an editorial as follows:

We have received a communication containing the history of twenty-five fatal accidents occurring to automobile wagons. Fifteen persons occupying these wagons were killed outright, five more died two days later, and three other persons were killed. Fourteen persons were injured, some seriously. A careful inquiry showed that in nineteen of these accidents the drivers had used spirits within an hour or more of the disaster. The other six drivers were all moderate drinkers, but it was not ascertained whether they had used spirits preceding the acci-

dent. The author of this communication shows very clearly
that the management of automobile wagons is far more dangerous for men who drink than the driving of locomotives on
steel rails. Inebriates and moderate drinkers are the most
incapable of all persons to drive motor wagons. The general
palsy and diminished power of control of both the reason and
senses are certain to invite disaster in every attempt to guide
such wagons. The precaution of railroad companies to have
only total abstainers guide their engines will soon extend to the
owners and drivers of these new motor wagons. The following
incident illustrates this new danger: A recent race between the
owners of large wagons, in which a number of gentlemen took
part, was suddenly terminated by one of the owners and drivers,
who persisted in using spirits. His friends deserted him, and in
returning to his home his wagon ran off a bridge and was
wrecked. With the increased popularity of these wagons,
accidents of this kind will rapidly multiply, and we invite our
readers to make notes of disasters of this kind.[1]

Unfortunately the editorial was deadly accurate in its
last prediction. It is estimated that roughly half of all traffic
deaths in the United States involve heavy use of alcohol on the
part of driver(s) and/or pedestrian(s). In 1973 this represented
approximately 27,800 lives.[2]

Scientific investigations of the role of alcohol in highway crashes began in the 1930s. Measures of blood alcohol
concentration made it possible to determine that drivers in
fatal crashes often had high levels of alcohol present in their
systems. Studies which have compared the blood alcohol
concentrations (BAC) of drivers in fatal crashes with those of
drivers not in crashes have shown that these high levels of
BACs are more characteristic of fatal crash drivers than of
drivers not in crashes.

A landmark study in this area is that of Borkenstein et
al., often referred to as the Grand Rapids study.[3] Conducted in
Grand Rapids, Michigan in 1962-63, this study involved collecting interviews, as well as BAC, from almost 6,000 accident-
involved drivers and over 7,500 control drivers. Limited data
on additional accident drivers were also obtained. Control
drivers were selected at accident sites at a time and day
corresponding to the time and day at which a previous accident

occurred. Interviewers received intensive training, and interviewees were guaranteed that information would be considered confidential. Almost 96 percent of those in the accident sample and almost 98 percent of control drivers cooperated with the project by providing information.

The major driver variables analyzed included BAC, age, estimated annual mileage of driver, education in years, race or nationality, marital status, occupational status, reported average drinking frequency, and sex. This carefully conducted study clearly demonstrated the importance of alcohol in accident involvement. Figure 7-1 illustrates the differences between accident and control groups by BAC. Drivers in accidents attained BACs higher than any found in control drivers. Analyses showed that for alcohol levels above .08 percent the differences between proportion of drivers in accident and control groups were statistically significant.

Accident and control groups differed significantly on each of the driver variables examined. However, further analyses showed that even when these differences were controlled, the higher BACs were associated with more frequent accident experience. Therefore the differences in alcohol involvement in the accident and control groups cannot be accounted for on the basis of these other variables. It was generally found that accident experience increases rapidly as BAC exceeds .05 percent.

In addition to considering accident involvement per se, the researchers also examined those drivers considered to have caused the accident. Figure 7-2 shows the relationship between BAC and the probability of causing an accident. There is a steep increase in relative probability above .08 percent BAC. This figure also illustrates a curiosity sometimes referred to as the Grand Rapids Dip. BACs between .01 percent and .04 percent are associated with lower probability of accident culpability than is the case at .00 percent BAC. The reasons for this finding are not clear. Borkenstein et al. can only conclude that BACs in this range are not inconsistent with traffic safety.[5]

Further findings of the Grand Rapids study indicate that drivers with relatively high BACs (.08 percent and above) are more over-represented in single vehicle crashes than in

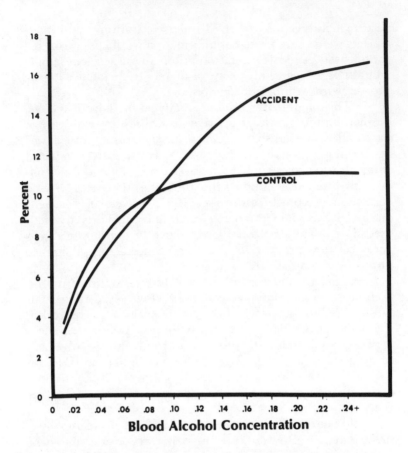

Figure 7-1. Cumulative percent at or below specific alcohol concentrations for accident and control groups.[4]

multivehicle crashes (although they are over-represented in both). Drivers at this level tend to have more severe crashes than drivers at lower BAC.

Other "controlled" studies confirm and extend the major findings of the Grand Rapids study. A recent project conducted in Vermont by Perrine et al. focuses on the behavioral and medical aspects of alcohol and highway safety.[7] The project was charged with determining, "the extent to which drinking and driving problems involve alcoholics and other abnormal drinkers, and the ways by which these individuals

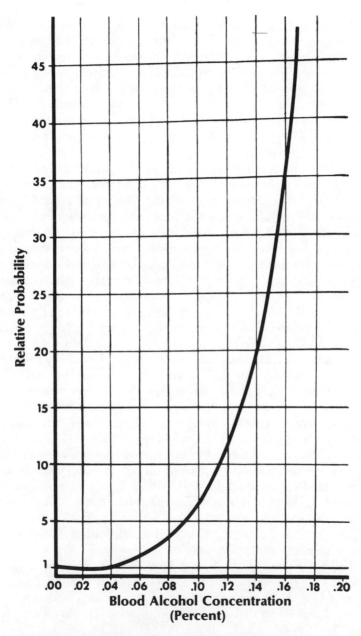

Figure 7-2. Relative probability of causing an accident.[6]

can be identified." Like the Grand Rapids study, the Vermont project included crashes from throughout the twenty-four hour period and from all days of the week. However, the Vermont project focused on injury and fatal crashes only. It was also conducted in a rural area rather than an urban one where most such investigations have been made. Since most traffic fatalities in this country occur in rural areas (even though most of the population resides in urban areas), the Vermont project may have greater generality.

The project included both drinker subjects who were studied under controlled laboratory conditions and driver respondents, including the following: fatally injured drivers (information obtained from survivors); a roadblock comparison sample for fatally injured drivers; clear record drivers (a subset of the roadblock comparison sample); drivers injured but not killed in crashes; a roadblock comparison sample for injured drivers; another clear record driver group derived from the roadblock comparison group for injured drivers; drivers cited for DWI (driving while intoxicated); and drivers cited for a serious motor vehicle violation other than DWI. The latter two groups were selected from official records. Information on BAC was available from all groups except the drivers injured in crashes and the drivers cited for a violation other than DWI.

The project was extensive and the findings were many, but one of the major conclusions was that BACs below .05 percent do not represent an appreciable increase in the probability of being involved in and being responsible for a fatal crash. However, BACs of .08 percent and higher are associated with increased risk. At .08 percent the risk of being responsible for a fatal crash is about four times that with no alcohol present, at .10 percent it is about seven times, and at .15 percent about twenty-five times the risk when no alcohol is present.

In 1968 the Department of Transportation delivered to the Congress a report on alcohol and highway safety.[8] On the basis of a review of all the available information, this report found that of drivers not in crashes between 1 and 4 percent have BACs of .10 percent or higher. (Many such studies select control drivers at the same site and time of day that a serious accident has occurred. Since serious accidents are more likely to occur on nights and weekends, and since more people are drinking at these times, the reported percentage of control drivers with high BACs may be higher than would be true of all drivers across time.) Of drivers killed in single vehicle crashes, 48 to 57 percent have BACs at or above .10 percent. Thus it can be seen that while only 1 to 4 percent of the population at risk are found to have such high levels, they account for about half of single vehicle crashes in which the driver is killed. Of drivers killed in multivehicle crashes, 44 percent of those considered to be at fault have BACs at or above .10 percent, compared to 12 percent of those drivers considered not at fault. Of all fatal crashes in which the driver is killed, between 39 and 50 percent were found to have BACs at or above .10 percent. This compared with 6 to 10 percent in run of the mill crashes. (It should be noted, however, that while this latter percentage is low, the actual number of such crashes is quite high.)

Thus far the focus has been on alcohol involvement of drivers. Each year in the United States approximately one-fifth of all traffic deaths are accounted for by pedestrians. There are three identifiable subgroups in these pedestrian deaths, namely, the very young (children), the very old, and the alcohol-impaired (usually falling in the middle and late middle age range).[9] To determine whether alcohol is over-represented in pedestrian deaths, one must have control data. Haddon et al. conducted a controlled investigation of fatal pedestrian accidents in Manhattan.[10] The cases studied included fifty pedestrian deaths age eighteen or older who died as a result of being struck by a motor vehicle at known sites in Manhattan between May 3 and November 7, 1959. Post mortem examinations provided BAC. The control group was obtained by going to the accident site on a subsequent date but on the same day of week and time of day as the accident occurred. Most control interviews occurred within four weeks of the accident. Interviews and breath specimens were obtained from the first four adult pedestrians of the same sex as the deceased who reached the site. Thus there were 200 control cases matched to the fifty accident cases on the basis of sex, accident site, and time of day and day of week of accident. The interview included questions concerning place and length of residence, place of birth, age, present occupation, and marital status. Sex, apparent race, appearance and apparent sobriety, date, location, time of interview, and weather were also recorded.

Of the deceased pedestrians, 26 percent showed no alcohol present, while 47 percent had BACs of .05 percent or higher. Forty-two percent were at or above .10 percent, and 32 percent were at or above .15 percent. On the other hand, 67 percent of the control group had no alcohol present, 16 percent had BACs at or above .05 percent, 8 percent at or above .10 percent, and 6 percent at or above .15 percent. The differences between control and accident cases were significant whether or not the two groups were matched by age and sex. In contrast to the findings from drivers in the Grand Rapids and Vermont projects, this study of pedestrian fatalities showed that the risk associated with alcohol first becomes significantly increased at the low BACs, namely, .01 percent to .04 percent. The pedestrian fatalities with little or no alcohol present were significantly older than control cases with little or no alcohol. Such age differences between accident and control cases disappeared at the higher BACs suggesting that the pedestrian deaths were composed of two discrete groups, each with an increased risk, namely, the elderly pedestrian with little or no alcohol and the middle-aged pedestrian with higher BACs. Haddon's findings have been confirmed by subsequent studies of pedestrian deaths.[11]

Thus it has been well established that alcohol plays a major role in traffic fatalities. Before any clear causal relationship is assumed, one should note that there may be a number of confounding factors in the data. For example, it has been reported that with vehicle speed at time of crash controlled, driver injury is more likely to occur if alcohol is present, and this effect is more pronounced for serious injury.[12]

Likewise, if many drunk drivers are actually problem drinkers or alcoholics (as has been reported), it may be that their recuperative potential is less than that of a nonalcoholic given the same injury. Thus the drinking driver may be more likely to end up a fatality than the nondrinking driver. Others have suggested that the drinking driver is merely expressing his basically antisocial personality in both his drinking and his driving. Smart claims that alcoholic drivers have more than their share of accidents when they are sober as well as when they are drunk.[13] If this is the case, simply preventing the drinking before driving will not solve the highway safety problem. Waller, on the other hand, is of the opinion that the pharmacologic effect of alcohol plays a more important role than personality factors in most drinking driver crashes.[14] It is evident that we need to know much more about the drinking driver.

Who Are the Drinking Drivers?

Most adults in the United States drive and most of them also drink alcoholic beverages. Furthermore, most of them at some time combine both drinking and driving. Thus, if we see as our goal the elimination of driving after drinking, we must say with Pogo, "We have met the enemy and they is us." Indeed, the traditional approach to the alcohol-traffic accident problem has been to admonish, "If you drive, don't drink." Since there is evidence that most of us do both and that, furthermore, most of us do not get into serious trouble doing both, the slogan has fallen on deaf ears.[15]

The problem is clearly more complex than the sloganeering would lead us to believe. Both the Grand Rapids study and the Vermont project found that low levels of alcohol were not associated with increased risk of crash. Thus the data support the experience of the majority of drivers. The controlled studies show that high risk of crash is associated with excessive use of alcohol, probably higher BACs than most social drinkers ever attain. These heavy drinkers do share some characteristics in common.

The Grand Rapids study reports higher BACs among males, and the Vermont project reports higher quantities and frequencies of drinking among males than females. Both studies show that drinking and driving is concentrated in the middle-aged groups, especially the twenty-five to forty-four year range. Likewise the Vermont data show that drivers age twenty to fifty-nine are more likely to have positive BACs. However, both studies indicate that younger drivers get into trouble at lower BACs. In the Michigan study drivers who were widowed, separated, or divorced were more likely to have alcohol present. In Vermont marital status was analyzed only for drivers age twenty-five and over. The marital status of roadblock subjects was about the same for those with no alcohol present as for those with high BACs. However, drivers fatally injured who had alcohol present were much more likely to be unmarried (single, widowed, divorced, or separated). At levels at or above .10 percent both DWI and fatally injured drivers were more likely to be unmarried than roadblock drivers. Concerning occupational levels, in the Michigan study the lower occupational classes were over-represented at high BACs, while in Vermont they were over-represented among roadblock drivers with no alcohol present. Both studies reported a positive relationship between high BACs and an index of frequency of drinking (Vermont used both quantity and frequency to compute an index). Both studies report an association between high BACs and a preference for beer. Drinking drivers are more likely to be present on the road during nighttime hours and on weekends, including Friday night.

While differences can be identified between drivers with high BACs and those without alcohol present, most drinking drivers (even those at the higher BACs) do not become involved in crashes. What variables differentiate the drinking driver who gets into difficulty from the drinking driver who does not? Table 7-1 summarizes some of the findings from the Vermont project. These data are based only on those subjects in each group who were found to have BACs at or above .10 percent

Table 7-1
Comparisons of Legally Impaired Drivers (BAC .10+)
Age 25 or Older in Three Populations.*

| Characteristic | Driver group | | |
	Roadblock	Fatal	DWI
BAC of .20 or more	0%	46%	61%
Married	88%	72%	52%
Upper occupational level	41%	50%	10%
Moderate or heavy drinker	50%	77%	83%
1 Suspension	21%	21%	64%
1 Citation last 5 years or more.	28%	17%	67%

*Compiled from data presented in Perrine et al.[16]

and who were age twenty-five or older. It can be seen, first of all, that although roadblock drivers included in this table had BACs of at least .10 percent, none was so high as .20 percent, compared to 46 percent of fatal accident drivers and 61 percent of DWI drivers. The roadblock drivers were the most likely to be married, with the DWI the least likely. A curious finding concerned occupational level, with the fatal accident drivers showing the highest percentage in the upper level, five times the percentage for the DWI drivers. The roadblock drinking drivers were least likely to be classified as moderate or heavy drinkers, with the DWIs the most likely to be so classified. DWIs also exceeded the other two groups in number of previous suspensions and number of citations in the last five years. On the basis of far more data than those presented here, Perrine et al. concluded that, "with only a few exceptions the data suggest that there are major similarities between DWIs and driver fatalities who had alcohol. We must conclude that to a substantial degree, these two groups of high alcohol drivers are probably drawn from a single population."[17]

In an earlier paper Waller arrived at a similar conclusion based on examination of several populations of drivers, including persons convicted for drunk driving, drivers cited for moving violations other than drunk driving, drivers involved in an accident but not arrested for drunk driving (divided into those who had been drinking and those who had not), and drivers with no accidents or violations during the previous three years.[18] He examined the driver records of these individuals plus information available about the number of contacts and reasons for contacts with the county welfare and probation departments, the alcohol rehabilitation clinic, the state mental hospital, family service agencies, and police departments. Almost two-thirds of the drunk drivers and half of the drivers with accidents after drinking could be identified as problem drinkers on the basis of information available in the public records referred to above. This was in contrast to 3 percent of the "clean" record drivers, 8 percent of the drivers with violations other than drunk driving, and 14 percent of the nonalcohol accident drivers. Alcohol appeared to be a major part of the lives of the drunk drivers. After reviewing the findings, Waller concludes that so far as problem drinking is concerned the drinking accident-involved drivers and the drivers arrested for drunk driving represent similar populations. It should be noted that Waller's study compared drivers arrested for drunk driving with drivers in alcohol-involved accidents, while the Vermont project compared DWI drivers with driver *fatalities* who had been drinking.

Others are not so convinced of the similarity between the DWI and the drinking driver fatality. A study in Southern California by Pollack et al. found that most fatality drinking drivers had never come to public attention through their driving convictions. They conclude that,

> The drinking drivers convicted by our courts are *not* likely to be those killed in subsequent fatal accidents . . . drinking driving does not act by itself as a causative agent in fatal automobile crashes but interacts with other variables that characterize the fatal accident-bound driver, even though heavy drinking immediately prior to the fatal crash is a decisive factor in promoting the accident.[19]

Smart and Waller present a provocative discourse on this point.[20]

Hurst, in his review of controlled studies of alcohol in highway crashes, suggests that DWI drivers, who appear to be heavier and more practiced drinkers, may have developed compensatory behavior to protect them from crashing.[21] Such a compensating driver may drive more slowly and erratically, thus attracting the attention of the officer. Such driving, however, would not be so likely to result in a crash, or if a crash occurred, in a fatality.

A corollary to such a hypothesis is that the drinking driver fatalities are less experienced drinkers and are therefore more impaired at the higher levels of alcohol. Hurst presents evidence that supports this line of reasoning. Using the data from the Grand Rapids study, he has plotted the relative probability of crash involvement at varying BACs for subgroups defined by drinking frequency, as shown in Figure 7-3. The drivers who drink most frequently have a lower probability of crash involvement at zero level of alcohol but also show a lower acceleration in probability of crash involvement as alcohol level increases. Thus the more practiced drinker

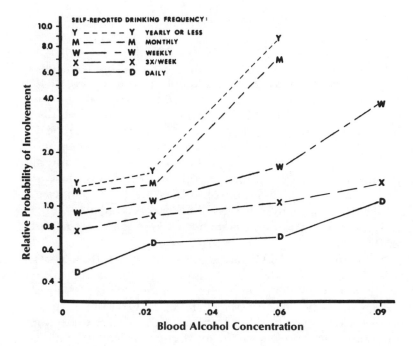

Figure 7-3. Relative probability of crash involvement (by drinking frequency group) as a function of BAC where 1.0—relative probability of composite group at zero alcohol.[22]

appears less likely to become involved in a crash than the less practiced drinker *with the BAC controlled.* Figure 7-3 shows BACs only up to .09 percent. The BACs of drinking drivers in fatal crashes are often far above this level, and it is difficult to imagine drivers who show BACs above .20 who are not fairly experienced drinkers.

Probably the single most important finding to emerge from the controlled studies is that the drinking driver who gets into difficulty (either DWI or serious injury or fatal crash) is driving at a BAC far above that found in most drivers on the road at the same time and place. Thus, while most adults at some time combine drinking and driving, most adults are not candidates for drinking-driving problems. This finding has been used to attempt to muster public support for strong measures for dealing with the drinking driver.

Countermeasures

The Federal Highway Safety Act of 1966 required a thorough study of the relationship between alcohol consumption and highway safety. The resulting report, referred to earlier, provided the basis for developing an alcohol countermeasure program.[23] In 1970 the first of a planned total of fifty-two alcohol safety action projects (ASAPs) were initiated. These were to be comprehensive community programs financed by federal funds with the hope that state and local funding would replace federal support at the end of the first three years. The first group of ASAPs are now completed, while the last are still underway. This undertaking is by far the most expensive effort ever launched to combat alcohol-related traffic deaths.

Briefly, the ASAPs attempt to accomplish three goals. The first of these is the *identification* of the problem drinker, through on-road screening programs, more extensive testing of drivers in crashes, per se laws whereby a BAC of .10 percent or higher would be considered evidence of driving under the influence without the need for supporting evidence of impairment, records from social service agencies, court records, and records from treatment facilities. Once the target group has been identified, the second goal of the ASAPs is *decision*. The information compiled in the identification phase must be evaluated by the courts and the licensing agencies to determine a course of action. If a case is handled by the courts, the decision may include input from a presentence investigation, from probation departments or from other sources and the decision may include assigning a defendant to treatment. If the case is handled by the licensing agency rather than the court, the decision may include input from medical review boards. The third and final goal of ASAP is *action* aimed at reducing the driving of problem drinkers, reducing the heavy drinking of any drivers or reducing both. Strictly from a highway safety point of view, the goal would be to reduce drinking and driving in combination rather than to reduce either alone.

How effective is the ASAP approach? Data from the first nine projects indicated some degree of success. However, the major program contributing to the apparent success was that in Oregon and there were serious questions as to whether the observed drop in fatalities in that state could be attributed to ASAP. It is probably accurate to say that the ASAP effort has encountered almost every barrier possible to effective evaluation. Part of the problem came from lack of clarity in original goals, incompatibility of goals ("selling" a program so that states and municipalities would assume funding while at the same time trying to do an honest evaluation of it), changes in goals along the way, and uncontrollable shifts in major background variables (e.g., changes in the BAC at which one may legally drive). We will probably never know for sure how effective the ASAP approach was or what parts of it were more promising than others.[24]

While a large number of possible countermeasures have been suggested, few have been subjected to careful evaluation.[25] Many of the suggested countermeasures fall into one of two major approaches, namely, legal and educational. The legal approach has great appeal. Many feel that it is easier to pass a law than it is to educate the public. Yet passing laws is not an effective approach if public opinion does not support the law. Our nation's experience with prohibition is a case in point. Indeed, the perceived harshness of the penalties for drunk driving may result in a reduction in convictions. Several years ago I was attending a luncheon at which a governor addressed the group on highway safety and in particular on the importance of cracking down on the drinking driver. He admonished the judges in the audience to find defendants guilty rather than allow them to plead to a reduced charge (usually reckless driving). The judge on my left turned to me and explained that almost invariably when he finds a defendant guilty of drunk driving, an appeal is made for a jury trial, and juries will rarely convict in such cases. Hence the guilty judgment leads to the defendant's being acquitted, while a judgment of reckless driving means he suffers at least some penalty. Thus harsher penalties alone cannot be expected to be effective.

A study in Denver, Colorado, addressed itself to the effectiveness of different types of penalties for drunk driving offenders.[26] The judges involved agreed to assign penalties of a fine, conventional probation, or rehabilitative probation, according to a determined schedule, to drivers convicted of driving under the influence (DUI) for the first time. Judges did not always adhere to the schedule, and some defendants were given jail sentences. The outcome of the study was that there were no significant differences in subsequent crashes, moving violations, or DUI convictions for the three treatment groups. Furthermore, drivers sentenced to jail did not differ from the other groups in their subsequent records. Thus the harshness of the penalty per se did not appear to be associated with the effectiveness of the sentence. Of interest also is their finding that defendants represented by legal counsel, although having poorer driving histories, were more likely to be found not guilty or to have their charges reduced or dismissed.

Legal controls on the sale of liquor may be expected to have some effect on consumption. Recent changes making eighteen-year-olds legal adults and eligible to purchase liquor may have resulted in an increase in alcohol-related traffic deaths among teenage drivers, although not to the extent initially anticipated.[27] Whether the presence of open bars, or liquor-by-the-drink sales, is related to traffic fatalities cannot be clearly ascertained because of the many other factors that differentiate the areas where the different systems prevail.

One measure aimed at reducing the combination of drinking and driving is the limited license: the court may allow a convicted drunk driver the privilege of driving within specified restrictions. The purpose of such a license is to spare the defendant and his family undue hardship, particularly where a driver license is necessary to enable continued employment. Ideally the defendant could continue to drive to and from work during daylight hours when drinking should be less of a problem. However, he would be prohibited from engaging in driving for social purposes where alcohol may be more likely to be involved. Such a law was passed in North Carolina effective July 2, 1969, applying to persons convicted of DUI for the first time.

While the courts did not always abide by the spirit of the limited license law and reputedly issued some driving privileges that could hardly be considered restrictive (e.g., anywhere in the United States), by and large the intent of the law was honored. Examination of driver records of those arrested for DUI prior to and after the implementation of the new law showed that, first, the availability of such a driving privilege was associated with an increase in the proportion of DUI arrests resulting in conviction and a corresponding decrease in the proportion of reduced charges.[28] In addition, those drivers given the limited privilege experienced no more crashes or violations than the general driving population in the subsequent year. However, they did show a higher frequency of subsequent DUI convictions. Nevertheless, drivers given the limited privilege averaged more accidents and violations than comparable drivers who had lost their driving privilege entirely prior to the new law. Whether the level of accidents and violations observed among these limited-license drivers is a reasonable price to pay for their opportunity to continue to work and participate in society is a value judgment that must be made.

Perhaps one of the most intriguing countermeasures to alcohol-related traffic fatalities is the British Road Safety Act of 1967. Heralded as the answer to the drinking driver problem, the act provides that a driver involved in a traffic violation or accident may be required by an officer to take a roadside screening breath test to determine the extent of alcohol present in his body. If the test is refused or failed (i.e., showed a BAC of .08 percent or higher), a blood test may be required. If the blood test shows a BAC at or above .08 percent, the driver is considered guilty of a crime, the punishment for which includes a mandatory license suspension for one year. As can well be imagined, the enactment of such a law was accompanied by controversy, but the initial effects looked promising. Evaluation of such legislation is not nearly so simple as it may seem. However, Ross conducted a careful investigation of the impact of this piece of legislation, examining not just the changes found in alcohol-related highway crashes, but also the changes in other types of highway crashes, in drunk driving charges, in amount of driving, in court sentences, in liquor consumption, and in a number of other factors considered relevant.[29] He concluded that British drivers were indeed reducing the amount of driving done after drinking, although neither drinking nor driving was reduced as an independent activity.

Unfortunately the initial positive impact of the law did

not last. This diminishing effect Ross attributes to the low probability of detection, so that drivers soon learned that the danger of apprehension was not great. He argues that the effectiveness of such legislation is to a large extent dependent upon a highly perceived probability of apprehension. A high probability of apprehension combined with relatively moderate punishment is more effective than a low probability of apprehension combined with highly severe punishment, according to Ross. To date, our drunk driving laws more closely approximate the latter condition.

Much has been made of the fact that the United States allows unduly lenient BACs compared to European countries where more stringent standards prevail. A brief review of the laws controlling alcohol and driving in a number of European countries is presented by Herrick.[30] His report leads one to exercise great caution before concluding that because a country has a law on the books therefore that law is enforced. For example, while France enacted legislation in 1970 providing for prosecution of drivers above .08 percent BAC, in practice there is little enforcement or for that matter little incentive to enforce such a law where wine appears to be a way of life. On the other hand, Sweden, where a BAC of .05 percent is grounds for a conviction of drunk driving, apparently enjoys widespread public support for their laws, with many citizens pushing for even stricter legislation and more severe penalties. However, Swedish authorities are concerned with the fact that under the present system 40 percent of the people sentenced to jail are sentenced for drunk driving. The jails are already bulging and could hardly accommodate the business that would be created by stricter penalties.

An interesting characteristic of the Swedish system is that fines are levied as a percentage of income, so that variations in the socioeconomic status of the offender become less relevant. The fines that are levied are high, running as much as 10 percent of one's annual income. Whether or not such laws are a contributory factor, Sweden reports only about 10 percent of their traffic deaths as being alcohol-related.

Laws are important and can accomplish much. However, there is also a need for education. The apparent success of the Swedish system is attributed in part to the fact that the

Swedish people recognize the importance of the problem and are willing to support countermeasures. Educational efforts must include informing the public of the nature and extent of the problem. Many feel that the general public would be more receptive to stricter legislation if they understood better that it is the driver who has been drinking excessively who is a major problem rather than the driver who has had one or two drinks. There remains much misinformation on the part of the voters in this regard. In addition, educational efforts can be focused more specifically on the offender himself. Such efforts often take the form of rehabilitative programs.

The identification of the role of the drunk driver (and pedestrian) in fatal highway crashes has led to predictions that if we can identify and treat this small group of drivers we will solve much of the highway safety problem. Such thinking is probably unduly optimistic. Estimates of the extent of alcoholism vary widely, usually ranging somewhere between 8 and 12 million persons in this country. This would approximate 7 or 8 percent of our adult population. But suppose we take a much more conservative estimate of 2 percent. We might conclude then that 2 percent of the drivers (essentially all adults) account for 50 percent of the traffic fatalities. What a rare opportunity! If we can identify and treat this 2 percent, we can eliminate half our traffic deaths.

Campbell and Levine have described this kind of thinking as the percentage fallacy.[31] It appears promising until it is translated into actual numbers. Applying the 2 percent figure to North Carolina's 3 million drivers, we find that 60,000 drivers are accounting for half the traffic deaths in 1973, or about 944. Thus we must treat successfully 60,000 drivers to eliminate 944 fatalities. Obviously the vast majority of the 60,000 drivers are not going to be involved in traffic fatalities, so that we will be hard put to subject them to whatever special treatment we may have in mind. Rehabilitative measures for the drinking driver are expensive and their efficacy is questionable at best. It would be difficult to justify the expenditure of large sums to treat huge numbers of drivers (most of whom will not get into difficulty) using measures that we cannot demonstrate to be effective. As yet we have no silver bullet.

Where do we stand in regard to alcohol and highway

safety? We know far more about the problem than we did a decade ago. The encouragement and support of the federal government has led to widespread efforts, some of which may provide leads. At this time, however, we should probably encourage the approach espoused by D.T. Campbell.[32] He recommends that society, and in particular the administrators of society, should focus on the seriousness and importance of the problem rather than advocate a particular solution. Such a stance enables the evaluation of alternative countermeasures while avoiding false promises leading to inevitable disillusion. In the field of alcohol and highway safety we have had more than our share of false promises. We need to be able to persist in our efforts to find ameliorative measures while we avoid the temptations of simplistic answers.

CHAPTER 8

How Risky Is Drinking?

John A. Ewing, M.D.

IN THE PRECEDING chapters, we have looked at medical, forensic, psychiatric, and highway safety aspects of drinking. All show the risks entailed in excessive drinking. Also, in chapter 6, I discussed safe versus dangerous drinking. In this chapter I will try to review evidence which can help to answer the average moderate social drinker who asks, "Is even the little drinking I do dangerous?"

Sources of information with which to answer this question come at present mainly from actuarial studies, the science of epidemiology, and clinical reports. Much of this is well reviewed in a recent U. S. government report.[1] Here I will simply pick out highlights which will satisfy the curiosity of the average reader.

Insurance Company Studies

Reports from the insurance industry have to be taken with caution when applied to drinking populations. To begin with, those who apply for insurance are a self-selected group, that is they are not necessarily representative of the population as a whole. From the applicants, companies select those whom they want to insure. Thus, actuarial findings may not apply to the total population in general. Early insurance company reports tended to compare total abstainers and all drinkers, lumping within the latter group the whole spectrum of drinking practices. However, since prohibition ended, the reports have generally compared "standard" risks and "substandard" ones. The latter policyholders were those whose records included adverse information about their drinking. For such information to get on the record, the drinking must have gone significantly beyond normal practices. From such studies, there is clear evidence of greater mortality (ranging from a ratio of 2.14 to 5.54 times greater) than in standard groups. The ratios are particularly high in those called "spree drinkers" by Menge[2] and in the younger age groups.

Clinical Samples

These consist of various followup studies of patients actually treated for alcoholism, and they do consistently show higher mortality rates than controls.[3] Obviously, patients treated for alcoholism are not necessarily representative of the class "alcoholics," and even more so these data do not say anything about the risks to health of moderate drinking. A recent British study has come up with similar findings showing the actual deaths among men at more than twice the expected rate and among women at more than three times.[4] It should be noted, however, that these deaths are by no means all the product of alcohol's effect upon the body. The leading causes were in fact accidents, poisoning, violence, and suicide.

Even among young alcoholics, mortality rates exceed those of the general population. Schuckit and Gunderson have studied young Navy and Marine Corps alcoholics, finding an annual death rate of fifteen per 1,000 hospitalized alcoholics.[5] Most deaths resulted from accidents or suicides followed by liver cirrhosis and alcohol-related gastrointestinal disease. The death rates in these young servicemen were about seven times higher than in nonalcoholics of comparable age in the same military services.

Community Studies

These studies involve comparing health and mortality rates with drinking patterns and avoid the errors implicit in looking only at those with alcoholism. Shurtleff, from a Framingham, Massachusetts, study demonstrated that the data tended to show an excess mortality in both abstainers and high volume drinkers.[6] The latter showed the highest excess mortality at younger ages while the abstainers showed the highest at older ages. In a study done in California, Belloc measured drinking in terms of the amount usually drunk per occasion (of the beverage drunk in the largest amount).[7] Heavier drinkers showed a higher mortality among younger men but no clear pattern existed for other sex and age groups. However, there was a slight tendency for light drinkers to show the lowest mortality on an age-adjusted basis.

The government report "Alcohol and Health" provides preliminary findings from a study by Room and Day, not yet published.[8] Four separate samples of the general population are involved, including two samples of adults in San Francisco and two nationwide samples of adults. One of each sample is limited to men, age twenty-one to fifty-nine years. They have been followed for varying lengths of time, ranging from four to eleven years. In terms of overall frequency of drinking, the lowest mortality rate in each sex and age group is at an intermediate drinking level. Under age sixty, the highest death rates occur at the highest frequency of drinking; above age sixty, the highest death rates are among abstainers. As in previous studies, there is a consistent tendency for those who are currently abstainers to show a higher mortality than those who are currently moderate drinkers.

In this study, frequent heavy drinking is measured by the frequency with which the respondent drinks five or more drinks on an occasion. Such relatively heavy drinking is so rare among women over fifty and men over sixty that mortality rates cannot be computed. However among younger subjects, an increased mortality rate does appear to relate to frequent heavy drinking. Even when the comparison only includes those who rate themselves currently as in good health, abstainers show a higher mortality rate than moderate drinkers.

These recent findings corroborate the report on alcohol and longevity by the distinguished biologist Raymond Pearl, which was published as early as 1926.[9] Although that study has been criticized, it has never been disproved. Using standard actuarial methods, Pearl constructed life tables for groups of abstainers, moderate drinkers, and heavy drinkers in an effort to determine the influence of alcohol on mortality. His classification included both drinking frequency and drinking quantity dimensions. In general, moderate drinkers had a lower mortality rate than abstainers and, among men, moderate steady drinkers had lower mortality rates than heavy occasional drinkers. The heavy occasional drinker is the binge or spree drinker already identified by Menge. Among men of all ages, the moderate steady drinkers had the most favorable mortality rates among all drinking categories. In the older age groups, the heavier drinkers showed the lower mortality rates, a finding which has appeared in subsequent studies. Heavy drinking might act as a selective process to kill off less healthy heavy drinkers at an earlier age. However, it may simply indicate good health at that time, with people in poor health having given up their drinking because of their ill health.

Specific Causes of Death

The recent government report provides useful data with regard to death by "natural causes" as opposed to the violence, poisonings, and such conditions already alluded to. In the first place, the excessive use of alcohol, especially when combined with tobacco, has been implicated in the development of certain cancers of the respiratory tract and upper gastrointestinal tract.[10] Nonwhite men appear to be especially susceptible. Next, there is the issue of alcohol and the heart which has already been discussed in chapter 4. Although alcoholic cardiomyopathy is a real alcohol-related problem, there is some evidence that alcohol may not be a significant risk factor associated with heart attacks of the type known as myocardial infarction or coronary thrombosis. Indeed, some studies have suggested that moderate alcohol use may be actually associated with a lower risk of such a heart attack. Interestingly enough, there is some evidence pointing to higher rates of heart disease among *former* drinkers and clearly this subject calls for much more research before any final conclusions can be drawn.[11]

Summing Up

The evidence to date fails to point to moderate alcohol use as a consistent villain in terms of man's health or longevity. Clearly, heavy drinking, and probably the periodic binge drinking so typical of alcoholism, can be extremely destructive. This is in terms of medical complications, psychiatric problems, exposure to violence and hazards on the highway. The government report from which we have quoted widely in this review sums up as follows:[12] "The data on general mortality suggest that for amount of drinking, apparently unlike amount of smoking, there may be some kind of threshold below which mortality is little affected. In the absence of further evidence, in fact, the classical 'Anstie's Limit'[13] seems still to reflect the safe amount of drinking which does not substantially increase the risk of early death."

Let me add a few words of additional caution to the reader who has followed these arguments thus far. If a physician has identified medical complications which are either secondary to alcohol use or liable to be aggravated by alcohol use, then his advice to cut down or abstain totally should be followed completely. Likewise, those who have experienced the loss of control over drinking and social and family and work-connected problems of alcoholism should recognize that for them total abstinence is indicated. No one should use the information supplied above (that the mortality of drinkers is lower than that of abstainers and exdrinkers in terms of coronary heart disease, and that overall mortality rates are higher in abstainers than in moderate drinkers) to argue against total abstinence when this is indicated. One of our own studies has suggested that just stopping excessive drinking may be associated with excess mortality,[14] but this might comment more upon lifestyle than upon any "hazard" from "not drinking."

Indeed, the issue of lifestyle needs to be considered in relation to all of the remarks contained in this chapter. For instance, when all the information is collected, it may become apparent that those who espouse moderate drinking and who succeed in maintaining this level of drinking are also people who live moderately in other health related aspects of their lives. Possibly being an ardent abstainer is associated with a particular psychological set and style of life which combine to produce certain tensions which are themselves basically unhealthy. In one of our studies in which we looked at indices of mental health in teenagers, we found evidence to suggest that having a totally abstaining parent could be as emotionally traumatic as having a heavily drinking one.[15]

Clearly further research is called for and will be done. However, to the moderately drinking reader, even if a daily drinker, I have to say that there is no evidence right now that would point to his habit as being particularly dangerous to his health.

PART III

Psychosocial Aspects of Drinking

DESCRIPTIONS OF DRINKING are not complete until they include the context in which the behavior occurs. Therefore, this section not only presents data on various age groups in the United States but also discusses the psychosocial and cultural factors that influence drinking both formally and informally.

Dr. Ira Cisin is Professor of Sociology at the George Washington University where he is head of the Social Research Group. He has done extensive research on drinking practices for the California Department of Public Health.

Dr. Gerald Globetti is a sociologist with the University of Alabama. Previously he was Director of the Center for Alcohol Education at Murray State University. Dr. Globetti has conducted much research on teenage drinking problems.

Beatrice Rouse and Dr. Ewing have already been introduced in Part I as editors of this book.

Dr. Kenneth C. Mills is a research psychologist who took his early training with research in alcoholism treatment but has gradually moved into more basic research issues. These include developing an animal model of voluntary alcoholism which shares measures with the human situation. Dr. Mills is with the Center for Alcohol Studies and Assistant Professor of Psychiatry at the University of North Carolina in Chapel Hill.

CHAPTER 9

Formal and Informal Social Controls over Drinking

Ira H. Cisin, Ph.D.

CULTURAL ANTHROPOLOGISTS ARE fond of telling us that, with perhaps one or two exceptions, any constellation of behavior that we can dream up will turn out to be normal behavior in some society somewhere in the world at some time in history. If there is one universal characteristic that pervades mankind, it seems to be the urge to manipulate the behavior of other people. This urge that seems to move us in all societies at all times operates on both the individual and the societal level. On an individual level, we do not need Eric Berne or Stephen Potter to remind us that we are continually playing games with one another, continuously acting in such a way that others will do what we want them to do. On a societal level, we need not subscribe to unattractive concepts like the "group mind" nor need we abandon attractive notions like "free will" to recognize that any organized society, if it is to survive, will reward behaviors of which that society approves.

Sociologists tend to distinguish between two kinds of mechanisms that we—the society—use to control, manipulate, or influence one another's behavior. These mechanisms may be broadly categorized as formal and informal social controls. This chapter examines these mechanisms in general as well as the role alcohol plays in our society, the drinking habits of Americans, and the mechanisms which our society uses to control or manipulate the use of beverage alcohol. This information should provide a backdrop useful in evaluating empirical evidence concerning the impact of law on various aspects of drinking.

Most social influence takes place through the operation of customs, folkways, mores—the ways of behaving that are encouraged or demanded by the society or its members. These informal mechanisms are transmitted through the socialization process. As we grow up in the society, we are reminded in a variety of ways by our parents, our peers, our churches, and our schools that certain modes of behavior are preferred and certain modes of behavior are disapproved. We are subjected to praise, to sanctions, to various kinds of reinforcements, rewards, and punishments, as we are molded into conformity with the demands and expectations of the society. The process is informal and, in many cases, inconsistent and chaotic. It may or may not be particularly effective, but it goes on all the time and we are all products of it.

In the discussion of the mores of a society, it is not unfair to distinguish between the behavioral mores and the lip-service or aspirational mores. Frequently a society which actually condones or accepts a certain kind of behavior will go out of its way to formally denounce that behavior. In our society, possibly as a function of time lag and slow change, we pay lip service to some Victorian notions, while it takes a Kinsey to remind us what we really do with our spare time. This hypocrisy—let us call it by its right name—usually takes the form of protecting our children or protecting the weak. We find ourselves denouncing the portrayal of violence on television when, in fact, we recognize that millions of us thoroughly enjoy the vicarious pleasure of watching the bad guy get his just desserts. We denounce pornography—yet, breathes there a man with soul so dead that he does not sneak a peak at the center spread of *Playboy*? Somehow, we rationalize the fact that we set standards, impose restrictions, or try to impose restrictions on our children or others that we never met and that we do not really expect them to meet. Such are the paradoxes of organized society and its social control mechanisms.

The informal mechanisms of social control are all-pervasive, influencing every aspect of human behavior. They are effective when the society truly wants them to be effective; they are ineffective when the society is ambivalent, split, in transition.

The formal mechanisms, on the other hand, are thought by some to be the rules which the society has agreed must not be broken. There is no clear pattern or theory to describe just exactly how members of a society decide which behaviors should be subjected to formal mechanisms of social control. Through popular demand, through pressure, or by some other means, men decide that a particular piece of behavior is so heinous, so objectionable, so damaging, or threatening to the general welfare that formally it must be declared illegal. Indeed, the passing of a law may simply represent decision on the part of the members of the society that the informal punishment process is ineffective as a deterrent, and the punishment process must be formalized to be effective; or it may simply mean that we want to impersonalize the punishment process by turning it over to a caretaker. In any case, we think of the legal process as a formalization of the general process of social control.

The legal process has many of the same characteristics that we find in the mechanisms of informal social control. Thus, it is not at all unusual for us to pass laws that represent aspiration or lip service rather than reality. These might be referred to as esthetic laws—they look good on the books, we think—but no one has any intention of enforcing them, or at least of enforcing them rigorously. In a similar category are the laws which facilitate prosecution by outlawing behaviors that are auxiliary to or incidental to the mores we are trying to enforce. Legislation against conspiracy falls in this category. So do the vagrancy laws that are rapidly disappearing or the loitering laws that are taking their place; these seem to be society's way of saying there are certain kinds of people we do not want on our streets.

There is no limit to the kinds of behavior we can think to outlaw, thus relieving ourselves of the responsibility of enforcing social control and passing the responsibility to our hired hands—the police and the courts. Sometimes we have a tacit understanding that they will not do anything about the problem—certainly not enforce the law against us; sometimes we just shift the burden of an unpleasant or onerous or clearly inhumane task, like driving the hippies out of town. But I am not cynical about law. Most of our laws represent what we really want our society to be like. We pass them with the full intention that they be enforced, in the sincere belief that our society will be somehow better if these laws are enforced. I do not really know how our drinking laws fit into this scheme; they probably have aspects of all the categories mentioned.

Whether we are talking about informal or formal social control, drinking behavior has been a prime target for control in our society and in many other similar societies. In general, our efforts to control have fallen into four general categories: we have tried to exercise control over (1) who is entitled to drink; (2) how much we are entitled to drink; (3) the conditions under which we can drink; and (4) the consequences of drinking.

1. *Who is entitled to drink?* Most jurisdictions have laws covering the sale of alcoholic beverages to minors. Some jurisdictions attempt to prevent parents from serving alcohol to their children even in the privacy of their homes. Not so long ago there were places where sale of alcoholic beverages to members of certain ethnic groups was prohibited. There are many places where, at least on the books, a bartender is forbidden by law to sell alcohol to an intoxicated person—and, although the custom never took hold in this country, there exist areas where so-called "known alcoholics" are blacklisted in the bars. Wisely or unwisely, we seem to be committed to protecting our children from public drinking, whether or not we are doing anything in the home or school to prepare them for later experience.

2. *How much are we entitled to drink?* The charge of public drunkenness is becoming less popular as a legal charge, but there seems to be some agreement, both formal and informal, that it is not fitting for a person to appear in public in an inebriated condition, whether or not he does any damage to anyone or anything.

3. *Under what conditions can we drink?* This is the area where most experimentation has occurred in our laws. Interest-

ingly enough, except for the well-enforced custom that we do not drink on the job (unless we are entertaining a client), there seems to be little effort at informal social control over when, how, and what we drink. This is the area where we have tried most cleverly to attain what we consider socially desirable ends by means of legislation. Most jurisdictions have laws covering hours of sale, presumably in order to prevent impulse drinking and thus indirectly rewarding those who stockpile. Many jurisdictions control the price of alcohol, presumably to remind us that drinking is a luxury, not a necessity, and subtly punishing us for "wasting" our money.

Perhaps the most popular kind of restrictive legislation is that which controls the manner in which we are allowed to drink outside our homes. Many jurisdictions have restrictions on drinking in vehicles; some jurisdictions require that drinks be sold only in places that also serve food. And, of course, we have the brown-bag jurisdictions, where restaurants are forbidden to serve liquor by the drink, but the customer is welcome to carry his own bottle and serve himself. Variations on this procedure occur where the customer is not allowed to carry his bottle but must store it in a locker at the club or restaurant; or the customer is allowed to pour from his own bottle, but the bottle must be kept under the table. In addition, there are the jurisdictions where there is no drinking allowed outside the home. In short, the cultural anthropologists would have a field day: name the variation and somewhere it is the law.

4. *What consequences of drinking are unacceptable legally?* We have almost universally passed laws governing the consequences (and in many cases, the presumed consequences) of drinking. Charges of drunk and disorderly are made "to keep the public peace." Driving while intoxicated is universally outlawed as a device to prevent accidents, on the well-established evidence that the probability of automobile accidents is increased when a driver has a significant amount of alcohol in him. By a simple extension of this preventive logic, it has become quite popular in many jurisdictions to define a specific blood-alcohol level as "presumptive evidence" of intoxication whether or not there is evidence of impaired driving skill.

As an example of how seriously our society considers

this, the Department of Transportation has sponsored counter-measure programs designed to get problem drinkers off the road. These efforts have not taken the form of specific legislation but are a determined effort to prevent from driving those persons who have drunk more than a little alcohol. The programs are built on the premise that a significant number (there is some dispute about the proportion) of highway deaths and other accidents are caused by habitual problem drinkers rather than by social drinkers. Building from this premise, individual communities are assisted financially to identify their problem drinkers and to take whatever steps are necessary to prevent the alleged problem drinkers from driving. The logic of these programs, their possible impact on alcoholic rehabilitation, and their constitutionality are still to be tested.

Now, it is not always clear what objectives the various laws in the above four categories are thought to serve; nor, more importantly, is it clear what objectives they are achieving. We do not have clear experimental evidence; but we have a great deal of information analogous to what the scientist would call a natural experiment. The systematic evaluation of this evidence is indeed a worthy objective.

From this quick overview of the subject of social control in the area of drinking behavior one can see that, if social control is to be effective, the manipulators of the control mechanisms must have not only clear objectives but a clear view of their subject. To serve this goal my colleagues and I undertook our national study of drinking practices.

In addressing ourselves to the question of what role alcohol plays in our society, one cannot help being reminded of the famous drunken Porter's scene in Macbeth. The Porter, after complaining about what we would now call a hangover, asserts: "drink, sir, is a great provoker of three things." And MacDuff, who seems to play straight man to the other characters in this play, naturally asks: "What three things does drink especially provoke?" To which the Porter responds:

> Marry, sir, nose-painting, sleep, and urine. Lechery, sir, it provokes, and unprovokes: it provokes the desire, but it takes away the performance. Therefore much drink may be said to be an equivocator with lechery: it makes him, and it mars him; it sets him on, and takes him off; it persuades him and dis-

heartens him; makes him stand to, and not stand to; in conclusion, equivocates him in a sleep, and, giving him the lie, leaves him.

After almost four hundred years, this is still a pretty good description of the effects of alcohol on the drinker: nose-painting, sleep, and urine, and, of course, the equivocation of lechery.

Although these may be the effects, these are not necessarily the functions the drinker seeks. We know enough about the psychology of the self-fulfilling prophecy to realize that the functions sought are the functions achieved. If one drinks, as some persons do, to pep himself up, if he believes that alcohol acts as a stimulant, increases his manliness and makes him the life of the party, no amount of biochemical evidence that alcohol is a depressant is going to prevent the alcohol from acting as a stimulant on him. This is not just the phenomenon of the depression of inhibition; it is the well-documented psychological phenomenon, analogous to the placebo effect, that drugs will have the effect that the drug-taker expects them to have. I do not deny biochemistry; I do not deny the physiological impact of drugs; I do say that the psychological impact may be of over-riding importance.

If I had to sum up in a word the effect that our society seeks in alcohol, the word would be "ice-breaking"—the relief of tension in social situations, the lubrication of social interactions. Ogden Nash has put it most succinctly in his poem "On Icebreakers":

> Candy
> Is dandy;
> But likker
> Is quicker.

Whether we are talking about seduction, consummating a business deal, or merely overcoming the shyness that many of us feel in social situations, we know that alcohol helps to speed up the processes of social interaction, and we take advantage of this knowledge to help us to break the ice.

Whether the facilitation or acceleration of social interaction is a good thing or a bad thing, the facts are that the social facilitation reasons seem to characterize the great majority of drinkers. This is not to deny the existence of antisocial or antiadjustment reasons that characterize the small proportion of drinkers who are not in the mainstream of the society, whose drinking is deviant not only in amount but, more importantly, in the psychological importance that it has for them. The normal drinker will drink to increase his contact with the society around him; the alcoholic, on the other hand, seeks isolation from the society, seeks to forget, seeks to reduce his contact with the society.

Our research over the past several years has been concerned with descriptive studies of American drinking practices in the general population, in a society where drinking is habitual behavior for a considerable majority of the population and where alcoholism is a relatively rare phenomenon. Alcoholism is not an unimportant phenomenon: alcoholism is a social problem, an esthetic problem, and a blot on our society. I applaud the valiant efforts of those who try to prevent the occurrence of this problem and to mitigate its effects when it does occur. However, when we look at the phenomenon called drinking, and when we observe this phenomenon in the general population, we find that the great majority of the adult population uses alcohol, that the great majority of the drinkers seem to achieve a reasonably harmless social facilitation through drinking, and that only a small minority of the drinkers seem to get into serious trouble.

My colleagues and I have conducted a series of studies to describe drinking practices of the adult population of the contiguous United States (excluding Hawaii and Alaska).[1] These studies have been sponsored by the National Institute of Mental Health. Although our main focus has been upon nationwide studies, companion studies of individual communities have been conducted under the same sponsorship by our group at the George Washington University and by a local group in the San Francisco Bay area through the Mental Research Institute of Palo Alto and Berkeley. Don Cahalan has been the project director in Washington; Genevieve Knupfer has been project director on the West Coast.

The main thrust of these studies has been on the who, what, when, where, and why of drinking. Who are the drinkers? What kinds of people drink? What do they drink?

With whom do they drink? On what occasions do they drink more or less than usual? Where does all this drinking take place? And what is the motivational pattern underlying the drinking?

The details of the methods used in our national study of drinking practices and the record of our findings are carefully documented in the book *American Drinking Practices.*[2] For our purposes here, let us concentrate on the functions that alcohol plays for our society and the kinds of expectations or norms society imposes on us.

1. *Alcoholism is associated with sex norms.* Alcohol has been male behavior for a long while, and it is still predominantly male behavior. The use of alcohol is part of women's emergence into first-class citizenship: a much larger percentage of women seem to be drinking these days than was true a generation ago. Women in general, however, tend to drink more moderately than men.

2. *Alcohol is associated with the relationships between men and women.* For example, in our study we found that when men were asked about the frequency of their wives' drinking, their responses in the aggregate almost perfectly matched the frequency of drinking which married women respondents reported for themselves. However, when women were asked about their husbands' drinking, the frequencies which they reported were at a lower level than the ones which the men in the sample reported for themselves. These findings indicate that husbands tend to know about their wives' drinking, but the wives do not know all there is to know about their husbands' drinking.

3. *Alcohol is part of our age norms.* Fewer older persons drink, and relatively fewer older women drink than is the case with older men.

4. *Alcohol helps to differentiate social status.* Within each age and sex group, fewer of those with lower social status drink than those of upper status. So, drink is not necessarily the curse of the working class, but the pleasure of the leisure class.

5. *Alcohol characterizes the process that sociologists have loosely called "urbanization."* We find that drinking differs a great deal between cities and suburbs and rural areas.

6. *Alcohol consumption serves to emphasize religious and*

ethnic differences. In a society struggling toward melting-pot integration, the subcultural differences in drinking patterns which we have found help to emphasize the subcultural differences which still exist.

7. *Finally, a word about the role of alcohol in alienating children from their parents—the part alcohol plays in the socialization process.* In our values as parents and educators, we have a responsibility for the socialization of our children, a responsibility for preparing them for life in the world. Part of our job is teaching children how to handle dangerous activities like driving, swimming, drinking, and sex. We behave toward our children as though there were really two different kinds of dangerous activities. Driving and swimming fall into the first type: we carefully teach our children that these are dangerous activities, and we deliberately set out to be sure that they know there is a right way and a wrong way to participate in these activities.

On the other hand, when we look at the other kind of dangerous activities, exemplified by drinking and sex, we seem to know only one word: "Don't!" We do not bother to say there is a right way and there is a wrong way; we just say "Don't!" In spite of the fact that our society fails to make abstainers out of our children, we continue to say "Don't!" We do not really want to produce abstainers; we have the illusion that they will follow our advice and be abstainers (in the case of sex, until marriage; and in the case of alcohol, until maturity) until they reach the magic age at which they can handle these activities. But as to the rights and wrongs of handling it when the great day comes, we choose to keep them in the dark. Now this is sheer hypocrisy. We are slowly awakening to the fact that we owe our children sex education in the home and in the school—education not dominated by the antisex league. We should be brave enough to tell them the truth; that drinking is normal behavior in the society, that moderate drinking need not lead to abuse; that drinking can be done in an appropriate civilized way without shame and guilt. Perhaps greater socialization in the direction of moderate drinking is part of the program we need for prevention of alcohol problems in the future.

I would now like to sum up some of our conclusions from our studies of drinking behavior in the United States:

1. Drinking is typical behavior for most adults in the United States, with both total abstention and heavy drinking (especially for escape from life's problems) being atypical.

2. Whether a person drinks at all appears to be primarily a sociological and subcultural variable rather than a psychological variable. This is evident from the great differences in incidence of drinking by sex, age, social status, degree of urbanization, and religion—all primarily sociological variables—and the relatively small associations that we have found between drinking and several psychological tests.

3. However, among the limited psychological measures we used in this national survey, certain measures of individual personality *are* useful in explaining variations in *heavy* drinking (and presumably, in problem drinking). These include measures of alienation from society, psychoneurotic symptoms, and psychological involvement with alcohol as evidenced by "escape" drinking.

4. Heavy drinking and "escape" drinking tend to vary inversely with the degree of social control which appears to be exerted upon the individual by the society.

5. Heavy and "escape" drinking also vary according to what Erich Fromm calls "the process of alienation." The "heavy escape" drinker in this survey was found to be generally unhappy with his progress in life, more likely than others to exhibit neurotic symptoms, and more dependent upon external aids to alleviate depression or nervousness.

6. We cannot tell from this single study whether the proportion of heavy drinkers is increasing or decreasing. The fact that the per capita consumption of alcohol in the United States has been holding fairly constant in the face of an apparent increase in the proportions of persons drinking (especially among women) indicates that the increase in the number of drinkers must be balanced out to some extent by a lower average rate of consumption. On the other hand, certainly the increase in the proportion of drinkers does increase the number who are subject to the risk of becoming heavy drinkers. It may be that whether there is a higher or lower

proportion of heavy drinkers in the future is more dependent upon broad considerations of mental health within the society as a whole than it is upon whether there is an increase in the proportion of drinkers. For example, we have seen in this survey and in other studies that Jews and those of Italian descent have a relatively low rate of heavy drinking despite the fact that they have a high percentage of those who drink at least a little.

In summary, we conclude that drinking is individually learned behavior, perhaps chaotically learned in our society; that drinking almost always occurs in a social setting; and that an individual's drinking behavior at any one time seems to reflect his early training, his momentary needs, his long-term psychological needs, and the social context in which he finds himself or into which he has thrust himself.

Let us return briefly to a point that is vitally relevant to the topic of law and drinking: having a law on the books is in no sense a guarantee that anyone's behavior will be changed. As mentioned earlier, we have many laws that apparently no one wants enforced. But suppose the society does have a law that it wants enforced; is that enough to get the job done? The answer is obviously no. While the effectiveness of the deterrent purpose of punitive laws is a factor in this failure, we should also be aware of our tendency to regard the law as a monolithic institution, when indeed we should be talking about the legal system.

The law is not a simple institution in our society or in any other; rather, the law is a complex interaction of cooperating and opposing forces. Enforcement of the law requires a sequence of steps which starts with the willingness of a policeman to make an arrest or to lodge a charge and includes the skill of the policeman in gathering evidence; the willingness and the skill of a prosecutor in preparing a case; the willingness of a judge to mete out punishment; and, frequently, the willingness of a jury to convict.

Policemen complain that there is no point in arresting under certain laws because the prosecutors will not prosecute or the courts will not convict; prosecutors point out that they cannot build airtight cases unless the police know how to collect evidence or unless the judges are willing to be sympathetic; and it comes as no surprise when the judges point out that they cannot convict on poorly presented cases with inadequate evidence. Add to this the fact the jurors may be asked to try cases in which the individual juror may be saying to himself: "There but for the grace of God go I," and you may get the feeling of an Alice-in-Wonderland quality about some of our drinking laws and their enforcement.

Let us consider specifically the laws about drunken driving, which are taken seriously in most jurisdictions, but which, in the opinion of some experts, are simply not being enforced. This point is made quite dramatically in a recent article by Richard Zylman which deserves much wider circulation because of its sociological importance. Zylman is a research specialist at the Rutgers Center of Alcohol Studies; his credentials include experience as a member of the Wisconsin State Patrol and participation as Field Research Supervisor of the famous Borkenstein study of drinking and driving in Grand Rapids, Michigan.

In analyzing the data from Grand Rapids, Zylman had isolated a group of 188 drivers involved in collisions who had blood alcohol levels above 0.15, the presumptive level in that jurisdiction. Note that all these drivers had been in collisions, all had been tested, and all had the requisite blood alcohol level. Thus, every one of them was eligible for the charge of driving while intoxicated (DWI). Faced with these drivers, the police of Grand Rapids made DWI arrests in just about half the cases. The other half were either cited on lesser charges or not charged at all. Zylman hastened to report that the Grand Rapids police force is well trained and well disciplined, that they were among the first to use breath-testing devices and that they have long experience in this type of enforcement. He concluded that the 50 percent enforcement rate can be assumed to be well above the average for other jurisdictions. Then, how do we explain this lack of enforcement of a law that is apparently taken quite seriously by society? Zylman suggests several explanations, three are quoted here for the challenge that they offer:

> 1. As penalties go up, the enforcement level goes down. Drinking driving laws fall into this category . . . the penalties for DWI are stiff, usually including a substantial fine, fre-

quently a jail sentence, almost always the suspension of driving privileges, a considerable onus, and a large increase in insurance rates. Such cases are usually contested, resulting in a trial requiring a good deal of time, effort, and expertise on the part of the arresting officer.

2. The laws of most states specify a blood-alcohol-concentration at or above which the driver is "presumed" to be under the influence of or impaired by alcohol. In practice this presumption is effective in most courts only if the arresting officer can not only produce the results of a chemical test but also testify as to some overt drunken behavior, e.g. staggering, vomiting, abusive language, impaired speech (and, conversely, in many cases, such clinical symptoms are not accepted as valid evidence of intoxication without a chemical test).

3. There is generally a lack of conviction among police officers, prosecutors and judges as to the effects of alcohol. Although most of them drink frequently and a few of them extensively, with rare exceptions these officials have no point of reference; they have never had themselves tested at various blood-alcohol-concentrations to learn what it feels like to be at 0.08, 0.10, or 0.15 percent . . . most policemen and almost all prosecutors and judges have had only superficial and frequently conflicting information about the effects of alcohol and its relationship to crash involvement. The result is that there is not only a lack of conviction as to the effects of alcohol, but in many instances the police, prosecutors, and judges have indicated that they thought the law was bad.[3]

Enforcement of the drunk driving laws appears to be haphazard, half-hearted, and lax. If this is the situation with respect to laws on which it is safe to assume the society is serious, what can we expect from the legal system with respect to laws that many members of the society refuse to take seriously? Perhaps the lesson to be learned is that having a law on the books is far less than half the battle. If we are to use the legal system as a mechanism of social control, then we must be assured that the legal system, in all its ramifications, can cope with society's wishes and can indeed handle the problem.

CHAPTER 10

Prohibition Norms and Teenage Drinking

Gerald Globetti, Ph.D.

THROUGHOUT HISTORY DISPARATE values have been assigned to the use of intoxicating beverages. Alcohol has been praised as a medicine, as a social lubricant which facilitates communication and strengthens group bonds, and as a behavior modifier that relieves the individual from the tensions of daily living. Despite these ascribed values, however, drinking has often been regarded as a bane, and attempts have been made to regulate or to abolish it.

Experimentation in an effective legal framework to prescribe conduct regarding beverage alcohol has crowded much of American history. No system, however, has proven either entirely satisfactory or outstandingly successful. There are several obvious reasons for this situation. First, social control is difficult to handle via legal means when the item in question permits both use and abuse. Many of the regulations focus upon the abusive drinker and, therefore, often inconvenience or alienate persons who traditionally conform to rules. The problem of penalizing the majority because of the noxious behavior of a few makes enforcement difficult. Furthermore, there are mounting and contradictory pressures on law-making agencies from both temperance and liquor forces. Consequently, laws reveal a lack of consistent policy and design; they appear to be more the result of compromises, special concessions, exceptions, and arbitrary decisions. Thus, the legislative wisdom behind many liquor laws has been viewed with widespread skepticism. Likewise, statutes abridge the right of personal privacy. In American society, what one eats, wears, and thinks is generally considered private and immune to outside interference.[1]

The question of whether one set of legal precepts is more effective than another in suppressing abusive drinking is difficult to answer since comparisons have been largely untested by research or extensive empirical trial. The ideal measure of a system's efficacy is to investigate the drinking habits of homogeneous subpopulations who reside in communities of similar dimensions but with varying legal restrictions. Such designs are obviously difficult to approximate in real life situations. One partial indication of effectiveness, however, is to measure the costs and benefits of enforcing particular legal sanctions.[2] Laws in themselves can create undesirable or unintended results. Therefore, they must be weighed against the price the community is willing to pay to have them enforced. Accordingly, the intent of this paper is to investigate the social and cultural factors associated with the drinking patterns of a sample of young people in a community characterized by prohibition norms, and then, to examine these findings in the light of this cost-benefit criterion.[3]

The Problem and Its Setting

Cultural variation has been treated as an important factor in a number of current theories regarding the use and the misuse of beverage alcohol. The major assumption underlying these theories, normally designated as the sociocultural approach, is that within the cultural system of a group of people, there is a general ethos or sense of decorum concerning the role of alcohol which in turn determines the type of response men make toward it.[4] Put in another way, the common fabric of values, symbols, and meanings shared by a group governs the drinkers and drinking styles.[5] Explanations of an individual's use or nonuse of intoxicants, therefore, can be accounted for in large measure by the cultural prescriptions for alcohol intake that are included in the social groups of which he is a member.

Within American society, these cultural attitudes run the gamut from absolute prohibition to permissiveness toward moderate drinking.[6] One reflection of these differences is revealed by studies of the drinking patterns of rural and urban residents. In farm and small community areas, fewer people use alcohol and imbibe less frequently than do urban people. This pattern probably indicates the strong influence in the rural environ of ascetic Protestantism, a belief that the indulgence of the senses is bad and that alcohol promotes sensualism.[7]

Unfortunately, there have been few investigations of the use of alcohol among young people reared in rural or small community areas. In the main, previous studies have been conducted in urban or metropolitan centers and have consistently recorded a positive relationship between community size and the proportion of young people who use alcohol. The focus of this study is on the drinking practices of a sample of high school students in a relatively small Mississippi community which represents the prototype of the abstinence cultural attitude. The locality has a trade center of approximately 18,000 from which most of the high school students are drawn. The population is made up largely of persons who migrated from the immediate rural surroundings. Not surprisingly, the community is homogeneous in terms of those religious groups which strongly censure all forms of alcohol intake. Drinking as a custom is not entwined with family and religious institutions.[8] Thus, the strong rural belief that to drink is to surrender to impulse, coupled with the tighter social controls found in small communities, should operate to deter the use of alcohol by students. Imbibing among the students in this locality is not only an illegal activity, as defined by state law, but also a taboo one.

The sample included 275 students who were chosen randomly from grades nine through twelve. The respondents were interviewed in a large conference room in groups of twenty-five. They were not permitted to discuss the questions among themselves and complete anonymity was assured.

Two forms of data are examined. The first is an analysis of the events and circumstances which surround the act of imbibing within this abstinence milieu. The second is an examination of the social adjustment of drinkers as compared to abstainers. Drinking among young people in a situation governed by abstinence norms is assumed to be a possible manifestation of a general pattern of deviance.

Findings

Drinking Patterns

Drinking behavior was operationalized by the item "Did you have the occasion to drink (beer, wine, or spirits) during the year immediately preceding the survey?" Students who gave an affirmative response were asked to answer additional questions with respect to the frequency of alcohol use, type of beverage consumed, and where and with whom drinking occurred. The results are shown in Table 10-1.

The data revealed that the Mississippi students departed from previously reported findings on several factors associated with drinking styles and the drinking situation. For example, only 40 percent of the respondents were classified as users. This small percentage may be explained in part by the rural character of the community studied.

Light alcoholic beverages, notably beer, were preferred by over half of those who imbibed. These drinkers usually were introduced to alcohol outside the home and continued to secure their beverages from a bootlegger or other illegal sources. They drank without parental knowledge and approval, most frequently in a sub-rosa situation with their age peers, and they were not governed by agencies which ordinarily affect restraint. This pattern is somewhat in contrast with that found elsewhere.[9] Previous studies indicate, for example, that

Table 10-1
Classification of Students' Use of
Beverage Alcohol by Situational Factors

Situational Factors	N	%
Source of Alcoholic Beverages		
Parents and/or older relatives	18	16
Friends same age or older	32	30
Bootlegger	46	42
Other (outside home)	12	12

Drinking Companions

Friends same age	53	49
Older friends	14	13
Parents or older relatives	17	15
Alone	4	4
Other (outside home)	21	19

Parental Knowledge and Approval

Both parents approve	12	11
Only one approves	5	5
Both disapprove	39	37
Do not know	49	47

Frequency of Alcohol Use

Frequently (once a week to several times a week)	30	28
Occasionally (once to three times a month)	35	33
Seldom (once or twice a year to once every two months)	42	39

Personal and Social Complications Index

Low	40	36
Moderate	54	49
High	17	15

Excessive Use of Alcohol Index

Nonexcessive	79	71
Mildly excessive use (drunk or high once during month preceding survey)	20	18
Excessive use (drunk or high two or more times during month preceding survey)	12	11

Effects of Alcohol Index*

Low	52	47
Moderate	48	43
High	11	10

Emotional Support Index**

Low	85	77
Moderate	16	14
High	10	9

* Items on this index included: "I drink: because it gives me a better appetite; because I like the taste; in order to get high or drunk; when I am in a bad mood." Low (students who did not drink for any of these reasons); Moderate (students who drank for one or two of these reasons); High (students who drank for three or four of these reasons).

** Items included: "I drink: to get along better on dates; because it makes it easier to do things which I know I should not do; when particular things are bothering me; as an aid in forgetting disappointments; in order not to be shy; when I am uncomfortable around people; because I need it when I am tense and nervous; because it makes me feel good." Low (students who drank for none of these reasons); Moderate (students who drank for one or two of these reasons); High (students who drank for three or more of these reasons).

the first personal use of alcohol by the young is typically reported to be in the home with parents or relatives present.

Evidence gathered by others suggests that drinking under these conditions insulates the act of imbibing from social controls and, therefore, may engender a more frequent and abusive use of alcohol.[10] The data of this research seem to give some support to this statement. Nearly three in ten of those who imbibed said that they drank from one to several times a week while over three in five said that they had experienced social complications as a result of drinking—such as getting in fights, destroying property, experiencing blackouts, damaging friendships. The limited research done in the area of problem use among adolescents shows the incidence of this type of drinking to be between 5 to 10 percent.[11] When asked about their motivations for using alcohol, approximately one-fifth to one-third replied that they did so in order to remove themselves from reality or to handle psychological tensions. Another indication of alcohol abuse was revealed; that is, about 30 percent of the users were classed as excessive drinkers, those who had been inebriated once or twice during the month immediately preceding the survey.

Caution must be employed in statements to the effect that alcohol use in an abstinent setting perpetuates a high incidence of problem drinking; the various studies do not report measures of teenage drinking styles in a manner that allows for specific comparison. The only point that can be made with a degree of certainty is that the students in this study who do drink usually do so under surreptitious conditions without observing normal propriety. Furthermore, they appear to be circumventing the social control mechanisms of such significant primary groups as the home, the church, and the community. It might be surmised that the needs of the alcohol users are not being met by these groups and, consequently, they lack adjustment to them. To this end, the social adjustment of the students was examined.

Social Adjustment

Social adjustment was measured by a deviant behavior index, a parent-child relationship index, and a religious participation index. The items included in these measures formed the adjustment index. The index of deviant behavior was constructed from questions used by Deschin et al., in their study of teenagers with venereal disease in New York City.[12] The questions were: Have you ever driven a car without a license? taken little things that did not belong to you worth less than $2.00? played hookey? purposely damaged property? run away from home? picked fights? driven over the speed limit? The expected relationship was observed in that a higher percentage of users than nonusers made high scores on this index. See Table 10-2.

The parent-child relationship index[13] contained the following items: How frequently have you felt that you were not wanted by your (father, mother)? Who do you think is your (father's, mother's) favorite? How close are you to your (father, mother)? How often do you do things with your parents?

Table 10-2
Classification of Students by Drinking Behavior
and Scores on Selected Indexes of
Personal Social Adjustment

Scores on Indexes of Adjustment	Nonusers		Users	
	N	%	N	%
Deviant Behavior				
Low	151	67	73	33
High	13	25	38	75
N=275 X^2=30.327 d.f.=1 P=.001				
Middle-Class Value Orientation				
Low	19	59	13	41
High	145	60	98	40
N=275 X^2=.0008 d.f.=1 P=.95				
Parent-Child Relationships				
Poor	41	50	41	50
Good	123	64	70	36
N=275 X^2=4.507 d.f.=1 P=.05				
Church Participation				
Low	85	55	72	45
High	77	66	39	34
N=275 X^2=3.790 d.f.=1 P=.10				
Average Monthly Church Attendance				
Low (0-4 times a month)	85	52	77	48
High (5 or more times a month)	73	71	30	29
N=265 X^2=8.859 d.f.=1 P=.01				

Answers were classified as favorable or unfavorable and assigned on the basis of continuum. As parent-child relationships improved from poor to good, the percentage of users decreased.

The final measure of social adjustment was concerned with the students' involvement in church sponsored organizations. The abstainers were significantly more active in church participation than were the drinkers.

Discussion and Implications

The results of this study lead to the conclusion that the circumstances which surround the act of teenage drinking within the abstinence setting of a small Mississippi community are somewhat different from those reported elsewhere. What speculative extrapolations of these findings can be made regarding the cost-benefits of the prohibition norms on teenage drinking? First, although fewer Mississippi students imbibe, the drinking styles disclose several "unhealthy" dimensions that frequently are associated with alcohol abuse. As a rule, users do not have parental permission to drink, and, for the most part, they identify with churches that condemn alcohol on moral grounds. They drink in a secretive manner. A significant number imbibe without the control of normal propriety and are exhibiting several personal and social complications as a result. This suggests that less drinking can be expected in an abstinence setting; but among young people who drink, alcohol problems may be relatively frequent. Stacey and Davis in an evaluative review of adolescent drinking studies in several countries gleaned a similar conclusion. Restrictive methods control the nature of the drinking occasion and the places where drinking may take place, but they often lead to an increase in the problem use of alcohol.[14] In terms of the cost-benefit criterion, we exchange an over-all reduction in the number of drinkers for a higher percentage of acute cases.

Secondly, what a young person is taught to expect from alcohol has the possibility of becoming a self-fulfilling prophecy. A teaching which implants a repugnance to drinking tends to identify the drinking act with personal and social disorganization. It may, therefore, suggest an inebriety pattern for drinking and actually foster behavior that it most deplores.[15] In addition, negative teaching may encourage rather than deter use. In these cases drinking can be more readily identified as a symbol of rebellion against parental and adult authority. The nature of rebellion tends to gain strength and intensity from disapproval and repression.

Other costs are more apparent. Most of the students who drink, having to secure beverages from a bootlegger, must drive an automobile sometimes over long distances. This is certainly conducive to automobile accidents which is one of the major concerns facing alcohol educators today. These conditions also lead to heavy and intensive drinking. As one student summed it in Straus' and Bacon's study of a college located in a dry community, "If you have to drive fifty miles you're not going to have just one beer." Some drinking Mississippians say, "When we drink, we mean business." This "business" drinking is, in part, a result of the circumstances which limit the person's ability to secure alcohol at convenient times. Within the cost-benefit frame, therefore, restrictions have the primary effect of determining where drinking takes place and the channels through which alcohol is obtained. Thus, where legal sanctions are severe, alcohol is secured via a bootlegger, or through an older person, and consumed in sub-rosa situations. Studies by Bruun and Hauge in Helsinki, Copenhagen, Oslo, and Stockholm and by Sweicicki in Poland have all shown that rigid regulations on teenage use increase illegal purchase and drinking out of doors. Alcohol use, therefore, is not controlled by agencies of restraint.[16]

Another nonintended consequence, although subtle, is the impact of these laws on the attitude of many young people toward the law in general. The legal restrictions did little to control the students' ability to procure beverage alcohol. Thus, many young people showed a disrespect and disregard for community law. Moreover, the students were highly sensitive to the state's unique system of liquor control at the time of the survey. Mississippians during this period spoke with two voices regarding alcohol, the one proclaiming the virtues of prohibition, the other negating them with a black market tax levied against the illegal sale of liquor. This state has always been noted for its peculiar prohibition law. It banned liquor but there were no state agencies empowered to enforce the statute. Consequently, enforcement was left to the individual counties which if they wanted liquor could simply elect a "wet" sheriff.

Mississippi was receiving at the time of this study approximately 7 million dollars a year revenue from illegal whiskey. Most of this revenue came from a "black market tax" which was enacted by the legislature in 1944 as a levy against the sale or distribution of goods prohibited by law. This inconsistency did not appear odd to many Mississippians; it was matter-of-factly accepted. Consequently, any resemblance between the letter of the law and the way many Mississippians acted in relation to alcohol use was purely coincidental. One can hardly fail to conclude that such conditions are not conducive to healthy socialization in a society based upon respect for law.

The laws and the enforcement practices associated with them have implications for alcohol education. An accompanying survey revealed that the students were eager to learn about alcohol. Yet few were receiving such information and the quality of that transmitted was questionable. A significant number of the students who discussed drinking and alcohol use with their parents or other adults said that the information given emphasized the evil nature of alcohol and neglected objective and scientific data. This grossly oversimplifies alcohol's complex properties and fails to impart constructive attitudes by which a child can make a wise decision regarding its use.[17] Most alcohol educators stress that programs should not employ or evoke a strategy of fear in teaching about alcohol. These types of pseudoeducational practices may only implant an admiration for intoxicated behavior since the adolescent is often intrigued by forbidden pleasure and fascinated by danger with little concern for its consequences.

Moreover, the authoritarian approach to instruction about alcohol has not been effective, as illustrated by the number of adult users who disregard the threats made in fear-arousing pronouncements.[18] Such an approach, however, does have the consequence of instilling a sense of guilt about drinking even in moderation. This feeling is a result of a rural heritage which values hard work, is suspicious of fun, and is preoccupied with impulse control. Thus, many of the states' adults describe their drinking in a defensive manner. As someone once expressed it, "We drink wet but think dry." What most of the students received was an indoctrination rather than an education about alcohol, summed up in the statement "Thou Shall Not," which to many of the adolescents translated into the eleventh commandment, "Thou Shall Not Get Caught."

Conclusion

Applying the costs-benefits criterion to an analysis of teenage drinking in an abstinence setting would suggest an overbalance on the cost side. If this is the case, then the task becomes one of finding better and more effective means to prepare these young people to participate in a drinking society.[19] One way is to be realistic in our instruction about alcohol. The prohibitionist's voice is out of date. Yet much of our so-called alcohol education of young people today still carries with it the burden of the prohibitionist voices of the past. Indeed the prohibitionist tendency is still quite strong within most of us when we find ourselves cast in the role of a parent or a community elder.[20] This negative kind of teaching runs counter to the experiences of a great many young people and has the adverse consequence of substantially reducing the credibility and believability of adults on other matters. Drinking is acceptable behavior in our society, and done in a moderate manner, it has no dysfunctional effects. It is time to teach our young that they can live safely in the presence of alcohol.

Finally, to demonstrate that something is not good or has few benefits does not necessarily imply that its opposite is by definition good or beneficial. Permissiveness regarding teenage drinking is not the answer either. The majority of our young people want guidelines for behavior. But as they grow older they want guidelines with reasons, and they want to participate in establishing them. To be effective, prevention must be based on each person's decision not to abuse alcohol because it is incompatible with his own goals. Adolescence is a period when the individual searches out and examines issues. Educational efforts, therefore, should present all sides of the argument fairly and attempt to stimulate the young person to play the role of the final arbiter. Certainly there is need for control over the use of beverage alcohol, but the control that is needed must be asserted from within the individual, not merely imposed upon him from without. What is needed in addition to sagacious laws is sound public education about alcohol.

CHAPTER 11

College Drinking and Other Drug Use

Beatrice A. Rouse, M.Ed.
John A. Ewing, M.D.

A STUDENT DRINKING song reads:

> Loud let the glasses clink
> Drink deep, nor spare the flowing bowl
> The man who fears to drink
> Has no true soul.

> This is the student's hour
> The stern professor's work is done
> We own no other power
> Save wine and song.[1]

Drinking by college students is legendary in many countries, yet much is still to be learned about it in scientific terms and even more needs to be understood by the general public. But students are not only drinking, some are also taking marijuana and a variety of other drugs. This "psychedelic revolution" has led people—not only in the general public but also among health professionals and college administrators—to perceive college *drinking* in a different light.[2] Even when the drinking is clearly excessive, some people—including parents observing their own youths—breathe a sigh of relief that the students are using alcohol rather than marijuana. Others, recognizing the *potential* for abuse of any drug in the hands of immature and inexperienced individuals, view with alarm any use of either drug by students. Still others, who consider marijuana and other drugs a minor problem compared with alcohol, overstate the case of problem drinking among college students in order to make their point.

Because of the anxieties and misconceptions that surround many discussions of teenage drinking and other drug use, the emphasis in this chapter is on presenting data—especially data drawn from national, representative samples and other in-depth scientific studies. Before examining the effects of the college experience on students, however, the first question explored is whether those youths who enter college differ initially in their drinking habits and drug use from others of the same age.

National Comparative Study of College and Noncollege Teenagers

In 1966, a national study was initiated which investigated, among other things, alcohol and other drug use in a sample of boys who were then in the tenth grade.[3] In the spring of 1970, these teenagers were surveyed for the fourth time. Of the 1,796 teenagers studied at that time, 46 percent were in college, 31 percent were civilians and employed, 9 percent were either unemployed or still in high school, 8 percent were in the military and 6 percent were attending a technical or vocational school. Those in the military had the heaviest use of alcohol and tobacco and the highest rates of nonusers converting to the use of alcohol, tobacco, and illegal drugs.

Attitudes toward the use of the various drugs as well as the accessibility of illegal drugs were similar in all groups. Of all the drugs, alcohol use was the least disapproved by the youth for their own age group. Fifty-eight percent disapproved of smoking a pack or more of cigarettes daily, 67 percent disapproved of regular marijuana use, 47 percent disapproved of experimental marijuana use and only 35 percent disapproved of drinking more than once a week.

Table 11-1 shows the drug usage rates for the different groups. These rates include experimental use of the various drugs because so many studies of illegal and harmful drug usage include as a user the person who took the drug only once. A more meaningful comparison, however, would be of the rates of regular usage. In this study, the only drugs used regularly by the youths were alcohol, tobacco and marijuana. Rates of regular drinking, which was defined as more than once a week, were lowest in college students: 38 percent of the students, 48 percent of the civilian employed and 55 percent of the military drank regularly. This study compared college freshmen with their high school classmates who had not gone to college.

National Studies of Undergraduates

What happens to the college students' drinking after being exposed to college? This question was explored by a national study of college campus lifestyles and drug use.[4] The total sample contained 7,948 men and women but only freshmen and juniors were sampled. Information was gathered concerning social rules, disciplinary policies, and actual administrative practices regarding drug use. These institutional characteristics were then to be related to the students' percep-

Table 11-1
Comparison of College Freshmen's Drug Usage Rates
With Their Classmates Grouped by After-High School Status

	After High School				
Drugs*	College (N=827)	Employed (N=559)	Military (N=144)	Trade School (N=115)	Other (N=151)
Alcohol	78%	81%	85%	85%	81%
Tobacco	57%	77%	82%	67%	83%
Marijuana	35%	31%	36%	30%	45%
Amphetamines	11%	15%	19%	7%	22%
Hallucinogens	10%	11%	14%	4%	21%
Barbiturates	7%	10%	11%	4%	19%
Heroin	1%	4%	1%	—	6%

*Rates for alcohol use include those who drank at least three times a year; all other drug rates include experimental use.
(Source: Lloyd Johnston, *Drugs and American Youth*. A report from the "Youth in Transition" project, Ann Arbor, Mich.: Institute for Social Research, 1973.)

tions and drug use. Only preliminary results are presently available. Using the definition of "at least once weekly" as regular use, the following rates were found: 58 percent used alcohol regularly, 14 percent used marijuana, 4 percent used pills (amphetamines and barbiturates) and 2 percent used psychedelics.

While public attention focused on marijuana and the use of other illegal drugs among college students, some researchers were comparing the rates and adverse effects of the illegal drugs with that of alcohol. In a study of 10 undergraduate campuses of a large mid-Atlantic state university, heavy drinkers were compared with heavy marijuana users.[5] Heavy use was defined as three or more times a week. Of the 6,110 students in the study, 91 percent drank and 23 percent used marijuana. Among the drinkers, 23 percent drank 3 or more times a week, 51 percent drank no more than twice a week and 26 percent drank occasionally. Among the marijuana users, 17 percent took it at least 3 times a week, 26 percent no more than twice a week and 57 percent used marijuana occasionally.

Heavy use of either alcohol or marijuana was associated with problems. Poor relations with parents, homosexual activity and psychiatric difficulties were related to heavy use of marijuana. Increased physical difficulties, on the other hand, were related more to heavy use of alcohol. In addition, those who drank for the purpose of intoxication were also more likely to use marijuana. The study concluded: "whatever the hazards of heavy marijuana use, it does not now constitute a public health problem of the same magnitude as alcohol."[6]

Nevertheless, in the late 1960s and early 1970s, as illegal drug use swept the nation,[7] we heard again and again that older people had their drug—alcohol, and the younger generation had theirs—pot. This claim often was not substantiated. Many of the earliest studies conducted during this period to examine college drug use did not gather data regarding drinking. Often, if the data were available, the relationship between drinking and marijuana use was not examined.

In a study which compared the rates of drinking and other drug use among colleges no data were presented as to the drinking status of marijuana users in each college. Instead, overall rates of drinking and marijuana use were compared.

The study indicated that the college with the lowest rate for marijuana use had the highest rate of drinking among its students. In this college, 28 percent had used marijuana ever and 92 percent of the students drank. Yet the college with the highest rate of marijuana use had almost as high a rate of drinking as the college with the lowest rate of marijuana use. The highest rate was 49 percent of the students having ever used marijuana, and in this college 86 percent of the students drank.[8]

Studies which did examine the relationship of drinking to marijuana and other drug use did not confirm the generation gap and did indeed find the use of alcohol associated with marijuana.[9] In fact, marijuana users were more likely to be frequent drinkers than were non-marijuana users. Any study of the effects of either alcohol or marijuana should, therefore, take into account possible synergistic effects due to combined drug use.

Factors Affecting Drinking and Drug Rates in Different Colleges

Additional factors to be taken into account in the interpretation and comparison of drinking studies among college students are the social pressures of the particular time period and the influences from regional community mores and drinking patterns. Demographic characteristics of both the geographic region and the particular college are also important.

The change in drug use patterns over time was examined in 3,010 undergraduate men and women of a mid-Atlantic university.[10] When all classes were surveyed in 1969, 86 percent of the students drank, 67 percent smoked, 24 percent used marijuana, 14 percent used depressants, 13 percent used amphetamines, 5 percent used hallucinogens, and 3 percent used narcotics. When the freshmen were resurveyed in 1972 (their senior year), they had changed their drug use. As seniors in 1972, they were not only more likely to decrease their illegal drug use in comparison to their own freshman levels, but also in comparison with seniors in 1968. Throughout the years, however, the most commonly used substances were alcohol and tobacco.

In addition to the increase or decrease of drinking or other drug use that may occur because of prevailing social influences at particular time periods, there are college characteristics and regional differences which also should be taken into account. A variety of institutional factors affect drinking and other drug usage rates in a student population. These include the kind of college, its administrative position and actual practice regarding various drugs, and the selection criteria used for admitting students. These factors exist within the college community; factors within the larger community are also important. These are often reflected in regional differences in drinking and drug practices and attitudes.

National studies of drug use have found the rates for adults, youth, and high-school students ever using marijuana and ever using LSD were highest in the West and lowest in the South. In 1972, for example, the overall rate for adults over 18 years old ever using marijuana was 14.7 percent. The rate for the West was 33 percent, for the North Central 15 percent, Northeast 14 percent and the South 8 percent.[11]

A national study of drinking practices found that 32 percent of the adult population does not drink but that regions differ considerably in their rates of abstention. The highest rate of abstention is found in the East-South-Central region with 65 percent nondrinkers. The lowest rate is found in the Middle Atlantic region with 17 percent nondrinkers.[12]

In order to determine if differences in the distribution of religion or other factors account for these regional rates, one can compare the rates within a single factor that might be influencing the rates to see if the regional differences still exist. For example, one can compare white Protestants in the South with white Protestants in other regions. In 1966, a Gallup poll found almost twice as many abstaining white Protestants in the South as elsewhere. In addition, 44 percent of those in the South favored a law forbidding the sale of all beer, wine and liquor throughout the nation. On the other hand, only 20 percent of the white Protestants in non-Southern states favored total prohibition. Further analysis of these data indicated that these regional differences in reported abstention rates and attitudes regarding prohibition could not be explained on the basis of educational, occupational or urban/rural differences.[13]

Not only are there regional differences in drinking attitudes which may affect student drinking but there are also differences in availability of alcoholic beverages and in legal drinking practices.

North Carolina—A Case Study

North Carolina, for example, has special conditions regarding drinking. These somewhat unusual policies regarding the availability of beverage alcohol have existed essentially since the repeal of prohibition.[14] A few other states, particularly in the Southeastern United States, have had similar policies. The most outstanding feature is the total absence of bars or taverns for the sale of mixed alcoholic drinks and the unavailability of mixed drinks in eating places. Alcoholic spirits may be purchased only by the bottle; the purchaser must then make his own arrangements for the drinking occasion. He may take the bottle home with him, to his hotel room, or into certain eating establishments which have special permits. There he may pour himself a drink from the bottle but he must pay the restaurant for set-ups, which involve the glass, ice, and any mix needed.

One curious phenomenon which expresses much of the social ambivalence around the whole matter of drinking is that the drinker may be breaking the law if the bottle is put in full sight of others.[15] If he keeps it in the paper bag which is supplied when it is purchased from the liquor store, with at most only the neck showing, however, he is perfectly legal! Thus, the practice is known as brown-bagging. Another kind of cover for the bottle is also acceptable. Many of these commercially available covers do not hide their function as a carrying case for liquor; still, they are acceptable because the important thing is that the bottle not be in full view of the general public.

Only some of the 100 counties in the state have voted to permit the sale of alcoholic beverages within their boundaries. Where this is in effect, the sole outlets are the state operated stores which sell alcoholic spirits and nothing else. Customers, who must be twenty-one years of age or over, are limited to the purchase of one gallon at a time.[16] Since most of these stores are placed in shopping centers with plenty of parking areas, the purchaser can easily buy a gallon, place this in his car, and return for a second gallon. This is perfectly legal. It is not legal however, for him to drive home with more than one gallon in the car without a special permit. Furthermore, if a person is transporting over one gallon of alcoholic beverages without a permit, the car may be seized, and, upon a conviction in the case, be sold at public auction.[17]

In spite of the extraordinary complications around the purchase and consumption of alcoholic spirits, the acquisition of weaker beverages is relatively easy. Beer, fortified wines, and table wines are freely available in almost any grocery store or supermarket. The one gallon rule, however, is also supposed to apply to wines. Anyone who is eighteen or over may purchase and consume these weaker beverages. Although there are no bars in the state, licensed restaurants may legally serve wine or beer with meals. One also can find various beer taverns or establishments which sell relatively little else. Part of this legal laxity toward beer and wine compared with hard liquor may be attributable to the fact that alcoholic beverages as defined by the state law include only those containing more than 14 percent of absolute alcohol by volume.[18] According to the law in North Carolina, therefore, beer and many of the table wines are not alcoholic beverages.

Another expression of the tremendous social ambivalence toward alcoholic beverages is the fact that this state is one if not the largest producer of illegally distilled alcoholic beverages in America. This illegally produced liquor is called moonshine. Moonshine is sometimes referred to as bootleg liquor, which is the more general term. Bootleg liquor includes not only liquors illegally produced but also liquors which have been legally manufactured, but illegally sold or transported for sale. The term is derived from the alleged practice of mountaineers concealing the illicit liquor in the leg part of their boots. Moonshine is produced particularly in the mountainous areas where the pioneer spirit dies hard and where it appears that the revenue agents are seen as enemies to be tricked. The primary states where illegal liquor has been seized are shown in Table 11-2.

The same area is sometimes known as the Bible Belt because of the strength and persistence of fundamentalist

Table 11-2
Seizures of Illegal Liquor in Selected States in 1974

Top 5 States (by mash)	Stills (number)	Mash (wine gal.)	Stills (% total)	Mash (% total)
Georgia	487	259,816	27%	38%
N. Carolina	408	132,490	23%	19%
Alabama	376	106,271	21%	16%
Virginia	52	49,985	3%	7%
Tennessee	151	39,495	8%	6%
Total Top 5 States	1,474	588,057	81%	86%

Percentages represent proportion of all stills and mash seized in the United States in 1974.
Source: Department of the Treasury, Bureau of Alcohol, Tobacco, and Firearms, *Alcohol, Tobacco, and Firearms Summary Statistics, Fiscal Year 1974,* AFTP 1323.1(4-75), p. 65.

religious groups. Special religious groups exist with practices not shared by the larger churches. Even in the 1970s we occasionally learn of the existence of snake handling cults; various states of religious ecstasy and hysteria, including speaking in tongues, are still not uncommon. Less extreme, but no less vociferous, against the use of beverage alcohol are various better known religious denominations including the Southern Baptists.

One fascinating and extraordinary alliance springs up any time there is a possibility of loosening beverage control laws. This alliance is between bootleggers and religious leaders. Although their motivations are diametrically opposite, they both work against the relaxation of stringent beverage control laws. The bootlegger finds his best market where legal whiskey is not available. The religious position tends to ignore the existence of the bootlegger and to be against legal liquor on principle.

In the state legislature a burning issue has been the legality of liquor-by-the-drink. North Carolina remains predominantly a rural state with 5 million inhabitants, but some of the cities are becoming larger, and they are concerned about attracting tourists and conventions. Thus, cities and tourist resorts are gradually building up pressure toward the legalizing of liquor-by-the-drink. In 1973 this failed once again, in a referendum, in spite of the fact that the proposal offered local option and the drinks would have been sold only under rigorously controlled conditions with meals in certain restaurants. In one of our studies, involving interviews of scientifically selected samples in an urban and a rural county, we found age differences in attitudes toward legalizing liquor by the drink.[19] Perhaps as the present older generations die out they will eventually be replaced by a majority of voters who are not opposed to liquor-by-the-drink.

While it is not possible to purchase a mixed drink in restaurants legally, various practices, such as "bottle clubs," have arisen so that for all practical purposes liquor by the drink is available. One can become a member of a "bottle club" by renting a locker in a restaurant and storing one's liquor bottle. Then, whenever a drink in that restaurant is desired, the bottle is removed from the locker, the drink served and the bottle returned to the locker until the next time. This is perfectly legal as long as the individual's name is clearly displayed on both the locker and the bottle or bottles.[20]

At the Center for Alcohol Studies in North Carolina, one of our interests is measuring current behavior connected with alcohol as it occurs in the context of rigid legal controls. As these controls are altered we hope to be in a position to monitor their effects, and, by supplying meaningful scientific data, assist state legislators in intelligent law making.

Drinking and Other Drug Use in a Southeastern University

A series of studies were conducted in a large coeducational state university in the Southeast within approximately the same time period. These included research on both undergraduate and graduate students in 1969-71 and a followup of undergraduates in 1971-72. In addition to the usual demographic variables of interest, specific variables such as risk-taking, driving under the influence, alienation, and serious suicidal thoughts were also examined.

Undergraduate Men[21]

Specially trained medical students administered a comprehensive pretested and standardized questionnaire to a random sample of undergraduate men in a confidential interview situation. The response rate was 77 percent and 138 men were interviewed.

Ninety-three percent of the students drank and 30 percent had tried marijuana at least once. The drinking categories used and the number of students in each are shown in Table 11-3. These categories were based upon a similar study conducted in the West Indies by Beaubrun.[22] Total amount consumed was calculated from a detailed examination of the kinds of beverages consumed, the usual amount and frequency of each beverage type, and the volume equivalents of absolute alcohol. Amount of drinking was found to be significantly related to religion, father's social class, family position, place of residence at college, and other drug use.

While the religion in which the student was reared as a child showed no particularly strong relationship to either drinking or marijuana, change in religious status was significant. Those students who either abandoned formal religious affiliations or changed to another denomination were more

Table 11-3
Number of Undergraduate Men in Each Drinking Category with Equivalent Amounts of Absolute Alcohol and Types of Drinking Patterns for the Past Year

Drinking Category	Number of Students	Absolute Alcohol*	Example of Drinking Patterns
Abstainer	10	None in last year	No drinking
Light	21	4,000 ml.	Glass wine on most days or whiskey twice a week
Moderate	34	4,000-16,000 ml.	2 bottles table wine a week or 2 glasses of bourbon most days
Medium-heavy	27	16,000-33,000 ml.	6 large beers a day or 4 sherries a day or 3 whiskeys a day
Heavy	46	33,000 ml.	4 whiskeys daily or 2 bottles whiskey a week or 2 cases beer a week

*Amount of absolute alcohol is derived by taking the percent alcohol of total volume for each beverage type.

182   PART III: PSYCHOSOCIAL ASPECTS OF DRINKING

likely to both use marijuana and drink greater amounts of alcohol. Among the religious denominations, Lutherans and Methodists were more likely to change and Baptists were least likely to change. There was also a strong relationship between drinking and father's social class as measured by the Hollingshead's Two Factor Index.[23] For example, 38 percent of the abstainers, 52 percent of the moderate drinkers, and 74 percent of the heavy drinkers came from the upper socioeconomic status.

Family position was related to smoking, drinking, and taking marijuana. Nonsmokers and nondrinkers were more likely to be an only child. Those who continued to take marijuana, in contrast, were more likely to be first born.

Place of residence was also related to drinking. The university provides dormitories, but only freshmen students are required to live in them. After the first year of studies, students may elect to live in private accommodations or in fraternity houses. Abstainers and light drinkers were more likely to be living in a dormitory. No abstainers were found living in fraternities. This finding is not surprising as fraternity groups have the reputation for much partying and heavy drinking. Either heavy drinkers tend to go to live in fraternities or those living there tend to become heavy drinkers. A study of 1,294 students in a Northwestern state university also found this association between campus residence and amount and frequency of drinking.[24]

The relationship between drinking and pledging a fraternity or sorority was studied in 629 college freshmen on campuses with such organizations.[25] Of the 121 who drank in high school 36 percent pledged; of the 146 who started their drinking in college, 30 percent pledged and of the 362 who remained nondrinkers as college freshmen, 16 percent pledged. This association between drinking and fraternity affiliation existed regardless of the student's socioeconomic status.

Drinking frequency was associated with marijuana use as shown in Table 11-4. For this study, marijuana users were defined as anyone who had tried the substance at least once. Of the forty-two students who had used marijuana, eighteen stopped and twenty-four continued its use. The characteristics found in this study to be positively associated with marijuana use were similar to those found in a national study.[26] Marijuana users were more likely to come from an upper class background with higher family income, and either to have no present religion or to have changed religious affiliation. The fathers of marijuana users tended to be light or social drinkers and were less likely to be heavy drinkers than the fathers of those students who had never tried marijuana.

An examination of the reasons for drinking shows that the greater the amount consumed, the larger the number of reasons given. The rank order of reasons given by all students from most to least popular was: (1) to celebrate, (2) to relax, (3) because others are drinking, (4) because of the taste, and (5) to feel good. Heavy drinkers were more likely to report drinking in order to relax: 52 percent of the heavy drinkers reported drinking because they were restless and tense, 28 percent because they were down in spirits, and 15 percent to forget their worries. Overall, the purpose of college drinking appears to be to experience good fellowship rather than to experience relief from individual symptoms, such as might be expected in the pre-alcoholic individual.

Among the heavy drinkers, seventeen reported that they had drunk in the morning to steady their nerves or to get rid of a hangover. Ten of these also reported having shaky hands after drinking and four reported that once they began drinking, they found it difficult to stop. In comparison with a small random sample, those students reporting the use of "eye openers" were more likely to have heavy drinking fathers, to have mothers with permissive attitudes toward the student's drinking and to have been in an auto accident because of drinking. They were also more likely to give reasons for

Table 11-4
Drinking Frequency of Male Undergraduate
Marijuana Users and Nonusers

Drinking Frequency	Users (N=42)	Nonusers (N=96)
Most days	21%	9%
1-2 times a week	62%	57%
Infrequently	17%	24%
Never	—	10%

drinking that involved symptom relief. Sixteen drank to feel good, sixteen to relax, fourteen to liven up things, nine when restless and tense, and eight to help sleep.

Age of first regular drinking reported by the students suggests that age of drinking laws are not effective in preventing under-age drinking. While most states do not permit teenagers under eighteen to drink, the average age for first regular drinking for these college men was seventeen years. Age of first regular drinking was related to drinking category. Heavier drinkers began drinking earlier than the other drinking categories. The average age for first regular drinking among heavy drinkers was sixteen years.

Undergraduate Women[27]

A confidential interview was conducted by trained women research assistants who administered a comprehensive, pretested, and standardized questionnaire and a list of activities used to cope with anxiety and depression. The research materials were completed by 184 randomly selected women students; their ages ranged from seventeen to twenty-seven years, with a mean of 20.5 years. The response rate was 92 percent.

The use of alcoholic beverages was examined in a number of ways in order to determine whether marijuana users had indeed made marijuana, rather than alcohol, their drug of choice. The total alcohol intake for the last year was significantly greater for marijuana users than for nonusers. Total intake was calculated from a detailed examination of the kinds of alcoholic beverages consumed, the usual amount and frequency of each beverage type, and the volume equivalents of absolute alcohol.

Marijuana users reported drinking significantly more regularly and more frequently than nonusers. Sixty-nine percent of the users and only 50 percent of the nonusers drank at least once a week. As with the men students, the more regularly the women drank, the more reasons they gave for drinking. It is interesting to note that among the women there was a tendency for more marijuana users (16 percent) than nonusers (7 percent) to drink to alleviate menstrual distress.

The marijuana users' own appraisal of their drinking appeared to be consistent with the greater amounts they reported. Significantly more users considered themselves frequent, moderate drinkers while more of the marijuana nonusers considered themselves abstainers. None of the students characterized themselves as heavy or excessive drinkers.

Marijuana users had begun drinking alcoholic beverages (discounting occasional sips during childhood) at a significantly earlier age than nonusers. The mean age of first drinking for marijuana users was 17 years and for nonusers 18 years. Also, those who continued to use marijuana had begun drinking at a significantly earlier age than those who had discontinued its use.

The women students were asked to indicate whether each of fourteen listed coping activities had been helpful to them when they were depressed or nervous. Table 11-5 indicates all those activities which were found helpful to a statistically significant different degree by the two marijuana groups. Users were more likely to find drinking, smoking, sexual activities, and medicines other than tranquilizers helpful. Nonusers, on the other hand, felt helped by religious activities. The activities used most often by the users when depressed or nervous were smoking and solitary activities; in contrast, nonusers more often resorted to physical activities as a means of coping.

Graduate and Professional Students[28]

Health professional students, law students, academic men, and academic women were stratified and randomly sampled. The overall response rate was 85 percent. The

Table 11-5
Activities Which Women Undergraduates Found
Helpful When They Were Depressed or Nervous

Activity	Marijuana Users (N=58)	Never Used Marijuana (N=126)
Drinking	64%	29%
Smoking	60%	31%
Sex	29%	13%
Religion	24%	58%
Taking nontranquilizing medicines	12%	4%

response rate and number of students in each group were comparable. Data were gathered on 169 students by trained women graduate assistants who administered a comprehensive, pretested, and standardized questionnaire in confidential interviews. The students ranged in age from twenty-one to fifty-two years with a mean of 26.3 and standard deviation of six years. There were no statistically significant age differences between the men and women or between the four graduate groups.

A variety of mood modifying drugs had been used by the graduate students. Marijuana had been used by 31 percent, amphetamines by 17 percent, LSD by 4 percent, and mescaline by 3 percent. Ninety-five percent currently drank alcoholic beverages, and 4 percent reported they had drunk to excess within the past year.

Table 11-6 shows the drinking frequency for graduate students classified by whether they had ever used marijuana or not. The association between drinking and marijuana use was less strong in graduate men than women. Among the undergraduates in this same college population, the association between marijuana and drinking had been stronger and held for both men and women.

Most graduate students found drinking helpful in relieving their depression; those who had ever used marijuana found it as helpful as those who had never used marijuana. The percent of graduate students in these marijuana groups who had found a variety of activities helpful is shown in Table 11-7. Except for religious activity, the association between

Table 11-6
Drinking Frequency of Graduate Student
Marijuana Users and Nonusers

| | Men | | Women | |
| | Used | Never used | Used | Never used |
Drinking Frequency	(N=47)	(N=82)	(N=11)	(N=29)
Most days	45%	51%	27%	10%
One to two times a week	51%	40%	18%	48%
Rarely or never	4%	9%	55%	42%

marijuana use and various coping activities differed for men and women.

An index of problem drinking applied to the separate graduate groups indicated more law students having drinking difficulties than any other graduate group. Among the law students, 12 percent reported problems associated with drinking. No more than 3 percent of any other graduate group, in contrast, reported such problems.

Followup Study of Undergraduates[29]

Two years after the initial studies of undergraduate men and women, a random sample of undergraduates was mailed pretested questionnaires to be completed anonymously. The questionnaire covered the student's background, drug use, and perceptions of risks associated with various drugs, including alcohol. Questions regarding possible indicators of alienation as well as Srole's Scale of Anomie were included.[30] Questionnaires were completed by 257 men and 117 women. This sample of 374 students represented a response rate of 83 percent.

The overall proportion of students who had ever used

Table 11-7
Activities Which Graduate Students Found
Helpful When They Were Depressed or Nervous

	Men		Women	
	Used Marijuana	Never Used Marijuana	Used Marijuana	Never Used Marijuana
Activity	(N=47)	(N=82)	(N=11)	(N=29)
Talking it over(a)	51%	74%	100%	93%
Being alone(b)	70%	73%	64%	93%
Sexual activity	62%	54%	55%	24%
Drinking	51%	45%	73%	66%
Smoking(b)	45%	39%	73%	28%
Religious activity(c)	6%	24%	—	45%
Other medicines(b)	2%	6%	45%	14%

(a) differences between marijuana groups were statistically significant (p <.01) for only the men
(b) differences significant (p<.02) for only the women
(c) differences significant (p<.02) for both men and women

marijuana had increased in both men and women in the two year period. The increase, however, was greater among men.

Regular and continuing use of marijuana, however, was not accompanied by any reduction in the use of the "older generation's drug," alcohol. Students who reported having taken marijuana no more than twice in their lives were defined as experimenters. Thirteen students not currently using marijuana had used it much more often than that and, accordingly, were not considered experimenters for the purposes of this study. Those who continued to use marijuana were grouped by frequency of use. Of the 131 continuers: 42 percent used it no more than twice monthly, 40 percent used it weekly, and 18 percent took marijuana most days or everyday.

Other drugs used, even experimentally, are shown in Table 11-8 by marijuana group. Nonmarijuana users had used only alcohol, amphetamines, and sedatives while the marijuana users reported the use of a spectrum of drugs with alcohol heading the list. The use of LSD, cocaine, opium, and heroin was primarily experimental, that is, used no more than twice in their lives. Seven students, however, had taken LSD about once a month. Marijuana users were also likely to drink beer and wine and to drink them frequently.

Risks of Drinking and Drug Use Perceived by Undergraduates[31]

A study was conducted to determine whether marijuana

Table 11-8
Percentage of Undergraduates in Each Marijuana
Group Who Had Used Other Drugs

	Other Drug Use by Marijuana Group		
Drug	Continued (N=131)	Experimental (N=54)	Never Used (N=189)
Alcohol	100%	100%	86%
Hashish	85%	44%	—
Amphetamines	50%	20%	3%
LSD	28%	—	—
Sedatives	24%	13%	7%
Opium	14%	—	—
Cocaine	9%	—	—
Heroin	2%	—	—

users took the drug because they enjoyed taking risks or whether they simply did not perceive much risk to be involved. The various types of risks involved in the nonprescription use of drugs were defined as follows: legal risk in terms of arrest and punishment, emotional risk as a threat to mental stability, physical risk as detrimental to bodily health, and social risk as disapproval by friends.

Table 11-9 shows the percentages of undergraduates who had perceived the various types of risk to be at least moderate for the nonmedical use of the different drugs. It is interesting to compare the risks perceived for hard liquor and marijuana. Seventy-eight percent of the students felt there were physical risks to health associated with drinking but only 38 percent thought such risks were associated with marijuana. Also, more students thought there were emotional risks associated with drinking than with marijuana.

Almost all marijuana users and nonusers perceived heroin, opium, and cocaine to involve substantial levels of legal, emotional, physical, and social risks.

A comparison of the perceptions of risks associated with marijuana between users and nonusers indicated that marijuana use appears to be more a function of seeing fewer risks than of wanting to take great risks. Significantly more nonusers perceived great risks of all kinds associated with taking marijuana. The primary risk seen by users to be associated with marijuana was that of arrest and punishment. Legal risks,

Table 11-9
Percent of Undergraduates Perceiving Various
Types of Risks Associated with Nonmedical Drug Use

Drug	Legal	Emotional	Physical	Social
		Risks		
Heroin	95%	92%	94%	88%
LSD	91%	90%	85%	74%
Opium	89%	82%	84%	75%
Cocaine	86%	80%	79%	73%
Marijuana	82%	45%	38%	32%
Amphetamines	73%	84%	87%	53%
Barbiturates	63%	83%	85%	51%
Hard liquor	26%	67%	78%	31%

however, appear not to be a sufficient deterrent. Perhaps as Brill, Crumpton, and Grayson found, these students did not feel bound to obey laws they consider unreasonable.[32]

Drinking, Driving and Drug Use[33]

A behavioral aspect of risk-taking, that is, driving after using drugs, was examined in the men undergraduates. Many of the women indicated that they did not drive or did not have cars; consequently, women were not included.

Seventy percent of the total sample of men admitted that they drove after drinking, 26 percent after using marijuana, 20 percent after alcohol and marijuana together, and 5 percent after alcohol with amphetamines. Most of the students admitted that the drugs used had an adverse effect on their driving. Those who had used marijuana, especially those who used it most days, were more likely to drive after drinking and after using any of the combination of drugs listed.

Because marijuana users were more likely to drink and drive as well as use the other drugs and drive, they seem liable for risks in addition to the legal, emotional, physical, and social risks already mentioned. These added risks involve the actual driving situation. While laboratory studies of the effect of marijuana on driving are few and inconclusive, there are many documenting the detrimental effects of alcohol on driving.[34] The other risk is the increased possibility of detection because of the expanded law enforcement campaigns for highway safety. Indeed, Klein reported that 53 percent of the chronic users in his study had been stopped by the police while under the influence of marijuana.[35]

Personal and Societal Inadequacies

Feelings of Alienation

Many have proposed that excessive drinking is a response to personal inadequacies or psychopathology.[36] Illegal drug use has also been perceived by researchers and theorists as a response to a deficiency within the individual drug user.[37] Others have proposed that young people, particularly college students, are responding to the inadequacies of society in dealing with changing conditions and in maintaining the integrity of its members. The illicit drug user is seen as viewing society's values and norms as irrelevant for the future and resorting instead to the immediate gratification of drug use.[38] This rejection of society's values, especially regarding illegal drugs, has been studied as part of deviant behavior,[39] unconventionality,[40] and alienation.[41]

Alienation is a complex concept which involves feelings of estrangement and lack of power, as well as rejection of society's values and norms.[42] It may well be also related to the issue of risk-taking. Brown has suggested that:

> if . . . there is a significant disorganization and deterioration of the social structure which defines and transmits norms, customs, mores in a meaningful fashion, as well as a basic cultural value void, there is really little risk in opting out. In fact, radical experimentation may very well be, in the long run, the most functional response to a socially anomic situation.[43]

If drug users are alienated, then they may both perceive and experience less risk in "dropping out" of society.

Halleck has described how both psychological and social stresses can combine to produce the clinical picture of alienation in the student.[44] At college, the student has the freedom to choose his friends, leisure activities, and career; for many students this freedom is new. He is also faced with challenges to his earlier values and beliefs both in the classroom and out. If he has not learned to exercise and trust his own judgment, if he has been made to feel guilty for valuing his own feelings, and if he has conflicts regarding his dependency needs, then he will be especially troubled on a campus with little structure and few guidelines and restraints. Both the opportunities and the challenges of college life, consequently, may make the unprepared student, whether male or female, at high risk for joining the drug subculture or for resorting to heavy drinking. The use of a pharmacological agent may help alleviate the student's anxieties and other difficulties. Drinking or drug taking, however, may also facilitate the student's acceptance into some groups.

While studies have focused on relationships between

alienation and illegal drug use,[45] it is also important to determine the relationship between student alienation and drinking.

In the undergraduate followup study described above,[46] various indicators of alienation were examined in relation to both marijuana and drinking. One indicator was the Srole Scale of Anomie which contains five items measuring pessimism, distrust, and political powerlessness.[47] Agreement with three or more of the items was used as an indicator of alienation. This measure as well as others are shown in Table 11-10. All chi-square analyses comparing the three groups on each indicator were statistically significant at least at the .05 level.

Only 24 students in the sample had abstained from both alcohol and marijuana. These students were comparable on the measures of alienation to the group who only drank, but they have not been included in the subsequent analysis and discussion.

Three drinking and drug groups are compared in Table 11-10. On all measures, those who drank but used marijuana only once or twice experimentally were significantly less alienated and had less difficulty achieving a sense of their own identity.

When those who continued to use marijuana were examined in terms of their drinking frequency, 65 percent of those who drank only occasionally reported difficulty in belonging. Less than half of those who drank regularly reported such feelings. The difference, however, was not statistically significant.

Table 11-10
Percent of Undergraduates in Each Drinking/Drug
Group Who Agreed with the Alienation Indicator

Indicators	Drinker and Marijuana Continuer (N=131)	Drinker and Marijuana Experimenter (N=54)	Drinker and Marijuana Nonuser (N=162)
High Srole Anomie Score	17%	2%	11%
Difficulty belonging	39%	17%	24%
Difficulty achieving identity	19%	6%	10%
Serious suicidal thoughts	14%	4%	6%

The role of drinking or of marijuana use in determining feelings of alienation is not clear. Why did fewer marijuana experimenters report such difficulties? Perhaps these experimenters had the confidence to try something new and to evaluate their activities independently of either parental or peer pressures. Perhaps they used the drug to confront themselves or others, to take risks not readily available elsewhere to achieve a meaningful experience. As Brown has said:

> risk taking is essential to human development and particularly to the process of individuation and identity in the adolescent. . . . Without confrontation there is no relevant experience, no meaningful evaluation of self-competence, and ultimately no development of self nor of a sense of societal responsibility.[48]

If the college student is searching for meaningful experiences, what are they? How does drinking or other drug use help? What relatively safe alternatives can society provide that can enhance personal growth and contribute to the successful functioning of a worthwhile society?

The finding that experimental marijuana users reported less alienation than either nonusers or continuing users is reminiscent of Maddox's findings regarding drinking and self-esteem.[49] Increased drinking levels were associated with increased negative self-evaluation. Light drinkers showed the most favorable and stable self-evaluations. Both abstainers and heavier drinkers, on the other hand, increasingly indicated more negative self-evaluations as they progressed through college. The light drinkers were interpreted as representing the "optimum solution": "On the one hand, the lighter drinker meets the modal peer-group expectation by drinking, while on the other hand, he drinks in a way which has some chance of being personally and socially justified as respectable."[50] Such an explanation is appealing because it acknowledges the joint influences of society, peer groups, and individual needs.

Drinking, Drug Use, and Serious Suicidal Thoughts[51]

Students were also asked whether they had ever had serious thoughts about committing suicide since enrolling in college. College class was significantly associated with serious suicidal thoughts. Sophomores reported more than any other class: 19 percent of the sophomores, 10 percent of the seniors, 9 percent of the juniors, and 4 percent of the freshmen reported serious suicidal thoughts. Although more women than men reported such thoughts, the difference was not statistically significant.

Marijuana use was also associated with serious suicidal thoughts while in college. More continuing users reported such thoughts than any other marijuana group: 14 percent of the continuing marijuana users, 7 percent of the nonusers and 4 percent of the experimenters reported having had serious suicidal thoughts.

All of the 131 continuing marijuana users, all the 54 experimenters and 86 percent of the nonusers drank. Only three of the twenty-four nondrinking, nonmarijuana users reported suicidal thoughts. The frequency of drinking among those students who had continued to take marijuana was also associated with serious suicidal thoughts. Those who drank regularly about once or twice a week reported more such thoughts: 27 percent of the weekly drinkers, 14 percent of the occasional drinkers, and 13 percent of the almost daily drinkers reported serious suicidal thoughts. The differences between these drinking frequency groups of marijuana users, however, were not statistically significant.

College Drinking Among Blacks and Other Ethnic Groups

There is a paucity of reliable, objective data on drinking among blacks.[52] Most of the research on college drinking has been conducted among predominately white institutions. Even when blacks have been included in such samples, usually there have been too few to make reliable estimates regarding their drinking behavior.

Most of the studies specifically of blacks have made statements regarding black-white differences in drinking without collecting the necessary data in their study. Instead, inappropriate comparisons of their findings on blacks have been made with white samples that were not only studied with different instruments and methodology but were as much as ten years older, were noncollegians in a different geographic area or had been studied at least a decade earlier.[53]

Three studies, however, should be noted: a national study which compared American black and white college students with students of various other nationalities, a study of black and white attitudes about alcohol in a Southern college, and a followup study of blacks in a college that was predominately black.

Rates of drinking and intoxication for blacks and various nationalities were ascertained in the national study of college drinking initiated in 1947 by Straus and Bacon.[54] White students whose families had been in this country for a minimum of three generations were classified as Americans. All other nonblack students were classified on the basis of their families' country of origin. Data were presented on only those ethnic groups containing at least fifty students. Those classified as Jews, Mormons or of mixed nationalities, however, were not included in this analysis.

Drinking rates among male students were available for nine ethnic groups. Russia was the country of origin with the greatest proportion of student drinkers and was followed in descending rank order by France, Italy, Germany, Scandinavia, Ireland, Britain, Africa, and America. Ninety-two percent of the students of Russian origin, 89 percent of French, 84 percent of Irish, 81 percent of British, 81 percent of American blacks, and 75 percent of American whites drank.

Drinking rates among women students were available on only five of these countries. Eighty-one percent of the women of German origin drank, 66 percent of British origin, 64 percent of Irish, 61 percent of American whites, and 43 percent of American blacks.

A comparison of the American white women and men students indicated comparable rates of drinking. Among the blacks, however, far fewer women than men drank.

Intoxication rates among the ethnic groups were also compared. Intoxication was separated into two levels: being tight and being drunk. Being tight included definite unsteadiness and loss of control, possible aggressive behavior, and slight nausea. Being drunk included the more extreme levels of intoxicating effects short of passing out. The data presented here are only for male drinkers.

More male drinkers of British origin (83 percent) reported having been tight than Germans (81 percent), American blacks (79 percent), American whites (77 percent), Irish or Italian (70 percent). White male drinkers of British origin were also more likely to report having been drunk (66 percent). More American whites (60 percent) than American blacks (55 percent) reported such behavior.

The attitudes toward drinking of twenty-four black and twenty-four white male undergraduates at a Southern campus were compared by Maddox and Allen.[55] Utilizing a modification of the Murray Thematic Apperception Test and a one and a half hour interview, they found that the whites provided more elaborate detail in their responses, but that the attitudes regarding alcohol of both blacks and whites were similar. Both were ambivalent toward drinking, saw alcohol as a means of modifying reality, and perceived the overall consequences of drinking to be negative.

Later, a followup study of black college students was conducted in a predominantly black Southern college.[56] Black male students were studied as freshmen in 1963, as sophomores, and again as seniors in 1967. The sample consisted of 262 blacks, with a median age of 18.7 years at entry into the study. The response rate was 91 percent. The majority of students were Baptists and residents of the predominantly rural state. Trained black upperclassmen from the same college interviewed the students regarding their drinking, self-esteem, and socioeconomic background.

As freshmen, 21 percent were abstainers, 37 percent were light drinkers, and 42 percent were heavier drinkers. Little change in the overall drinking prevalence occurred in the sophomore year. In the senior year, only 109 of the original sample remained. Among the seniors, 6 percent were abstainers, 38 percent light drinkers, and 56 percent heavier drinkers.

Students were not only more likely to drink as seniors but also to drink for different motivations. As freshmen, they drank primarily for social reasons; as seniors they were more likely to drink to modify reality.

Dropping out was associated with heavier drinking. Of those who dropped out in their freshman year, 53 percent were heavy drinkers. Dropouts also tended to have lower self-esteem and to be preoccupied with alcohol.

Data were also available on changes in drinking status on 103 of the black males who reached their senior year. Of the twenty-six who were abstainers in their freshmen year, four remained abstainers, seventeen became light drinkers, and five became heavy drinkers. Of the forty-one initially light drinkers, one became an abstainer, ten remained light drinkers, and thirty became heavy drinkers. Of the thirty-six initially heavy drinkers, one became an abstainer, eleven became light drinkers, and twenty-four remained heavy drinkers. Overall, 50 percent of the students increased their drinking.

Important differences may exist between blacks and whites in their drinking attitudes, behaviors, and complications. Up-to-date scientific research is needed, however, to determine if and what differences exist.[57] Such research should be more than just comparative studies of the sociocultural influences on drinking attitudes and behavior. Research is also needed to suggest effective prevention and intervention strategies concerning both psychosocial and physiological complications from drinking and intoxication.

Comparative studies of white and black college students need to take into account the factors affecting drinking rates that were discussed in this chapter. Other factors are also important that relate specifically to the study of different ethnic groups. These include the race/sex of the interviewer, the wording used in the questions, the difficulties involved in determining comparability of family socioeconomic status among minority groups, and the racial composition of the college and its administration.

Black-white differences should be studied because they may provide a clue as to some of the mechanisms leading to the development of alcoholic persons as well as insight into the socialization of persons into the drinking or nondrinking role.

The Relationship of Student Drinking to Drinking Patterns in Later Adulthood

Fillmore recently reported an exploratory twenty year

followup study of a sample of students who had attended college during the late 1940s and early 1950s.[58] The initial study was conducted by Straus and Bacon and was comprised of a sample of 17,000 students representing twenty-seven American colleges and universities.[59]

Fillmore sampled from the 11,914 students who had initially volunteered for a followup study when they completed their questionnaires during 1949-1952. This step was conducted to determine the feasibility of locating and gaining the cooperation of the people after twenty years. Of the total 896 people sampled, 84 percent of the men and 80 percent of the women were located.

Of those located, a sample of 278 people was drawn, and 206 of these participated in the followup study. The majority completed a mailed questionnaire but seventy of them were interviewed by telephone. Questions included the respondent's drinking frequency, the quantity per occasion of the most frequently drunk alcoholic beverage, frequency of intoxication, and indicators of problem drinking.

The measure of problem drinking used was based on the definition of the Cooperative Commission: "a repetitive use of beverage alcohol causing physical, psychological, or social harm to the drinker or to others," and adapted from Cahalan's national study of problem drinkers.[60]

The measure of problem drinking used was comprehensive. It comprised such indicators as psychological dependence on alcohol, frequent intoxication, binge drinking, belligerence associated with drinking, and behavior symptomatic of alcoholism. Alcohol-related social and personal problems on the job, at school, and with friends, neighbors, or relatives were also considered. In addition, health, financial, and legal problems were also included if they were alcohol related. Thus, although clearly not unassociated with alcoholism, the term "problem drinking" is not necessarily synonymous with "alcoholism."

Fillmore expressed appropriate cautions regarding the findings of this exploratory study because of the unrepresentativeness of the sample and the relatively small follow-up group. In addition, no information was presented on blacks. Nevertheless, some interesting findings can be noted.

Of the 109 men followed, 42 percent had been problem drinkers while in college. Twenty years later, however, only 17 percent were so classified. Of the ninety-seven women, 11 percent had been problem drinkers in college and 12 percent were problem drinkers twenty years later. Among both men and women, those who had been problem drinkers in college were more likely to be problem drinkers in their later adulthood. Of those who were abstainers or nonproblem drinkers in college, no more than 10 percent became problem drinkers. Among the problem drinkers in college, on the other hand, 28 percent of the men and 33 percent of the women were still problem drinkers twenty years later.

Interesting relationships between problem drinking and the quantity and frequency of drinking were noted. For example, many of the problem drinkers in college did not drink extremely heavily or frequently; problem drinkers in later adulthood, however, did. Quantity of drinking, particularly for men, was a better predictor of problem drinking than was frequency of drinking. Fillmore concludes that a mere count of the amount of drinks or the number of drinking occasions is limited in its power to describe and explain drinking behavior:

> Quantity and frequency of drinking seem to be on a different level of questioning than is the problem-drinking measure. Although all three variables "count" and quantify behaviors, a problem-drinking set of questions is more intimately tied to human experience. It gets into the reasons and inner context of the act. . . . It asks, "What does drinking do for you and what do you do after drinking has done it for you?"[61]

Further, she emphasizes the importance of individual attitudes toward drinking, of the drinking context and of sociocultural influences in both understanding and predicting an individual's future drinking behavior.

Fillmore examined the relationship between college drinking to later problems with a prospective study using data on collegian drinking gathered while the people were still in college. In contrast, Trice and Belasco dealt with the same question but started with alcoholics and asked them to recall their college drinking.[62]

In an admittedly nonrepresentative sample using questionnaires from 552 Alcoholic Anonymous members, they found the influence of college drinking to depend on the person's career pattern. Alcoholic college graduates who entered clerical, service, and semiskilled occupations were more likely to report alcohol-related social complications while in college. Those who entered executive or professional positions did not report such problems.

Alcoholism among the executives and professionals was felt by the researchers to have been due to job-related factors. For the executives, these related to the organizational structure and its accompanying power struggles. Internal job factors rather than organizational structures were felt to be contributing to alcoholism in professionals. Occupational obsolescence was the most frequent contributing factor cited for this group.

The role of college drinking in the development of later alcoholism for the executive/professional group differed significantly from that of the nonprofessional group. It would be interesting to determine to what extent the college drinking problems of the nonprofessionals prevented their entering more advanced occupational levels.

Drinking and the New Collegians

Changes in the composition of the student body, faculty, and administration have occurred since Straus and Bacon's national study of college drinking behavior. Currently a greater proportion of young people are attending institutions of higher education accompanied by changes in attitudes, values, and background characteristics that affect rates of drinking and intoxication.

In 1950, 14 percent of the persons eighteen to twenty-four years of age were enrolled in institutions of higher education. Further, 68 percent of the college population were male and 49 percent were enrolled in public institutions.

The rate of young people attending colleges has increased steadily since then until in 1973 it was 32 percent. In the mid-1970s, only 56 percent of the college population were male and 75 percent were enrolled in public institutions of higher education. Also, 10 percent of the college population were nonwhite, 24 percent were married with their spouse present, and only 23 percent had home residences in nonmetropolitan areas.[63]

In addition to more women and minority groups participating in the college experience, more international students were found on the campuses of the late 1970s. In particular, more American students came in contact with exchange students from Middle and Far Eastern countries where drinking is less prevalent. Contact with these students may promote less interest in drinking among the American students. It might be, however, that American drinking practices will be carried back by the international students and adopted by these Eastern countries.

Students entering the colleges of the latter part of the twentieth century will also have had a wider spectrum of drugs from which to choose as well as had experience with a variety of drugs in addition to alcohol. In a national study of 13,122 students from grades seven through twelve, for instance, 29 percent reported experience in the last six months with marijuana and 4 percent with hard drugs.[64] Use and abuse of alcohol by the new collegians, therefore, need to be evaluated in terms of the alternative drugs available to them.

As economic conditions fluctuate, drinking among college students will probably respond accordingly as does the drinking of the general adult population. These conditions also affect the young adult's career possibilities and attitudes toward desirable lifestyles. Attitudes toward health and the care of one's body have already begun to change. Health food restaurants on college campuses, for example, have been established by college students or young entrepreneurs, not by individuals of their parents' generation wishing to encourage good nutrition.

With changes occurring in such aspects as the composition, experiences, and career opportunities of the student body, as well as economic conditions, college administrative structures, attitudes toward health and the use of other drugs, one would expect to see changes in the student's use and abuse of alcohol. Whether or not drinking patterns will conform to these expectations remains to be seen. In any event, these changes afford alcohol researchers further opportunities to test and refine their theories. Meanwhile, social scientists, college administrators, educators, and others maintain a continuing interest not only in describing collegian drinking behavior but also in studying and evaluating the influence on college drinking of peer pressures, parental training, collegiate regulations and societal norms.

CHAPTER **12**

Does Your Moderate Drinking Indicate Psychological Dependence on Alcohol?

Kenneth C. Mills, Ph.D.

"I'll be sober tomorrow, but you'll be crazy the rest of your life."[1]

—W. C. Fields

MANY ARTICLES ABOUT alcohol look at the serious problems of alcohol use, the developing alcoholic, and the medical implications of simply consuming too much liquor. There is an immense amount of data dealing with the effects of alcohol on the human, and methods which deal with the alcoholic are the topic of much expert attention. For most people the one or two drinks before dinner or the few glasses of wine before bed are not considered a problem. The beer with lunch is certainly not viewed as a threat to personal development. Appropriately, professional attention to the consequences of moderate alcohol intake has been minimal. But few alcoholics or problem drinkers started out with the goal of developing an obvious alcohol problem.

Drinking alcohol is a behavior, and like other behaviors it is subject to repetition. The idea that we practice our drinking is not new, but seldom is the practice thought of as leading to more developed performance. When dealing with moderate alcohol intake, practice reaches into the area of psychological dependence or psychological addiction. Both are nebulous terms. When dealing with behavior the effects of drinking are not clear-cut, the reasons for drinking are not obvious, and the consistency of the drinking pattern is not easily discernible.[2] The discussion of psychological dependence rests more upon speculation than data, but some interesting and revealing ideas are starting to emerge.

Within the context of drinking which might be considered inconsequential, this chapter deals with the subtle relationships between drinking and behavior. The purpose is not to point an accusing finger at your drinking, but to explore some of the consequences of drinking which are considered socially acceptable. Instead of exploring your relationship with your mate, your children, your parents, your social environment, or your boss, I want to describe how you might relate to alcohol. Perhaps my outlook is dismal for the alcoholic. I don't intend to say that successful treatment after years of drinking is impossible, but as many alcoholics will tell you, controlling your drinking before the onset of severe signs of dependence is certainly more desirable than waiting until the signs are obvious. I am assuming that people don't typically worry about their drinking until the problems become noticeable and it is easier to change your definition of *noticeable* than it is to change your drinking after years of practice. The relationship between behavior and your use of alcohol is not easy to see in the early stages. My contention is that simply counting your drinks is not adequate to assess the role of alcohol in your life. Instead, defining the function of drinking relative to specific behaviors will reveal subtle relationships which will be useful for self-control.

Five Stages

I find it convenient to view a person's relationship with alcohol as moving through five operational stages: exposure, definition, function, priority, and exclusion. *Exposure* places the person in contact with an alcohol-using culture. Alcohol is a passive part of the environment. Similarly, *definition* describes the alcohol relationships which are possible, contexts in which they occur, and how others have defined those relationships.

During the *function* stage a person establishes an active relationship by drinking. Involvement in the alcohol-using culture is no longer as an observer, but as a participant. Voluntary consumption in a variety of situations begins to define a functional relationship between specific behaviors and the effects of alcohol. As the functional relationship grows, the pharmacology of alcohol can move to the foreground and alcohol can take *priority* over other relationships. This is a gradual process and typically alcohol is intermingled with a large proportion of the drinker's life activities. Alcohol seems to become a significant part of the person's total environment until drinking is the overwhelming characteristic of the individual. This is the final phase, apparently defined by physiological limit, and is labeled as the *exclusion* phase. Alcohol has gained top priority and excludes other relationships, including family, work, social events, and involvement with oneself. This is usually what our society labels as the alcoholic phase. This chapter deals primarily with the development of drinking behavior in the initial function stage before the obvious indices of priority and exclusion are apparent.

Concepts

At this point, let me emphasize that when one examines alcohol use relative to the behavior of an individual, concepts which lump people together lose much of their utility.[3] One of these concepts is the term *alcoholic*. People, especially those who drink, often want reassurance that they are not in danger of being classified alcoholic. A person drinking a fifth a night alongside several six packs will often argue that he is not an alcoholic because he doesn't drink in the morning. Perhaps what Alcoholics Anonymous refers to as *hitting bottom* is realizing that your definition of *alcoholic* no longer allows you to exclude your own drinking behavior. You will not wake up one morning and become an alcoholic, but you may wake up and realize that your long-term relationship with alcohol is now a source of serious concern. If you view your relationship with drinking on a functional continuum and the behavior of taking one or two drinks as a less practiced form of the behavior of drinking to oblivion, then the consequences of all types of drinking are important, not just the consequences of so-called *alcoholic patterns*.

Functions

Specifically, recognize three functions that alcohol can have for an individual. First, it is now common knowledge that alcohol acts as a central nervous system depressant and affects a host of behaviors including walking, talking, driving, and thinking. Second, and most obviously, alcohol rewards, or, in the jargon of a behavioral approach, reinforces. Third, and probably the most overlooked, alcohol becomes a permissive signal for other behaviors. This relationship is simply conjunctive: given the stimulus alcohol, a new set of behaviors become available.

The three functions—eliciting, reinforcing, and discriminative—form a composite for every individual who drinks alcohol. The composite is sometimes popularly tagged as psychological dependence. An alternative concept is behavioral dependence, which denotes the strategy of listing out the functional relationships between alcohol and various behaviors. Behavioral dependence is not conceived as a "real" phenomenon resembling physical dependence, typified by withdrawal and convulsion, but rather it is an approach to allow you to ask about the specific consequences of your drinking.[4]

Important, also, is the behavior which leads to drinking in the first place. All drinking, and all drug use for that matter, is preceded and maintained by behavior. Understanding behavior which precedes and supports chemical intake is critical to any ideas we may have about prevention of future similar behaviors. If the scientific world came up with a drug which cancelled the addictive effects of alcohol, we would still have to deal with alcohol-seeking behavior. The focal point of the research would no longer be alcohol but rather that element of human behavior which requires chemical reassurance.

Alcohol Excludes

The next question you may ask, and rightly so, is if any drug will reassure the human, why is our culture specifically so laden with alcohol-related problems? What factors dictate the choice of alcohol, and are these factors unique to alcohol? Although these questions cannot be unequivocally answered without more research, a tentative answer can be offered by stating that alcohol is not unique and alcohol is everywhere.

First, alcohol is a drug. It produces a pharmacological effect which a large number of people prefer to the nondrug state. Alcohol also produces the reactions characteristic of other addictive drugs—withdrawal, death on overdose, physical dependence, and dose dependence (tolerance).[5] And as with most drugs which become abused, alcohol is fun! People seldom drink large quantities of alcohol simply to quench their thirst.

Second, alcohol is legal, portable, inexpensive, easily available, and socially acceptable. This is in contrast to other drugs which are often expensive, both financially and socially.

The rewarding function of alcohol is apparently the best reason for drinking and the most dangerous. Man derives his rewards from an infinite variety of sources, such as food, the work environment, and interpersonal relationships. Man also has an elastic ability to fit into almost any social relationship, a flexibility which has likely helped to define man as the most advanced being. There are, nevertheless, strong exceptions to the principle of human flexibility, and these arise when man plays with ethanol. As alcohol increases its role in your life, it excludes other sources of reward, diminishing the flexibility characteristic of human behavior.

With initial use of alcohol, the reward for some stems simply from the drug effect. In many cases, drug-effect rewards seem to be natural rather than learned.[6] For others, pleasure from alcohol requires considerable exposure or exposure to other drug sources. In any event, alcohol for the beginning drinker rewards in a specific setting at a specific time—for a while.

As time goes by, and, of course, as the frequency and quantity of drinking builds, alcohol moves to a more prominent position in a person's milieu of rewards. The priority assigned to alcohol increases. The availability of alcohol may come to outweigh the availability of social encounter because for many the rewards of alcohol become more attractive. For example, consider the drinker who substitutes conventional forms of social time-out, such as vacations or hobbies, with an alcohol time-out. The appealing thing about drinking to achieve time-out is the total predictability of the drug's effect. The drinker knows before he starts drinking that the effect is going to be relatively pleasant, and the effect is going to be the same as last time. Drinking doesn't require planning to the same extent that a vacation or a simple gathering of friends would. Drinking seldom fails; the effects are immediate and the outcome is literally guaranteed. If you decide tomorrow night to relax by going to a movie, to forget about the problems of the day, to remove some of the unpleasantries around you, the movie may or may not achieve the desired effect. The movie may, to your dismay, increase your tension by increasing your awareness of other areas of your life with which you are having difficulty or by just simply being the most boring movie you have ever seen. But seldom does the effect of drinking fail to achieve the desired result: the relationship between time-out and a specific dose is easy to establish. But not for long. The dose requirement changes to achieve the same effect, and this tolerance introduces new problems which in a sense were not spelled out in the original guarantee.

Gradually alcohol takes on a changing role: instead of simply offering more varied opportunities for temporary escape, as is often the case with social drinking, alcohol becomes the overriding principle in any effort toward developing alternatives to tension. Recent research indicates that a person's inability to establish a social relationship is brought about by the increasing use of alcohol.[7]

Functionally, excessive drinking is not loss of control, but, in fact, it is increased control by a single source of reinforcement. Other reinforcers—derived, primary, social or otherwise—lose the capability of controlling behavior when alcohol or any drug source is a predominant feature in one's life. It is difficult to distribute love, attention, money, titles, rank, or privilege to a person when his needs embrace a drug supply.

Getting Alcoholed

As an attempt to strip alcohol of its often assigned magical properties, let us consider an effect which we will call *alcoholed*. Being alcoholed arbitrarily refers to the extent that alcohol in your system acts to control your behavior. The term is not to be confused with the blood alcohol level, that is, the amount of alcohol in your blood supply.

A scale of getting alcoholed could be defined for each individual, closely interwoven with the end products of drinking. Extremes of the scale would be designated by little change from sober behavior (perhaps a few verbal comments not typical of the individual) to the bizarre repertoire often associated with heavy drinking, including fighting, screaming, or even prolonged silent withdrawal. Getting alcoholed between the extremes of the scale would call up different and varying behaviors, some unique, some bizarre, depending on the experience of the person in handling the effect of the drug in various environments. This analogy is merely to say that getting alcoholed is a stimulus. Getting alcoholed, as a result of widespread use and acceptability in our culture, changes the consequences of behavior. The alcoholed state sets the occasion for other behaviors. A green light is a stimulus that says go. A red light says stop. When the stimulus changes, the consequences of behavior change. Similarly, getting alcoholed is a stimulus to both the drinker and those in his environment. He is allowed, at times, to show disinhibition. At other times, say at work, being alcoholed must not show. Getting alcoholed to 5 is a different stimulus from getting alcoholed to 20 and different again from 80 on our theoretical scale of 1 to 100.

Craig MacAndrew and Robert Edgerton in their book, *Drunken Comportment,* deal with alcohol use as a stimulus.[8] They provide an exquisite comparison of how individuals in various cultures respond to getting excessively alcoholed, to a high level of 80 or greater. They argue convincingly that the oblivion or time-out aroused by alcohol becomes a distinct stimulus for each culture. In some cultures getting drunk calls up inhibition and in others disinhibition of behavior.

Much of the evidence for the stimulus interpretation of drug effects also comes from the animal laboratory. Animals have been trained extensively to discriminate between drugs, to discriminate drugged from nondrug states, and to discriminate doses of the same drug.[9] The term *discrimination* is used to denote the ability to tell the difference between events. Drug discriminations are usually accomplished using procedures specifically designed to test an animal's relationship to his external environment. Certain drugs, including alcohol, however, have the capability to exert as much or more control over behavior as any external stimulus.

This fact says a lot for alcohol use in people. Although the effect of alcohol on the nervous system is quite specific, behaviors which can be unleashed by a particular dose of alcohol are quite variable from person to person, from culture to culture, and from time to time.

Why worry about the stimulus function? It is apparently not the stimulus function which deals out social and individual problems. People alcoholed to 80 frequently are in oblivion, and alcohol has most likely lost its stimulus function, at least for the more subtle aspects from lower doses.

Most drinkers know, consciously or unconsciously, that different alcohol quantities provide innumerable opportunities for consequences to occur—different consequences which are not available without drinking. Following selected alcohol doses, you may choose the occasion, the time, the place, the participants, and if you are a clever drinker, make up your own set of rules for new and unique consequences to occur. Access to sex, violence, sedation, solitude, and social insult are offered. These scenes are not new to most drinkers, but they are dose related. Behavior becomes a function of dose.

Generalization

Early in your drinking history, alcohol as a stimulus sets the occasion for specific behaviors—perhaps a few unrestrained comments or a few social advances. The learning organism, however, tends to change its reactions to stimuli over time. One change is labeled generalization.[10] Generalization is used to denote a process which is the opposite of discrimination; generalization is not being able to distinguish a difference. In order not to overload our brain with infinite stimuli different to every situation, we group stimuli that will be taken care of by the same response. Often this response is drinking.

Generalization is apparently working in many aspects of how we greet our external world, including verbal behaviors, motor behaviors, or coping behaviors. In coping, generalization is obviously useful in that we do not have to greet every new stressful situation as a unique threat. Generalization is not unique to people. Most, if not all, mammals do it. Pigeons trained to respond for food under a green light will also respond to a blue light, but not as readily. They will respond at a moderate rate to yellow and even less to red.[11]

This same process, which can be seen to be a great energy saver, can also run amok. The stimuli that set the occasion for alcohol can be grouped. More things can come to bring on drinking. More things, in turn, can happen when drinking occurs. Generalization, while once useful, is now detrimental.

Consequences: Before and After

We have drawn the distinction, theoretically at least, between alcohol as a stimulus which produces a unique set of consequences and the effects of alcohol as a consequence of behavior. The distinction is functional in that the same event, the effect of the drug, has several meanings. Food acts as a reinforcer in that it fills the person who is hungry, but at the same time gathering for dinner or lunch can set the stage for a social occasion with different consequences than simply a full stomach. A drug, such as alcohol, like the food, can act as both the stimulus and reinforcer with functionally distinct properties.

However, when we use the principle that behavior produces consequences we must incorporate different types of consequences as the causal principle for change. If the consequences of a behavior, such as touching a hot stove, are immediate, the learning is rapid. If, however, the behaviors are not clear-cut and distinct and the consequences are delayed, then the person's ability to distinguish between different behaviors is reduced.

Unfortunately, most people do not think of the consequences of alcohol or drug use from a stimulus context. We tend to ask "What are the effects of taking the drug?" or "How will the drug affect subsequent behavior?" This is not limited to the layman's view of drug usage, for the professional literature is most often concerned with the effects of a drug on physiology, motor performance, or some previously established behavior. This is different from asking why an individual took the drug in the first place. What were the conditions or the behaviors which preceded the drug intake, and the effect the drug had on these behaviors? In a sense, this is thinking backwards. If a person is having a drink after getting home from work, we are now asking how the alcohol is affecting what has happened during the work day rather than trying to assess what effect the alcohol is going to have later in the evening.

If we postulate that the negative consequences of behavior for the human are cumulative, regardless of the source, then we can have behavioral arrangements for the concept of anxiety. Limiting our analysis to one day in a person's life would reveal that he or she may be exposed to a variety of situations in which an infinite number of behaviors are performed. The consequences of daily behaviors will range theoretically from extremely positive to extremely negative, but not typically and not every day. The chances are that the daily consequences of your behavior will be within a narrow range. Unless you lead the life of a television detective, during the course of a day the difference between behaviors which produce negative and positive consequences will often be very difficult to distinguish. We live in a world of social consequences, subtle consequences where the differences between positive and negative are often impossible to discern. We deal with concepts such as sincerity, where a compliment delivered as a positive consequence can be interpreted as an insult. The nature of the social environment is ambiguous. When we are having a drink at the end of the day, we may not be responding to fatigue, but the cumulative impact of the social environment. In addition to postulating that the effect of alcohol is a delayed consequence of behaviors during the day, the reward function of the drug dictates that the nature of the delayed consequence is positive. Whatever the negative consequences which occurred during the day, and especially those linked to subtle behaviors, they now stand a chance of becoming linked with the positive effect of taking a few drinks.

This is arguing that the alcohol changes the consequences of behavior. The negative, ambiguous, social consequences of behavior have added up and the feelings the person is getting at the end of the day are not clear-cut. As discussed earlier, this is anxiety, and alcohol is efficient at relieving the tension which does not have an easily identifiable source. We can cope with the clear-cut sources; if the kids are screaming, send them outside; if the dishwasher is broken, fix it. But if the source of anxiety is next to impossible to identify, it is just as impossible to deal with. With time and after attempts at altering the social environment, the diffuse problems will become more clear-cut and the unidentifiable will become identifiable. The person will be able to deal, avoid, or eliminate the problems and endure the process labeled as coping. However, a repeated daily dose of alcohol, especially an increasing dose, may influence a person's ability to deal with consequences. At this point we are speculating, but the idea that a drug has the capability to remove the cumulative negative consequences has some disturbing implications. Although the person's ability to endure an aversive environment might be increased, his capability in telling the difference between negative and positive consequences is diminished. He or she no longer has to cope with the negative consequences of behavior. They do not have to alter the environment, the social environment, to make the negative consequences go away. The alcohol can make the consequences go away. The drug, the alcohol, replaces behavior.

Cultural Approval

But our culture extensively approves the use of alcohol to make the consequences of behavior more delectable. The social consequences of moderate alcohol intake, for whatever reason, are negligible. Thinking about alcohol as reducing your capacity to make distinctions, to tell differences, and to make decisions may alter the personal consequences of alcohol use. It may not.

Apparently it is easy to learn the relation that drinking removes unpleasant consequences of daily life.[12] The important feature is not that you drink alcohol, but that you drink and discover that it can relieve unpleasant feelings. Because it works, you can now apply the relationship of "alcohol-relieves-the-uptights" to other bothering aspects of your life. A functional relationship between alcohol and behavior can be established. Given the opportunity the relation can be applied to a complaining mate, financial pressures, the inability to sleep, and so on. The concept of generalization returns: what is learned under one set of conditions *can be* and *is* used under other conditions. Notice, however, that this is not simple generalization either to the stimuli produced by anxiety or to alcohol. Certainly these phenomena occur. All stress can be perceived as equally terrifying. All alcoholed effects can be felt as similar, especially at high doses. The new form of generalization is to the functional relation between the removal of stress and being alcoholed. Alcohol has now taken on a new dimension in relating to the outside world: it has become prominent. One simply learns to use the relationship between anxiety removal and alcohol intake to the fullest extent. In a real sense, using a learned escape and applying it to a wide variety of circumstances becomes almost too efficient. Ironically, a serious drinker's flexibility in coping is limited to the number of environments capable of signaling drinking and not the number of different reactions to those environments. The drinker has in effect learned to handle all problems with a single solution. Alcohol is flexible. It can match the salience of practically any environment, not by acting on the environment but by simply making it go away. The flexibility that once characterized the total person now characterizes only their relation to alcohol.

From the individual drinker's point of view, alcohol works. It requires much less effort to drink than it does to establish new social outlets or to work out long-term problems. Alcohol, however, only works when it is around. Alcohol is fickle over time. Obviously, the relation with alcohol must be re-established each time you meet.

Alcohol Rather Than . . .

A question often raised by many is how much liquor can be consumed safely—usually on a daily basis. The answer from a behavioral point of view is that it's not altogether the quantity that you drink, but the circumstances under which you drink. If you take several drinks daily, and this drinking always follows a fight with your mate, it should be considered risky behavior because the consequences of fighting become related to the pharmacology of alcohol. Typically a fight produces negative feelings and the participants will strive to reduce these feelings in the future. This may involve redefining the relationship or even one partner avoiding contact with the other. When, however, drinking always follows fighting, then the consequences of fighting are positive. This increases the probability of fighting in the future, rather than precipitating alternatives to the conflict. The essential feature of a behavioral approach to drinking is that it offers early alternatives to resolving life strains without alcohol, while choices are still possible to make. Once you become physiologically dependent, alternatives which you perceive as more satisfying than the drug source are few and far between.

Safe Drinking

How, then, can the everyday drinker use alcohol safely? More critically, how can you use alcohol and be aware of indications of behavioral dependence? Ask yourself several questions and phrase them so that an honest answer is possible. First, when you drink, what feelings are you trying to change? Can these changes in feeling, tone, mood, or behavior be achieved *without the alcohol or any other chemical intervention?* The only test is to achieve the desired changes at least once without the drug. If you find the change you want is impossible, then the chances are good you are fostering behavioral dependence. If those desired changes include a large measure of stress and escape from stress (including boredom) be alert to your drug use.

In addition, each time you take a drink, however small, admit that you are using a drug. You may prefer the taste of beer, but be aware that beer, too, is a drug. The liquor industry may not find this interpretation particularly appealing or helpful to sales, and you may not receive a lot of social support for this notion, but your first concern should be your own relation with alcohol. Admitting that alcohol, in any form, is a drug will also allow you to identify the pushers in your environment. Pushers are not only those who profit from the sale of alcohol but also those who do not enjoy drinking alone. Their goal is the same: for you to consume a larger quantity of the approved drug supply and this often confirms that they are not drinking too much. A partially effective method for controlling the pusher is to decide exactly how much alcohol you want to consume before you enter the drinking environment and before you take your first drink.

To take the next step, define the dose needs in your life. You may find it helpful to list out the number of circumstances in your daily routine which are occasioned by alcohol as the stimulus. Are the different events which you experience becoming dose related? Don't leave out fantasies of upcoming events at which alcohol will be a central theme or an essential ingredient. If you catch yourself wishfully thinking of achieving a certain level of getting alcoholed in upcoming situations, then be aware of alcohol's importance to you.

Finally, and most important, try to assess your use of alcohol in any attempts to avoid coping. If the relationship has become alcohol rather than conflict, alcohol rather than relating to your peers, alcohol rather than tedium, then your awareness and decisions to continue to use alcohol should become increasingly conscious and overt. This is critical, even if your first drink is an alternative to coping, for preventing the alcohol relationship from becoming the exclusive one.

PART IV

Social Policy and Drinking

THIS SECTION EXAMINES the complex interplay between laws and drinking and considers how present knowledge might, or might not, significantly influence one of man's favorite activities, alcohol consumption.

Professor Ben F. Loeb specializes in public law and government. He is Assistant Director of the Institute of Government at the University of North Carolina and serves as a scientific consultant to the Center for Alcohol Studies, and to the Alcoholic Beverage Control and Highway Safety Committees of the North Carolina General Assembly. His chapter examines the interrelationship between existing alcoholic beverage control laws and drinking behavior.

Chapter 14 is written by researchers on the staff of the Addiction Research Foundation (ARF) in Toronto, Canada. The senior author, Robert Popham, a graduate in biology and anthropology of the University of Toronto, is a member of the Expert Panel on Drug Dependence of the World Health Organization. He was a recipient of the Jellinek Memorial Award for Contributions to the Study of Alcoholism in 1972. Wolfgang Schmidt, a graduate of the University of Graz and of Toronto, is director of social and epidemiological studies in

218 PART IV: SOCIAL POLICY and DRINKING

the Foundation. Jan de Lint taught anthropology for several
years in the University of Toronto, and both he and Dr.
Schmidt have published extensively on epidemiological aspects of the problems of alcohol. Their best-known recent
work includes research on the distribution of alcohol consumption in society and on the mortality experience of alcoholics.

Robin Room is a sociologist who has been engaged
since 1963 in studies of drinking practices and problems in the
general United States population. He is the co-author with
Don Cahalan of *Problem Drinking Among American Men,* the
author of various articles on drinking practices and problems
and the minimization of alcohol problems, the editor of *The
Drinking and Drug Practices Surveyor,* and a Lecturer in the
School of Public Health at University of California at Berkeley. He is currently co-directing a study of drug use among
young American men, and directing an analysis of cross-
national data on drinking practices and problems. In his
chapter, Mr. Room provides a scholarly review of the major
positions on the relation between alcohol control laws and
drinking and he offers a critique of each position in terms of
available data.

Wayne Womer, D.D., is the Executive Director of the
Middle Atlantic Institute for Alcohol and Other Drug Studies,
Inc. and Director of Education and Church Relations of the
Alcohol-Narcotics Education Council, Inc. of Virginia
Churches, both of Richmond, Virginia. In his chapter, he
turns to an actual field experience, looking at what happened
in Virginia when major legal changes were invoked. He also
supplies an interesting historical survey of drinking in Virginia throughout its modern history.

The final chapter in this section is by Professor Frank
Grad of Columbia University who directs the Legislative
Drafting Research Foundation there. Dr. Grad has been active
in developing model laws to help us deal better with the
problems of alcoholism and his contribution on this topic
serves to demonstrate his wide understanding of the problem.

CHAPTER 13

Relationship of State Law to Per Capita Drinking

Ben F. Loeb, Jr., J.D.

THE PURPOSES OF this chapter are: (1) to examine the alcoholic beverage control laws of several states, with a view to ascertaining whether there is any relationship between the law of a given jurisdiction and the per capita liquor consumption of the inhabitants of that jurisdiction, and (2) to relate the experience of these states to national trends. The liquor-control acts of eight states will be surveyed, with all major geographical regions of the country represented. Three of these states have government-owned liquor stores (control states) and the other five have privately owned stores licensed by the state (license states). Per capita consumption figures given will be for the year 1970, unless otherwise indicated, and will include the data for distilled spirits (hard liquor) only. Those jurisdictions with a large tourist industry, or having other factors present which might account for an unusually high or low per capita consumption, have been intentionally omitted from consideration. For this reason the District of Columbia, which has an apparent per capita consumption three times the national average, is not included in this study. Nor is Utah, which has a consumption level less than half the national average.

The states to be analyzed, in order of declining per capita consumption, are: Alaska, New Jersey, Illinois, Colorado, Arizona, Oregon, North Carolina, and Iowa. Table 13-1 shows the 1969 and 1970 consumption figures for all the license states and Table 13-2 for all the control states.[1] References are to apparent consumption because there is no way to take fully into account such factors as purchases by out-of-state residents or illegal purchases of nontaxpaid liquor. Consumption figures are given in terms of wine gallons, which consist of four quarts each, as with all United States standard liquid gallons.

Table 13-3 shows the number of retail liquor licenses issued in each license state.[2] Table 13-4 shows the liquor licenses for control states. On-premises licenses authorize liquor sales by the drink, and off-premises licenses permit sales by the bottle only. Some states issue one license which allows both types of sales on the same premises.

Alaska

Alaska is a license, as opposed to control, state and has a quite high per capita consumption of liquor. (See Table 13-1) In this state, licenses are issued by an Alcoholic Beverage Control Board. A beverage dispensary license may be acquired for on-premises sales of liquor-by-the-drink[3] and a retail license for liquor store sales by the bottle for off-premises consumption.[4] A club license is available to certain organizations that have been incorporated for at least two years; but sales may be made only to club members and their families.[5] The sale of liquor is on a local-option basis and may be prohibited in a given area altogether.[6]

One interesting provision of the Alaska law concerns the hours for sale. The statutes provide that "no person may consume, sell, or give . . . any liquor on any licensed premises between the hours of 5 A.M. and 8 A.M."[7] Why write into statutory form a law that is effective for only three hours out of twenty-four, particularly when the prohibited period is generally used for sleeping anyway? Except during the hours noted above, liquor may be sold at any time on any day (including Sunday) except on election days—and even then sales may resume after the polls close.

Table 13-1
Apparent Consumption of Distilled Spirits For License States
Calendar Years 1970-1969 [a]

License States	Rank in Consumption 1970	Rank in Consumption 1969	Consumption in Wine Gallons 1970	Consumption in 1969	Percent Increase/ Decrease	Per Capita 1970	Per Capita 1969
*Alaska	47	48	945,370	898,384	5.2	3.13	3.19
**Arizona	32	32	2,967,269	2,648,286	12.0	1.67	1.56
*Arkansas	39	39	1,865,031	1,783,362	4.6	0.97	0.89
*California	1	1	45,070,650	44,013,195	2.4	2.26	2.26
*Colorado	25	25	4,254,048	4,147,701	2.6	1.93	1.98
*Connecticut	17	17	7,276,811	7,505,861	(3.1)	2.40	2.50
**Delaware	41	41	1,583,166	1,540,051	2.8	2.89	2.85
*Dist. of Columbia	21	19	5,730,253	6,111,564	(6.2)	7.57b	7.66b
*Florida	4	6	18,031,618	15,710,834	14.8	2.66	2.47
*Georgia	16	8	7,453,253	7,007,387	6.4	1.62	1.51
*Illinois	3	3	24,213,606	24,619,182	(1.6)	2.18	2.23
*Indiana	19	21	6,164,823	5,765,986	6.9	1.19	1.13
*Kansas	36	33	2,410,475	2,400,965	0.4	1.07	1.03
*Kentucky	24	24	4,450,543	4,336,585	2.6	1.38	1.34
*Louisiana	22	22	5,281,620	5,253,429	0.5	1.45	1.40
**Maryland	12	12	8,748,466	8,194,173	6.8	2.23	2.18
**Massachusetts	10	10	12,732,230	12,767,031	(0.3)	2.24	2.34
*Minnesota	18	15	7,027,234	7,617,302	(7.7)	1.85	2.06
*Missouri	13	13	7,724,043	7,631,270	1.2	1.65	1.64
*Nebraska	34	35	2,478,081	2,322,900	6.7	1.67	1.60
*Nevada	33	34	2,498,767	2,357,709	6.0	5.11	5.16
**New Jersey	5	4	16,288,922	16,572,143	(1.7)	2.27	2.32
**New Mexico	42	42	1,530,291	1,395,915	9.6	1.51	1.40
**New York	2	2	43,365,269	41,993,080	3.3	2.38	2.29
*North Dakota	45	45	1,031,120	1,044,460	(1.3)	1.67	1.70
*Oklahoma	28	28	3,568,490	3,355,029	6.4	1.39	1.31
*Rhode Island	38	38	1,866,877	1,801,267	3.6	1.97	1.98
*South Carolina	23	23	5,187,268	4,863,361	6.7	2.00	1.81
*South Dakota	46	46	972,355	1,012,581	(4.0)	1.46	1.54
*Tennessee	27	26	3,765,694	4,028,396	(6.5)	0.96	1.01
*Texas	9	9	13,689,637	13,290,390	3.0	1.22	1.19
*Wisconsin	11	11	8,867,418	8,452,439	4.9	2.01	2.00
TOTAL LICENSE			279,040,698	272,442,218	2.4	1.98	1.96

a Source: *Distilled Spirits Industry Annual Statistical Review, 1970.*
b Per capita consumption for District of Columbia calculated using population of only the District of Columbia but the gallonage for the Metropolitan Area (includes Virginia and Maryland suburbs as well as visitors).
*Based on tax collections.
**Based on gallonage shipments of wholesalers.

221

Table 13-2
Apparent Consumption of Distilled Spirits For Control States
and Grand Total for All States
Calendar Years 1970–1969[a]

Control States	Rank in Consumption 1970	Rank in Consumption 1969	Consumption in Wine Gallons 1970	Consumption in Wine Gallons 1969	Percent Increase/ Decrease	Per Capita 1970	Per Capita 1969
Alabama	26	27	3,862,956	3,749,627	3.0	1.12	1.06
Idaho	49	49	852,600	816,376	4.4	1.20	1.14
Iowa	30	30	3,152,684	3,075,511	2.5	1.12	1.11
Maine	40	40	1,667,559	1,593,230	4.7	1.68	1.63
Michigan	7	7	15,055,823	14,568,480	3.3	1.70	1.66
Mississippi	35	36	2,457,992	2,313,504	6.2	1.11	0.98
Montana	44	44	1,144,966	1,098,296	4.2	1.65	1.58
New Hampshire	29	31	3,370,779	2,879,275	17.1	4.57	4.02
North Carolina	15	16	7,583,955	7,582,980	—	1.49	1.46
Ohio	8	8	14,045,628	14,434,784	(— 2.7)	1.32	1.34
Oregon	31	29	3,135,465	3,120,181	0.5	1.50	1.54
Pennsylvania	6	5	16,187,669	15,781,625	2.6	1.37	1.34
Utah	48	47	927,278	908,584	2.1	0.88	0.87
Vermont	43	43	1,240,265	1,189,884	4.2	2.79	2.71
Virginia	14	14	7,717,265	7,743,309	(— 0.3)	1.66	1.66
Washington	20	20	6,024,060	5,893,903	2.2	1.77	1.73
West Virginia	37	37	1,996,362	1,897,694	5.2	1.14	1.04
Wyoming	50	50	615,959	592,557	3.9	1.86	1.85
TOTAL CONTROL			91,039,265	89,239,800	2.0	1.47	1.44
TOTAL LICENSE			279,040,698	272,442,218	2.4	1.98	1.96
GRAND TOTAL			370,079,963	361,682,018	2.3	1.83	1.80

[a] Source: *Distilled Spirits Industry Annual Statistical Review, 1970.*

Table 13-3
Retail Licenses for Sale of Distilled Spirits in License States

State	Number of Licenses				1970 Census (Thousands)	Number of Licenses per 1,000 population			
	On-Premise	Off-Premise	On and Off-Premise	Total Licenses		On-Premise	Off-Premise	On and Off-Premise	Total Licenses
LICENSE STATES									
Alaska	596	319		915	302,000	1.97	1.06		3.03
Arizona	416	1,043	1,260	2,719	1,772,000	0.23	0.59	0.71	1.53
Arkansas	194	604		798	1,923,000	0.10	0.32		0.42
California	12,082	10,498		22,580	19,953,000	0.61	0.53		1.14
Colorado	2,108	1,020		3,128	2,207,000	0.96	0.46		1.42
Connecticut	2,654	2,140		4,794	3,032,000	0.88	0.71		1.59
Delaware	254	278	215	747	548,000	0.46	0.51	0.39	1.36
Dist. of Columbia	663	382		1,045	757,000	0.88	0.50		1.38
Florida	554	534	3,799	4,887	6,789,000	0.08	0.08	0.56	0.72
Georgia	457	1,153		1,610	4,590,000	0.10	0.25		0.35
Hawaii	648	530		1,178	770,000	0.84	0.69		1.53
Illinois			21,127	21,127	11,114,000			1.90	1.90
Indiana	1,187	1,471	2,662	5,320	5,194,000	0.23	0.28	0.51	1.02
Kansas	718	1,080		1,798	2,249,000	0.32	0.48		0.80
Kentucky	857	764	151	1,772	3,219,000	0.26	0.24	0.05	0.55
Louisiana		1,447	5,564	7,011	3,643,000		0.40	1.53	1.93
Maryland	577	1,035	2,633	4,245	3,922,000	0.15	0.26	0.67	1.08
Massachusetts	5,039	2,048		7,087	5,689,000	0.89	0.36		1.25
Minnesota	1,482	625	948	3,055	3,805,000	0.39	0.16	0.25	0.80
Missouri	3,124	2,854		5,978	4,677,000	0.67	0.61		1.28
Nebraska	258	591	1,407	2,256	1,484,000	0.17	0.40	0.95	1.52
Nevada	639	322	411	1,372	489,000	1.31	0.66	0.84	2.81
New Jersey	1,252	2,017	8,874	12,143	7,168,000	0.17	0.28	1.24	1.69
New Mexico	114	123	1,164	1,401	1,016,000	0.11	0.12	1.15	1.38
New York	23,221	5,257		28,478	18,191,000	1.28	0.29		1.57
North Dakota		72	923	995	618,000		0.12	1.49	1.61
Oklahoma		801		801	2,559,000		0.31		0.31
Rhode Island	1,336	338		1,674	950,000	1.41	0.36		1.77
South Carolina		899		899	2,591,000		0.35		0.35
South Dakota	546	560		1,106	666,000	0.82	0.84		1.66
Tennessee	157	471		628	3,924,000	0.04	0.12		0.16
Texas	1,682	3,187		4,869	11,197,000	0.15	0.28		0.43
Wisconsin	11,707	1,173		12,880	4,418,000	2.65	0.27		2.92
TOTAL LICENSE	74,522	45,636	51,138	171,296	141,427,000	0.53	0.32	0.36	1.21

223

Table 13-4
Retail Licenses for Sale of Distilled Spirits in License States

State	Number of Licenses				1970 Census (Thousands)	Number of Licenses per 1,000 population			
	On-Premise	Off-Premise	On and Off-Premise	Total Licenses		On-Premise	Off-Premise	On and Off-Premise	Total Licenses
CONTROL STATES									
Alabama	872	105	.....	977	3,444,000	0.25	0.03	.....	0.28
Idaho	658	117	.....	775	713,000	0.92	0.17	.....	1.09
Iowa	3,211	199	.....	3,410	2,825,000	1.14	0.07	.....	1.21
Maine	515	88	.....	603	994,000	0.52	0.09	.....	0.61
Michigan	7,232	2,447	.....	9,679	8,875,000	0.81	0.28	.....	1.09
Mississippi	302	507	.....	809	2,217,000	0.14	0.23	.....	0.37
Montana	1,437	147	.....	1,584	694,000	2.07	0.21	.....	2.28
New Hampshire	650	57	.....	707	738,000	0.88	0.08	.....	0.96
North Carolina	—	308	.....	308	5,082,000	.....	0.06	.....	0.06
Ohio	11,097	370	.....	11,467	10,652,000	1.04	0.04	.....	1.08
Oregon	1,013	178	.....	1,191	2,091,000	0.48	0.09	.....	0.57
Pennsylvania	20,358	729	.....	21,087	11,794,000	1.73	0.06	.....	1.79
Utah	146	101	.....	247	1,059,000	0.14	0.10	.....	0.24
Vermont	607	57	.....	664	445,000	1.36	0.13	.....	1.49
Virginia	434	237	.....	671	4,648,000	0.09	0.05	.....	0.14
Washington	1,255	273	.....	1,528	3,409,000	0.37	0.08	.....	0.45
West Virginia	818	146	.....	964	1,744,000	0.47	0.08	.....	0.55
Wyoming	131	75	480	686	332,000	0.39	0.23	1.45	2.07
TOTAL CONTROL	50,736	6,141	480	57,357	61,758,000	0.82	0.10	0.01	0.93
TOTAL LICENSE	74,522	45,636	51,138	171,296	141,427,000	0.53	0.32	0.36	1.21
GRAND TOTAL	125,258	51,777	51,618	228,653	203,185,000*	0.62	0.26	0.25	1.13

Source: *Distilled Spirits Industry Annual Statistical Review*, 1970.

In recent years Alaska has reduced the age requirement for buying and consuming liquor from twenty-one to nineteen years; but a person under nineteen is not even allowed on premises holding a liquor license unless accompanied by a parent, guardian, or spouse who has attained that age. The only category of persons to whom sales are prohibited is those already intoxicated.[8]

Alaska has 3.03 liquor licenses outstanding for each 1,000 inhabitants. (See Table 13-3.) This is by far the highest ratio of licenses to population in the United States, and it could be a factor in the state's high per capita consumption level. Also contributing to Alaska's relatively high per capita liquor consumption are the following: (1) *Long hours of sale.* Not many states allow sales for twenty-one hours a day. In North Carolina, for example, all alcoholic beverage control stores are required by law to close by 9 P.M. and may not reopen until 9 A.M. the next morning. (2) *No prohibited days of sale.* In many states liquor stores remain closed on Sundays, and often on a number of holidays as well. (3) *Age requirement.* Reduction of the legal age increases purchase and consumption. Most states still require that a person be twenty-one before he is eligible to purchase hard liquor.

New Jersey

New Jersey has a per capita liquor consumption of 2.27 gallons per year, which is well above the national average for license states. (See Table 13-1.) Several different types of retail liquor licenses are available in this jurisdiction, including the following:

1. *Plenary retail consumption license.* The holder of this license is authorized to sell liquor by the drink for consumption on the premises, or by the bottle for consumption off the premises.

2. *Plenary retail distribution license.* The holder of this license is authorized to sell liquor for off-premises consumption only, and all liquor must be sold in its original container.

3. *Club license.* This license authorizes only sales by the drink for on-premises consumption; and no sales may be made except to club members and their guests. The New Jersey system, like that of most other states, has local-option features.

For example, the governing board of any municipality may enact an ordinance prohibiting the issuance within its corporate limits of any one or all types of the retail liquor licenses listed above.[9]

In New Jersey to sell liquor to any person under twenty-one years of age is a misdemeanor. For the purpose of establishing age, identification cards are issued by the clerk of each county upon application of anyone twenty-one years of age or older. This card contains the holder's date of birth, photograph, and signature. Any licensee who mistakenly sells liquor to a minor because of a failure to request proof of age incurs the same criminal liability as one who intentionally sells to a minor.[10]

One rather unusual feature of this state's liquor law concerns days and hours of sale, with these important determinations being left largely to local governments. It is provided by statute that:

> The governing board or body of each municipality may, as regards said municipality, by ordinance or resolution, limit the hours between which the sale of alcoholic beverages at retail may be made, prohibit the retail sale of alcoholic beverages on Sunday. . . .[11]

And, in addition to the authority of the municipal governing board noted above, New Jersey law also provides for municipal referendums on Sunday sales and hours of sale—with the voters in effect taking the decision out of the hands of the governing board.[12]

While permitting local option on various types of retail sales, state law imposes by formula a limit on the number of establishments that may sell liquor by the drink or by the bottle in a given locality. As amended in 1969, the law now provides that no new retail consumption license shall be issued in a municipality until the number of such licenses is fewer than one for each 3,000 inhabitants; and no new retail distribution license shall be issued until the number of licenses is fewer than one for each 5,000 inhabitants.[13]

Because of the local-option features of the New Jersey system it is difficult to categorize its liquor control laws as being on either the liberal or conservative side. The structure certainly appears more conservative than that of Alaska, with its legalized sales twenty-one hours a day. Also, the New Jersey requirement that a person be twenty-one to make purchases is, of course, not exceeded anywhere in the country. However, Table 13-2 indicates that there are 1.69 liquor licenses per 1,000 population. This compares with a national average of 1.13. The availability of liquor through these numerous outlets may contribute to the high per capita consumption.

Illinois

Illinois is another license state with a per capita liquor intake well in excess of the national average. (See Table 13-1.) Retail liquor licenses for on-premises consumption may be obtained from the State Liquor Control Commission for restaurants, hotels, and clubs;[14] and these establishments are defined in a manner to insure, so far as possible, that their primary purpose is not the sale of liquor.[15] However, there is no provision, such as exists in Colorado, requiring that liquor be served only with meals.

Local-option provisions allow municipalities with a population of 200,000 or less to vote as a unit on the question of prohibiting the sale of liquor. In cities with a population in excess of 200,000 the vote takes place on a precinct basis; and under this system, a single city could have both wet and dry areas.[16]

Statewide law prohibits sales on election days and on Sundays. Cities and counties may, however, suspend the Sunday sale law by enacting an ordinance permitting such sales.[17] Hours of sale for on-premises consumption are not set by state law, but they are subject to local regulation.

Sales to certain categories of individuals are prohibited. It is unlawful to sell liquor to any: (1) person who is under twenty-one years of age; (2) intoxicated person; (3) known habitual drunkard; (4) spendthrift; or (5) other person who is insane, mentally ill, or deficient, or in need of medical treatment.[18] If the experiences of other states are any indication, then these prohibitions are almost totally ineffective except as they apply to purchases by minors.

Illinois has stringent laws relating to liquor in automobiles. The state vehicle code provides:

No person shall transport, carry, possess or have any alcoholic liquor in or upon any motor vehicle except in the original package, with the seal unbroken.[19]

The criminal penalty for violating this provision can range up to $500. This type of law, if properly enforced, discourages having an open bottle in an automobile. It would be far wiser, for example, to abandon or leave behind a partially consumed bottle of expensive whiskey, rather than to risk such a stiff fine. The transportation provision is probably intended to discourage drinking only while operating a vehicle, and it is unlikely that it has much effect on overall consumption.

In Illinois all licenses authorize both on-premises consumption and sales by the bottle for off-premises consumption. The ratio of liquor licenses to inhabitants is high even for a license state—1.90 as compared with an average of 1.21 for other license states. (See Table 13-3.) Per capita liquor consumption declined in this state during 1970 by 1.6 percent; but there is nothing to indicate that the decrease was caused by any change in the law. Perhaps this decline resulted from nationwide adverse economic conditions.

Colorado

Colorado is a license state also; but unlike the three previous jurisdictions examined, this state has a per capita consumption level below the national average for license states. Licenses are obtained from the Secretary of State, and retail licenses are of four general types: (1) liquor store, (2) liquor-licensed drugstore, (3) hotel and restaurant, and (4) club.[20]

An establishment licensed as a retail liquor store may sell the beverages in sealed containers only for consumption off the premises. Any drugstore licensed by the state may also secure a liquor license for sales in the original containers for off-premises consumption. Only liquor stores and drugstores are authorized to sell liquor by the bottle.[21]

A hotel and restaurant license authorizes sales of liquor by the drink, but drinks may be served only with meals.[22] Club licenses may also be obtained that authorize sales by the drink, but such sales may be made only to members and their guests.[23]

Colorado law does not appear to authorize bars where the general public can consume liquor only. In this respect Colorado law is more restrictive than many other states, including Alaska, New Jersey, and Illinois.

The liquor law of this jurisdiction is statewide, but any county or municipality is authorized to prohibit any type or all liquor licenses from being issued within its territorial limits.[24]

Liquor sales are restricted or prohibited altogether on Sundays, election days, and Christmas. On other days sales of liquor by the drink are prohibited from 2 A.M. to 7 A.M., and sales by the bottle may not be made between midnight and 8 A.M.[25] Sales to persons under twenty-one years of age, habitual drunkards, or anyone who is intoxicated are expressly prohibited.[26]

Colorado has enacted a variety of laws intended to encourage strict compliance with its liquor code. Among these are the following provisions: (1) making it unlawful to possess a container of liquor not bearing excise tax stamps; (2) prohibiting the consumption of liquor in any public place, except on premises having a liquor-by-the-drink license; (3) prohibiting an open liquor bottle on the premises of a retail liquor store or liquor-licensed drugstore; and (4) preventing liquor shipments by wholesalers on New Year's Day, Memorial Day, Independence Day, Labor Day, election day, Thanksgiving, or Christmas.[27]

Overall Colorado has a somewhat more restrictive liquor law, and a lower per capita consumption level, than the three states already analyzed. For example: hours during which sales are prohibited are set by state law, rather than left to local ordinance; a person must be twenty-one to purchase alcoholic beverages; drinks may not be served except with meals; and the voters in a given political subdivision can prevent sales altogether. These types of restrictions may account, in part, for Colorado's having a per capita liquor consumption level below the national average for license states.

It should be noted, however, that Colorado law has not prevented a proliferation of liquor outlets. This state has 0.96 on-premises licenses per 1,000 population (compared with 0.62 nationally) and 0.46 off-premises licenses (compared with 0.26 nationally). (See Table 13-2.)

Arizona

Arizona is the last of the license states to be analyzed. This jurisdiction has a per capita consumption average of 1.67 gallons, compared with a national average of 1.98 gallons for license states and 1.47 for control states.[28]

In Arizona licenses are issued and revoked by the State Liquor Board, which is a division of the Department of Liquor Licenses and Control. Types of licenses include:

1. Restaurant licenses, which authorize liquor sales solely for consumption on the licensed premises. To qualify as a restaurant, the establishment must be regularly open for the serving of meals and must have suitable kitchen facilities.[29]

2. Hotel-motel licenses, which authorize sales of liquor by the drink. To qualify for this license, the hotel or motel must have a restaurant in which meals are regularly served.[30]

3. Club licenses, which authorize liquor-by-the-drink sales to members and bona fide guests.[31]

4. Off-sale retailer licenses, which may be acquired by liquor stores for sales of beverages in the original package to be consumed off the licensed premises.[32]

5. On-sale retailer licenses, which authorize both sales in the original container for consumption on or off the licensed premises and sales by the drink for on-premises consumption.[33]

A formula is set out in the statutes to limit the number of on-sale retailer and off-sale retailer licenses that can be issued in a given county. For on-sale licenses, the ratios are as follows: (a) one license for each 1,000 inhabitants for the first 24,000 inhabitants; (b) one license for each 2,000 inhabitants for 25,000-100,000 inhabitants; and (c) one license for each 2,500 inhabitants over 100,000. A similar formula is provided for off-sale or liquor store licenses. These license restrictions based on population do not apply to club, hotel-motel, or restaurant licenses.[34]

Sales are prohibited for both on-premises and off-premises establishments from 1 A.M. to 6 A.M. on weekdays and to noon on Sundays. Liquor sales are also prohibited while the polls are open on election days. Consumption on premises licensed for liquor-by-the-drink sales is unlawful after 1:15 A.M.[35]

In Arizona the legal age for purchasing liquor is twenty-one.[36] Thus Arizona's law, in this respect, is more restrictive than that of several states, including Hawaii, Louisiana, Nebraska, New York, and Maine.[37]

The consumption of liquor in public places, except for licensed premises, is expressly prohibited. Sales to intoxicated or disorderly persons are unlawful; and it is a violation for a licensee to allow such a person to remain on the licensed premises.[38] Liquor cannot be purchased on credit, except when served with a meal that is also charged or when included with a hotel or motel bill.[39] There are 1.53 liquor licenses per 1,000 population, which is well above the national average. (See Table 13-3.)

All of the states thus far examined are license states, and all permit liquor-by-the-drink sales in one form or another. The remaining states to be mentioned are control states with government owned liquor stores. Table 13-2 shows that the control jurisdictions, on the average, have a lower per capita consumption level than the states in which stores are licensed. Thus it is no coincidence that the low-consumption states in this study are all control states.

Oregon

Oregon has government-owned liquor stores and a per capita liquor consumption level that is well below the national average of 1.83 gallons. (See Table 13-2.)

This state has three types of liquor-by-the-drink licenses. The Class A license may be issued to private clubs, veterans' and fraternal organizations, and commercial establishments where food is cooked and served. Licensees must purchase all liquor from the State Liquor Control Commission and may resell it by the glass for consumption on the licensed premises. The Class A license does not allow dancing or any live entertainment on the premises.[40] A Class B license differs from a Class A only in that it allows dancing and other "proper forms" of entertainment on the licensed premises. A Class C license is issued only for private clubs or for fraternal and veterans' organizations. Oregon law limits the total number of licensed premises to one for each 2,000 inhabitants of the state.[41]

Any county or municipality having a population of 500

or more may conduct a local-option election on the question of liquor-by-the-drink sales. In the event of a negative vote in a given locality, all types of by-the-drink sales by all types of licensees are prohibited.[42] In addition liquor-by-the-drink sales are not allowed anywhere in the state from 2:30 A.M. until 7 A.M. and during polling hours on election days.[43]

Sales of hard liquor by the bottle are the exclusive prerogative of the Oregon Liquor Control Commission. The commission is directed by statute to establish control stores and warehouses in such places as are required by public convenience and necessity. One rather interesting provision of law requires the commission to obtain, upon request of an individual, any particular kind or brand of whiskey that is obtainable anywhere in the United States.[44] By way of comparison, the North Carolina Alcoholic Beverage Control (ABC) Board determines what liquor may be sold in control stores, and a disappointed customer's only recourse is to make his purchase outside the state.

Among the restrictions placed on the state-owned ABC system are the following: (1) liquor-control stores may be prohibited in any given city or county by local act; (2) advertising of liquor or the control stores is expressly prohibited; (3) all liquor stores are required by state law to remain closed on Sundays, election days, and legal holidays.[45]

In Oregon it is unlawful to sell or serve liquor to a person under twenty-one years of age. This age restriction is imposed by all of the control states except Maine, which permits sales to persons who have reached their twentieth birthday.[46] Sales to intoxicated persons are also unlawful; and licensees are prohibited from maintaining a noisy, lewd, disorderly, or unsanitary establishment.[47] A violation of the Oregon liquor-control law can result in a substantial penalty. A fine of $500 and a jail sentence of six months may be imposed for a first offense, and a $1,000 fine and one-year sentence for a second offense.[48]

Factors that may contribute to Oregon's relatively low per capita consumption include its state-owned distribution system, local-option provisions making it possible for a community to prohibit liquor-by-the-drink establishments, and an age requirement of twenty-one to purchase alcoholic beverages.

North Carolina

North Carolina is a control state with an annual per capita consumption level of only 1.49 gallons. In this state the liquor-control stores may sell only by the bottle, and as a matter of practice containers of less than one pint are not stocked.[49]

Control stores in North Carolina are established on a local-option basis, and all counties are dry until there is an affirmative vote "for county liquor control stores."[50] The general state law does not provide for municipal liquor store elections because it was originally intended that all referendums on this question be on a county-wide basis. Over the years, however, the legislature has passed many special acts authorizing citywide referendums, and presently there are about as many city liquor stores as county.

Liquor-by-the-drink, as of this date, is not authorized. As a substitute for by-the-drink purchases, North Carolinians have over the years developed a practice known as brown bagging—which simply means taking one's bottle of liquor with him in a brown paper bag. This custom has now been written into the statutes and is described more fully in chapter 11. Certain types of establishments may acquire a permit authorizing consumption of hard liquor on the licensed premises. Among the types of places eligible for such a permit are restaurants and private clubs. And, in the case of clubs, a member's liquor may be stored in a locker on the premises.[51]

Liquor-control stores, whether city or county, are required to close by 9 P.M. and must remain closed until 9 A.M. the next day. Also, sales are totally prohibited on Sundays, election days, and a number of holidays.[52] While the state has set rather conservative hours for liquor stores, the hours set for establishments licensed for on-premises consumption are not conservative. There are absolutely no closing hours for these brown-bagging establishments; and liquor may be lawfully consumed on the licensed premises twenty-four hours per day, 365 days a year. For liberal hours, this tops even Alaska, where establishments are required to close for at least three hours each day.

The ratio of liquor licenses to population in this state is 0.06, which is far below the national average. To state this another way, North Carolina, with a population exceeding 5 million, has only 308 liquor stores and no by-the-drink licensees. (See table 13-4.)

North Carolina, like a number of other states, has tight restrictions relative to the transportation of liquor in a motor vehicle. Only one gallon may be transported in any one vehicle at any time and all open bottles must be kept outside the passenger area—in other words, they must be put in the trunk.[53] Sales to persons under twenty-one are prohibited, and theoretically those convicted of such crimes as public drunkenness and driving under the influence may not purchase liquor.[54]

North Carolina's low per capita consumption of hard liquor may be attributable to such factors as the absence of privately owned liquor stores, the prohibition of liquor by the drink, the requirement that a purchaser be at least twenty-one years of age, and a rather tight control over liquor advertisements. As noted above, liquor-by-the-drink may be just around the corner for some areas of the state. In addition, the 1971 session of the General Assembly made other liberalizing changes in the liquor-control law. It will be most interesting to see whether these changes are followed by a sharp increase in per capita consumption.

Iowa

Iowa, a control state with a local-option liquor-by-the-drink law, has one of the nation's lowest per capita liquor consumption levels.

The Iowa Liquor Control Commission is empowered to establish state liquor stores and to determine the cities and towns in which these stores are to be located.[55] Unlike some control states, Iowa does not provide for local-option elections with respect to the opening and location of these state-owned package stores. Sales by stores are prohibited on Sundays, legal holidays, election days, and any other days designated by the Liquor Control Commission.[56]

Three principal types of liquor-by-the-drink licenses are issued in this state. A Class A license may be obtained by a club and authorizes the sale of liquor to members and their guests.

A Class B license may be issued to a hotel or motel, and a Class C license to a commercial establishment.[57] Apparently a commercial establishment need not serve food in order to qualify for a liquor license.

Municipalities and counties must expressly approve the issuance of all liquor-by-the-drink licenses, and a local governing board can decline to approve any such license for an establishment located within the territory over which it has jurisdiction. A referendum may be held in a given area to determine voter sentiment on liquor-by-the-drink, but the vote is advisory only and does not bind the city or county governing board.[58]

Sales by the drink are prohibited between 2 A.M. and 7 A.M. on weekdays, and from 1 A.M. on Sunday until 7 A.M. on the following Monday.[59] Sales to persons under the age of twenty-one are unlawful, but the law allows a minor to drink in his own home with his parents' permission.[60]

Consumption of liquor on a public street or in any other public place (except for licensed premises) is prohibited. Public intoxication is likewise unlawful, and conviction can carry a penalty of $100 and thirty days in jail.[61]

The Iowa Liquor Control Act contains one unusual provision concerning indemnity for one injured by an intoxicated person. Any person who is injured in his person, property, or means of support by one who is intoxicated has a cause of action against any licensee who sold or gave liquor to such person while he was intoxicated. To insure that a licensee can satisfy a judgment obtained pursuant to this provision, Iowa law requires all liquor licensees to furnish proof of financial responsibility. This can be done by means of a liability policy or by posting a bond.[62]

Liquor licenses are not required for some places and purposes. Thus private social gatherings on premises not open to the public are not subject to Iowa's licensing law. Also, persons attending a convention or other meeting may bring their own liquor rather than making by-the-drink purchases.[63]

Iowa's ratio of off-premises (liquor-by-the-drink) licenses to population is 0.07 per 1,000, compared with a national average of 0.26.

National Trends

I

First, it should be noted that per capita consumption has been steadily increasing in the United States since the end of prohibition. Table 13-5 shows that in 1934 only twenty-eight jurisdictions had legal liquor, and per capita consumption was only 0.65 gallons.[64] Five years later there were forty-six wet states, and per capita consumption had risen to 1.08. By 1950, forty-seven jurisdictions had hard liquor and per capita consumption was up to 1.29. Since 1965 there have been no totally dry states, and per capita consumption continues to increase each year. The liquor intake per person has more than doubled since 1935, and the end is not yet in sight.

Table 13-5
Apparent Consumption of Distilled Spirits Since Repeal

		States		Per
Year	Wine Gallons	Number [a]	Population	Capita
1934...........	57,964,788	28	88,706,909	0.65
1935...........	89,670,446	41	109,041,649	0.82
1936...........	122,117,965	43	113,235,914	1.08
1937...........	135,352,692	44	116,716,065	1.16
1938...........	126,892,827	45	120,711,232	1.05
1939...........	134,653,694	46	124,554,618	1.08
1940...........	144,991,927	46	125,662,000	1.15
1941...........	158,156,921	46	127,019,000	1.25
1942...........	190,248,257	46	127,736,000	1.49
1943...........	145,529,454	46	127,657,000	1.14
1944...........	166,679,635	46	126,779,000	1.31
1945...........	190,130,760	46	126,338,000	1.50
1946...........	230,981,503	46	133,988,000	1.72
1947...........	181,645,635	46	137,397,000	1.32
1948...........	171,021,257	46	140,082,000	1.22
1949...........	169,545,152	47	144,353,000	1.17
1950...........	190,019,680	47	146,823,000	1.29
1951...........	193,766,629	47	149,007,000	1.30
1952...........	183,686,737	47	151,385,000	1.21
1953...........	194,663,221	47	153,983,000	1.26
1954...........	189,470,688	47	156,873,000	1.21

1955..........	199,570,748	47	159,959,000	1.25
1956..........	215,225,286	47	162,832,000	1.32
1957..........	212,073,384	47	165,875,000	1.28
1958..........	215,465,819	47	168,788,000	1.28
1959..........	225,453,345	48	171,904,000	1.31
1960..........	234,714,557	49	176,512,262	1.33
1961..........	241,449,065	49	180,082,000	1.34
1962..........	253,700,966	49	182,879,000	1.39
1963..........	258,979,291	49	185,687,000	1.39
1964..........	275,861,906	49	188,365,000	1.46
1965..........	292,987,572	49	190,785,000	1.54
1966[b].......	307,756,120	50	195,139,000	1.58
1967..........	323,498,937	50	197,124,000	1.64
1968..........	344,067,256	50	199,082,000	1.73
1969..........	361,682,018	50	201,130,000	1.80
1970..........	370,079,963	50	202,415,000	1.83

[a]Includes District of Columbia as a state; excludes Hawaii.
[b]Includes gallonage for Mississippi, July—December.
Source: *Distilled Spirits Industry Annual Statistical Review,* 1970.

II

As noted before, states with government-owned liquor stores on the average have lower per capita consumption levels than states with privately owned stores. This fact is well illustrated by Table 13-2, which shows a national average of 1.83 gallons per person, a license state average of 1.98, and a control state average of 1.47. Thus the license states have an average per capita consumption level approximately 25 percent higher than control states.

III

Apparently there is also a relationship between the number of retail liquor establishments in a given state and that state's consumption level. Among the license states, for example, only Alaska, Nevada, and Wisconsin have a ratio of more than two licensees per 1,000 inhabitants, and each of these jurisdictions has a per capita consumption level considerably above the national average. By way of comparison Arizona, Oklahoma, and Georgia, three license states with a low license-to-population ratio, also have relatively low per capita consumption levels. (See Tables 13-1 through 13-4.)

IV

The data contained in Tables 13-3 and 13-4 show that only Oklahoma, South Carolina, and North Carolina still totally prohibit liquor-by-the-drink sales: Tables 13-1 and 13-2 show that all three of these states have low per capita consumption levels. In fact, North Carolina, which is the highest of the three, has a level some 20 percent below the national average for all states. The argument is often made that allowing liquor to be purchased by the drink, rather than only by the bottle, promotes moderation. This may be true, but it apparently does not promote low per capita consumption.

Conclusions

From the foregoing the following general observations can be made:

1. As more jurisdictions have legalized liquor, the nationwide per capita consumption level has increased dramatically.

2. States with privately owned liquor stores tend to have a higher per capita consumption level than those with government-owned stores.

3. Per capita consumption tends to be greater in those states with a high ratio of liquor outlets to total population.

4. States without liquor-by-the-drink establishments tend to have lower consumption levels than those with liquor-by-the-drink.

Besides these trends, there is some evidence of a relationship between high per capita consumption and such factors as late closing hours for liquor outlets and the lowering of the age requirement for purchases of hard liquor.

The general conclusions outlined above are based on broad trends, to which there are numerous exceptions. Alabama and Iowa, for example, both have liquor-by-the-drink, but still have a consumption level below North Carolina, which now permits sales by the bottle only.

Despite these exceptions, however, the conclusion seems inescapable that liberal liquor laws and high per capita consumption levels go hand in hand. What cannot be presently answered is whether enactment of permissive liquor laws is the cause or the result of an increasingly wet American electorate.

CHAPTER 14

Government Control Measures to Prevent Hazardous Drinking

Robert Popham, M.A.
Wolfgang Schmidt, D.JUR.
Jan de Lint, M.A.

OVER THE YEARS a substantial part of the research endeavour of the Addiction Research Foundation of Ontario has been concerned with the causes of regional and temporal variation in the prevalence of alcohol consumption and alcohol problems. Among the possible contributing factors which have been studied, special attention has been given to certain legislative and other governmental measures intended to prevent the problems of alcohol. Our purpose is to review this aspect of the work and discuss its practical implications. However, it should be stated at once that none of our results to date suggest any means of prevention in the absolute sense of the term. But they do indicate how—at least in theory—further increases in prevalence might be prevented, and even a limited reduction brought about.

The Primary Data

From an epidemiological standpoint, the initial task was to establish that there was, in fact, substantial variation in rates of alcohol problems from one place or period to another. For this purpose suitable indices were required since the prevalence of these problems is not regularly reported as such

by any jurisdiction. Following the lead of earlier workers—
especially E. M. Jellinek[1]—we began by gathering and evaluating statistics of alcoholic beverage sales, arrests for drunkenness and other alcohol-related offences, hospital admissions for
alcoholic conditions, mortality from causes associated with
heavy alcohol use such as liver cirrhosis, and various other
regularly reported alcohol-associated events. We did this for
many countries and parts of countries, and for as many years
back in time as we could in each case.[2]

Considerable work was done with these data but for
present purposes just two results are important:

1. We satisfied ourselves that, despite certain shortcom-
ings, several of the statistics could be employed as valid indicators of the magnitude of alcohol problems in an area. Most
particularly, reported liver cirrhosis mortality proved to vary
in close association with variations in the prevalence of alcoholism. This association was assumed by Jellinek in order to
develop an alcoholism prevalence estimation formula;[3] it has
been verified since through case-finding surveys and other
methods in Ontario and elsewhere.[4]

2. We found considerable differences in the indicators
from one area to another, and in most jurisdictions there was
also substantial variation through time. This variation was not
due primarily to errors in the indices but presumably to real
variation in the amount of alcohol consumed and in the
prevalence of alcohol problems.[5]

The Monopoly System, Outlets, and Hours of Sale

The next task was to examine certain control measures
widely believed to affect the prevalence of alcohol problems.
For this purpose, jurisdictions having a government-con-
trolled monopoly system were compared with those in which
liquor sales were in the hands of private enterprise. The old
questions of hours of sale and outlet rates (that is, the number
of stores and public drinking places per unit of population)
were studied; and we looked at the effect of diversification of
licensed drinking places, notably, the introduction of cocktail
and dining lounges in Ontario.

Table 14-1
Mean Apparent Alcohol Consumption in Spirits, Wine, and Beer, Liver Cirrhosis Mortality and Index of Urbanism for 17 Monopoly and 30 License States of the U.S.A. 1964

	Monopoly States		License States		t-test
	Mean	S.D.	Mean	S.D.	
Spirits Consumption[1]	3.45	1.22	4.03	1.63	N.S.
Wine Consumption[2]	0.59	0.29	0.83	0.44	N.S.
Beer Consumption[3]	4.04	1.21	4.17	1.25	N.S.
Total Alcohol Consumption[4]	8.08	2.28	9.07	2.93	N.S.
Liver Cirrhosis Mortality Rates[5]	15.5	3.92	18.6	6.34	N.S.
Index of Urbanism[6]	26.41	13.13	35.00	16.25	N.S.

[1] Based on data in *Apparent Consumption of Distilled Spirits, 1964*, Distilled Spirits Institute, Washington, D.C.

[2] Based on data in *Wine Institute Bulletin, 1964*, Wine Advisory Board, San Francisco, Calif. California, which is a license state, has been omitted in the case of wine consumption. When included the t-test shows a significant difference at the 5 percent probability level.

[3] Based on data in *Brewers Almanac, 1964*, New York, N.Y.

[4] All consumption figures are expressed as liters of absolute alcohol per capita population aged eighteen and older.

[5] Based on data in *Liver Cirrhosis Death Rate of Population Twenty-one Years and Older, 1964*, U.S. Dept. Health, Education and Welfare, Washington, D.C.

[6] From W. Schmidt and J. Bronetto, "Death from Liver Cirrhosis and Specific Alcoholic Beverage Consumption: An Ecological Study," *American Journal of Public Health* 52(1962): 1473-1482.

Generally, these variables did not seem to be related in any important degree to the indicators of alcohol problems employed. As shown in Table 14-1, the monopoly states of the United States of America (about one-third) did not differ significantly from the license states in level of consumption or liver cirrhosis mortality. The slightly larger values for the license states may reflect the differences in urbanism between the two groups. This factor is well known to be associated with variations in alcohol consumption and alcoholism;[6] but its influence may depend primarily on the higher income levels prevailing in more urban areas.[7]

Similar findings have been reported by Simon with respect to per capita consumption under each system[8] and by Jellinek who analyzed trends over the period 1930 to 1945. Jellinek could find no evidence of an effect on "rate of inebriety," and in the case of consumption trends he concluded that "the monopoly system did not prevent fairly large increases; nor did the license system lack small increases."[9] However, in contrasting monopoly and license states, one is not comparing "control" with "no control." There are many important differences in the administration of the monopoly system among the states which have adopted it.[10] And there is evidence that in countries with a government monopoly which has emphasized vigorous control rather than maximization of revenue, a substantial decrease in alcohol consumption and attendant problems may be achieved.[11] But in these cases, the question is whether or not the particular controls which proved effective could not have been exercised as well under a licensing system as under state ownership.

Hours of sale in both package stores and public drinking places are now, and have been for many years, widely regulated in the belief that this is an effective control measure. In Toronto, an apparent correlation with tavern closing hours was found in the pattern of arrests for drunkenness exhibited between 8 A.M. Monday and 8 A.M. the following Sunday. However, when arrests were plotted for each hour from 8 A.M. Sunday to 8 A.M. Monday morning—during which time all taverns were closed—an almost identical pattern emerged.[12] This suggests that hours of sale reflect the drinking habits of the community rather than the reverse. On the other hand, the closing hours which prevailed at the time of the study had been in force for many years and originally may have shaped the characteristic pattern observed.

The effects of hours of sale deserve further research, preferably utilizing jurisdictions in which there have been substantial changes and for which statistical indicators of drinking and alcohol problems are available for long periods

before and after. Certainly in the United Kingdom, where
closing hours have been deliberately manipulated in an effort
to control insobriety, there is some conviction that this is an
effective approach. For example. Shadwell contends that measures such as "shorter hours and higher taxation . . . have
proved really efficacious, while other—particularly state
ownership and control, the reduction [in number] of licensed
houses, alteration of premises, disinterested management and
supply of food—have failed to exert any perceptible influences
on sobriety and public order."[13]

Over the centuries governments have frequently sought
to minimize the prevalence of insobriety by reducing the
number of sales outlets, especially those for on-premise consumption. The assumption appears to be that the more places
there are for people to drink, the more they will consume and
the more drunkenness there will be. The available data for
Canada did not support this assumption.[14] Indeed, for the
provinces and major cities, the highest drunkenness rates
tended to occur where there were fewest outlets per unit of
population. In Ontario, prior to prohibition in 1916, alcohol
consumption, liver cirrhosis mortality, and drunkenness conviction rates were all comparatively high; so also were tavern
rates. But following the reintroduction of on-premise outlets
in 1934, the number of such establishments per 100,000 has
remained much below pre-prohibition rates. Yet the indicators
mentioned have all achieved levels during the last twenty years
markedly higher than in any previous period for which figures
are available.

The results of a correlation analysis of data for England
and the United States are shown in Table 14-2. All four
coefficients are nonsignificant, and those for England again
suggest a slightly inverse relationship. This has also been
reported by mass observation for a different series.[15] The
reason, as suggested by Ahlström-Laakso, may be that fewer
taverns mean fewer places to become drunk unobserved by the
police, and a greater probability that heavy drinking will occur
in parks and other public places.[16]

A closely related question concerns the consequences of
tavern diversification. Beginning in 1947, cocktail and dining
lounges were permitted in Ontario. Essentially, this meant a

Table 14-2
Correlations Between Outlet Rates and
Indicators of Alcohol Problems in
England and the United States

Series	No.	Variables	Linear Coef.
English county boroughs	84	Convictions for drunkenness and on-premise licenses per 10,000 population[1]	-.18
English counties (excl. boroughs)	52	Convictions for drunkenness and on-premise licenses per 10,000 population[1]	-.19
States of the U.S.A. (incl. D.C.)	49	Taverns per 100,000 and alcohol consumption per capita aged 15 and older[2]	+.16
States of the U.S.A. (incl. D.C.)	49	Taverns per 100,000 and alcoholics per 100,000 aged 20 and older[2]	-.01

[1] Based on data in Home Office Licensing Statistics 1938, H.M. Stat. Off., London 1939, tables H and J.

[2] Based on population and tavern data in Beverage Distilling Industry: Facts and Figures 1934-1945, Lic. Bev. Ind., New York 1946, p. 164 et seq.; and on consumption and alcoholism rates in E. M. Jellinek, "Recent Trends in Alcoholism and in Alcohol Consumption," Quarterly Journal of Studies on Alcohol 8(1947):1-47, tables 10 and 17.

slight increase in outlet rates, the sale of spirituous liquors for on-premise consumption, and higher standards of decor for the establishments licensed to sell such beverages. Pre-existing outlets catered primarily to the working classes; the new establishments were intended to attract a middle-class patronage.

In a preliminary attempt to study the effects of these innovations, changes in consumption, drunkenness, and alcoholism rates before and after 1947 were examined. Trends in the adjacent Province of Manitoba—where no significant changes in liquor legislation had occurred over the period—were included by way of control data. The results are shown in Table 14-3.

Table 14-3
Comparison of Changes in Consumption, Drunkenness, and Alcoholism Rates in Ontario and Manitoba Before and After the Diversification of Taverns in Ontario 1947[1]

Year	Alcohol Consumption[2]		Drunkenness Convictions[3]		Alcoholism Rate[4]	
	Ontario	Manitoba	Ontario	Manitoba	Ontario	Manitoba
1939	3.55	2.09	650	185	1095	930
1946	5.82	4.27	962	502	1150	970
1947	6.50	5.27	996	463	1290	925
1954	7.73	6.00	1070	672	1860	1460
% Change (1939-1946)	+64	+104	+48	+171	+5	+4
% Change (1947-1954)	+19	+ 14	+7	+45	+44	+58

[1] The data used and primary sources are to be found in R.E. Popham and W. Schmidt, *Statistics of Alcohol Use and Alcoholism in Canada 1871-1956.* (Toronto: University of Toronto Press, 1958).
[2] Liters of absolute alcohol per capita aged 15 and older.
[3] Per 100,000 persons aged 15 and older.
[4] Estimated by means of the Jellinek Formula adapted to Canadian data and expressed as alcoholics per 100,000 aged 20 and older. See R.E. Popham, "The Jellinek Alcoholism Estimation Formula and Its Application to Canadian Data," *Quarterly Journal of Studies on Alcohol* 17(1956):559-593.

The more rural character of Manitoba and its lower average income level are reflected in lower rates throughout than in Ontario. However, with the exception of alcoholism rates, the percentage increases were much greater in both provinces before than after 1947. From 1947 to 1954 consumption increased somewhat more in Ontario than in Manitoba, but drunkenness and alcoholism rates showed greater increases in Manitoba.

Findings similar to these have been reported by others. Thus, Bryant could find no evidence that increases in consumption or alcohol-related offences could be attributed to the introduction of liquor-by-the-drink in the state of Washington.[17] With respect to the reduction of outlet rates, we have already alluded to work in the United Kingdom. In the United

States, Entine concluded that limiting the number of package stores did not reduce off-premises consumption.[18] On the other hand, Simon found per capita consumption to be related positively to outlet rates, but felt, on further analysis, that this variable was "more likely to respond to consumption, rather than be a cause of consumption."[19]

Finally, a word should be said about the case of extremely low accessibility. The variation in number of outlets with which we have been concerned ranges from situations where they are ubiquitous to those where some customers are mildly inconvenienced. In certain areas, such as parts of northern Canada, the nearest outlet to some communities may take a costly day to reach. Under these circumstances, the introduction of new outlets may have an appreciable effect on consumption. Indeed, the results of Pekka Kuusi's famous sales experiment in rural Finland would seem to support this conclusion.[20] At the same time, there was little evidence of an increase in alcohol problems and some evidence of a compensatory decline in illicit production.

The Effect of Relative Price

At first the failure to find a clear and positive relationship between outlet rates and our indicators of alcohol problems was rather puzzling. As previously noted, regulation of the number of outlets as a measure to reduce consumption and insobriety is often encountered in the history of alcohol legislation. And among members of the public there is a widespread notion that this aspect of accessibility is an important factor in alcohol problems. However, local opinion is divided on the topic: some cite the "forbidden fruit" concept and argue that if alcohol were everywhere available man would not desire it so much and would drink in a moderate and civilized manner. Others argue that an increase in accessibility would simply increase his temptation to drink and so there would be more abuse.[21]

We came to feel that the problem lay in the assumption underlying both of these views, notably an assumption fostered especially by the temperance movement in this and other countries, that the demand for alcoholic beverages is qualitatively different from that for other commodities and consequently not subject to the same factors as affect the demand for other consumer goods. For example, probably no one would expect an increase in the number of television stores to increase the prevalence of television sets. Actually, if there are too few stores some customers simply will be inconvenienced, and if there are too many some stores will go out of business. We think the situation is about the same in the case of alcoholic beverage outlets (at least, within certain limits: the effect of total prohibition or extreme rarity is a special case). On the other hand, just as one would expect sales of television sets to be influenced by their cost, so also this would seem a likely, if not obvious, determinant in the case of alcoholic beverage consumption.

Certainly governments have recognized for centuries that the taxation of alcoholic beverages is a lucrative source of revenue. And there are probably few, if any, jurisdictions today (where such beverages are legally sold at all) in which there is not some tax imposed upon them. However, it is now rather uncommon to find price control through taxation justified as a means to reduce consumption and inebriety. In older statutes and government reports this was quite frequently done. To give one local example, in the Third Report of the Liquor Control Board of Ontario 1929, the following assertions are made: "Economic conditions, rather than laws, influence the gross sale of liquor . . . Beyond all doubt consumption increases with low prices, and decreases with high prices." And with reference to decreased drunkenness in the United Kingdom, despite the comparatively large number of outlets, it is said: "While propaganda has been carried on against drunkenness, the best informed workers and observers are generally of the opinion that the higher cost of spirits coupled with industrial conditions and unemployment largely contribute to the decreased consumption" (p. 10).

With a few notable exceptions,[22] contemporary students of alcohol problems have given little or no attention to the effects of price variation. There have been several econometric studies, but these have been concerned mainly with methodological and theoretical questions, and they consider only per capita consumption as a dependent variable.[23] Accordingly, it seemed to us worthwhile to extend Seeley's earlier work on the topic, and to deal with the principal issues raised by the results. The important variable, as Seeley had noted, was not absolute price but price relative to income, that is, the apparent ability to buy. Hence, this index was used throughout: the average price of a given quantity of alcohol expressed as a fraction of average disposable (real) income.[24] In Figure 14-1, the remarkably close association of alcohol consumption and liver cirrhosis mortality and the inverse relationship with relative price are shown graphically for a period of forty years in Ontario. The data upon which the graph was based are provided in Table 14-4.

The interrelationships of the three variables, as reflected in both temporal and spatial series, were also examined for as many other jurisdictions as the relevant data could be readily obtained.[25] The results are summarized in Table 14-5.

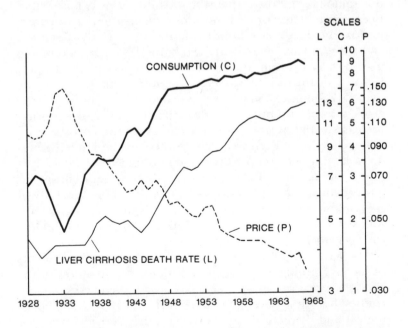

Figure 14-1. Alcohol price and consumption and liver cirrhosis death rates, Ontario, 1928–1967.

Table 14-4
Consumption of Alcohol, Relative Price of
Alcohol and Deaths from Liver Cirrhosis,
Ontario 1928-1967

Year	Alcohol Consumption[1]	Relative Price[2]	Deaths from Liver Cirrhosis[3]
1928	2.81	.102	4.4
1929	3.09	.099	4.1
1930	3.00	.101	3.8
1931	2.64	.112	4.0
1932	2.05	.148	4.2
1933	1.77	.153	4.2
1934	2.09	.137	4.2
1935	2.41	.112	4.2
1936	3.05	.097	4.2
1937	3.36	.086	4.5
1938	3.68	.085	5.0
1939	3.55	.082	5.2
1940	3.64	.074	5.0
1941	4.00	.068	4.9
1942	4.73	.063	5.0
1943	4.91	.064	4.8
1944	4.46	.069	4.6
1945	4.86	.064	4.9
1946	5.82	.069	5.4
1947	6.50	.065	6.0
1948	7.09	.057	6.5
1949	7.18	.058	7.2
1950	7.23	.055	7.7
1951	7.23	.052	7.5
1952	7.32	.051	7.7
1953	7.64	.055	8.3
1954	7.73	.056	8.7
1955	7.55	.047	8.8
1956	7.91	.045	9.4
1957	7.86	.044	10.3
1958	7.96	.043	11.0
1959	7.77	.043	11.5
1960	8.14	.043	11.8
1961	8.14	.043	11.6
1962	8.23	.041	11.3
1963	8.46	.040	11.4
1964	8.73	.039	11.9
1965	8.77	.038	12.6
1966	9.18	.039	12.9
1967	8.91	.035	13.2

Table 14-4 (continued)

1 Liters of absolute alcohol per capita aged 15 and older.
2 Average price of 10 liters of absolute alcohol divided by personal disposable income.
3 Centered two-year moving averages of deaths from liver cirrhosis per 100,000 aged 20 and older, corrected to allow for the effects of the Sixth Revision of the I.L.D.C.D. For sources of primary data for this table see note 1 to Table 14-3.

In most cases the index of alcoholism (liver cirrhosis mortality) is significantly associated with apparent per capita consumption and is an inverse function of relative price. There are exceptions. In Finland and the United Kingdom, where the level of consumption is comparatively low, the associations are less striking. And in the United Kingdom a negative correlation is obtained for the consumption and alcoholism indices. There are probably several reasons for this, including insufficient variation to fulfill the assumptions underlying this type of correlation analysis.[26] Nevertheless, the overall picture is clear. In general, where or when relative price is high, these indices of consumption and alcoholism are low and vice versa.

Thirty years ago, Jolliffe and Jellinek argued that the death rate from liver cirrhosis was closely related to alcohol consumption rates.[27] Since then a substantial body of epidemiological evidence has been accumulated to support this contention.[28] Nevertheless, a criticism still commonly heard is that a chronic disease cannot be expected to respond so quickly to transitory changes in the etiological factor. However, as Terris has pointed out, in the case of liver cirrhosis:

> This phenomenon is consistent with the clinical course of the disease. In many cases the cirrhotic process can be halted and decompensation prevented by avoiding further use of alcohol. Conversely, resumption of heavy alcohol use after a period of abstinence can decompensate a previously injured liver in a relatively short period of time.[29]

In practice, one would expect a slight lag in the mortality trend since advanced cases probably will die prematurely even in the absence of drinking. Such a lag is quite evident in the Ontario trend.

A further illustration of the role of relative price is provided by the international data in Table 14-6. As already

Table 14-5
Correlations Between Alcohol Comsumption, Liver Cirrhosis Mortality, and
the Relative Price of Alcohol in Various Temporal and Regional Series[1]

Series		Coefficients of Correlation		
		Consump- tion & Mortality	Consump- tion & Price	Mortality & Price
Temporal				
Canada	– 21 years	+ .96*	– .99*	– .93*
Nova Scotia	– 22 years	+ .68*	– .98*	– .82*
Quebec	– 16 years	+ .57*	– .90*	– .63*
Ontario	– 21 years	+ .96*	– .94*	– .90*
Manitoba	– 22 years	+ .88*	– .94*	– .90*
Saskatchewan	– 17 years	+ .75	– .78	– .66
Alberta	– 21 years	+ .94	– .95	– .86
United States	– 25 years	+ .60	– .79	– .92
Australia	– 22 years	+ .65	– .46	+ .06
Belgium	– 25 years	+ .75	+ .42	– .80
Finland	– 25 years	+ .78	– .37	– .34
France	– 12 years	+ .94	– .99	– .96
Netherlands	– 28 years	+ .43	– .54	– .11
Sweden	– 26 years	+ .52*	– .75*	– .38*
United Kingdom	– 21 years	– .68	+ .04	– .59
Regional				
9 Provinces of Canada		+ .81	– .92	– .79
46 States of the U.S.A.		+ .76	– .80	– .71
11 European & Other Countries		+ .78*	– .57*	– .71*

[1] For sources and tabulations of the primary data employed, see the reference to the original studies cited in the text. In all cases the consumption index comprised reported sales in units of absolute alcohol per capita of drinking age. Death rates were unstandardized but expressed in terms of the adult population. The price index was the average price of a unit of absolute beverage alcohol divided by the average disposable income per adult. All of the time series were for periods ending in the mid or late 1950s. The coefficients followed by an asterisk are second order. Generally, however, curvilinear analysis did not explain significantly more variation than linear correlation.

indicated, in countries where alcoholic beverages are relatively cheap, the per capita consumption is usually high. However, the association is certainly not perfect and such exceptions as the Netherlands are especially noteworthy.

Specific Consumption and Differential Taxation

We felt that before relative price control could be accepted as a potential means to control the prevalence of alcoholism, two further questions in particular must be answered. The first was the validity of the common assertion that the different types of alcoholic beverages are not equally to blame for pathological drinking. Frequently this view reduces to the contention that beer is the drink of moderation and spirituous liquor is the real culprit. This view has often been embodied in reports and briefs to government on the liquor question; and a few students of alcohol problems have argued in a similar vein.[30] If true, then *differential* taxation might be preferred so as not to penalize unnecessarily the moderate drinker, that is, the user of a beverage shown to be relatively harmless.

Again we examined the literature and documentary statistics for many different jurisdictions but this time taking into account the class of alcoholic beverage favoured: beer, wine, or spirits. On an international basis we failed to find evidence to indict any one class of beverage over another;[31] in some areas beer was the exclusive beverage of choice of many pathological drinkers, for example, Australia,[32] Czechoslovakia,[33] and southern Germany;[34] nor was the prevalence of alcoholism by any means low in these areas. In our own clinical alcoholic population in Ontario, beer was commonly the principal beverage used by the patients.[35] And in the medical literature generally, there was a substantial body of evidence implicating heavy beer consumption in ailments such as liver cirrhosis and myocardial disease.[36] Wallgren and Lelbach have recently reviewed the experimental and clinical data bearing on this question and concluded that type of beverage is largely irrelevant. Total absolute alcohol consumed was the significant variable.[37]

Table 14-6
Cost of Beverage Alcohol,
Consumption and Liver Cirrhosis Mortality
in Various Countries

Country	Alcohol Consumption[1]	Relative Price[2]	Deaths from Liver Cirrhosis[3]
France	24.66	.016	51.7
Italy	18.00	.027	30.5
Portugal	17.57	.023	48.0
Austria	14.47	.025	38.5
W. Germany	13.63	.026	29.0
Australia	10.71	.029	7.8
Czechoslovakia	10.27	.080	14.8
Canada	8.95	.029	11.6
Belgium	8.42	.022	14.2
United Kingdom	7.66	.057	4.1
Rep. Ireland	7.64	.092	5.0
Denmark	7.50	.069	11.6
Netherlands	6.19	.028	5.7
Finland	4.16	.117	5.4

[1] Liters of alcohol per capita aged 15 and older. See: J. de Lint and W. Schmidt, "The Epidemiology of Alcoholism," *Biological Basis of Alcoholism*, ed. Y. Israel and J. Mardones (New York: Wiley, 1971), pp. 423-442.

[2] The cost of 10 liters of absolute alcohol as contained in the least expensive beverage available to the consumer divided by personal disposable income. Data were obtained through personal communications with the appropriate government departments in each country.

[3] Per 100,000 aged 20 and older. Data were obtained from the *Demographic Yearbook 1966*, United Nations, N.Y., 1967.

Table 14-7 shows that when consumption is held constant by pairing countries with a similar per drinker rate, liver cirrhosis death rates show little relationship to the contribution of spirituous liquors.

Of special interest are the figures for Belgium and

Table 14-7
Liver Cirrhosis Mortality, and the Contribution
of Spirituous Liquors to Total Consumption
in Countries with Similar Per Drinker Consumption Rates

Country	Per Drinker Consumption[1]	% Contribution of Spirituous Liquors to Total Consumption	Liver Cirrhosis Mortality[2]
Austria	16.0	18.2	38.5
W. Germany	16.0	21.2	29.0
Luxembourg	12.5	13.0	37.2
Hungary	12.5	21.8	14.4
United Kingdom	10.9	14.2	4.1
Rep. Ireland	10.9	34.4	5.0
Denmark	9.4	17.2	11.6
Belgium	9.3	15.0	14.2
Finland	5.9	46.7	5.4
Norway	5.9	45.8	5.3

[1] Consumption data were obtained from: *Dutch Distillers Association Annual Report for 1968*, Schiedam, April 1969. The percentage of users among persons aged 15 and older was estimated from available survey data for each country.

[2] Per 100,000 aged 20 and older. Data were obtained from the *Demographic Yearbook 1966*. United Nations, N.Y., 1967.

Denmark. In these countries large increases in the cost of spirituous liquors led initially to a considerable decline in overall consumption. Moreover, in Denmark at least, this was apparently responsible for a sharp drop in the prevalence of delirium tremens.[38] It may well be that the frequency of certain acute alcoholic states can be affected through a reduction in access to spirituous liquors. The increased cost of spirits seemed to induce a compensatory shift to beer, and in the long run, a substantial prevalence of alcoholism was again achieved.

Currently, the evidence most frequently cited in support of arguments for a tax differential favoring beer has been that generated by the experiments of Goldberg and his associates on relative intoxication potential.[39] Recently, this work was more or less replicated by a Canadian group with similar results.[40] The experiments demonstrated that a higher peak blood alcohol level and correspondingly greater psychophysical impairment were achieved after the ingestion of spirits than after ingestion of the same quantity of alcohol in beer. The validity of this difference, under the experimental conditions imposed, has been generally accepted by workers in the field for some years. Indeed, it is in accord with an established pharmacological principle respecting the effect of the concentration of alcohol ingested on rate of absorption. However, the relevant questions are whether the finding is likely to be applicable to actual human drinking habits and whether any meaningful difference which may exist is reflected in the type or prevalence of alcohol problems encountered.

As to the first question, the experimental conditions would seem to have been far from realistic analogues of most human drinking practices. A single, large dose of beverage alcohol had to be consumed in a short period of time, and no further drinking was permitted. In addition, drinking took place after a protracted fast (usually at least twelve hours). The largest difference was obtained when the distilled beverage was taken undiluted—a mode of consumption still common in Scandinavian and Slavic countries but comparatively rare elsewhere. Kalant and LeBlanc have just recently completed a comparison of the effects of beer, wine, and spirits in which subjects achieved substantial blood alcohol levels through progressive drinking.[41] The minimum time since the subjects last ate was forty-five minutes. Under these more realistic circumstances, differences among the blood alcohol curves for the three classes of beverage virtually disappeared; nor were any significant differences in impairment found on the performance tests employed.

With respect to the second issue—the social significance of any difference in effect between spirits and beer—the results of a careful study of the role of alcohol in traffic accidents, conducted by Borkenstein and his colleagues, are particularly enlightening.[42] This study determined the blood alcohol levels of a large sample of drivers in accidents and of a control sample of drivers stopped at random within the constraints of an appropriate statistical design. The drivers were all interviewed to determine the type of alcoholic beverage they typically consumed. The results confirmed earlier work in that a higher overall proportion of drinking drivers was found in the accident group, and the probability of accident involvement increased rapidly with higher blood alcohol levels. But in addition, significantly more of the accident drivers (64 percent) than of the control drivers (58 percent) reported beer to be their beverage of choice. Conversely, fewer in the accident (30 percent) than in the control group (36 percent) reported spirits to be their customary beverage. It was further shown that the proportion of the control group who described themselves as beer drinkers increased greatly with higher blood levels. Among those not found to have been drinking at the time of the test, the ratio was 1.5 beer drinkers to one spirits drinker; among those with blood alcohol levels of .08 percent or higher, the ratio was 4:1.

These results certainly do not provide ground for complacency among those who contend that beer is a harmless drink of moderation. This is not to say, however, that the study is entirely conclusive. Although the likelihood of a discrepancy in most cases seems small, the possibility cannot be altogether discounted that a driver's beverage of choice was not the beverage which produced the blood alcohol level detected. Also it may be argued that the reports of beverage preferences were influenced by a belief that beer is less impairing than spirits. An accident driver, in particular, might feel that reporting beer rather than spirits consumption would be less damaging to his position. However, the investigators made every reasonable effort to divorce themselves from the activities of the police, and to reassure drivers that information given would have no bearing on official investigations.

We conclude that the available evidence, pertaining to both acute and chronic effects, offers little to justify the view that beer is a comparatively harmless beverage of moderation while spirituous liquor is a comparatively harmful beverage of excess. At the same time, if the stomach is empty and there is determination to become as drunk as possible in as short a time as possible, a distilled beverage is to be preferred. For the same reason, the theoretical risks of severe alcoholic states such as delirium tremens or acute alcohol poisoning may be greater in the case of spirits. However, in practice, these risks have not been convincingly shown to materialize as significant social problems. On the other hand, a dependence on alcohol can be maintained as well on beer or wine as on spirits. Indeed, the beverage of choice of an alcoholic seems to roughly reflect the beverage preference dominant in his sociocultural milieu, with a distinct tendency toward the cheaper source of alcohol when his financial resources are limited.[43]

With respect to the last point, a detailed analysis of data for the United States showed that the best index of liver cirrhosis mortality was per capita wine consumption.[44] The reason appeared to be that alcoholics consume a larger proportion of all wine sold than of spirits and beer. The most likely explanation for the attraction of wine to these drinkers was its relatively low cost. This interpretation was in accord with the results of a direct study of alcohol buying in Ontario.[45] There too, certain domestic dessert wines were the cheapest source of alcohol (on a cost per ounce of pure alcohol basis) of any beverage.[46] The vast majority of consumers of such wines were found to be chronic drunkenness offenders, skid-row alcoholics, and other impoverished pathological drinkers. Thus, we were brought back to the relative price of alcohol, regardless of its beverage source, as the significant factor.

The Distribution of Consumption

A second important question needed to be settled before the practical implications of the role of cost in alcohol problems were pursued further. This concerned the relation between general drinking and drinking by alcoholics in a given population. To the old-time temperance worker, there was an obvious, close connection between the two. For him *alcohol* was the cause of alcoholism: man was basically weak and subject to temptations which would lead him astray. Accordingly, it was only necessary to avoid drawing his attention to alcohol, preferably to make alcohol totally unavailable to him, and there would be no alcoholism. But with the rise of the disease concept of alcoholism—stimulated not a little by the teachings of Alcoholics Anonymous—a rather different view as to the causes of alcoholism has emerged.[47] Alcohol has become merely the material cause of alcoholism as the motor vehicle is the material cause of traffic accidents. The real or efficient cause lies in the person of the alcoholic; he is somehow unique—different either in his physical or mental makeup—and by virtue of the difference, he is driven to use alcohol to excess and be labeled as suffering from a disease. Thus drinking itself is commonly seen as symptomatic, as a *consequence* rather than a cause of an underlying disease process.[48]

Now from the standpoint of this conception of alcoholism, it follows that the intake of alcohol of those suffering from the disease will be quite different from that of the nonalcoholic population. As they are allegedly unique in personality or biological characteristics so, it is assumed, will they be unique in their drinking. This conception, common among workers in the field, implies a bimodal distribution of alcohol consumption in the population as a whole, the alcoholics constituting a small group off by themselves. This view is depicted graphically in Figure 14-2.

If the distribution were in fact bimodal, then it would be difficult to see why control measures designed to reduce overall per capita consumption should necessarily affect the alcoholic, other than to put him to a little more trouble than before to meet his abnormal craving. In other words, one would not expect the prevalence of alcoholism to respond to the same factors as influenced the consumption of other drinkers. However, a prodigous amount of work with the beverage sales slips for five Ontario communities revealed that the distribution, in that province at least, was not at all bimodal.[49] The were fully described by the Ledermann curve (a model of the lognormal type), as shown in Figure 14-3.

Since then, the curve has been found to give a reasonable fit to the distribution of blood alcohol levels in a large sample of nonaccident drivers in Michigan.[50] Prior to these investigations, the same curve had been demonstrated by its inventor to hold for drinking in Finland, France, and Sweden, and for one sample in the United States.[51] This means that it applies equally well to populations which differ greatly from one another in attitudes toward drinking, beverage preferences, drinking habits, and most important, attempts to prevent alcoholism through legislative controls and educational efforts. Our conclusion is that, for practical purposes, the essential character of the distribution is unalterable and *the prevalence of consumption by those we label "alcoholic" is inextricably linked to general consumption.*[52]

The more darkly shaded area in the tail of the curve in Figure 14-3 comprises those who, in 1968, consumed an average of fifteen centiliters of alcohol daily or more. This level of consumption agrees well with the reported intake of alcoholics in clinical samples in Ontario, France, West Germany, and Australia.[53] Furthermore, the number of such consumers indicated by the distribution differs little from alcoholism prevalence estimates based on mortality data.[54] A second level has been indicated on the curve at ten centiliters daily (about nine ounces of whiskey or sixty-six ounces of 5 percent beer). We have tentatively designated consumption at or above this level as hazardous. Our justification lies in data on the alcohol intake of persons suffering from liver cirrhosis. In particular, Pequignot's study indicates a significantly elevated risk of the disease at this point.[55]

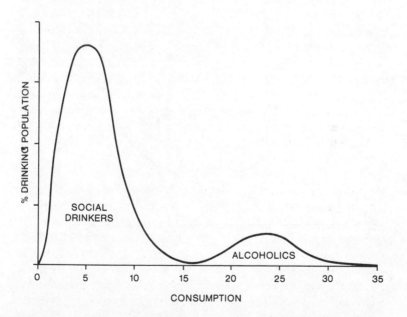

Figure 14-2. Distribution of alcohol consumption expected on the basis of the disease concept of alcoholism.

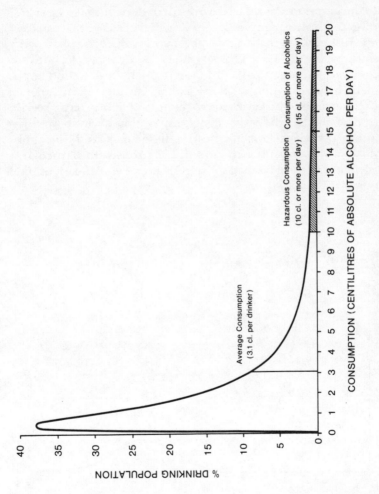

Figure 14-3. Actual distribution of consumption, Ontario, 1968.

In view of these findings, the only feasible approach to the reduction of hazardous drinking (including alcoholism) is to effect a decrease in the level of consumption of the population as a whole. This would mean shifting the distribution to the left which would not change its lognormal character. But the result would be a decline in the number of persons in the tail end, that is, in the number of hazardous consumers. We believe that an increase in relative price is one factor which can cause such a shift.

Discussion and Conclusions

We do not contend that the relative price of alcohol is the only important variable responsible for differences in alcoholism prevalence. However, it seems to be one of the most powerful, statistically speaking, and the one which, in theory, is most easily manipulated. Certainly, a strong effect on indicators of alcoholism is also exerted by the level of acceptance of drinking in a society, although the two factors are probably not strictly independent. Thus, indices such as proportion of total abstainers, responses to attitude surveys on drinking, and voting behavior on alcohol control issues have been shown to vary with alcoholism rates.[56]

It is probable that some of the international variation shown in Table 14-6 is attributable to this factor. For example, the Netherlands appears as a notable exception because consumption is low despite a low relative price. In that country there is comparatively little tolerance for drunkenness and, although there are marked differences between Catholic and Protestant levels of acceptance, the strongly disapproving Calvinists of the rural north keep the consumption of the country as a whole at a low level.[57]

On the other hand, there appear to be no instances of high consumption in the presence of a high relative price. Nor is this solely because acceptance and price may be negatively correlated in some degree. Southern Ireland, for example, may be safely designated a high acceptance area, but contrary to a common belief among both the lay public and students in the field, consumption and alcoholism rates are low. This is in accord with the high price of alcohol relative to the average income level of the Irish.[58]

The example of Ireland raises another matter of relevance: the tendency to confuse problems of acute intoxication (or in Jellinek's terms—"occasional excess"[59]) with problems of heavy chronic consumption. In the case of Ireland, undue emphasis has been placed on the deleterious consequences of the occasional massive intake as evidence of a high frequency of alcoholism.[60] In contrast, both Italy and France are often cited as models of civilized drinking, that is, by implication, widespread drinking but few alcohol problems. In fact, both countries have high rates of alcoholism as reflected in mortality and other statistics although obvious drunkenness is comparatively rare.[61] Also instructive is the situation in Finland where the alcoholism rate is low, as would be expected from consumption and relative price data.[62] But, as Kuusi pointed out many years ago, whatever is consumed tends to be concentrated in a short period rather than taken in small quantities over several days.[63] The result is a problem of "explosive intoxication" or in other words, violent behavior as a consequence of acute intoxication.[64]

The confusion of these problems may account in part for the persistent interest in differential taxation favoring beverages of low alcohol content. As noted in a previous section, the introduction of a heavy tax on spirituous liquors may lead to a reduction in certain problems of severe intoxication. But so far as chronic heavy intake of alcohol is concerned, beer or wine will serve as well. Therefore, in the long run the deterioration to health is apt to be as serious a problem as before. Moreover, the two types of problems overlap to a considerable degree. For example, in Ontario at least 28 percent of alcohol-impaired drivers in traffic accidents were estimated to be alcoholics in the clinical sense of the term.[65] Also, alcoholism by definition involves a history of frequent impairment with attendant personal and social problems. Accordingly, it is all but inconceivable that a measure which reduced the prevalence of alcoholism would fail to reduce problems of intoxication.

In our view, a price system aimed at prevention and in accord with the evidence presented would involve:

1. A price structure such that the cost of any given quantity of alcohol was the same for the cheapest source of

alcohol in each class of beverage: beer, wine, and spirits. Prices would then be scaled upward in each class depending upon the producers' values for different brands. Probably the cost of alcohol in the cheapest spirituous liquor would ordinarily be taken as the base figure.[66]

2. Adjustment of prices as often as required to maintain a constant relationship between the cost of beverage alcohol so established and average disposable income.

3. The ultimate establishment of an optimum relative price level in an effort to minimize the prevalence of hazardous consumption. Liver cirrhosis mortality rates might be employed as one index of achievement in this regard. The optimum level would have to be determined for each jurisdiction and, in addition to research findings, would need to take account of various practical, ethical, and political factors. Some of these are touched upon in the discussion which follows.

We are fully aware that in many jurisdictions there would be strong resistance to the utilization of this mode of control. Such resistance is apt to be especially stubborn where social acceptance of drinking is high. Three of the objections which have been raised to the suggestion in Ontario deserve comment here.

First, it is argued that elevated prices would lead to widespread illicit production which would negate the effect sought. This consequence is probably exaggerated, since even during the later years of prohibition in North America and the allegedly ubiquitous bootlegger and speakeasy, liver cirrhosis death rates were lower than before or since.[67] If enforcement is reasonably vigorous, the relative price of illicit alcohol will likely be high to compensate for the risks involved in its production and distribution. Accordingly, a practical consideration in the establishment of an optimum relative price level would be to find a point high enough to hold down consumption but low enough to avoid a substantial illicit trade.

In any case, the objection rests in part on a misunderstanding of what is being suggested in the way of price manipulation. It is not proposed that legal alcohol be rendered virtually inaccessible through cost. This, like prohibition, would ignore the many benefits—social and psychological—which undoubtedly accrue to the moderate use of alcohol. We believe that personal adaptations to higher price levels could be made without serious sacrifice of such benefits. For example, the regular tavern patron might simply reduce his drinking speed, and the cocktail hour might involve one-ounce instead of two-ounce drinks. The main point is that an ethical question is involved: How much harm are we willing to tolerate in return for how much benefit?[68] In our judgment, substantial improvements in the health status of many jurisdictions could be achieved through suitable price increases and without undue loss of the rewards associated with drinking.

A second objection is that price control will not affect the alcoholic; he will simply turn to illicit sources, nonbeverage alcohols, or crime to get the money for a legal supply. In part, this objection is simply contradicted by a wealth of evidence. Liver cirrhosis mortality has been shown to be a good index of the number of alcoholics in a population (whether or not they happen to suffer from the disease); and the frequency of this cause of death is in fact highly sensitive to the effect of relative price on general consumption. Nevertheless, these findings do raise a question respecting the current conception of the alcoholic, and it is this which underlies the objection.

We do not doubt that most of those persons now labeled "alcoholic" are clinically ill—by virtue of the consequences of long-term heavy consumption, and sometimes also because of pre-existing physical, mental, or social problems. However, we are not aware of any compelling evidence that there is a *unique* predisposing factor or an irreversible change due to chronic intake, which renders the individual permanently incapable of controlling his alcohol consumption. The long search for distinctive psychological and physical features has produced essentially negative results.[69] As Keller has noted, many differences have been found between alcoholics and nonalcoholics, but these either are of no etiological significance or are nonspecific, that is, found also in other deviant and psychiatric populations.[70] Indeed, Jellinek once remarked that drinking and damage are about all that alcoholics have in common.[71] The notion of permanent loss of control has been challenged on clinical grounds,[72] and there is now experimental evidence that the reversibility of physical dependence on alcohol lies in the realm of learning.[73] All this is to say nothing of the fact that the response of alcoholics to newer treatment modalities, which rely entirely on the manipulation of environmental contingencies including the cost of alcohol, has been by no means discouraging.[74]

In any event, the principal aim of a preventive measure is to affect the incidence (new cases) rather than the prevalence of a condition. Since the death rate of alcoholics (from all causes) is more than double that of the general population, natural attrition alone would rapidly diminish prevalence if the inflow of new cases could be prevented.[75] Here relative price control might be expected to have its most significant effect.

The third objection again takes us out of the realm of science and into those of ethics and political philosophy. An increase in relative price would penalize the poor man and leave the rich man unaffected. One can but agree that an increase would hurt the poor man more, as presumably do all forms of taxation. However, a benefit would not necessarily be conferred on the rich. In the United Kingdom, where relative price is high, liver cirrhosis seems to have become largely a rich man's disease.[76] We would also question the assumption that the rich man is unaffected by price increases. This will depend on his attitude toward money and on just how rich he is. In Canada at least, the number who theoretically might be quite unaffected on financial grounds by a substantial price increase comprises a small fraction of the population.

This objection also raises a more general ethical question: should legislation ever be employed to protect public health? If so, then it is simply a matter of how many will be helped and not of class discrimination. We suspect that objections such as this would seldom be heard if relative price control were seen as a valid health measure. At present it is not likely to be viewed in this light in most North American areas, and consequently, it will not be politically feasible to implement.

Our general conclusion is that in the manipulation of the relative price of alcohol, governments theoretically have at their disposal a powerful instrument to control the prevalence of hazardous drinking including alcoholism. However, at the present time there are apt to be formidable political and emotional obstacles to the use of this instrument. The most practical approach to their removal would appear to be a vigorous educational program designed to generate public recognition of the hazards of heavy consumption and the preventive value of this mode of control. Price increases would have to be seen as having a protective function and not as just being another device of government to increase its revenue.

CHAPTER 15

Evaluating the
Effect of Drinking
Laws on Drinking

Robin Room, M.A.

ANYONE WISHING TO analyze the relation between laws and drinking behavior is faced with a somewhat discouraging task. In the first place, there is a large mass of historical records relevant to the subject, stretching back to Biblical times and including a vast diversity from the last century or so but few of these records allow any trustworthy conclusions on the effects of laws on drinking behavior. Time and again, when confronted with assessing the effects of a particular law, one is left wondering whether the law is a cause of change in behavior or an effect of antecedent changes in public sentiment. Was the decline in consumption in both the United States and throughout Europe in World War I a direct result of wartime restrictions? Were both the restrictions and the decline independent results of focused patriotic fervor and increased social cohesion in wartime? Or were both the result of changes in habits and sentiment that started in the prewar years?[1] The answer to all three of these questions, and to others like them, may well be "Yes, at least in part." All that analysis has accomplished is to beg the more difficult question of assessing the relative importance of the various chains of causation involved.

In the second place, the behavior involved is extremely complex. There is a wide range of possible meanings to the act of drinking—a wider range, perhaps, than for any of the other behaviors which have been the traditional objects of sumptuary legislation. State liquor control laws usually state in their preamble that their object is to promote temperance, and they leave it essentially at that. This is, to say the least, not specific about the kinds of behavior the laws are intended to affect and effect. Such behavior has a number of different possible dimensions. Let us examine a few. First, there is the act of drinking itself. What is the goal of the law: abstinence rather than drinking; infrequent rather than frequent drinking, say once a week instead of twice a day; small rather than large amounts on an occasion—say, two drinks instead of twelve—or diminishing the intoxicating potential of the occasion, perhaps by stretching out its duration, by substituting a beverage with a lower alcoholic content, or by lining the stomach with food? On most of these dimensions, the range of possible human behavior is enormous—a minute between drinks or a year, a dash of alcohol or a bottle, a drunken feast or skipping meals while drinking.

Besides the act of drinking itself, there is the matter of who does the acting. Is drinking to be a privilege of the socially enabled—is it to be denied to youth and discouraged in the poor and among women? Third, there are the circumstances of the act—in a public or a private place, in a restaurant or a bar, with friends or with family or alone, while watching television or passing the bottle in a public park. And, finally, of course, there are the personal and social consequences of the act— drunk driving, accidents, cirrhosis, loss of control, break up of families, loss of job and of friendships, alcoholic psychosis— the whole dreary litany of possible bad ends the drinker can come to.

No doubt all these dimensions of drinking behavior bear some relationship to each other, but the relationship is certainly not uniform and direct. Historical instances abound in which legislation which promoted temperance on one of these dimensions hindered it on another. To cite one small example, the lately repealed laws closing bars at six o'clock in much of Australia, instituted as temperance measures by popular referendum during World War I, certainly got the working man out of the pub and perhaps home to his family in time for dinner; but they also produced the custom known as the six o'clock swill, the main object of which was to pour as much beer as humanly possible down one's throat in the hour between the end of work and closing time. When one is gauging the effects of a law, then, even a law ostensibly narrow in scope, the analysis is complicated by the necessity of ranging widely across the kinds of dimensions of drinking behavior enumerated and presenting a kind of balance sheet of the various resulting changes in behavior.

A third factor inhibiting analyses of the relation between drinking laws and drinking behavior has been the preemption of scholarly attention and allegiance in alcohol studies, roughly since the coincident rise of Alcoholics Anonymous and the Yale Plan Clinics, by issues of social policy and provisions for alcoholism, viewed as a disease. Disease concepts of alcoholism, in defining the "problem" to be an attribute of the affected individual[2]—whether the "problem" is seen as an allergy, as an acquired tissue tolerance, or as a psychological dependence—have resulted in a de-emphasis of the context of social drinking out of which the institutionalized alcoholic emerges. They have also often carried the implication that there are two entirely different classes of phenomena, "normal drinking" and "alcoholic drinking," each irrelevant to the other. If loss of control is the salient issue, the actual amount and context of drinking are essentially immaterial. With this assumption, combined with the understandable priority assigned to research in the prevention and treatment of alcoholism, questions of the relation between legal and social arrangements and drinking behavior have generally been seen by researchers as just not an important topic for research.

The final discouragement in analyzing the relation between drinking laws and drinking behavior is its probable irrelevance to the policy-making process. The behavior of legislators, in this as in many other areas of sumptuary legislation, is determined not so much by considerations of rational policy—such as a consideration of the law's actual effects on behavior—as by the necessities of symbolic action: how will a particular vote on a piece of legislation look to his constituents and what will future opponents be able to make of it? For a

long period in American history, as Gusfield has cogently
argued, "the liquor question" was the touchstone of an earlier
manifestation of what has lately been christened the "social
issue" in American politics—of a struggle for primacy in social
status between opposed tendencies in styles of life—small town
versus city, "old American" versus immigrant, the South and
Midwest versus the Northeast.[3] The "liquor question" may
now generate less political heat, the temperance movement
may be a shadow of its former self, but the prudent legislator
knows there is a large reservoir of sentiment, both dry and wet,
in the voting population, so that he will generally lose the least
votes by doing nothing.[4] In many states, the liquor control
laws are essentially unchanged from their original passage on
the repeal of prohibition.

   When public policy is to be controlled by symbolic or
moral considerations, facts are an irrelevance, and those who
insist on discussions of rational considerations are if anything
an annoyance. As seen recently in reactions to the national
commission on pornography and the law—and as Socrates
found out long ago—the very act of turning cherished assumptions about causes and effects into hypotheses to be tested may
be viewed as an affront to the moral order.

   The cumulative result of these discouragements and
difficulties has been a small amount of learning from a large
amount of experience. In spite of the considerable intervening
history, understanding in this area has not greatly improved
since, say, the work of the Committee of Fifty to Investigate the
Liquor Problem at the turn of the century. It is still, then, a
time for modest beginnings rather than augustan summations.

   This paper is limited to a consideration of drinking
laws and control measures which bear upon the general adult
population, basically by manipulating the conditions of
supply and the price of alcohol. I do not consider control
measures which are aimed at specific portions of the
population—for example, prohibitions of serving alcohol to
certified alcoholics. Specifically aimed control measures, once
widely used in Scandinavia and parts of North America, have
been on the decline in recent years, partly because they have
been found to be generally ineffective.[5]

Existing Data vs. the Ideal

The kinds of data that are available for a consideration of the effects of generally applicable drinking laws on drinking behavior are, as I have mentioned, usually less than conclusive. In general, they fall into one of three categories: correlations of trends through space and time in various kinds of social statistics; measurements of behavior at a given point in time by surveys and other cross-sectional methods; and collocations of more or less systematic observations. None of these three categories of data is suited to establishing the nature and direction of causes and effects. Before making what I can of the data I found, then, I will spell out the nature of the data I would like to have found.

A model study of the effects of law on behavior, enabling one to get at least some leverage on the vexing problems of which is causing what, would require measurements of behavior, attitudes, and other data, both before and after the change in law, in the population affected and in an equivalent population not affected by the change in law. The "after" measurement should not be too soon after the change in law. National prohibition in the United States is a notable example of the common pattern of liquor law changes being more successful in accomplishing their aims in their first couple of years than thereafter. On the other hand, the longer the elapsed period, the larger the sample attrition, and the greater the likelihood of the intrusion of extraneous events. Given a desire to study the effects of introducing liquor-by-the-drink, for instance, and given sufficient funds, I would seek out a state or localities where liquor-by-the-drink was about to go into effect. I would select a matched state or localities where there was no liquor-by-the-drink, and preferably also places where liquor-by-the-drink already existed, matched as far as possible on size, composition, dry sentiment, and anything else I could think of which might conceivably affect the comparisons. I would certainly include some urban and relatively wet neighborhoods, since the little work in this area has been done exclusively on rural and relatively dry communities. I would conduct survey and other studies before and after the change in law. And I would not expect the results of my work miraculously to cure the politicians' headaches by defusing all controversy on the subject.

There is to my knowledge exactly one published study of the effects of change in alcohol control policies which fills the model criteria I outlined above, a study of the effect of opening a state beer and wine package store in Finnish rural communities.[6] The study in fact found important shifts in drinking behavior in the communities where the stores were opened. But, as the author himself noted, "after five laborious years," the results of the study did not eliminate "divergencies of opinion." "If, let us say, at the Ikaalinen church village-market town the total consumption of alcohol among men increased during the period of the experiment by 40 percent, the use of illicit liquors was reduced by 50 percent, and excessive drinking remained more or less unchanged," there remains the question of "what alcohol policy value should be attached to this finding?"[7]

General Theories of the Effect

Christie and Bruun have noted that discussions of alcoholism have been much afflicted with "fat words."[8] To the extent that there have been any general discussions of United States liquor control policies in the last forty years, they tend rather to be afflicted with fat theories—theories of the relation between drinking laws and drinking behavior which are inflated beyond the reach of the supporting evidence. I shall tease out three such grand hypotheses from the snarl of occasional literature on the subject, discuss their implications and assumptions, and attempt some preliminary evaluations of how well they fit the available evidence.

The Null Hypothesis

The first hypothesis to be considered, among those which can be found in the literature, is essentially a null hypothesis: that liquor control laws have no effect at all on drinking behavior, particularly on drunkenness and alcoholism. This hypothesis is a favorite of the alcohol beverage industry, which is quite comfortable with a great conceptual gulf fixed between normal social drinking—which the industry proudly serves—and alcoholic drinking—which the industry deplores. Reacting to the New York State Moreland Commission's plans to study the effect of the liquor control laws on behavior, a liquor industry spokesman fulminated that "the problems of alcoholism and driving while intoxicated have nothing to do with the N.Y. State Liquor law, and never were intended to. As a matter of fact, I was amazed that the Commission had to spend the time and money to have a survey made to reach that startling conclusion. Anyone could have told them that."[9]

Ironically, Selden Bacon, whose study the liquor industry spokesman was attacking, has come quite close to embracing this hypothesis. Thus he has described as "inadequate or fallacious" the proposition that "the use and the evils of alcohol can be controlled by controlling production and sales, particularly the latter"; the conditions of sale, he affirms, are *"at best* peripheral to either *use* or *problems* of beverage alcohol"[10]; indeed, "for persisting, complex social problems . . . law can only play minor roles except for special purposes and short periods."[11]

There are two major lines of argument used in support of this hypothesis. One of them, used by the liquor industry spokesman later in the speech we have quoted, is simply to make reference to the "failure" of national prohibition in the United States. The problem with this argument is that prohibition did not fail, if by this is meant that it had no effect on drinking behavior. For one thing total consumption was actually lower during prohibition than before or after. In a careful and elegant study, Warburton concluded, on the basis of several independent methods of estimating consumption, that

> during the early years of prohibition the per capita consumption of spirits was reduced approximately to two-fifths, and that of beer to one-fifteenth the pre-war level. In the four years from 1927 to 1930, . . . the per capita consumption of spirits averaged about 10 percent and of wine about 65 percent greater than from 1911 to 1914, while the consumption of beer was about 30 percent as great. The total consumption of liquor, expressed in terms of its content of pure alcohol, dropped during the early years of prohibition to one-third the pre-war level, . . . [and then rose to] two-thirds as great as prior to World War.[12]

Even if it is contended that the changes in consumption reflected historical trends to which prohibition was irrelevant—not a particularly convincing argument—it can hardly be denied that prohibition had some effects on behavior, even if not necessarily the intended effects. For one thing, as Warburton's estimates show, turning alcoholic beverages into contraband shifted the bulk of production and thus of consumption into the most easily produced and most concentrated forms.

The second line of argument, that adopted by Selden Bacon, is that the state liquor control systems now extant in the United States have "no demonstrable effect on the direct problems of alcohol or on the rate of consumption of alcoholic beverages."[13] The evidence offered in support of this, however, is actually directed at a quite different proposition, which is that the *differences* between the state liquor control systems now operating in the United States do not seem to result in demonstrable differences in social statistics on consumption or problems.

This second proposition derives some support from my reanalysis of data from Bacon's study and other sources:[14] interstate variations in control systems were entirely secondary to such factors as urbanization in the extent of their association with consumption and problems statistics; and they do not show strong associations either with trends in these statistics over time. I also attempted to measure differences at the level of individual behavior under different control systems in roughly comparable milieux, using the southern rural segment of a national survey.[15] The numbers involved were small and the findings equivocal, but in general it might be said that there was no strong evidence that control policies were having their intended effects: southern rural male white drinkers living in areas with no liquor-by-the-drink were if anything more likely than those living in places allowing bars to do their drinking "most often" in bars or restaurants.

Since the comparisons are across space rather than through time, and of static rather than changing control systems, these findings are not really conclusive regarding the second proposition. It may be, for instance, that the control systems are responsible for holding down differences in behavior which would otherwise emerge. Christie has argued on the basis of comparisons of Scandinavian statistics that a strict control system may both reflect and cause extreme drinking behavior in the population controlled.

> A strict system of legal and organizational control of accessibility of alcohol seems to be related to low alcohol consumption, but also to a high degree of public nuisance. The causal chain probably goes like this: A drinking culture with a large degree of highly visible, non-beneficial effects of alcohol consumption leads to a strict system of control which somewhat reduces total consumption, which again influences and most often reduces the visible problems. But also, the system of control influences visible problems—sometimes probably in the direction of increasing them.[16]

In comparisons of the southern region with other regions of the United States, there are patterns which suggest analogies with Christie's comparisons for Scandinavia.[17]

Even if the second proposition did turn out to be true— even if differences between state control systems in the United States do not affect individual drinking behavior—this is no proof of the original proposition, that liquor control systems have no effect at all. As Kettil Bruun has stressed, comparisons of the control systems themselves must pay at least as much attention to the actual functionings of the system as to their abstract legal framework.[18] U.S. control systems may well be more alike in their actual functioning than their legal frameworks would imply.[19] An institutional manifestation of this convergence is the Joint Committee of the States to Study Alcoholic Beverage Laws. Over the last twenty years, the executive officers of all the state control systems have been able to get together, with support from the alcoholic beverage industry, on studies of aspects of the control system.[20]

The only conclusive test of the original proposition that control systems have no demonstrable effects on behavior is, of course, to see what happens when control systems are changed. As noted, the one fully controlled study did find changes in behavior in rural Finland.[21] The evidence for urban areas is less formally established, but it is convincing. The introduction of controls in a situation of complete laissez-faire in eighteenth century London did result in changes in behavior.[22] In the detailed accounts of the interaction between regulations and behavior in the day-to-day work of the Central Control Board (Liquor Traffic) in Britain during and after World War I,[23] there is abundant evidence that many regulations affected behavior. However, in such a situation of crisis consensus and flexible powers, the behavior also clearly affected the regulations. And in the United States, as we have seen, prohibition appears to have affected both the patterns and the magnitude of consumption.[24]

In its unvarnished form, the hypothesis just will not bear the weight of detailed scrutiny. A more reasonable restatement of the hypothesis, in the light of experience, would be that severe liquor control laws—those which cause more than inconveniences—have less affect on behavior than their proponents expect, and they tend to have adverse side effects which may come to be seen as outweighing any benefits. In a situation of limited consent, only limited regulations—and not all even of these—will have their intended effect, and they will thus be limited in their effects.

The "Constant Proportion" Theory

A second major hypothesis in the literature is what we might call the "constant proportion" theory: the proportion of excessive drinkers in a population directly depends on the amount of drinking in the population. This hypothesis has recently been restated by the staff of the Addiction Research Foundation of Ontario (ARF) with some emphasis. They discuss proposed changes in Canadian drug control laws in the light of experience with alcohol:

> Any factor which raises average per capita consumption by the whole population also raises the proportion and absolute number of heavy users. . . . All users fit on a single curve falling smoothly from a high frequency of very light consumers at one end, to a small frequency of very heavy consumers at the other end. . . . Anything which raises the level of [social] acceptance tends to displace the whole curve towards the higher-consumption end, so that a larger absolute number of users exceeds the limit of "low risk" consumption. Legal measures, social controls, and educational programs may

therefore have to be aimed at reducing the general level of acceptance and use, if they are to have any success in reducing frequency of heavy use.[25]

This hypothesis is directly opposed to the general liquor industry theory, already alluded to, that normal drinking and alcoholic drinking have no relation to one another.

The "constant proportion" hypothesis is, of course, close to the rationale which underlay the temperance movement. If, as the early temperance movement quickly concluded, attempting to solve the liquor problem by reforming drunkards was like trying to catch all the fish in the sea with a fishing rod, perhaps the only sure and certain solution was to dry up the sea. Drunkenness would only be eliminated by procuring abstention for all—at first, by voluntary pledges of abstention, and later, by legal enforcement. In fact, a version of the "constant proportion" hypothesis was invoked by an abstinence advocate in his "exposé" of the Cooperative Commission's report:

> It is very likely that the total number of drinkers would be increased if the Commission's recommendations are carried out. Therefore since we know that approximately 10 percent of all social drinkers seem destined to become problem drinkers or chronic alcoholics, how can we hope by the recommendations of this REPORT to *decrease* the number of problem drinkers?[26]

In fact the evidence for the hypothesis is not conclusive. The evidence cited by the Addiction Research Foundation statement in support of the "constant proportion" hypothesis is a study of the distribution of sales of wine and liquor-by-the-bottle in the provincial liquor stores in Ontario. Forty-two percent of all buyers bought only one bottle in a month, 20 percent bought two, 11 percent bought three, 7 percent bought four, and the remaining 20 percent were distributed in a long tail, in a curve which the authors describe as resembling the "logarithmic normal curve" which Sully Ledermann had previously found in his primarily French data.[27] On this basis, it is proposed that the logarithmic normal curve is generally "applicable to North American drinking behavior."[28] By implication in the original study but explicitly in the recent ARF staff statement, the curve is proposed to be immutable, so that a rise in per capita consumption will automatically lead to a rise in alcohol problems.

The major conceptual problem with this chain of reasoning is familiar: essentially static findings of the distribution of drinking that exists in a population at a given point in time are somehow transformed into data which "establish" the manner in which changes must inevitably occur. The major practical problem is that the ironclad curve of distribution proposed just does not fit the variations in consumption patterns which can be found in different populations. For instance, in a national U.S. sample, comparing males age 21 to 59 in the highest and lowest socioeconomic status groups, 64 percent of all highest status current drinkers drink with at least moderate volume, and of those drinking with at least moderate volume, 55 percent drink with high volume. A smaller proportion (49 percent) of lowest status current drinkers drink with at least moderate volume, but of these a higher proportion (65 percent) drink with high volume.[29]

To question the interpretation placed upon these studies of the distribution of consumption is not, of course, to deny the value of the studies themselves. They have taught alcohol researchers a valuable lesson, which the alcoholic beverage industry learned long ago: that a small proportion of the population is responsible for the bulk of the total consumption of alcohol[30]—from a U.S. national survey, I made a rough estimate that 6 percent of the population accounted for 41 percent of the consumption, and 10 percent accounted for 60 percent.[31] And they have demonstrated that, at least with the scales used, the distribution in the populations studied is unimodal—there is no "bump" at any particular higher level of consumption. As de Lint and Schmidt note, this suggests that there is no distinct pattern of alcoholic drinking which is set apart from the continuum of normal drinking.

The distribution curves found in these studies might profitably be viewed in the light of an older and more general formulation, Allport's "J-curve hypothesis of conforming behavior."[32] On the basis of studies of the distribution, for instance, of the timeliness of workers' arrivals at their job,

Allport formulated the hypothesis that "in a field of conforming behavior, the distribution of degrees of conformity upon their appropriate telic continuum is in the form of a curve of positive acceleration"—in other words, a "J-curve" which much resembles the distributions found for alcohol consumption. By a "field of conforming behavior" Allport means that there are definite norms involved, to which at least one-half of the population adheres. By "the appropriate telic continuum," he means that the distribution must be plotted on a scale of constantly decreasing conformity, so that all conforming behavior is in the first category or so. Looking at the Ontario distribution in this light, one might speculate that the norm of behavior operating is the purchase of no more than one or two bottles a month, and that the "appropriate telic continuum" is therefore in the neighborhood of the scale used in the study—that is, bottles per month. If the scale used had been, say, ounces per year, the distribution might well be quite different—in fact, Ledermann and Allport agree that its general shape will be skewed and leptokurtic.

The advantage of this perspective is that it directs attention away from numerological formulae and the aesthetics of curve-fitting and back to the substantial questions of the nature and strength of drinking norms and their relation to conforming and deviating behavior. Allport, for instance, proposed that the distributions he found were the result of the interplay of four "component distributions," representing the factors of "the conformity-producing agencies, the common biological tendencies, the personality-trait distribution tendency, and simple chance." These are not necessarily the most appropriate factors for explaining the distribution of alcohol consumption, but they certainly suggest some directions in which to look.

There is what would seem on its face to be somewhat better evidence for the ARF staff thesis of a direct relationship between per capita consumption and the proportion of excessive drinkers, if liver cirrhosis deaths can be taken, as is by now traditional, as an indicator of excessive drinking. In a whole series of studies covering many years, analysts—many of them, as is also traditional in the alcohol literature, quite unaware of each others' existence—have shown that per capita consumption, particularly of wine and spirits, tend to vary from year to year in the same population closely with cirrhosis deaths.[33] The correlations found have been consistently high. Several investigators have independently observed that cirrhosis death trends appear to lag consumption trends by about a year. Although such a short lag is surprising, since death from alcoholic cirrhosis is undoubtedly the outcome of a lengthy process, Terris has argued that this "is consistent with the clinical course of the disease. In many cases the cirrhotic process can be halted and decompensation prevented by avoiding further use of alcohol. Conversely, resumption of heavy alcohol use after a period of abstinence can decompensate a previously injured liver in a relatively short period of time."

On the face, then, these data would seem to offer indisputable evidence of a strong relationship between even short-term variations in the same population in per capita consumption and excessive drinking. I am, however, inclined to dispute. As I have already noted, consumption of alcohol is concentrated so that a small proportion of the population accounts for a large proportion of all consumption. Up to one-half of the total consumption is contributed by excessive drinkers, so that per capita consumption is at least partly a measure of excessive drinking. Further, relatively small changes in the drinking patterns of excessive drinkers will have a disproportionate effect of changes in per capita consumption. If light drinkers cut down from a couple of drinks a week to a couple of drinks a month, the effect on per capita consumption will be much less than if excessive drinkers cut down from getting drunk every day to getting drunk three times a week. Change in per capita consumption over time would seem, therefore, even more likely than per capita consumption per se to be primarily a reflection of the drinking patterns of excessive drinkers. I contend, then, that correlations of variations in cirrhosis deaths and per capita consumption, and particularly correlations over time in the same population (except perhaps in times of large scale shifts in consumption patterns) are high because they are both largely measures of the same thing—the drinking patterns of excessive drinkers.

The Inoculation Theory

The third major hypothesis in the literature might be

called the "inoculation" theory: the hypothesis that the proportion of excessive drinkers can be reduced by increasing the
proportion of the population practicing certain styles of
moderate drinking—perhaps by teaching teenagers how to
drink. This is, broadly speaking, the position of the two books
resulting from the work of the Cooperative Commission on
Alcoholism:[34] "while it is impossible to foretell whether . . . a
policy of both encouraging and discouraging certain types of
drinking . . . would lead to an increase or decrease in the
proportion of drinkers, it is likely that they would decrease the
number of problem drinkers."[35] Morris Chafetz, until recently
the director of the National Institute of Alcohol Abuse and
Alcoholism, also espouses this idea: "By providing educational
information and experience with their peers in group settings
at school, and by integrating their drinking experience with
family use as well, immunization against unhealthy, irrespon-
sible drinking behavior can be provided as a bulwark against
alcoholism."[36]

The evidence for the "inoculation" hypothesis is primarily drawn from comparisons of the drinking patterns of
different cultural groups. Usually, the patterns of one or
another culture or subculture are pointed to as an example of
what is desired for the United States as a whole. There is no
doubt that there are substantial cultural differences in drinking
patterns—variations on each of the dimensions of the act of
drinking enumerated above. Plausible hypotheses have been
advanced to account for many of the differences. The problem,
in fact, is that there are entirely too many plausible hypotheses
and that the task of sifting through them for those that are not
only plausible but verifiable has barely begun. Again, systematic studies of the correlates of changes over time are lacking,
so that the advocates of the "inoculation" hypothesis, too, are
left in the untenable position of basing conclusions about
change on essentially static data.

Even if cultural determinants of drinking patterns can
be identified, there is a further problem with the "inoculation"
hypothesis—that these determinants may well be quite difficult to change. As Hiltner noted in his comments on Chafetz:

> With limited exceptions, the types of cultures in which the
> relaxed-sip-with-food approach is manifested consistently are
> (to use the categories of Apollonian and Dionysian as deve-

loped by Ruth Benedict for anthropological studies) all much
more Apollonian than are most American or Western European
cultures . . . . What Chafetz seems, in effect, to be proposing is
that we try to produce an Apollonian attitude about
drinking—in a culture which is, in most other respects,
strongly Dionysian. Can one such factor be shifted without
some supporting shift in at least many other factors? The
answer may not be an impossibility, but the difficulties are very
great.[37]

A further difficulty, I suspect, is that some drinking patterns commonly ascribed to cultural styles might better be
viewed as products of the position in the social system in
which the members of the culture find themselves. For
instance, it is hard to imagine what the cultures of many
extraordinarily diverse American Indian tribes—not to mention the Australian aborigines—could have in common to
explain their common pattern of widespread disruptive drinking. But it is easy to see what they have in common in terms of
position in the social system. They are all peoples engulfed by
a dominant and colonizing nation-state which denies their
traditional tribal values and yet offers no functional position
in which they can conform to its values. If this is true, the
remedies for the drinking patterns are not so much difficult as
costly—and at the expense of the dominant society: a restruc-
turing of social relations, rather than the manipulation of
cultural values, appears to be indicated.

Toward a Synthesis

All in all, the available evidence does not allow of any
definitive verdict on either the "constant proportion" or the
"inoculation" hypothesis. They both offer fertile fields for
further research, with important policy implications. However, the most likely result of this research, in my opinion, will
not be a final proof of one and disproof of the other. Apparently the "constant proportion" and "inoculation" theorists
are focusing on different aspects of alcohol problems as their
criterion of individual behavior. Thus the criterion for the
"constant proportion" theorists tends to be the long-term
medical complications of chronic excessive drinking, associated with wet environments, while the "inoculation" theor-

ists concentrate on the social disruptions of explosive but often intermittent drinking associated with dry environments.[38] Clearly the discussions focus on quite different aspects of the potential legal and social control systems. Future work therefore seems most likely to result in the specification of definitions and conditions under which each of the possible relations between drinking controls and drinking behavior—positive, negative, and null—hold true.

There is, as mentioned at the outset, a plethora of scattered evidence available in the historical record from which this process of specification can start. A summary of the British experience with considerable experimentation with legal controls during and after World War I gives us a good idea of the kinds of relationships likely to be involved in the various methods of legal restriction and channeling of the general supply of alcohol, short of prohibition:

> The people . . . submitted to limitation and reduced facilities, but deprivation they would not tolerate. . . . Under peace conditions the volume of intemperance can be kept far below the former level by means of shorter hours and higher taxation . . . . These measures have proved really efficacious, while others—particularly State ownership and control, the reduction of licensed houses, alteration of premises, disinterested management and supply of food—have failed to exert any perceptible influence on sobriety and public order.
>
> But . . . however desirable the suppression of intemperance may be and however efficacious the methods just indicated, there are limits to their application; they cannot be effectively and safely pushed beyond a certain point. During the war they were carried as far as they could be without provoking reaction, and an attempt to carry them further had to be given up because of the resistance aroused. Nor is the issue merely one between liberty and sobriety; it is also one between increasing and diminishing sobriety. The assumption that measures which within limits conduce to sobriety by making excess difficult will continue to do so in proportion to their stringency is a fallacy. It has often been put to the test of experience, and always with the same result. When drinking by legalized channels is made too difficult, recourse is had to illegal ones, and the practice tends to spread with disastrous effects. . . . There are limits to the compulsory suppression of drinking,

and . . . when carried beyond those limits it defeats its own
object by tending to promote more injurious forms of drinking
and evasion of the law by common consent. Nor is it possible to
counteract those tendencies in a free country for three reasons:
namely, the ease with which alcoholic drink can be produced,
the lucrativeness of the illicit traffic, and the refusal of society
in general to regard drinking as a crime, whatever the law may
say.[39]

The Effect of Prices on Drinking

As in the above quotation, discussions of the effectiveness of means of limiting "intemperance" by liquor control
policies have generally centered around restrictions of
supply—in space or in time—or of the relative price. Restrictions of supply also function as increases of the effective price,
whether by restricting competition,[40] by creating a contraband
market with a risk cost included in the price, or by increasing
transportation costs (in money and time) of the beverage to the
consumer or the consumer to the beverage. For the remainder
of this discussion, therefore, I will focus on the evidence
available concerning the relation between changes in the
effective price of alcohol and drinking behavior.

In a comparison of a number of countries, Popham,
Schmidt, and de Lint have found a strong relation between relative price and per capita consumption.[41] It is tempting to conclude from this that raising the price lowers the consumption;
but this again is basing a dynamic conclusion on a static
finding. The causation may indeed be more in the opposite
direction. Governments are chronically short of money and
historically have found sumptuary taxes such as those on
alcohol very attractive: such taxes yield large revenues and can
be justified as serving the public welfare. Thus the taxes on
alcoholic beverages generally exceed the cost of production.
The only obvious limit to the rate of alcohol taxation is the
extent and depth of popular attachment to alcohol, which
makes itself felt in a variety of ways—whether at the polls, by
less formal methods of resistance, or through home brewing
and the support of moonshine and bootlegging operations. In
comparisons between countries, then, the relative price of
alcohol may well be more a reflection of, than a control on,
habits of consumption.

Dynamic data are available from a number of econometric studies of alcohol sales, primarily concerned with using regression equations to gauge the effect of variations over time in price and disposable income on per capita alcohol consumption.[42] The results vary quite widely, but the general weight of evidence seems to be that alcohol consumption is more influenced by income than price—that is, hard times have more effect than taxes—but that is not particularly "elastic" with respect to either. This means that it would require a rise in price of considerably more than 10 percent to effect a 10 percent decline in consumption.

One problem with these studies, at least for the United States, is the lack of a full range of experience which can be assumed to be relevant to modern times. Once the analyst excludes the special conditions of prohibition and the Second World War, he is left with six years of experience in the 1930s, plus the experience of the postwar period. And for all consumer commodities in the United States, "the postwar data are dominated to a considerable extent by trends . . . [by] the persistent upward movement in many of the consumption series. . . . Sustained economic growth is fine from a social point of view, but it makes life difficult for the econometrician."[43] Thus Houthakker and Taylor find that the postwar data taken alone yield a positive price elasticity for alcohol—which, taken literally, would mean that a rise in price led to a rise in consumption.

There are some further problems with the application of the results of regression analyses in discussions of public policy. The models used in these analyses make a number of assumptions about the variables involved which may well not hold for alcohol consumption. For instance, the degree of change in a predictor is assumed to have a monotonic and simple relation (linear or logarithmic, usually) with the degree of change in the criterion. But, there are suggestions in the alcohol literature, as in the summary of British experience quoted above, that a severe measure may have a reversed effect from a mild measure. It is also assumed that effects are symmetrical, so that a rise in price will affect consumption to the same extent but in the opposite direction from a fall in price. But if some members of the population can indeed be said to lose control over their drinking behavior—which implies that the behavior is more easily acquired than shed—it seems likely that the conditions for decreasing consumption would differ considerably from the conditions for increasing consumption.

A useful characteristic of the econometric studies is that they do allow for looking at alcohol consumption in the context of other consumer behavior, as Popham, Schmidt, and de Lint urge, rather than simply assuming "that the demand for alcoholic beverages [is] qualitatively different from that for other commodities and consequently not subject to the same factors as affect the demand for other consumer goods." Houthakker and Taylor's analysis, which presents equations for each of eighty-two classes of personal consumption, includes in its model a "stock coefficient," which estimates the relative predominance in each class of consumption of "inventory adjustment" versus "habit formation"—that is, whether the fact of consumption in the immediately preceding time period tends to predict lesser or greater consumption in the succeeding time period. For example, buying a car last year could predict not buying one this year, because you already have a useful one (inventory adjustment), or it could predict buying another one this year because you like having a new car (habit formation).

As would be expected, alcohol consumption is estimated to be quite strongly subject to habit formation—more strongly, in fact, than tobacco products consumption. But there are eight other categories of consumption with higher habit-formation estimates than for alcohol. Furthermore, Houthakker and Taylor find that overall, "habit formation quite clearly predominates in United States consumption" and that the extent of predominance has increased over time. Sixty-one percent of total consumer expenditure is in the forty-six categories showing habit formation, while only 28 percent is in the fifteen categories showing inventory adjustment. It is suggested that increasing affluence is responsible for the rise in habit formation, so that a rise in disposable income means that clothes buying, for instance, becomes less a function of the wearing out of the stock on hand and more a function of expressive impulses and buying habits. At least within the terms of Houthakker and Taylor's analysis, then, expenditures on alcoholic beverages do show a considerable degree of habit formation, but in this they do not differ from a large and increasing preponderance of all consumer expenditures.

The major drawback of the econometric studies as evidence on the relation between control measures and drinking behavior is that they typically tell us nothing about variations in effects between subgroups of the total population. Even if one knows that an increase in price tends to cause a somewhat smaller decline in the total consumption, one does not know who is drinking less. Yet if a control policy is aimed, for instance, at reducing excessive drinking, it would clearly be important to know if it in fact affected only the behavior of light drinkers.

In this area, one is again in the realm of plausibilities rather than proofs. One thing which does seem clear is that change in the effective price affects the poor more than the rich. Advertisements for liquor addressed to the rich—for example, in the *New Yorker*—even make a virtue out of high price. Prohibition in the United States, in driving up the price of alcoholic beverages, seems to have accomplished a major shift in the distribution of consumption between the social classes. Under prohibition, the consumption of alcohol per capita by the working class declined by about 60 percent, but the per capita consumption "by the business, professional and salaried class [was] fully as great" toward the end of prohibition as at its inception.[44] This characteristic of raising the effective price will be regarded as a point in its favor by those, whether oligarchs or Marxists, who are particularly concerned to save working people from the evils of drink. From a populist perspective, or one of an insistence on equal protection of the laws, it tends rather to be an argument against. In any event, the net result of an increase in the effective price may be that the consumption, even though reduced, absorbs an increased proportion of the total family income. Thus Houthakker and Taylor, analyzing survey data on consumer expenditures, find for alcohol consumption, as befits a habit-forming commodity, that the proportion of income spent on alcohol became relatively higher for families whose income fell and relatively lower for families whose income rose.

On the crucial issue of differential effects by amount of

drinking, there is almost no direct evidence. Alcohol consumption is clearly more salient in general to heavy than to light drinkers. Heavy drinkers give more reasons for drinking than light drinkers,[45] and they are several times as likely as moderate drinkers to say they would miss drinking "a lot" if they had to give it up.[46] It is reasonable to expect, then, that the behavior of light drinkers will be the most amenable to change with a rise in the effective price. On the other hand, a great proportional change in the consumption of light drinkers will not greatly affect their family finances—or, as noted, the overall consumption statistics.

Increasing the effective cost of alcohol, then, will clearly pinch heavy drinkers much harder than light drinkers between two conflicting incentives—they have more to gain financially but also more to lose in gratification, from cutting down on consumption. The result will presumably vary from case to case. The consumption of affluent heavy drinkers, like that of affluent people generally, will no doubt be affected little. Terris notes that the cirrhosis death rate "is greatest in the lowest social class in the United States and in the highest social class in England and Wales," and that the relative price of alcohol is much greater in England and Wales than in the United States. "Spirits have been taxed out of the reach of the lower social classes in the United Kingdom, where only the well-to-do can really afford the luxury of dying from cirrhosis of the liver."[47] This pattern suggests that an increase in the general affluence of a society may result in a smaller proportion of heavy consumption being affected by control measures changing the relative price.

Poorer heavy drinkers will presumably take evasive action if possible, and their tenacity in this pursuit should not be underestimated. This is the segment of the alcoholic beverage market most affected by considerations of the "biggest bang for the buck," that is, the greatest amount of absolute alcohol for the lowest price. When strong wines were introduced in rural Finland at a price which made them the cheapest source of alcohol, "within a few weeks the . . . stores which so far had been dominated by beer became dominated by wine."[48] It seems plausible that the American "wino" would disappear if dessert wines became no longer generally the cheapest source of alcohol—but that he would be replaced by the inveterate drinker of what became the best bargain. Schmidt and Bronetto mention this factor in explanation of their finding that wine consumption trends are more highly correlated than beer or liquor trends with U.S. cirrhosis death rate trends.[49]

Clearly evasions by poor heavy drinkers have their limits, particularly without a supportive social context of moonshining, bootlegging and homebrewing. Really poor or destitute heavy drinkers may in fact be forced into relative sobriety by a substantial change in effective price, and conversely, in prosperous times, when there is a place for them in the labor market, really heavy drinkers will find it easier to drink to oblivion. Any gains even in this population, however, must be weighed against possible increases in poisonings from nonbeverage alcohol and of malnutrition from skimping first on food.

Conclusion

While general liquor control measures have the potential of affecting the whole population, their actual effects are different in different populations. Little enough is known about the net effects of control measures in the total population, but even less is known about their detailed effects in different segments of the population. Alcohol policies are in the end, of course, a matter of competing values and relative priorities. But it is hard to see how any policy, whatever its principles and aims, can make sense without just such a detailed knowledge of the shape of its practical effects.

As noted earlier, in the field of drinking laws and drinking behavior, the experience has been vast but the profit in terms of systematic understanding has been little. Hopefully, with some forethought, this equation may yet be reversed. A small amount of effort, when compared with the prodigious efforts which the experience already comprises, would go a long way toward clearing up some of the confusions and uncertainties found in this discussion. But this effort must be carefully planned, in terms of specific hypotheses to be tested and appropriate models for testing them. In particular, it should be emphasized that one cannot fully understand how and why behavior changes using static studies which describe conditions at a given moment in time. To understand change, one must study change.

CHAPTER 16

Drinking Laws in the Commonwealth of Virginia

Wayne W. Womer, D.D.

IF HISTORY IS the root of political science and political science the fruit of history, then an adequate understanding of current political problems requires a knowledge of their history. Liquor control in the Commonwealth of Virginia is no exception to this principle. To understand how and why Virginia legalized liquor-by-the-drink in 1968 we must know the evolution of different laws and concepts of liquor control there since the founding of the federal union.

Such a history includes not only legislative acts but also the attitudes of the Virginia population toward beverage control at various times. Indeed, as the late Dr. E. M. Jellinek, one of the founders of the Yale University Center of Alcohol Studies, observed: "The attitude of the people in any given state regarding the use of alcoholic beverages has more bearing on the consumption of alcoholic beverages than state laws."

Obviously, the problem confronting administrators of liquor control, whether they be judges or bureaucrats, has for a long time been real and difficult. It causes concern today, as it did in 1890 when the General Assembly recognized a growing dissatisfaction with the system under which licenses for the sale of ardent spirits were granted. Even as far back as 1779 the Virginia legislature was alarmed at "all manner of vice and immorality," and set about trying to restrain "so growing and dangerous an evil."[1] Governmental regulation of the liquor traffic has, in fact, been traced back into the dim past and furnishes the student with one of the best examples of public regulation that has been accepted as valid exercises of state police power.

Changes in the character of the so-called temperance problem occasioned by shifting social and technological conditions necessitated frequent reinterpretations of the objectives of regulation and the development of new control techniques. The legislative history of liquor control in Virginia for the past 175 years is thus in retrospect the history of the experimentation with various regulatory schemes designed to fit newly arisen social conditions.

The history of liquor control in Virginia can be divided conveniently into six periods. A brief summary of each period will help us to understand how the present law evolved.

The First Period (1789-1822)

Regulation in the first period followed the colonial pattern rather closely. The Liquor Control Act of 1792 was the first definitive liquor statute enacted after Virginia abjured its political allegiance to the mother country. However, the state did not repudiate the liquor control system it had used as a colony. On the contrary, it made several amendments.

The system of control lacked any separate liquor license; alcoholic beverages were made or sold under the same statutory conditions as governed other commodities. There was one important exception—sales of liquor for consumption on the premises could only be made by persons who were licensed to operate an "ordinary," a wayside inn which provided lodging for travelers. Liquor was considered a part of entertainment and diet for the traveler stopping at these ordinaries; selling liquor was therefore included among the privileges conferred by the license to operate an ordinary. The rationale appears to be that the ordinary constituted the traveler's home for the time of his stay and that persons should be allowed to do their drinking in homes. This principle is an early British custom and prevailed in modified form in the Alcoholic Beverage Control system in Virginia until about 1968.

In the first two decades of the nineteenth century the Virginia General Assembly made few changes in the 1792 law; later, however, the law was greatly modified as the colonial system began to feel the pressure of changing conditions.

The Second Period (1822-1873)

The second period may be described as the decline and fall of the ordinary, or the elaboration of the license system. The liquor license was firmly established as a separate privilege and soon extended to virtually all branches of the trade. In this transitional stage the legislature leaned heavily on the courts, giving them wide discretion to discover and enforce appropriate public policy. The Civil War hastened this development; so that by 1873 the liquor control system bore little resemblance to its predecessor of the first period. This period witnessed two major changes in Virginia's liquor control system. One involved the disappearance of many colonial regulations governing operation of ordinaries; the other was the rapid extension of the license system to almost every commercial liquor enterprise. Yet few control measures emerged; in fact, some old ones were dropped. Regulation probably lost some of its former effectiveness as courts assumed the burden of administering many new licenses.

During a relatively short period immediately following the Civil War, probably the most significant development occurred in the history of liquor control in Virginia. With two laws the General Assembly struck the death knell of the ordinary and ushered in the era of the saloon. An act of 1866 ended the ordinary's time-honored monopoly of sales for consumption on the premises by extending this privilege to eating houses. They were licensed to serve malt liquor, spirits, or cider with meals. Ordinaries, however, were still permitted to sell liquor with or without meals, and thus had this advantage over eating houses. The modern conception of a saloon as a place where any person can purchase liquor to be drunk on the premises without meals had no legal foundation as late as the 1860s. Yet the actual character of eating houses depended on the definition given the phrase "with meals." If such food as pretzels or sandwiches were accepted as meals, the saloon made its debut in 1866. All doubt was dispelled in 1872 when courts were authorized to license for on-premises sales

places other than eating houses and ordinaries. The saloon—
called a barroom—then became a legal reality in Virginia.

The Third Period (1873-1916)

The third period has been characterized as the heyday of
experimentation. It ended with the adoption of prohibition. If
there was one thing certain about liquor control in this period,
it was its changeability. During this era the search for more
effective methods of control led to the adoption of first one and
then another technique, some successful, others less so, until
the system grew into an exceedingly heterogeneous structure.
Many different kinds of licenses were legalized, the distinction
between on-premises and off-premises licenses disappeared,
the barroom began selling liquor for on-premises consumption, and this privilege was extended to the new malt-liquor
saloons. There was no injunction against the same person
holding licenses as a manufacturer, a wholesaler, and a
retailer, hence, the growth of the notorious tied-house system,
which led to many of the evils associated with the liquor traffic
during this period.

After a while when it became apparent that the law was
far too liberal and too many abuses were taking place, many
changes in the Liquor Control Act were made by the General
Assembly and many cases were brought to court. In the words
of the legislature:

> There exists in the cities of the Commonwealth a growing
> dissatisfaction with the system under which licenses for the sale
> of ardent spirits are granted; and the Legislature recognizes the
> justice of this complaint . . . and is disposed to surround the
> granting of these licenses with all the safeguards suggested by
> an enlightened and progressive public policy.[2]

Many reforms were tried. Finally local option was
adopted as a radical response to dissatisfaction with administration of the license system. This method enabled localities to
adopt prohibition by popular referenda. The first grants of this
local option privilege are found in three special acts passed by
the 1879 General Assembly. Making rapid progress, the movement chalked up seven more victories within the next five years
and then succeeded in obtaining the passage of a general local
option law that granted the privilege to every county, magisterial district, town, and city in the state.

Was the General Assembly going beyond its authority in turning over to the electorate responsibility for deciding whether there should be prohibition in a locality? This question was brought to the Supreme Court of Appeals and the answer was "no," upholding the constitutionality of local option. Local option has ever since (except during statewide prohibition) been an integral part of Virginia's liquor control systems.

Great experimentation in liquor control marked the period between 1900 and 1916, called the Prelude to Prohibition. Using local option, numerous communities became dissatisfied with liquor control and began to vote out the sale of alcoholic beverages. This, of course, put pressure on the General Assembly which finally organized a liquor monopoly for the magisterial district of Franklin and experimented with local dispensaries under community control. These actions did not solve the problem. A system of severe restrictions under the title of the Mann and the Byrd laws was then created to offset the inroads of local option in many of the communities voting dry. The General Assembly set up criteria concerning the kind of person who should receive a license to sell alcoholic beverages and increased the fee (known as the high license principle) making it difficult and costly to engage in liquor business.

The Mann law began conditioning the people in the state for prohibition. For the first time the General Assembly enacted a liquor law in response to growing pressure from the Anti-Saloon League. The provisions of this law seemed to say between the lines, "If you disobey these restrictions, prohibition is just around the corner." The league's leader, Bishop Cannon, claimed several years later that all "temperance legislation which has been passed by the General Assembly since 1902 has been passed either at the suggestion of or by the efforts of the Anti-Saloon League of Virginia."[3] All these restrictions, however, seemed rather fruitless.

The stage was now set for statewide prohibition, but just before the curtains dropped, the legislature bowed once more before the theory of high license. In 1910 it created a new type of license which limited the quantities of liquors to four and one-half gallons which the holder could ship on order to any person at a time. This required a fee of $1,000. The liquor tax on malt and other wholesalers was also greatly increased.

No important action was taken by the 1912 General

Assembly, but the year 1914 brought the question of prohibition squarely before the electorate. When one contemplates the
extent to which the state had gone dry by the end of 1913, the
question had only one possible answer. Ninety-five percent of
the state's area and 72 percent of its populace were under either
local option or no license. Consequently, in 1914 when the
enabling bill was introduced for the third consecutive session,
its passage was logical and almost a foregone conclusion. On
the fourth Tuesday of November 1914, by a margin of 30,365
male votes out of a total count of 158,137, the electorate
expressed itself in favor of prohibition. The governor then
proclaimed the election results, and liquor traffic became
illegal on and after November 1, 1916.

The Fourth Period (1916-1933)

The fourth period was the prohibition years. Prohibition in Virginia was launched under the egis of the Mapp Act,
which, approved by the governor on the tenth day of March
1916, became effective November 1 of the same year in accordance with the Enabling Act of 1914. After November 1 it was
unlawful to "manufacture, transport, sell, keep or store for
sale, offer, advertize or expose for sale, give away or dispense or
solicit in any way, or receive orders for or aid in procuring
ardent spirits, with certain exceptions."

Characteristic of prohibition laws, the greater portion
of the Mapp Act was devoted to regulations designed to prevent
abuse of the privileges exempted from the basic prohibition
policy. The act is, paradoxically, better remembered for its
permissions than its prescriptions. The provision that gave the
law its nickname, the One Quart Law, allowed persons to
import a quart of ardent spirits each month from sources
outside the state. They could either have it shipped to them by
common carrier or bring it into the state in their personal
baggage. Another exemption applied to persons who manufactured at home for their own consumption wine or cider from
homegrown fruit. The act also permitted persons to keep in a
bona fide home one gallon each of spirits and wine and three
gallons of beer, and to serve drinks to members of the family
and guests. Sacramental wine and sweet cider were entirely
exempted, and druggists were licensed to sell ardent spirits on

prescription. The manufacture and sale of ardent spirits and alcohol for drug stores and for many scientific and mechanical purposes was also licensed and subjected to strict regulation.

Federal laws soon curtailed or nullified many of these privileges. The Food Control Act prohibited the use of food in the production of distilled spirits after September 9, 1917, and authorized the President to reduce or prohibit the use of food in making beer and wine. War prohibition was next adopted, effective June 30, 1919, until the "termination of demobilization." It forbade the sale and importation (but not the manufacture) of intoxicating liquors for beverage purposes. This act definitely nullified the one quart privilege in Virginia. War prohibition was succeeded by the Eighteenth Amendment, which went into effect in January 1920, in accordance with its enforcing legislation, the National Prohibition Act. Strictly interpreting the new amendment, the act defined intoxicating liquor as that containing 0.5 or more percent alcohol.

A repressive law is of little value without effective means of enforcement. The General Assembly created an office of Commissioner of Prohibition and relied to a considerable degree on the enforcement activities of local officers implied from the meager appropriation of $25,000 to the Department of Prohibition and from the clause which empowered cities and towns to enact ordinances paralleling the Mapp Act.

During the period of the modified prohibition, the Mapp Act was amended only once, in 1922. The General Assembly in that year made three rather important changes in the administrative system. (1) It abolished the Department of Prohibition and transferred its functions to the Attorney General's office, and (2) it empowered law enforcement officers, under specified circumstances, to search and seize *without warrants*. (3) Finally, it authorized the Attorney General to institute ouster proceedings against any local officer who neglected his duty. Localities were assuaged, however, by being permitted to keep fines that they collected.

The passage of the Layman Act at the next session of the General Assembly in 1924 signified the end of modified prohibition and the beginning of strict, almost absolute, prohibition. Within the next decade prohibition reached its climax—and its denouement.

The Layman Act provided for almost any contingency that might arise in enforcing absolute prohibition. The monthly allotment clause was expunged from the law, and personal consumption was limited to liquors already on hand or used for medicinal and sacramental purposes. Druggists became subject to increased restrictions. Searches and seizures without warrant were extended to dance halls and rooms used in connection therewith. The law continued to induce activity on the part of local officers by holding out rewards for the capture of stills in addition to regular fees.

With minor exceptions, the Layman Act of 1924 remained unchanged up to the day of repeal, thus giving one the impression that it represented a final and all-out effort of the General Assembly to make prohibition work. Despite increased vigilance in enforcing the law, Virginia went the way of the nation when the time arrived to choose between prohibition and "a plan of liquor control."

The Fifth Period (1933-1950)

In the fifth period the question of legalized alcohol consumption in Virginia was raised again and the Alcoholic Beverage Control Board was established. After seventeen years of prohibition, in August of 1933 the Virginia General Assembly convened in special session to deal with the question of repeal. It did three things:

1) It legalized immediately the sale of alcoholic beverages containing not over 3.2 percent of alcohol by weight; 2) it provided for holding special election for choosing delegates to the ratifying convention and for choosing, in the event of national repeal, between state prohibition and some form of regulation; and 3) it created a committee to draft legislation for a plan of liquor control if the electorate favored state repeal.

When the Twenty-First Amendment was certified as part of the Constitution on December 5, 1933, the committee appointed by the General Assembly was able to come forward with the basis for a new law. The committee had reviewed the entire system of liquor control laws in the Commonwealth of Virginia since colonial days and considered the reasons for the success or failure of the laws. It tried to visualize the most ideal conditions under which alcoholic beverages might be sold without creating conditions which would bring public dissatisfaction and again result in many communities voting out the sale of liquor. After this study of the matter, the committee subscribed to eight fundamental principles which served as guidelines for producing a concrete legislative proposal.[4] These fundamental principles were:

1. The need for state or local revenue should be subordinated to the prime objective of "temperance, social betterment, and respect for law." The committee did not believe "that the system should be used to rehabilitate the finances of any class of citizen, any industry, or locality."

2. In order to merit the respect and support of a preponderant majority, the liquor control plan must be strong, liberal, and flexible. It should contain only "the main guiding principle" and should vest the control agency with "wide discretionary powers to modify the details as conditions demand."

3. "Local option should be a cardinal principle."

4. "The sale of alcoholic beverages should be brought out into the open and placed on a decent plane." Legal liquor should be dispensed at prices and under conditions which would discourage bootlegging.

5. "The private profit motive, with its incentive to stimulate the sale and consumption of liquor, should be reduced to a minimum."

6. The old saloon must not return.

7. Temperance can be promoted by a system which discourages the use of hard liquors and encourages the use of light fermented beverages.

8. "No system of liquor control will be entirely satisfactory to all citizens. . . . It should be designed as a workable compromise to insure the greatest good to the greatest number of citizens as a whole."

The framers of the liquor control act after the repeal of prohibition had sought to set up a system to avoid the abuses of former years so there would be no attempt to bring back statewide prohibition. Under the new liquor control act beer could be sold in eating places and was made readily available to the public. Hard liquor and fortified wine could be sold only under the direction of the Alcoholic Beverage Control

Board and in state stores where spirituous liquors could be available to the public if they wanted them but where no effort should be made to induce their purchase. This new law adopted at the end of prohibition stayed in effect until 1968 with little change or modification.

The Sixth Period (1950-1976)

The first significant change was the legalizing of liquor-by-the-drink which occurred in the sixth period (1950 to the present). The question arises as to why the state took thirty-five years to legalize liquor-by-the-drink. The kinds of people who lived in Virginia greatly influenced the history of liquor control in the state. When the evangelical church increased in membership throughout Virginia, their influence became pronounced. The denominations, largely Baptists and Methodists, belonging to the abstinence tradition, continually brought pressure to bear upon the General Assembly and were largely responsible for statewide prohibition in the earlier years. Their influence was strongly felt in the framing of the new liquor control act after prohibition which did not provide for liquor-by-the-drink. As the years passed, the character of Virginia rapidly changed: new industry was bringing in new people; affluence and the cult of permissiveness were rising and the authority of the church was declining.

A liquor-by-the-drink bill was introduced in the General Assembly in 1950 as a trial balloon. It received little or no support and brought much protest. For the next eighteen years each session of the General Assembly had to consider liquor-by-the-drink legislation. About 1962 an all-out effort was made to enact a liquor-by-the-drink bill; however, this failed. The evangelical influence, though still vocal, was shifting slowly.

In the 1960s new issues arose to engage people's attention; the focus shifted to war, poverty, and race. The issue of liquor-by-the-drink became old hat, and slowly the attitude developed that such a bill would eventually pass so why keep fighting it. The prohibition-minded denominations shifted their emphasis from abstinence to a kind of permissiveness called "the responsible use of beverage alcohol." The economic influence was pronounced in the demand for legislating mixed drinks. Counties, towns, and cities in the Commonwealth were hard pressed to find additional sources of revenue. Tourism, which is now big business, also demanded liquor-by-the-drink, not only to attract more tourists but to get them to spend more money in Virginia. So, in 1968, after much activity by the proponents between sessions, the General Assembly enacted the liquor-by-the-drink bill into law.

The 1968 liquor-by-the-drink bill is labeled as "Model Act." Seeking to prevent abuses, if possible, it bears the imprint of past history, of the concern of the citizens with strict control. The Alcoholic Beverage Control Board always had wide authority, made many regulations, and been strict. The highlights of the present act are as follows:

1. Any city, town, or county has to hold a local option election to legalize mixed drinks. Twenty percent of the qualified voters must sign a petition calling for such elections.

2. Mixed drinks can only be served with food. Food must comprise over 51 percent of the restaurant's business.

3. No table hopping. Customers must be seated at tables of more than two.

4. No standing or drinking at bar.

5. Restaurants to qualify for a license must be able to seat fifty or more.

6. All spirits must be purchased from the state stores.

7. Hours are the same as legalized by the community for beer and wine. No sales before 8 A.M.

8. Sunday sale is determined by the governing body of the community.

After local option elections were held, forty-five cities, towns, and counties voted for mixed drinks. Two cities (Danville and Salem), six counties, and one town voted against. Many other places held no election.

There has been no rush to secure licenses. In the fiscal period of 1968 to 1969, 345 active licenses were issued to restaurants for mixed drinks. In 1969 to 1970, a total of 434 licenses were in effect. At the end of the fiscal period 1971 there were 491 out of an approximate 1,500 to 2,000 that might be eligible. In 1972 there were 572 active mixed drinks licenses, in 1973 there were 655 and in 1974 there were 705. These are far below the number predicted.[5] There are about 9,000 public restaurants in Virginia—not all of which, of course, are eligible for a license. Many eligible restaurant owners have evidently been waiting to see if liquor-by-the-drink has been profitable to those who secured licenses. Here again, we can see the influence of the past; the English custom of home drinking that prevailed in the colony still persists.

Effects of Liquor-by-the-Drink

Proponents have argued that liquor-by-the-drink was available in the state before it was legalized. Opponents to the legislation have argued that it would lead to an increase in alcohol consumption, public drunkenness, and drinking drivers.

In evaluating the effects of this legislation, you will find the tables that follow most helpful, since they compare data over time.

Table 16-1 shows the number of gallons of spirits sold by the Alcoholic Beverage Control stores for the three years before liquor-by-the-drink and the six years after that legislation. The gallon measure rather than the amount of revenue is used for comparison to eliminate the effect of price changes and inflation. The percentage increase is the increase in sales over the preceding year. In 1968, when the liquor-by-the-drink became legal, there was a 6.22 percent increase over the previous year. This probably represents a stocking up of restaurants for their anticipated sales. In 1971, there was a decrease which was probably due to increased taxes and an economic slowdown at that time. Otherwise, these figures reflect an overall growth in sales rather than any sharp or particular trend.

Table 16-2 compares the number of persons committed to city and county jails and jail farms on charges of drunkenness and drunk and disorderly for the period of three years before and six years after the legalization of liquor-by-the-drink. As of 1972, the trend was to emphasize rehabilitation efforts rather than jail.

Table 16-3 shows the number of driving-under-the-influence convictions for the three years before and six years after liquor-by-the-drink legislation. The number of drivers and miles driven as well as the nature of the law enforcement are important factors to be considered and for which data are

Table 16-1
Virginia Sales and Consumption Data for Fiscal Years 1965-1974
(in gallons of distilled spirits)

Fiscal Period	Gallons of Spirits Sold[a]	Percent Increase Sold[a] (over previous years)	Per Capita Consumption Rate[b]
1965	6,284,939	–	–
1966	6,515,505	3.67	–
1967	6,779,185	4.05	1.53
1968	7,200,759	6.22	1.60
1969	7,481,520	3.90	1.66
1970	7,784,441	4.05	1.66
1971	7,743,022	–0.54	1.68
1972	8,069,462	0.50	1.71
1973	8,364,956	2.71	1.78
1974	8,503,197	1.65	—

[a] Source: Virginia Alcohol Beverage Control Board, *Annual Reports.*
[b] Source: Distilled Spirits Institute, *Annual Statistical Reviews, 1965-1974.*

not available. Not included, also, are those cases which might properly be labeled as driving under the influence but which received reduced or other charges.

Interpretation of all these data must take into account the amount of illegal alcohol consumed before the legislation and the increase in population after the legislation as well as the incompleteness of information available. The results at this point, however, seem inconclusive.

Now and in the Future

To understand the present system of alcohol control in Virginia requires a knowledge of its historical roots over the past 200 years. The past few years especially have brought more changes in the attitudes and habits of people—revolutionary changes when one considers that for thirty-five years Virginia allowed no sale of spirits by the drink.

Liquor-by-the-drink has now been legal in Virginia since July 1, 1968. This has not been long enough to establish any new definite trend in the drinking customs of Virginians.

There are now nine towns, twenty-five cities, and twenty-eight counties that have legalized mixed drinks. However, certain changes have taken place. The proponents of the mixed drinks law in 1968 stated that it was a model law that would prevent all the evils of the old time saloon. But, of course, no one proposed that it would be amended at a future date liberalizing this law. Consequently, this is what has happened.

First, the greatest change taking place is the number of convictions for driving under the influence. In 1968, 5,994 persons were convicted; in 1974, 15,311 persons were con-

Table 16-2
Number of Persons in Virginia
Committed to City and Count Jails and Jail Farms on
Charges of Drunkenness or Drunk and Disorderly from 1965 to 1974

Year	Number of Commitments
1965	44,474
1966	42,599
1967	41,350
1968	40,202
1969	41,314
1970	42,279
1971	42,440
1972	39,972
1973	39,577
1974	38,547

(Source: Virginia Department of Welfare and Institutions Annual Reports.)

victed.[6] This increase is partially due to changes in the law, to lowering the Blood Alcohol Content from .15 to .10, and to the legalization of the breath test; also to improved law enforcement and to the impact of the Alcohol Safety Action Program (ASAP) in populous Fairfax County.

Second, the percentage of votes in a locality necessary in order to call for a local option election is now 15 percent rather than 20 percent.

Third, the Alcoholic Beverage Study Commission to study the present Alcoholic Beverage Control Act has recommended the following changes to the Alcohol Beverage Control Board relating to the mixed drinks laws:

1) The original law required that mixed drinks only be purchased with a full meal. It is now recommended that club sandwiches, pizzas, and the like be regarded as a light meal providing full meals can be purchased.

2) It is also recommended that Counter Sales be permitted when such counter is used for serving food; before the patron had to be seated at a table.

3) That the original law permitting only one drink be now modified so that the customer can now have two mixed drinks in front of him, also that customers now be allowed to

Table 16-3
Number of "Driving Under the Influence"
Convictions in Virginia from 1965 to 1974

Year	Number of Convictions
1965	4,943
1966	5,763
1967	5,973
1968	5,994
1969	6,406
1970	7,359
1971	9,389
1972	11,703
1973	14,006
1974	15,311

(Source: Virginia Department of Motor Vehicles, Annual Reports.)

move from table to table.

4) Furthermore, the strict rule about advertizing shall be relaxed, particularly in the advertizing of mixed drinks.

Now is not the time, or place, to predict or prophesy, but merely to state historical facts. The many aspects of drinking behavior—law enforcement, education programs, religious policy, taxation, therapeutic programs, campaigns of politics, information and indoctrination—have all been present in the past and have had their share in influencing the current legal and social attitudes toward the use of alcohol beverages in Virginia. They will continue to do so in the future.[7]

CHAPTER 17

Legal Controls of Drinking, Public Drunkenness, and Alcoholism Treatment

Frank Grad, LL.B.

LEGAL REGULATORY CONTROLS of drinking behavior and the treatment of alcoholics have received much attention, but the role of the law in dealing with drinking problems is a fairly limited one. Law can affect behavior, and drinking behavior is no exception. To determine to what extent changes in behavior are due to legal pressures and to what extent such changes are due to changes in general social attitudes is difficult—and it is, of course, difficult to determine whether changes in the law are themselves due to changes in the mores and folkways, or vice versa. Religious attitudes, too, may have a great deal to do with personal behavior, and changes in patterns of sexual behavior, drinking behavior, and other aspects of personal conduct may well reflect changes in underlying social and religious attitudes. A waning of strict attitudes may in turn have an impact on the enactments of new laws as well as in changed interpretations and attitudes of enforcement of existing laws.

Whatever else may be true of drinking behavior, it is a personal matter whether one chooses to drink or abstain, or to drink to moderation or excess. As in other instances of sumptuary law, the purposes of the law need to be defined. It is not to reinforce religious attitudes. It is not to reinforce the attitudes of any one socially dominant group in the population, and it is not to protect individuals against their own folly. All of these purposes are better served by other social controls, whether religious, educational, or familial or reflected in the approval or disapproval of a particular person's social environment. The role of the law, it is here suggested, is simply to deal with those aspects of drinking behavior that cause demonstrable harm to society—and not only to the person whose behavior society may frown upon.[1] The law, then, must draw that rather delicate balance between personal liberty—to live as one wishes, even self-destructively—and the interest of society in protecting itself against physical aggression or other palpable injury.

To be sure, alcoholism does cause considerable injury (as do other diseases!) to society as a whole and to the immediate family of the alcoholic. For 1971, the national cost of alcoholism has been calculated as 25.3 billion dollars in lost work, medical expenses, and motor vehicle accidents. There are, according to most recent statistics, some 9 million alcoholics in the United States, and that number is increasing at the rate of some 250,000 persons per year—and each alcoholic is said to affect a minimum of five other persons.[2] If these figures are reliable—and there is no reason to disregard them—then alcoholism is a major national problem, adversely affecting better than one-fourth of the population and adding significantly to the sum total of national unhappiness.

Control of Liquor Sale and Distribution

Other chapters in this book address themselves in considerable detail to the subject of social control through the legal regulation of liquor distribution and sales.[3] Without attempting to respond in detail or to deal in an analytical fashion with the man; alternative devices for controls proposed, I suggest merely that the law has been no more successful in the regulation of drinking behavior through the control of the liquor business than it has been in its attempt to regulate drinking behavior more directly. That is not to say that the control of the liquor business has not served a number of desirable social ends. What is questioned here is the efficacy of such controls in substantially affecting drinking behavior. It has been demonstrated, of course, that absolute prohibition on liquor sales will reduce problem drinking.

> Rates of problem drinking apparently decreased substantially during the early years of prohibition, although, at least in part, this was a continuation of previous declines. Reported deaths from liver cirrhosis also declined, as did hospitalization for alcoholism. Arrests for public drunkenness were much lower than earlier. . . .[4]

This quotation from the authoritative 1969 report of the Cooperative Commission on the Study of Alcoholism points to the rather limited success of even so drastic a remedy as prohibition. Had prohibition been an effective, enforceable way of dealing with problems of alcohol use, then problem drinking, liver cirrhosis deaths, and arrests for public drunkenness should have been reduced to negligible proportions. What is surprising, then, is not that an absolute prohibition on selling and dispensing of liquor reduces excessive drinking, but rather that it has never succeeded in coming close to eliminating such behavior.

Although the intensity of the battle seems to have subsided, there is still a lively contest between those who want to see our laws wet and those who want to see them dry. Indeed, there is not a single state in the Union where liquor cannot be purchased, although there are still many dry counties and municipalities. Any attempt to go from dry to wet is generally fought by an unholy political alliance of temperance forces and bootleg interests. Our society will likely take the direction charted by the Cooperative Commission on the Study of Alcoholism—neither wet nor dry, but moist.[5]

There is also the question of the appropriate manner of regulating the distribution and sale of alcoholic beverages. Some advocate a state liquor monopoly, and some would leave the business in private, though thoroughly regulated, hands. Aside from the fact that in many monopoly states liquor is less expensive than in nonmonopoly states, who sells the bottles appears to have little effect on drinking behavior. If anything, an argument can be made that by providing liquor at a lower price, the state monopolies encourage rather than discourage liquor consumption, though again there is no convincing evidence of this. What is certain, however, is that the liquor business is profitable, regardless of who manages it. The states that have a liquor monopoly derive very handsome revenues, and it is likely that any serious attempt to try and cut down on liquor consumption would affect the tax structure in the monopoly states—that is, some taxes would go up to compensate for the loss in liquor revenue.

Another lively debate regarding the nature of liquor regulations is that between the by-the-drink and by-the-bottle jurisdictions. Aside from the inconvenience caused to drinkers by having to brown bag their liquor, it is questionable whether by-the-drink or by-the-bottle provisions have any major impact on drinking behavior—there are enough phony "private clubs" around in most of the jurisdictions that purport to prohibit by-the-drink sales to approximate the open bar situation in the jurisdictions that do not. There are some side issues, however. Some states that prohibit by-the-drink sales also prohibit carrying unsealed liquor bottles in motor vehicles. This places an obvious premium on disposing of liquor by carrying it inside the drinker rather than inside the bottle, and that probably encourages overconsumption.

Another argument frequently made is that by-the-drink sales encourage excessive drinking because, as closing time approaches you have, as in some Scandinavian countries, the phenomenon of the "six o'clock swill": an attempt is made to put away as much as possible before closing time. There is a nice question whether longer hours for bars and other by-the-drink places discourage swilling. Comparative studies are needed to determine whether there is a swill whatever the closing time. Is it not almost as likely that there will be a 1 A.M. swill as a 6 P.M. one?

The three principal objectives of present liquor control systems to prevent abuses in the liquor business have been listed as follows:

(1) Prevent abuses in the liquor business such as participation by criminal elements, solicitation for prostitution, and other illegal activites in bars, by "policing" the industry, including enforcement of minimum price and "fair trade" laws;

(2) Produce income for states and the federal government

through the sale and taxation of alcohol and through license fees; and

(3) Promote temperance.[6]

The last objective, while generally a part of the state's alcoholic beverage statute, plays little part in the work of the several state liquor authorities. Usually, the enforcement of laws against the serving of alcoholic beverages to minors and to intoxicated persons represents the full range of temperance activities on the part of the state agency.[7] On the whole, state regulations of the distribution and sale of alcoholic beverages have stressed the nontemperance-directed purposes.

The efforts to prohibit or control liquor-by-the-drink take on a great deal more meaning in the context of other regulatory concerns than in the context of controlling drinking behavior. Liquor-by-the-drink sales are generally cash transactions and the amount of liquor sold in this fashion is difficult to check or regulate. There is also the additional problem of "refilling," i.e., the filling up of bottles having name brand labels with less expensive liquor, or even with bootleg brands. The amount of cash generated in liquor-by-the-drink sales—just as in the case with cash derived from juke box, pinball machine, and other small cash transactions—can then be used by illegal business or racket interests to serve as a smokescreen for other transactions. Thus, liquor-by-the-drink sales create many economic and social problems, though it is questionable whether increased consumption of alcoholic beverages is one of them.

From the point of view of the efficacy of regulatory controls, it is important to define clearly the aims and purposes of the law. More stringent controls on the distribution and sale of alcoholic beverages and an elaborate administrative apparatus may well be necessary to deal with problems of crime control and illegal business operations—as well as to produce needed state and federal tax revenues. There is little reason, however, why these purposes, useful and valuable in themselves, ought to be diluted by any notion that these laws are capable of having any major impact on drinking behavior itself. If years of prohibition by constitutional amendment were unsuccessful in permanently influencing national drinking behavior, why is it reasonable to assume that lesser, indirect controls will be more successful?[8]

Regulation of Drinking Behavior
Through the Criminal Law

Although recent developments in a new direction will be noted, the majority of American jurisdictions still attempt to regulate drinking behavior through the criminal law.[9] Thus, although the consumption of liquor is usually legal and the use of alcoholic beverages at a variety of social events is socially sanctioned, the law does try to deal with certain aspects of the problem of excessive drinking. Note that drinking to excess has never been illegal in itself. Although there are many self-appointed guardians of the morals and social behavior of their fellow citizens, there is no legal prohibition on drinking to excess in the privacy of one's own home. Nor is there any effective regulation of excessive drinking in more public places as long as the drinker does not come to the attention of the police through some overt behavior. Thus, until some recent changes, the law's primary preoccupation in dealing with drinking behavior has been not the welfare of the drinker but the peace and quiet of the community. A person who chooses to drink to excess to the point of becoming an alcoholic need never come to the attention of public authorities, though his social relations may be adversely affected and though he may alienate or lose his family and his job. He may go right on conducting himself in this irrational manner as long as his behavior is quiet and subdued and does not bring him to the attention of the police.

Thus, the major effort of the criminal law in controlling drinking behavior deals only with a small minority of public drinkers who are noisy and otherwise offensive. There is a nice question of the precise aims of the criminal law in dealing with inebriates. Primarily, they appear to be sanitary and aesthetic—i.e., to keep the city streets free from annoying drunks.[10] Moreover, the criminal law is made to carry the burden of society's moral disapproval of excessive drinking behavior—regardless of whether, in any particular instance, it imposes a real danger or risk to the public.[11]

A number of categories of the criminal law have traditionally dealt with drinking. The mildest of these, which can still be found in some form in fourteen jurisdictions, is a prohibition on drinking in public.[12] Some states prohibit drinking in public outright, others specify particular public places such as churches,[13] public meeting halls,[14] wharves, trains[15] or even, in one instance, scholastic athletic events,[16] where no alcoholic beverages may be consumed. Thus a person who takes a sip from a hip flask at a school football game, regardless of whether he annoys or otherwise interferes with others, was, until recently, committing a misdemeanor punishable by up to sixty days in jail in the state of Maryland.[17] Few prosecutions for public drinking were made at this time. The offense of public drinking will generally not be prosecuted when a more serious charge may be brought.

The person who drinks in a public place is more likely to be arrested for being publicly intoxicated.[18] In the majority of jurisdictions that still retain the offense, the charge of public intoxication can be proved by showing that the defendant was in a public place and conducted himself in a manner which is normally associated with drunkenness, including incoherent or unusually loud talk,[19] unsteady or staggering gait,[20] or a disheveled appearance.[21]

Another offense which is found on the statute books of a majority of states is that of drunk and disorderly conduct,[22] generally considered a somewhat more serious offense than public intoxication. However, the penalties provided for each of these offenses are nonetheless rather similar, ranging in the several states from a fine of a few dollars to a high of $1,000,[23] and, alternatively, jail terms ranging from a few days up to one year.[24] The typical range of statutory penalties is from $25 to $300 and from thirty days to three months.[25] The fines *actually* imposed by the criminal court are apt to be minimal, and the jail terms imposed are likely to be for only a few days, regardless of whether the particular jurisdiction's law authorizes considerably heavier sanctions.

Although drunk and disorderly conduct is regarded as a somewhat more serious offense than public intoxication and although this is likely to be reflected in the actual fine or jail sentence imposed, there is little distinction between the kinds of behavior that may give rise to either charge. Drunk and disorderly conduct has been held to involve "boisterous or indecent behavior or discourse which is loud and profane"[26] or "falling prone while intoxicated."[27] It is hard to draw a distinction between a person who talks "incoherently or unusually loudly"—which is recognized evidence of public intoxication—or one who is engaged in loud or profane discourse. The difference between "staggering"—evidence of public intoxication—and falling prone is also likely to be one of degree rather than kind. Basically, which of the two charges will be brought against an offender will depend entirely on the arresting officer's judgment.[28] Apparently nothing is gained by retaining both of these rather undifferentiated offenses on the statute books, and furthermore drunk and disorderly conduct is an inappropriate charge in any event. If a person is clearly guilty of disorderly conduct, the fact that he is also drunk hardly adds an aggravating circumstance, nor does it make his conduct any more threatening to the public. If a person is not disorderly, then the fact that he is noticeably drunk should at most give rise to a public intoxication charge, if the criminal law is to be invoked at all.

Another category of criminal conduct that involves drinking is a charge of vagrancy. A number of vagrancy statutes define the person who is a "common drunkard" or a "habitual drunkard" as a vagrant.[29] Vagrancy prosecutions are gradually getting out of style. It is recognized that vagrancy is a difficult charge to sustain against constitutional attack on due process grounds, and the United States Supreme Court and the highest courts of a number of states have invalidated particular vagrancy laws as void for vagueness.[30] The original rationale for vagrancy prosecutions was that a vagrant was a person more likely to engage in criminal behavior than others.[31] First, it is difficult if not impossible to prove this, and second, the criminal law is designed to punish for past offenses perpetrated, rather than to impose sanctions prospectively, on the mere chance that the defendant might commit a crime in the future. Nonetheless, the inclusion of common drunkards in the outlaw category of vagrants is illustrative of early social attitudes reflected in the criminal law. Of recent, the terms "habitual drunkard," or "common drunkard" have been attacked as unduly vague, and courts have held such vagrancy statutes unconstitutional as void for vagueness.[32]

The entire matter of criminal prosecution for drunken-

ness offenses has an air of triviality, in spite of the fact that
drunkenness offenses—even excluding the offense of drunken
driving—until recently accounted for some 2 million arrests
annually. This means that better than one-third of all arrested
offenders were arrested for drunkenness offenses.[33] Although
the changes in the law of some of the states in the early
seventies have undoubtedly improved the situation, no precise
data are as yet available. The large number of drunkenness
arrests also mean that the police and the lower criminal
judiciary spent (and still spends) an inordinate amount of time
and energy in arresting and processing drunks without any
demonstrable social benefit. Study after study has shown that
arrest and criminal prosecution of drunkenness offenders is a
form of revolving-door justice which benefits neither the
offender nor the community. The same offenders are arrested
and put through the process time and again.[34] The well-known
cases of the late sixties that challenged the constitutionality of
criminal prosecution for public intoxication each involved
defendants that had been arrested, prosecuted, subjected to
correctional treatment, and released from forty to 200 times
previously.[35] The police inebriate is usually an alcoholic
whose drinking is of a compulsive nature and who is therefore
the least likely to be deterred by the usual apparatus of the
criminal law. There is evidence, too, that in practice the
criminal process reflects a great deal of social bias and is highly
discriminatory in its application. The skid-row alcoholic or
the lower-class problem drinker is likely to be arrested for
drunkenness offenses readily and frequently. A well-dressed
middle-class drinker on his way home from a party or a genteel
spree who is found in an intoxicated condition by a police
officer—and who has the price of a cab ride in his pocket—is
far more likely to be escorted to a taxi and to be sent home to
sleep it off. Of course, police arrest and jail provide at least
some minimal protection for the lower-class or skid-row
alcoholic who might not otherwise have a warm and relatively
safe place to recover from intoxication.[36] It is true that the local
drunk tank sometimes meets this minimal requirement, although it does not meet it very well. Intoxicated persons, and
particularly alcoholics who are taken in by the police, frequently suffer from injuries caused by falls or accidents or from

a variety of physical ailments. Many of them may succumb to delirium tremens or go into shock. The police lockup or drunk tank facilities normally do not provide medical care or even a minimal medical examination. Death in the drunk tank is not an unusual occurrence—prior to a change in the law toward greater treatment orientation, sixteen persons died in such facilities in one year in Washington, D.C.[37]

The criminal law offers no solution to the problem of excessive drinking. It neither deters the offender nor protects the alcoholic when he is in need of protection. The urgency and dimension of the problem compel us to turn to other solutions. One of the issues presented is whether punitive sanctions devised by law are either suitable or appropriate to drinking behavior. Most people would not get drunk regularly even if all legal penalties for drunkenness were removed. Persons who do drink to excess do so in spite of the threat of legal compulsions. In recent years the emphasis of the law has begun to change—the growing emphasis is less on punishing or correcting the drunkenness offender and more on providing facilities and opportunities for treatment.

Recent Developments in the Legal Treatment of Public Drunkenness Offenders

The Road to Powell v. Texas

The view of alcoholism as a disease rather than as a pattern of willful criminal conduct is indubitably part of a general movement in society to substitute treatment approaches for the punitive attitudes of earlier law. Essentially, the newer approach is to treat the social pathology rather than to seek out an individual and to punish him for particular conduct defined as an offense. An important judicial development in that direction occurred not in the field of alcoholism but in the field of drug use.

In 1962, in *Robinson* v. *California,* the Supreme Court had to decide on the constitutionality of a California statute which made it a criminal offense to be "addicted to narcotics."[38] In reviewing a conviction under that statute, the Supreme Court found that narcotics addiction was an illness and held that it was a violation of the constitutional protection against cruel and unusual punishment to penalize an addict not for any particular criminal act but simply because he was ill. The *Robinson* case came to be regarded as holding that a person could not be punished for being in a particular status of illness, i.e., for being an addict. The general doctrine was soon tested in a series of cases involving alcoholics. The case of *Driver* v. *Hinant*,[39] decided in 1965, involved an appeal from a public intoxication conviction by a defendant who had been convicted of this offense at least 200 times previously. The court held that the defendant as a chronic alcoholic could not be convicted of the crime of public intoxication because public intoxication was symptomatic of his disease and to convict him would run counter to the prohibition of the Eighth Amendment.

Shortly thereafter, the Washington, D.C., Circuit Court, in *Easter* v. *District of Columbia*,[40] reversed a similar conviction of a chronic alcoholic who had also been convicted of public intoxication on numerous prior occasions. A number of other courts followed suit, and the view was gaining currency in the late sixties that henceforth alcoholics could no longer be convicted for public intoxication.[41] Such a legal doctrine would not make criminal prosecutions for public intoxication invalid, but in every instance of such a charge a determination would have to be made whether or not the defendant was an alcoholic. If he was, he would have to be excused from criminal prosecution.

In the absence of a decision by the United States Supreme Court, the law remained in a state of uncertainty, but in response to some of the court decisions mentioned, a number of states began to move in a new direction of treatment rather than arrest for intoxicated persons. Maryland,[42] Washington, D.C.,[43] Hawaii,[44] and North Dakota[45] were the first jurisdictions to pass such laws. These new treatment laws—soon to be followed by other jurisdictions—were intended to abolish or limit criminal prosecution for persons charged with public intoxication and to provide reception and treatment services primarily in detoxification centers.

The development of the new laws that substituted treatment approaches for criminal prosecution of drunkenness offenses reflected the dissatisfaction with the criminal law rem-

edies, as well as growing belief that prosecution of alcoholics
for such offenses was likely to be held invalid, following the
doctrine of the *Robinson* case. This belief was shattered,
however, by the decision of the United States Supreme Court in
Powell v. *Texas*[46] in June 1968. That case, similar to the earlier
ones, had been appealed as a test case by a number of interested
organizations. It involved the conviction of Leroy Powell who,
similar to the defendants in the *Easter* and *Driver* decisions,
had had more than one hundred prior convictions for public
intoxication. The Supreme Court upheld the conviction in
spite of clear evidence that he was an alcoholic. The narrow
holding of the *Powell* case essentially consisted of a limitation
of the "status crime" decision in *Robinson*—the court held
that the conviction of an alcoholic for public intoxication did
not amount to cruel and unusual punishment under the
Eighth Amendment. The decision served to put a temporary
halt to the development of new treatment legislation in a
number of jurisdictions by removing the immediate pressure
for its enactment. It also raised a great many questions of
policy and law which will remain unresolved for some time.

There were no fewer than four opinions in the case: the
majority opinion, so-called, subscribed to by four judges,[47] a
separate concurrence subscribed to by one,[48] a separate concurrence by two judges who also subscribed to the majority
opinion,[49] and a dissenting opinion joined in by four judges.[50]
The dissenting opinion is most easily disposed of. The four
dissenters sought to follow the decision in *Robinson,* and the
earlier decisions in the *Driver* and *Easter* public intoxication
cases. The dissent accepted the notion that alcoholism is a
disease and that public intoxication is symptomatic of that
disease. To punish an alcoholic for public intoxication, the
dissenters asserted, runs afoul of the Eighth Amendment and
constitutes cruel and unusual punishment because it penalizes
the condition or status of illness. The majority opinion,
written by Mr. Justice Marshall, on the other hand, not only
rejected the notion that alcoholism is a disease and that public
intoxication is symptomatic of that disease, but also contained
a number of other challenging ideas. The majority opinion
clearly indicates the court's reluctance to interfere with the
criminal prosecution of public drunkenness offenders until

some alternate mode of treatment will have been established:

> It would be tragic to return large numbers of helpless, some-
> times dangerous and frequently unsanitary inebriates to the
> streets of our cities without even the opportunity to sober up
> adequately, which a brief jail term provides. Presumably no
> state or city will tolerate such a state of affairs.[51]

In addition to the unsuccessful search for immediate
and serviceable alternatives to criminal prosecution, the court
indicated its reluctance to deal with an issue of considerably
broader implication than the criminal responsibility of intoxicated alcoholics for drunkenness offenses. The court took
pains to state that conduct which is involuntary or which is
generated by compulsion is not necessarily immune from
criminal prosecution. There was evidence of the court's awareness that a holding that intoxicated alcoholics are not to be
held criminally responsible would amount to a declaration
that the law of criminal responsibility has constitutional
ramifications. The court clearly wanted to avoid the legal
implication that every time a defendant asserts that he was not
criminally responsible by reason of compulsion, involuntary
act, mental defect, or the like, a federal constitutional issue
would arise. Thus far it has always been held that rules of
criminal responsibility are matters of state law, and the court's
decision shows its reluctance to turn common evidentiary
requirements in criminal cases into constitutionally required
tests or responsibility.

The two judges who joined the majority and also wrote
a separate concurring opinion wished to limit *Robinson* even
more strictly and expressly disapproved of any purported
constitutional requirement that behavior is to be immune from
punishment because it is involuntary or the result of compulsion, however caused.

The opinion which turned the case against Powell,
however, was the separate concurring opinion of Mr. Justice
White.[52] He took a position which, in its result, joined him
with the judges upholding Powell's conviction, though his
opinion put him closer to the dissenters. He found, with the
dissenters, that alcoholism is a disease and that Leroy Powell
had no control over his drinking. But he joined with the

majority in affirming the conviction because, in his view, there was not sufficient proof that defendant's appearance in public was caused by the same compulsion that caused the intoxication. He found that though Powell may have been under a compulsion to drink, he was not under any compulsion to appear in public in an intoxicated condition. Thus, though Powell's conviction was affirmed, five out of nine judges of the United States Supreme Court did indeed find that alcoholism is a disease.

The decision in *Powell* v. *Texas* warrants two comments. First, the decision will not likely be overruled in the foreseeable future. Changes in the composition of the Supreme Court make it less rather than more likely that criminal prosecution of alcoholics accused of public intoxication will be invalidated on constitutional grounds. Moreover, regardless of the composition of the court, there is no strong judicial desire to change rules of criminal responsibility into constitutional requirements. Such a major change in the criminal law would also create major pressures on the court's procedures for review.

Second, although many advocates of improved treatment approaches to alcoholism viewed the decision in *Powell* as a near disaster, subsequent history has shown that its effect has not been adverse. Although the decision did for a while relieve the pressure on state legislatures to enact treatment legislation, the natural import of the case is really the other way. As previously noted, the majority opinion indicated that the court looked with favor upon the decriminalization of public intoxication if alternate treatment modes were available.

Finally, it should be stressed that the case has not prevented states from enacting proper treatment legislation. On the contrary, the opinion left the states free to decide for themselves whether they wanted to deal with public intoxication by way of criminal prosecution or by way of other treatment approaches.

Treatment Legislation of the Late Sixties

Previous mention has been made of the enactment, just prior to the decision in *Texas* v. *Powell*, of laws in the District of Columbia, Maryland, Hawaii, and North Dakota that, in varying degrees, substitute treatment approaches for the criminal prosecution of publicly intoxicated persons. The most detailed of these early treatment laws is that of the State of Maryland, which became effective in July 1968. Its detailed set of findings and declaration of purposes state that it is "expensive, burdensome, and futile" to treat publicly intoxicated persons as criminals, and it favored the removal of such prosecution from the criminal system. As one of its further findings, it states that chronic alcoholism is an illness properly treated "under public health, welfare, and rehabilitation procedures" and that "voluntary treatment for alcoholism is more appropriate than involuntary treatment." Significantly, it also states that:

> to control public intoxication and chronic alcoholism requires a major commitment of efforts and resources by both public and private segments of the state. An effective response to these problems must include a continuum of detoxification, inpatient and out-patient programs, and supportive health, welfare, and rehabilitation services, coordinated with and integrated into a comprehensive health plan that covers all of the State's citizens.[53]

A Division of Alcoholism Control is established in the Department of Mental Hygiene to be in general charge of the state's treatment and rehabilitation plans and efforts. The legislation predicates a variety of short-term and extended care facilities.

The Maryland law abolishes public intoxication as a criminal category and provides instead that "any person who is intoxicated in a public place may be taken or sent to his home or to a public or private health facility by the police or other authorized personnel." Alternatively, such a person who is "either incapacitated or whose health is in immediate danger may be taken to a detoxification center." A person is considered incapacitated when he is unable to make a rational decision about accepting assitance.

Provision is made, too, for the use of detoxification centers on a voluntary basis by intoxicated persons who simply report there. The physician in charge of the detoxification center determines whether a person is to be admitted as a patient, referred to another facility for care and treatment, or denied referral and admission. If he is admitted as a patient, he may be required to remain until he is sober and no longer incapacitated, but in no event may he be detained there for longer than five days, unless he consents to a longer stay. At the conclusion of a person's stay at the detoxification center, he may voluntarily request transfer to other, more long-term treatment facilities. Since public intoxication is no longer a crime in Maryland, a police officer cannot arrest an intoxicated person, but the law protects the officer by stating that in taking an intoxicated person to a detoxification center or to his home the police officer acts within his official duty.

When an intoxicated person has been taken into custody by the police for a criminal offense, the new law requires him to be taken to a detoxification unit or another proper medical facility "when his condition appears to be or becomes such as to require emergency medical treatment." This procedure may raise some questions with respect to the constitutional require- ment that a person charged with a crime be taken before a magistrate as soon as reasonably possible. The judgment of how soon it may be reasonably possible to take the arrested person before a magistrate depends, under the Maryland law, on a determination of his need for emergency medical treat- ment. The inclusion of persons charged with other crimes in the group to be treated at a detoxification center may, moreover, have an adverse effect on the open character of the facility and may discourage voluntary admissions.

The law provides that while in a detoxification unit, the patient is to be encouraged to consent to treatment at an appropriate in-patient or out-patient facility. Voluntary admission to such facilities is also provided for. If a patient is diagnosed as a chronic alcoholic and if he consents, "intensive treatment for the illness shall begin immediately at the in- patient center while a comprehensive individualized plan is being made for his future out-patient treatment." The law evidences a generous, social orientation with respect to out- patient and after-care treatment. No patient may be dropped from out-patient treatment, for instance, solely because of a relapse into intoxication after the onset of therapy. No specific method of treatment is required but "all reasonable methods of treatment" are to be used. For chronic alcoholics for whom recovery is unlikely "supportive services and residential facilities shall be provided so that they may survive in a decent manner." The statute also says that all public and private community efforts, including welfare services, vocational rehabilitation, and job placement, should be utilized to reintegrate chronic alcoholics into society.

In addition to these purely voluntary provisions, civil commitment is also provided for. Prior to the expiration of the five-day period of detention for detoxification, the state's Commissioner of Mental Hygiene, or the governing body of the locality which controls the detoxification unit, may ask that a person be committed for detoxification or for in-patient treatment and care for a period of thirty days from the date of original admission to the detoxification unit, if the judge determines: that the person (1) is a chronic alcoholic, and as a result of chronic or acute intoxication is (2) in immediate danger of substantial physical harm and (3) unable to make a rational decision about accepting assistance. Such a person may be released from commitment, if in the judgment of the medical officer of the facility where he is detained he is again able to make a rational decision about accepting assistance, unless he chooses to remain voluntarily. Again, the patient is to be encouraged to consent voluntarily to further treatment and rehabilitation.

Maryland provides, too, that a person charged with or convicted of a crime may be committed to a detoxification unit or alcoholism treatment facility in lieu of the usual commitment to a penal institution. While the law thus is made applicable in part to a person convicted of a crime, it is expressly made inapplicable to chronic alcoholics who have been found to be mentally ill under laws relating to the determination of mental illness. Such a chronic alcoholic is to be dealt with under laws applicable to mental illness.

Provisions are also made for a variety of alcoholism programs, for training of professional and nonprofessional alcoholism workers, and for alcoholism education. The law also instructs the Division of Alcoholism Control to proceed immediately to develop "a detailed and comprehensive intoxication and alcoholism control plan for the state."

The District of Columbia Alcoholic Rehabilitation Act of 1967[54] preceded the Maryland law by about a half a year. Although the provisions for emergency treatment of intoxicated persons are similar to those provided under the Maryland law, the District of Columbia statute does not go quite as far in decriminalizing public intoxication. The District of Columbia Code retained the crime of public intoxication, and any person who after examination in the detoxification center is found not to be an alcoholic may be returned to court to be prosecuted as a public inebriate after treatment at the center has been completed. Under the District of Columbia Code, the longest period of time a person may be detained in the detoxification center is three days, rather than five as in Maryland.

North Dakota[55] abolished the crime of public drunkenness in 1969, and authorized police officers to take intoxicated persons to jail, to a hospital, or to their homes. A person taken to jail may be held for no longer than twenty-four hours, and if taken to a hospital he may be held for up to seventy-two hours. While so held, he will be considered in protective custody.

The laws enacted in the late sixties—particularly those in Maryland and the District of Columbia—represented significant legislative advances and became the prototypes of subsequent model and state legislation.

Federal Legislation

Reflecting the growing recognition of the problem of alcoholism in the United States, the Congress enacted the Alcoholism Rehabilitation Act of 1968,[56] subsequently expanded by the Community Mental Health Center Amendments of 1970.[57] That legislation, though inadequately funded, recognized that public intoxication and alcoholism are public health problems which should not be left to criminal procedures. This first federal effort in the alcoholism area sought to aid in the development of community-based planning and treatment and rehabilitation programs throughout the country by the authorization of certain construction, staffing, and special project grants.

Impressed by the magnitude of the long-neglected national problem of alcoholism, the Congress, in the closing days of 1970, enacted the Comprehensive Alcohol Abuse and

Alcoholism Prevention, Treatment, and Rehabilitation Act of 1970.[58] The new "comprehensive" federal law, established the National Institute on Alcohol Abuse and Alcoholism within the National Institute of Mental Health, to carry the responsibility for alcoholism-related programs within HEW. The law also authorized the establishment of alcoholism prevention, treatment, and rehabilitation programs and services for federal civilian employees, to be operated by the Civil Service Commission in cooperation with the secretary of HEW. Provision was also made for grants and contracts for demonstration, education and training, and other special projects.

The most significant and far-reaching provision of the law, however, establishes a grant-in-aid program to assist the states "in planning, establishing, maintaining, coordinating, and conducting projects for the development of more effective prevention, treatment, and rehabilitation programs to deal with alcohol abuse and alcoholism." Allotments to the states are to be based on population, financial need, and their respective demands for more effective programs for the prevention, treatment, and rehabilitation of alcohol abuse and alcoholism.

In order to obtain federal grant moneys, a state must submit a state plan designating a single state agency for administering the plan with sufficient authority to carry it out. Such a state plan must also set forth, in accordance with criteria set by the secretary of HEW, a survey of need for the prevention and treatment of alcohol abuse and alcoholism, including a survey of the health facilities required to provide such services, and a plan for their development and distribution throughout the state. The plan must provide for methods of administration, for periodic review, and for maintenance of effort. Each state must also provide in its plan for a state advisory council on alcoholism, to include "representatives of nongovernmental organizations and groups, and of public agencies" concerned with the problem. Although substantial appropriations were authorized in the law for federal assistance, the actual amounts have thus far failed to meet the needs.

An indicator of a recently strengthened congressional commitment to the resolution of problems of alcoholism was the enactment, in May 1974, of an amendment of the Comprehensive Alcohol Abuse and Alcoholism Prevention, Treatment, and Rehabilitation Act[59] over the opposition of the administration, which would have preferred to phase out the program. The 1974 amendments strengthened the legislative findings of the dimension of the problem and reaffirmed and enhanced the grant-in-aid provisions of the law. Moreover, the National Institute on Alcohol Abuse and Alcoholism is no longer within the National Institute of Mental Health, but directly under HEW, thereby enhancing its status. Other provisions prohibit public and private general hospitals that receive federal funds from discriminating in their admission and treatment policies against persons who are alcoholics.

Most significantly, however, the act establishes a special program of grants for the implementation of the Uniform Alcoholism and Intoxication Treatment Act, endorsing the very features of the Uniform Act that are referred to later in this chapter. As a condition of receiving such a special grant of up to $100,000 per year, the state must have "repealed those portions of their criminal statutes and ordinances under which drunkenness is the gravamen of a petty criminal offense, such as loitering, vagrancy, or disturbing the peace." In addition to decriminalization, the states must, as a condition of the special grant, exercise a preference for *voluntary* treatment, and for outpatient or intermediate, rather than in-patient care. Moreover, treatment is not to be denied solely because of past treatment failures, or past withdrawals from treatment against medical advice. The state program is to have individualized treatment plans for each patient, and there is to be provision "for a continuum of coordinated treatment services so that a person who leaves a facility or form of treatment will have available . . . other appropriate treatment."[60]

The federal endorsement of the principles of the Uniform Act by way of the special grant program is gratifying, though it is too soon to tell whether the limited amount of the grant will persuade states to adopt the Uniform Act that would not have done so without the small federal inducement.

State Responses to Federal Legislation

As clearly was its purpose, the enactment of federal legislation with provisions for grants-in-aid for state programs generated a great deal of activity on the state level, and a variety of new state legislation was passed in the early seventies.

In the enactment of the new alcoholism legislation, the states were aided considerably by the earlier prototype legislation in Maryland and the District of Columbia, as well as by the adoption in 1972 of the Uniform Alcoholism and Intoxication Treatment Act by the Conference of Commissioners on Uniform State Laws.[61] The Uniform Alcoholism and Intoxication Treatment Act was based primarily on model legislation prepared by the Legislative Drafting Research Fund of Columbia University under my direction, following a study undertaken pursuant to contract with the National Institutes of Mental Health.[62] In turn, the concept of the Columbia draft was derived from the Maryland statute.

The Uniform Act abolishes criminal prosecution for public intoxication and other alcoholism-related offenses other than drunken driving. It provides for detoxification facilities to take the place of the drunk tank, and it limits admission for detoxification to forty-eight hours. An intoxicated person may be detained for five days for emergency care unless a petition for commitment has been filed, in which case ten additional days of civil detention are allowed.

The Uniform Act also provides for a variety of integrated treatment facilities, ranging from detoxification centers, out-patient care programs, and half-way houses, to full in-patient treatment facilities. The model law provides for freely available transfers from one institutional setting to another, depending on the patient's needs—when commitment is necessary, a patient will not be committed to a specific institution, but to the agency in charge, so that he may be assigned to the facility or program most suitable.

The Uniform Act expresses a preference for voluntary treatment and for treatment by consent whenever possible, and an alcoholic may be committed only if he "has threatened, attempted, or inflicted physical harm on another or is incapacitated by alcohol." Incapacitation is defined to imply lack of judgment as to the need for treatment, but a refusal to undergo treatment does not, by itself, constitute evidence of such lack of judgment. Commitment is also limited as to duration—the initial commitment is to be for one thirty-day period, which may be extended for two successive ninety-day periods. The functions of planning and research are delegated in the Uniform Act to a state commission on alcoholism, and to advisory councils.

Three states—Alaska,[63] South Dakota,[64] and Washington[65]—have adopted the Uniform Act by name. Some ten jurisdictions have adopted essentials in modified and more or less abbreviated form.[66] Maine[67] and South Carolina[68] have adopted the basic provisions of the Uniform Act but have retained criminal prosecution for alcohol-connected offenses. A number of states have adopted the provisions of a "single state agency"[69] required by the federal law, while others have adopted statements of policy without making new provisions for facilities,[70] or have provided for new facilities without new statements of policy.[71] Most of the legislation has been on the books for only a year or two, and it is as yet premature to speculate on its effectiveness. The evidence of good intentions reflected in all of this new legislation will hopefully be backed by an adequate commitment of resources, for otherwise the beneficiaries of the purported social legislation may well be worse off, being deprived even of the minimal protection previously afforded by the drunk tank.

Decriminalization

The majority of states retain criminal prosecution for public intoxication and other drunkenness offenses. In consequence of recent legislative enactments, eighteen states have wholly or partially decriminalized drunkenness offenses. Three states—California, Maryland, and New Mexico—have provision for the jailing of unmanageable (disorderly) drunks only. In New Mexico this is not an arrest nor is it followed by criminal charges;[72] in California, it is an option to be exercised only when the officer is not "reasonably able" to place the violater in civil protective custody;[73] in Maryland it is a misdemeanor punishable by a maximum of $100 and ninety days.[74]

Washington, D.C.[75] provides that a notice of violation be left with the chief medical officer whenever a public drunk is taken into custody for detoxification. The patient is then examined for alcoholism. If he is found alcoholic, the chief medical officer has discretion to review his record to determine if the charge should be filed; if not, the notice is served immediately upon detoxification. Delaware[76] makes alcoholism an affirmative defense to any public drunkenness charge. Connecticut[77] allows a similar defense at judicial discretion (with subsequent commitment to a treatment facility for a minimum of thirty days to one year maximum) when so requested by any alcoholic defendant or when the defendant has twice been found guilty of public intoxication within the preceding six months.

In Maine,[78] no criminal charges are filed whenever a person incapacitated by alcohol is taken to a detoxification center, but the criteria for such a procedure are not specified. Georgia[79] and Indiana[80] both allow judicial discretion to impose protective custody in lieu of criminal penalties for charges resulting from alcoholism. North Carolina[81] shifts this discretionary power to the police, although arguably such discretion is always implicit in the arrest procedure. Several states while adhering to the policy that alcoholism is a disease meriting medical attention have nonetheless retained criminal penalties for public drunkenness perhaps as a stopgap measure.[82]

It is questionable, in view of the fact that the overwhelming number of persons charged with public intoxication are alcoholics, whether a partial decriminalization is administratively justifiable. Since the 1974 federal legislation makes decriminalization a condition of additional federal grant money, more states may soon head in that direction.

Drunkenness Legislation and Class Bias

The law providing for prosecution of public drunkenness offenders and the newer legislation calling for treatment approaches share certain social biases. For instance, the Maryland legislation, as does the District of Columbia law, gives the police officer the choice of escorting the inebriated person to the detoxification center or of seeing that he gets safely home. The police officer will likely exercise the choice in the same way he has previously made decisions on arrest and prosecution of public inebriates. The well-dressed middle-class alcoholic, or the middle-class person intoxicated after a spree, is not likely to be arrested by a police officer. If he has the cost of a taxi ride in his pocket, he is far more likely to be sent home by cab to sleep it off. If, however, the offender is badly dressed, or has the appearance of a skid-row alcoholic, he will be arrested and processed through the criminal court system. The same essential bias is perpetuated under the new treatment laws, except that instead of arrest and prosecution the skid-row or lower-class inebriate will be taken to the detoxification center while his middle-class counterpart will be sent home.

Because of his drinking patterns, one being that he drinks less frequently in public bars, the middle-class alcoholic is less likely to come to the attention of the police than the lower-class alcoholic. The class bias on the part of the police has as its consequence the fact that we know far more about the habits and social profile of the so-called police inebriate or skid-row drunk than we do about the middle-class alcoholic.[83] By conservative estimate, there are some 9 million alcoholics in the country today—yet only a small proportion of these alcoholics ever come to the attention of the police.

The social bias implicit in the enforcement of all public drunkenness legislation raises some interesting questions regarding the basic purposes of that legislation. If the purpose is to provide opportunities to get as many alcoholics into treatment as possible then the legislation falls far short of the mark, because the practice of focusing on lower-class or skid-row alcoholics allows the middle-class alcoholic to continue to deceive himself and to escape treatment which might otherwise be available to him. If, on the other hand, the purpose of such legislation is primarily aesthetic or sanitary, it may well be considered a success. It does aid in keeping the city streets free from obstruction and from unsightly and discouraging looking people. In the future, treatment legislation ought to require that any intoxicated person, regardless of class or appearance, be taken to the detoxification center for necessary treatment and for possible intake in a more extended alcoholism treatment program.

Long-Term Treatment of Alcoholics— Voluntary or Compulsory

The short-term detention in a detoxification unit or the more extended commitment of alcoholics to a long-term hospital facility raise similar basic issues. Under all of the new treatment laws, a person taken to a detoxification center may be detained until the physician in charge of the center releases him, but no longer than a set number of days—five days in Maryland, three days in Washington, D.C., two days in the states that have adopted the Uniform Act, three days in a North Dakota hospital, or one day in a North Dakota jail. In spite of the socially protective language of the different statutes involved, the detention of an intoxicated person in a detoxification unit in legal terms constitutes a civil commitment without court order. It is analogous to the short-term detention without court order of persons considered to be mentally disturbed, who are held until some more permanent disposition can be made of them.[84]

In general, the law is wary of commitments without court order. Such a commitment is not likely to be upheld against due process challenges unless a clear necessity for the detention can be shown and unless it can also be shown that it is not possible to obtain a court order without defeating the purpose of the short-term commitment. To obtain a court order before a person is admitted to a detoxification unit would clearly be impossible. The very purpose of the institution is to provide care and treatment quickly and informally. On the other hand, to justify continued detention of a person in a facility requires a good reason, related either to treatment needs or to requirements of social protection. Thus, any detention for longer than the time needed to render a person capable of making rational treatment decisions would be subject to constitutional challenge, unless that release would create danger of physical injury to the public.[85] There has not been any such challenge to the Maryland law to date, but it would be hard to defend a five-day detention for purposes of detoxification. It would even be hard to defend provisions such as that in the District of Columbia for a three-day detention. How much time is needed to render a person free from the influence of alcohol?

The Uniform Act posits a maximum detention of two days, which arguably is closer to the maximum time needed for detoxification purposes.[86] The maximum time of detention should be capable of medical justification—i.e., there should be good medical authority to substantiate an assertion that the maximum length of detention provided by law is indeed the longest time it takes to restore a person to a position where he can make a rational decision about his treatment needs.

Similar questions are raised in the context of longer-term commitment of alcoholics, both as to the purposes of commitment and to the legal grounds on which such commitment may be based. Commitment must either relate to necessary protection of the public or to the treatment needs of the patient as more particularly defined. A five-day maximum period of detention cannot be justified on the grounds that the time is needed to persuade the patient to undergo long-term treatment on a voluntary basis or to afford the state's attorney general an opportunity to obtain a civil commitment order to detain him for longer treatment. Detention in the detoxification center is for the good of the patient and not for the convenience of the state; the maximum period for detention is not to be set, therefore, to provide adequate time to pressure or persuade the patient or to allow for the timely institution of civil commitment procedures.

Many states base commitment of alcoholics on what appear to be questionable legal and constitutional grounds. The District of Columbia law authorizes commitment for treatment up to thirty days in the case of the first or second such commitment within any twenty-four-month period, or up to ninety days in the case of the third or subsequent such commitment within any such period. The only determination the court must make for such a commitment is that the person is a chronic alcoholic and that as a result of chronic or acute alcoholism he is in danger of substantial physical harm. The only other requirement is that the person receive timely notice of the filing of the commitment petition before the hearing held by the court.[87]

In effect, this provision allows fairly long-term commitment of any alcoholic. An alcoholic may be regarded as in immediate danger of substantial physical harm as soon as he starts drinking. Consequently, an alcoholic may be committed under the law simply because he is an alcoholic. The grounds for commitment, moreover, are the alcoholic's danger to himself—the law does not require that he be in any way dangerous to the people around him. It is questionable whether the creation of danger to oneself is a constitutionally valid ground for commitment. A person who is suffering from acute appendicitis who refuses to consent to an operation is indubitably in immediate danger of substantial physical harm, yet the law does not authorize the commitment of such a person for compulsory treatment.[88]

Essentially the District of Columbia statute, as indeed other similar laws, permits the commitment of alcoholics for treatment simply because they are alcoholics. What has happened is that the law has substituted the language of social rehabilitation for that of crime or moral disapproval and, under the guise of beneficent interest, the state compels the alcoholic to undergo treatment whether he wants it or not. As a first step in the compulsory treatment process it is necessary, of course, to deprive him of personal liberty—which puts him in a position not too different from one who has been convicted of a crime.

Professionals in the field of treatment of alcoholism disagree as to whether *any* compulsory treatment can ever succeed. The point has already been made that the law does not compel anyone (other than a child or an incompetent) to undergo treatment simply because someone in legal authority has decided that it will do him good. An individual who has full mental and legal capacity to make decisions cannot be compelled to accept treatment for a physical ailment, and there appears to be no logical reason why an alcoholic should be compelled to do so for his disease.[89] More must be shown to make a legally and constitutionally justifiable case for compulsion.

Commitment may be justified on the ground that in addition to being an alcoholic the person has lost judgmental capacity to such a degree that he is incapable of understanding the need for treatment or of making a rational choice with regard to his treatment needs. This is the "incapacitation" that the Uniform Act refers to. If a person is incapable of making a treatment choice for himself because he has lost judgmental capacity for any reason, the state may make the choice for him, acting by proper commitment order.

Commitment may also be justified on the ground that a particular alcoholic represents a danger to society as a result of his condition. An alcoholic who has become physically aggressive in the past and who is likely to engage in assaultive or threatening behavior to others should be committed.

An alcoholic who has lost judgmental capacity should be subjected to commitment and compulsory treatment because he needs treatment and lacks the capacity to choose it for himself. A physically aggressive alcoholic should be committed to protect society—he is committed, not primarily for treatment, but in order to safeguard other persons. An alcoholic committed by reason of judgmental incapacity should be released as soon as he is again capable of making treatment choices for himself. He should also be released if further treatment cannot benefit him—since he has been committed for his own good, there is no reason to detain him any longer when it appears that further treatment cannot help him.

Decisions on the "right to treatment" rendered in other contexts are relevant here, too.[90] In dealing with a potentially assaultive alcoholic, however, commitment may constitutionally continue until he is no longer a danger to society, whether or not treatment has any reasonable prospects for success, because the treatment is not primarily to benefit him but simply to render him less dangerous. As a corollary, the judgment of risk or hazard of physical injury to society ought to be based in every instance on a sound judgment rather than on mere guesswork, however garbed in scientific jargon. A good argument can be made for the position taken by recent model legislation that physical danger should never be presumed unless there has been at least one prior episode of physical aggression. It would be too easy otherwise to put away alcoholics not because they are dangerous, but simply because somebody is afraid of them.[91]

There is a good deal of confusion of purposes in many of the present state commitment laws. While some of them provide for a variety of reasons for commitment, in many instances commitment is permitted simply because an alcoholic is "a danger to himself or others."[92] This leaves open the question whether the alcoholic is to be committed for his own treatment or whether he is to be committed because he represents a risk to the community. There are other laws which state the reasons for commitment in the conjunctive rather than in the alternative. This leads to similar lack of clarity in result. When the law says that the person is to be committed because he is an alcoholic who is a risk to others, is unable to take care of his own affairs, *and* is in need of treatment,[93] the precise grounds for commitment remain clouded in uncertainty.

Most state treatment laws provide maximum terms of commitment that are for longer than experience has shown to be needed for the treatment of alcoholics.[94] Fortunately, however, actual commitment practices differ, and most alcoholics are held for far shorter periods of time than commitment laws would permit.[95]

Reliance on voluntary treatment for alcoholism is increasing. This, however, is not as yet fully reflected in treatment legislation, though it is in the Uniform Act. Modern treatment legislation should provide that an alcoholic can choose to enter an institution and maintain guest status as would any other patient who enters a hospital to be treated for a disease. An alcoholic should not be under any necessity to commit himself voluntarily in order to obtain treatment. The difference between voluntary commitment and guest status is a rather significant one. In some states, the period of time for which an alcoholic may be held does not depend on whether his commitment is voluntary or involuntary.[96] An alcoholic on guest status is free to leave the institution whenever he chooses. An alcoholic who has voluntarily committed himself may sometimes be held in the same manner and for the same extended term as a person subject to compulsory commitment.

A great need exists for a variety of institutions, from out-patient care to half-way houses, to open institutions and to closed institutions. Major reliance should of course be placed on voluntary treatment in out-patient facilities or in institutions of the more open type. Alcoholics should not be committed by the court to a specific institution because it is unlikely that a court can make professional and fully informed judgments on the kind of treatment necessary for a particular individual. The treatment decision should be made after appropriate classification by persons trained in the field rather than by the committing judge. Hence, it is desirable, as is already done in a number of states and as has been proposed in model legislation,[97] that the alcoholic be committed to the care of the appropriate mental health or public health agency which may then decide whether he is to be treated as an out-patient or in an open or closed institution. The agency should also have the right to make necessary changes in the place and manner of the treatment. A person who does not comply with a reasonable out-patient regime, for instance, would then be subject to reassignment to a half-way house or in-patient facility, if necessary in the judgment of the agency to whose care he has been committed.

Reintegrating alcoholics into society is not simply a matter of more and better staffed treatment institutions.[98] The reintegration of alcoholics requires a far broader social effort that will involve many other care-giving agencies, both public and private, as well as other agencies not generally encompassed in the care-giving category. For an alcoholic to be reintegrated into society, he must be properly housed, and he must find a job. His other medical problems need to be taken care of and his family relationships will need to be rebuilt—and this rebuilding must be assisted by meeting the transitional economic, health, educational, and other problems of members of his family. The rehabilitation of the 9 million alcoholics in this country requires a major, costly, long-range effort. It is an effort which cannot be advanced by better laws to regulate the liquor industry or by stronger laws to convict, sentence, and jail the public drunk. The law can be of major help in creating a proper framework for that rehabilitative effort, but it must be backed by a major social commitment.

PART V

Summing Up

Ms. ROUSE AND Dr. Ewing have already been introduced in Part I as editors of this book and contributors of other chapters.

This final chapter is not intended to summarize completely the preceding ones. However, we realize that some readers prefer to read the end of a book first and for those who have turned here in the first place, we hope that this overview of drinking behavior and social policies will whet your appetite and attract you to all, or some, of the preceding chapters. For those who have reached this chapter as a logical sequence to the foregoing, we hope that you will read on.

The final chapter summarizes the most current research on basic questions regarding alcohol consumption and suggests issues for further investigation. In addition, a conceptual model is presented indicating, in broad terms, the influences and the consequences of drinking in our society.

The reader, however, is urged to consider the subject of drinking not only in the abstract but also in terms of his own drinking and the role he plays in the drinking of others.

Finally, in a review of social policies regarding alcohol, a variety of questions are raised including those regarding the

Part V: Summing Up

justification for legalizing alcohol consumption, the source of inconsistencies in the present statutes on drinking, and the effectiveness of legislation in controlling alcohol use and abuse. The final question, "What should be our social policy concerning alcohol?" requires the judgment of all citizens because drinker and nondrinker alike will be affected by it. Data are presented in this chapter comparing the use of alcoholic and nonalcoholic beverages. This and other information throughout the book should give the reader insight into the complexities of both the question and the answer.

CHAPTER **18**

An Overview of
Drinking Behaviors
and Social Policies

Beatrice A. Rouse, M.Ed.
John A. Ewing, M.D.

THE USE OF alcoholic beverages is not an isolated phenomenon in either American society or its members' personal
lives. Drinking is associated intimately with peoples' view of
themselves as individuals, their behavior toward others, and
their situational demands. Indeed, alcohol use is such an
integral part of American life that little or no explanation is
needed to clarify the fact that the title of this book, *Drinking,*
refers to the drinking of alcoholic beverages.

"Drinking" in some peoples' minds is equivalent to
"drunkenness"; this book, however, has examined the full
spectrum of alcohol consumption.

Drinking, Drunkenness, and Alcoholism

Drinking, drunkenness, and alcoholism are not the
same. Drinking does not necessarily lead to drunkenness, and
drunkenness does not always lead to alcohol addiction.

Drinking covers a wide range of activities characterized
by imbibing alcoholic beverages. The properties of alcoholic
beverages were described in chapter 1.[1] As noted in chapter 11,
however, in some states the legal definition of alcoholic

beverages excludes beer and table wines. The more general legal term is "intoxicating liquors" which includes all beverages with at least one half of 1 percent ethanol.

Ethanol (C_2H_5OH) is also called grain alcohol or ethyl alcohol and is the only kind of the various alcohols that can be consumed safely. Some members of the general public do not consider beer to be an alcoholic beverage. Nevertheless, beer does contain ethanol, and drinking excessive amounts can result in drunkenness and can lead to alcohol addiction.

Alcohol use varies and may include such drinking behaviors as the occasional sip on holidays, several drinks during an evening party, the habitual drink before dinner, drinking to intoxication, and the addictive drinking over which the person has lost control.

Distinguishing between the different types of drinking behavior is important. Physiological effects, attitudes, and social policies all may vary depending on the type of drinking behavior under consideration.

Drinking behavior is classified not only in terms of the amount consumed and the ability of the drinker to control his consumption, but also in terms of its appropriateness in time, place, and consequence.[2] A person taking a shot of whiskey in the afternoon, for example, is viewed differently, depending on whether the drinking occurs on the job or while relaxing on vacation. By the same token, a person intoxicated at night on the public streets is viewed differently from the person found drunk in the evening in front of his television.

When the amount of alcohol consumed results in blood alcohol levels exceeding .05 percent, then the drinker may be described as "high," drunk, or intoxicated, depending upon how much the blood level exceeds .05 percent alcohol. In some states, drivers with .08 percent blood alcohol levels are considered intoxicated by law and may be charged with driving under the influence of intoxicating beverages. In some countries, particularly Scandinavia, drivers may be so charged if found with a blood level of .05 percent alcohol.

Experienced drinkers may not show the common signs of intoxication until very high levels of blood alcohol. Although rare, cases have been recorded with blood levels that were .50 percent alcohol or more. Needless to say, these cases were either hospitalized or found at autopsy. Some of these cases, however, did survive. Both the psychological and physiological aspects of intoxication were described throughout this book, particularly in chapter 1.

Not only should drinking be distinguished from drunkenness, but also intoxication (or drunkenness) should be distinguished from alcoholism.

Definitions of alcoholism may vary among researchers and between countries. Jellinek, one of the early leaders in alcohol research, described various stages in the development of alcohol addiction.[3] He cautioned against the extensive use of the term "alcoholism" for a wide range of excessive drinking. Instead, Jellinek wished to preserve the term for well-defined types of excessive drinking in which physical or psychological pathology was involved. More recently the National Council on Alcoholism developed guidelines for helping the physician determine whether a patient had a pathological dependency on alcohol.[4] Definitions and causes of alcoholism were discussed in chapters 3 and 6. Although there are a variety of models describing alcoholism[5] the medical model is one of the most pervasive. Accordingly, the historical development of the disease concept of alcoholism was presented by the Howlands in chapter 3.

Per Capita Alcohol Consumption
in America and Other Countries

While drinking behaviors, intoxication, and alcoholism are causes for concern in the United States, compared to the apparent per capita consumption of alcohol in most other countries, Americans drink less. The per capita consumption is an estimate based on the census population of a geographical area rather than on the actual number of drinkers. The estimate has been calculated various ways: based on the entire population, based on those at least fifteen years old and based on those at least twenty-one years old.

In a study of twenty-five countries which based its estimates on the population at least fifteen years old, the American per capita consumption of alcohol exceeded only that of the Scandinavian countries, Great Britain, Canada, the Republic of Ireland, and Poland.[6] France ranked first in per capita consumption followed by Italy and Spain. France, in 1970, had an estimated per capita consumption for people fifteen years and older of twenty-four liters of absolute alcohol. Italy's per capita consumption was twenty-one liters, and Spain's was seventeen liters. The United States ranked sixteenth, with an estimated per capita consumption of ten liters of absolute alcohol.

One can determine how much these per capita consumption estimates of absolute alcohol represent of a particular alcoholic beverage by calculating the absolute alcohol equivalent on a weight to volume basis. The American per capita consumption of ten liters of absolute alcohol, for example, is equivalent to everyone at least fifteen years old drinking about two cans of beer a day. The French per capita consumption, on the other hand, represents about four small cans of beer, or more likely, sixteen to twenty ounces of wine every day.

American Drinking of Alcoholic and Nonalcoholic Beverages

Evaluating American drinking not only in terms of per capita consumption but also in terms of the various nonalcoholic beverages consumed may lead one to conclude as did G.R. Stewart almost a quarter of a century earlier:

> On the whole, however, in spite of the interest that attaches to the history of whiskey, beer, and wine, and in spite of the great quantities of them consumed, the most interesting fact about the drinking habits of the United States is that they are so little alcoholic; as against lakes of whiskey and beer may be set seas and whole oceans of water, coffee, tea, milk, and soft drinks.[7]

Table 18-1 shows recent statistics on the per capita consumption in the United States of a variety of alcoholic and nonalcoholic beverages. The data are subject to all the problems of per capita consumption estimates and say nothing about the purposes, situations, or consequences of the beverage consumed. Therefore, the reader is left to judge the relative importance of the various beverages and the place of alcoholic beverages in American drinking habits.

Other indicators of the relative importance of nonalco-

Table 18-1
**Per Capita Consumption of Alcoholic and Nonalcoholic Beverages
in the United States (1973)**

Beverages	Per Capita Consumption[a]
Milk and Cream[b]	61.5 gal.
Soft Drinks[c]	26.9 gal.
Malt Beverages[d]	20.2 gal.
Distilled Spirits[e]	1.9 gal.
Wines[d]	1.6 gal.
Coffee[b]	13.7 lbs.
Cocoa[b]	4.2 lbs.
Tea[b]	0.8 lbs.

[a] Per capita consumption estimates are based on the total U.S. population.
[b] Standard and Poors Industry Surveys. "Packaged Foods: Demands Remain Strong," In: *Food Processing-Canners, Meats, Dairy, Packaged Foods Basic Analysis*, 345 Hudson Street, New York, N.Y. 10014, June 12, (Section 2), 1975.
[c] Standard and Poors Industry Surveys. "The Outlook: Price Increases to Sustain Growth," *Soft Drinks-Candy Basic Analysis*, 345 Hudson Street, New York, N.Y. 10014, Nov. 28 (Section 2), 1974.
[d] United States Brewers Association, Inc. *The Brewing Industry in the United States Brewers Almanac, 1974*, p. 110, 1750 K Street, N.W., Washington, D.C. 20006, 1974.
[e] Distilled Spirits Council of the United States, Inc. *1973 Public Revenue from Alcohol Beverages*, p. 5, 1300 Pennsylvania Building, Washington, D.C., 20004, 1974.

holic and alcoholic beverages include economic factors. For example, income from the soft drink manufacturers' sales in the United States in 1970 was $4.7 billion and exceeded that of either brewery products ($3.7 billion) or distilled spirits ($1.8 billion). Soft drink sales also exceeded that of canned fruits and vegetables ($3.3 billion), confectionery products ($3.3 billion), frozen vegetables ($2.8 billion), and processed cheese ($2.2 billion).[8] The combined manufacturers' income for all alcoholic beverages, however, exceeded that of soft drinks and the other products.

Personal consumption expenditures are another economic indicator. Because data were not available on the various nonalcoholic beverages, the comparison is made with tobacco products. In terms of the amount of money paid by consumers in the mid 1970s, $20 billion was spent on alcoholic beverages compared with $13 billion on tobacco products.[9] Approximately 3 percent of the total expenditures on personal goods and services was for the purchase of alcoholic beverages. In recent years, this percentage of personal consumption expenditures has remained relatively constant.

Why the Interest in
Drinking and Alcohol Studies?

Alcohol would be an interesting subject for study simply because it is an integral part of the lives of so many people. A national survey of American patterns of alcohol consumption, for example, found that the majority of adults drink to facilitate their social relations and do so without problems.[10] Abstention and heavy escape drinking are both atypical patterns of alcohol use. Yet the number of men and women who drink excessively is sufficient to warrant public concern and to justify large research efforts into the pharmacological, sociological, psychological, economic, and legal aspects of alcohol use.

Excessive drinking may be variously defined as pointed out earlier in this chapter. One definition used by researchers is in terms of an average daily consumption of more than 15 cl (five ounces) of absolute alcohol. This represents a daily average of about nine small cans of beer or twelve ounces of 86 proof whiskey. Using this criterion, researchers estimated a rate of 2,690 excessive drinkers per 100,000 persons fifteen years and older in the United States.[11] Of course, the number of family members, friends, and associates affected by excessive drinkers is even greater.

Yet, estimates of alcoholism in the United States range from 4 to 6 percent of the adult population. Alcohol consumption alone, therefore, is not a sufficient explanation for alcoholism. A society's perceptions, attitudes, and practices regarding drinking are also significant factors in the development of alcohol problems. To deal effectively and appropriately with these problems requires an awareness of the use and meaning of drinking not only in our personal lives but also in our society.[12]

Many teenagers and adults who have lived successful, harmonious lives without alcohol find it difficult to understand the attraction of alcoholic beverages. They hear a drinker explain the thirst quenching and delicious properties of a beer after mowing the lawn or watching football and the abstainers wonder, "Why not ice tea or lemonade?"

Why Do Adults Drink Alcohol?

The reasons people drink are not only quite varied and complex but may change for any individual with age and either social or geographic mobility. The decision to be either an abstainer or a drinker is determined largely by sociocultural factors. The amount and patterns of drinking, on the other hand, are influenced largely by personal and situational factors.[13] As Cisin pointed out in chapter 9, an individual's decision to drink reflects influences from both the present and the past. These influences include the individual's early training, present social context, and momentary as well as longterm needs. Cisin also discussed the differences in social class, nationality, religious background, age, sex, and education found to be significantly related to variations in drinking patterns.

Friends and families also influence an individual's drinking behavior.[14] For the married, the most potent effect is exerted by the spouse. Wives vary in their responses, however, when their husbands begin to drink excessively. Some drink heavily to keep pace while others stop drinking altogether. More information is needed, on the other hand, as to the response of husbands to excessive drinking by wives.

Randall and Lester conducted some intriguing research indicating that social pressures may also affect the drinking preferences even of mice.[15] They used inbred strains of genetically predisposed drinking (C57BL) mice and nondrinking (DBA) mice. The newborn mice were raised by their own mothers for twenty days and then some were randomly chosen to be raised for seven weeks by mothers of the opposite strain.

The control groups were the litter mates who remained with their natural mothers. Young C57BL mice continuously raised by their natural mothers drank more than any other group. Young DBA mice raised by their natural mothers drank the least.

The findings regarding the experimental groups, however, were interesting. Mice from the drinking strain which were raised with nondrinking mothers reduced their drinking to half that of their litter mates raised with their natural mothers. Nondrinking mice raised with drinking mothers, on the other hand, drank twice that of their litter mates. The drinking levels of the mothers, therefore, appeared to be an important influence on the young.

People drink not only in response to social pressures but also because of an attraction to alcohol itself. While some people drink merely for the taste and some drink to elicit specific reactions from others, more drink primarily for the pharmacological effect they experience from alcohol. Furthermore, the greater the amount of alcohol consumed, the more reasons an individual will give for his drinking.

Whether people drink to achieve a particular pharmacological effect and whether alcohol actually produces that effect are two separate questions. For example, because many people have reported that they drank to reduce their tension and anxiety, a variety of studies were conducted to determine whether alcohol actually reduces tension and anxiety. Cappell and Herman reviewed the research findings from the wide variety of experimental situations using a number of different species of animals. They concluded that while the tension-reducing hypothesis regarding alcohol "may be quite plausible intuitively it has not been convincingly supported empirically."[16] An even more recent critical review of the laboratory work investigating the human response to alcohol concluded that there were still grounds for the tension-reducing hypothesis regarding alcohol.[17] There is some evidence, on the other hand, that suggests that alcohol may even increase feelings of conflict.[18]

Laboratory studies have indicated that individuals may differ from each other in their reactions to the same amount of absolute alcohol.[19] Even in a social setting, one can observe these differences. In order to achieve the same level of effects, such as relaxation and euphoria, moderate or frequent drinkers usually require a greater amount of absolute alcohol than do less experienced drinkers. Ethnic differences in metabolism or physiological reactions to alcohol may also account for these varying reactions among drinkers.[20] Drinkers themselves may notice that their reactions to alcohol vary with the circumstances. The social setting, the individual's drinking history, how much food is in the stomach, the person's body mass and his particular expectations regarding that drinking occasion are all influential in determining the specific effects experienced from drinking.[21]

Laboratory and social scientists are not the only observers studying drinking behavior among adults. Children and teenagers are also viewing adult drinking, trying to determine what role alcohol should play in their own lives and how they should behave while drinking.

The relationship between social class and various drinking behaviors in adults was seen in the following way by a high school student interviewed by Maddox and McCall in a study of teenage drinking:

> I think all groups drink . . . the high-ups in society drink as much as the lower groups but drink a better quality of stuff and know when to stop and can consume it better. The lower class group people drink a lot and don't know when to stop and are boisterous about it . . . . (the upper class don't) get out of hand because they are afraid they'll lose their society . . . . The people at the bottom, they don't care, because they don't have any place else to fall . . . .The middle class are in between. They know whether to drink and when to drink and how much to drink.[22]

Young people often are perceptive observers of adult behavior. Perhaps one way of determining a community's drinking attitudes and behavior is to observe the drinking attitudes and behavior of its teenagers. Whether or not their perceptions of adult drinking are accurate, their own drinking behaviors will be influenced by their perceptions.

Why Do Young People Drink Alcohol?

Studies of teenage drinking indicate that for those adolescents with healthy life adjustment, drinking serves primarily to symbolize the transition from the dependency of childhood to the independence of adulthood. Drinking for these youths becomes a signal to friends and family of a readiness to act independently and to accept responsibility for their own actions and decisions.[23]

The drinking behavior of healthy, well-adjusted adolescents is influenced by the attitutdes and values toward alcohol which are held among the important adults in their lives and within the community. This was confirmed by a study of drinking among teenagers in two communities which differed in drinking attitudes and legal availability of alcohol.[24] While there was less teenage drinking in the legally dry community, the more interesting finding was the association between drinking and student popularity. In the community where drinking was socially acceptable and legally available, student popularity and social involvement were positively associated with drinking. In the other community, however, the more popular and socially involved students were those who did not drink.

The social and cultural factors associated with teenage drinking in a community characterized by prohibition norms were studied by Globetti and described in chapter 10. An analysis of the conditions in which the teenagers in such a community did drink indicated that their drinking was insulated from the usual social controls over such behavior. Globetti suggested that while fewer people can be expected to drink in this kind of social climate, alcohol problems will be relatively more frequent in those people who do drink.

Drinking may be used as a way of tangibly rejecting authority and the rules of society. Such drinking behavior, however, is usually a manifestation of hostility and rebellion in general. Such rebellion is not restricted to teenagers nor is it reserved for drinking. Many such teenagers are people with problems who also happen to drink. It is just as important not to label youth by only one aspect of their behavior as it is with adults. These teenagers, therefore, should not be characterized primarily as problem drinkers. If not helped, they can become unhappy, hostile adults as well as problem drinking adults.

A study of institutionalized delinquents and students of comparable age found that more of the delinquents drank to relieve their tensions and anxiety.[25] Other differences were found between the 383 drinking students in grades seven through twelve and the 138 drinking institutionalized delinquents, especially in their first drinking experiences. Among the student drinkers, about 75 percent had their first drink in their own or a friend's home under adult supervision. Only 20 percent of the delinquents, however, had their first drink under such circumstances. The first drink was stolen by 13 percent of the students and 30 percent of the delinquents. While most of the reasons for taking their first drink were comparable, only 2 percent of the students reported that they wanted to get drunk when they took their first drink. In contrast, 18 percent of the delinquents reported that they took their first drink for the purpose of getting drunk.

Jessor and Jessor conducted a valuable longitudinal study of the transition from abstinence to drinking in a sample of junior high school students.[26] Because of the difficulties involved in obtaining parental permission, only 52 percent of the original sample were able to participate. Nevertheless, this study is important not only because it followed the students over time but also because it employed a sociopsychological framework to examine both the changes in drinking status and the time at which they occurred.

The 408 boys and girls who participated in the study for the entire four years were divided into five groups. Group I contained 22 percent of the sample and were those students who remained abstainers throughout the four years. Group II contained 9 percent of the sample and began drinking only in the fourth year. Group III contained 11 percent of the sample and began drinking in the third year. Group IV also contained 11 percent of the sample but began drinking in the second year. Group V contained 47 percent of the sample and were drinkers throughout the study.

Initially, the groups were comparable on measures of alienation, independence, church attendance, parental control, and compatibility between their friends' and parents' views. Various·nondrinking measures, however, were associated with the time at which the groups began their drinking. These measures included achievement, deviance, and religiosity. Drinking measures on which they differed included approval of drinking by parents and friends, models for drinking among friends, and attitudes regarding negative functions of drinking.

By the fourth year, the groups were also different in their rates of participation in other possible transition behaviors, such as sexual intercourse and the use of marijuana.

The study concluded that the transition from abstinence to drinking was "an integral aspect of personality, social and behavior change during adolescence" and was related to other

transition-marking behaviors. This relationship was expected
to be true in any society which considered drinking as an indicator of adulthood.[27]

Drinking among college students was examined in
chapter 11. A variety of national and regional studies were
discussed, including research on college drinking among
blacks and other ethnic groups. Rouse and Ewing presented
data from studies which compared college freshmen with their
noncollegiate high school classmates, which described not
only current but past collegiate drinking patterns, and which
related drinking to other drug use. In depth studies were also
presented of a college population in the Southeast where both
legal and bootleg alcoholic beverages are available. In addition, the role of college drinking in the development of alcohol
problems in later adulthood was examined.

The stereotype of college drinking as being predominately excessive, boisterous, and antisocial has not been
substantiated by national studies nor by the Rouse and Ewing
studies summarized in chapter 11. According to the results of
one national survey, "the major problem of college drinking
appears to lie in the confusion, conflict, and anxiety which
parents, college administration, faculty, public officials, and
students themselves experience over the question of drinking
by young people."[28]

Where Do Most People Drink?

While most Americans do their drinking in their own
homes or that of friends, there are a variety of places for
drinking in public. Marshall Clinard differentiated five types:
1) the skid-row bar, 2) the downtown bar and cocktail lounge,
3) the steak and cocktail places, 4) the night clubs and road-
houses, and 5) the neighborhood taverns.[29] The different
social classes vary in their preferred places. The stereotype is
that the lower class drink in taverns, the middle class in
restaurants and cocktail lounges, and the upper class at the
country club.

An interesting participant-observer study of the
different behaviors in various public drinking places was
conducted by Sherri Cavan.[30] Although patrons of lower class
public drinking places are thought to behave in less desirable

ways than the middle class, Cavan found that "quarrels of varying intensity, displays of affection, the prefabrication and embroidering of biographies, and activity typically characterized as the effects of overindulgence (loss of motor control, excessive depression, or elation)" were found in both upper- and lower-class public drinking places. Such effects of excessive drinking were also greeted with the same level of acceptance by witnesses to such behaviors in both places.

Activities other than drinking may be important to the patrons of public drinking places. Such activities include meeting new people, talking over personal problems with the bartender and other patrons, and engaging in the important exchange of information, ideas, and attitudes. The tavern, for example, may serve as a blue collar worker's club. There he can spend leisure time relaxing with friends and coworkers, discussing world events and problems of immediate concern, and playing games, music, or cards.[31] These basic social and psychological needs may be eliminated with the trend toward increased patronage of package stores. Increased package sales may result in more solitary drinkers imbibing excessively because there is no bartender available to suggest that the drinker "take it easy."

Why Do People Get Drunk?

Inexperienced drinkers may have an occasion or two of intoxication as they learn their limits. Some drinkers, however, get drunk in order to escape the reality of their situation, some to indulge in behaviors that otherwise would be considered inexcusable, and some to manipulate others. Any particular man's or woman's reasons may differ. The time-out phenomenon has already been discussed and laboratory observations of alcoholics suggest that "alcoholics frequently drink in order to regress, rebel, and more comfortably act out repressed impulses and wishes from their early lives."[32] The role of habit should not be overlooked and was discussed by Mills in chapter 12.[33]

McClelland has suggested that the excessive drinker is a man with an inordinate need for personal power who finds drinking an effective way to achieve a feeling of this desired power.[34] He proposes that men often become heavy drinkers in those occupations and endeavors which accentuate power and influence or those which constantly involve interactions which challenge a person's sense of power. The recommended therapy for this kind of excessive drinker is to help him find alternative ways of expressing his concerns for personal power, ways that are socially acceptable and less hazardous to himself and others.

A study testing the hypothesis that alcoholics have a greater need for power, especially direct influence over others, compared sixty-five alcoholic and fifty-six nonalcoholic clergy.[35] Although the groups were similar in their overall need for power, they differed significantly in the kind of power desired. The alcoholics were more likely to prefer personal power. The nonalcoholics, in contrast, were more likely to prefer socialized power, that is, indirect influence over others.

McClelland's power theory is somewhat at variance with the earlier dependency theory which postulated that drinking satisfied passive oral dependency needs which the drinker felt unable to acknowledge openly.[36] Transactional analysis theory, on the other hand, combines elements of both the previous positions. No one theory, however, will completely explain the problem drinker because there are a variety of problem drinkers, just as there are a variety of motivations and uses for excessive drinking.[37]

Drunkenness, for example, is also used as a way of communicating various messages that these drinkers feel unable to convey otherwise to people who are important to them.[38] The most common messages are refusal to accept responsibility, a plea to be taken care of, and a wish to punish someone else regardless of the personal consequences.

Three kinds of interactions were proposed by Steiner as games alcoholics play.[39] The first, "Drunk and proud of it," is a means of expressing aggression toward another without feeling guilty. The message conveyed is "I was bad and you couldn't stop me, ha ha." A remarkable account of an alcoholic with such a motivation has been written by Robert Straus.[40] This twenty-seven-year followup of an alcoholic portrays vividly one man's attempt to use alcohol to punish his mother. The second game, called "Lush," occurs when the alcoholic bids for attention by first hurting himself. The lush says, in effect, "I am loveless and depressed and you can't help me." The last game is "Wino"; this type of interaction begins when the alcohol consumption leads to severe physical consequences for the alcoholic. Wino is then in a position to say, "I am sick and you must medicate and take care of me."

These games are not reserved for the alcoholic. Any drinker can play and many problem drinkers do. The games themselves are not like solitaire; they require the participation of at least one other person. Sometimes the cooperation is unintended and sometimes unwilling, but nevertheless, it has to occur for the game to proceed.

One example of such an interaction is what Steiner calls a "gallows transaction." In this encounter the problem drinker is rewarded for his self-destructive behavior. The drinker, for instance, recounts his escapades on his week long drinking spree and his listeners smile or laugh in response. No matter how much the listeners might disapprove of this behavior in the abstract or how aware they are of the effects of such behavior on the drinker and his family, still they smile or even laugh merrily. The problem drinker may be hanging himself but he also has help to the gallows.

Really helping the problem drinker requires the aid of those around him or her. An important aid is for friends, family and coworkers to support with attention and approval the drinker's healthy behaviors and not reinforce the self-destructive acts. Treatment and rehabilitation efforts also must include helping the problem drinker find alternative means of communicating his important feelings and needs.

Under What Circumstances Do People Consume the Most Alcohol?

Some of the factors described earlier in this chapter which produce differences among individuals in their reactions to the same amount of absolute alcohol also influence how much alcohol they will actually consume on a particular drinking occasion. These factors include the individual's psychological and physiological state as well as the social context of the drinking.

A recently completed study has provided data regarding the association between the amount of alcohol consumed and such contextual factors as the time, place, duration, and interpersonal relations of the drinking occasion.[41] Dr. Thomas C. Harford, a research psychologist with the National Institute on Alcohol Abuse and Alcoholism, developed the theoretical framework, and Eva Gerstel served as project director of the study.

Residents in the metropolitan Boston area who were at least eighteen years old and who drank at least once a month were eligible to participate in this survey. Data on one week of drinking immediately previous to the interview were collected on 82 percent of those eligible. Of the 793 respondents, 633 provided complete data on four continuous weeks of drinking.

Various theoretical, methodological, and substantive issues were explored in this study and related findings will be available later. Only preliminary results regarding the frequency of each social context and the average amount of absolute alcohol consumed at each drinking event are presently available. These results should be qualified by the fact that the respondents were from a metropolitan area and were interviewed during the summer. Also, higher amounts of absolute alcohol were often reported by those few respondents for whom information on some of the contexts of their drinking was not ascertained.

Nevertheless, some interesting findings emerged. For this sample, the reports for one week of drinking did not differ significantly from those for the longer period. The one week of drinking covered 2,726 drinking events and reports from 717 drinkers. The four week period covered 9,252 events and reports from 629 drinkers.

Age was found to be related to both the total amount of absolute alcohol consumed over all drinking occasions and to the contexts of drinking. In terms of total alcohol intake, the highest level was found in the eighteen to twenty-five year olds. The twenty-six to thirty-five age group, in contrast, consumed about two-thirds the amount of total alcohol of the younger group. After age thirty-five, the total amount gradually increased until age sixty-two. This change in total intake is accounted for by an increase in the frequency of drinking rather than by an increase in the amount of alcohol per drinking event. After age sixty-two, another sharp drop in total alcohol intake occurred.

In terms of the drinking contexts, the number of drinking events lasting an hour or more and of those in the presence of large groups decreased with age. The frequency of drinking in private homes, with meals, and with relatives, on the other hand, increased with age.

Table 18-2 shows the frequency of each drinking context, the percent of the total absolute alcohol consumed in each context and the average amount of absolute alcohol consumed in each drinking context. The time and place of most frequent drinking was not usually the context in which the highest amount of absolute alcohol was consumed. For example, while most drinking occurred later in the day, the absolute alcohol of all beverages consumed during a drinking event tended to be higher during early morning drinking. Furthermore, drinking more frequently occurred in private homes and with relatives present. The absolute alcohol per drinking event, however, tended to be higher in public places, at parties, and without relatives present.

Why Do People Allow or Even Encourage Excessive Drinking?

Admittedly, it may be easier for a host or hostess to tolerate an excessive drinker than to tell a guest that his or her drinking is excessive, disruptive, or embarrassing. Perhaps, a "Yes, I mind very much if you're drunk" public education campaign would remedy this reticence.

Nevertheless, people do actively encourage or provoke others to drink excessively. Often it is for some of the very reasons that a person may choose to get drunk—that is, to excuse some behavior, to manipulate others, or to facilitate communication. The presence of an intoxicated person and his antics may be self-enhancing to the observer. Since everyone at one time or other is unable to solve all problems satisfactorily, to some it is comforting to have someone else behaving badly. This provides an opportunity for the observer to appear more favorable in comparison.

In addition, communication is often facilitated when the speaker is less self-conscious about making an unfavorable impression. When people, particularly those in authority, are intoxicated, others can speak more freely to them or in a more forthright manner with less fear of adverse consequences.

Table 18-2
Percent of Drinking Events and Amount of Absolute Alcohol (AA) According to Drinking Contexts

Drinking Contexts	One Week (N=717 Drinkers)			Four Weeks (N=629 Drinkers)		
	Drinking Events	Total AA	AA per Events (ozs.)	Drinking Events	Total AA	AA per Events (ozs.)
Day:						
Fri.-Sun.	53%	57%	1.61	52%	56%	1.52
Weekday	46%	42%	1.37	47%	43%	1.32
NA*	01%	01%	1.89	01%	01%	2.43
Time Drinking Initiated:						
P.M.	93%	90%	1.44	94%	93%	1.40
A.M.	06%	09%	2.41	05%	06%	1.94
NA	01%	01%	1.74	01%	01%	1.82
Duration of Drinking Event:						
<60 min.	62%	38%	0.93	59%	36%	0.88
≥60 min.	37%	61%	2.44	40%	63%	2.23
NA	01%	01%	1.24	01%	01%	1.97
Location:						
Private	66%	58%	1.30	67%	61%	1.29
Public	33%	41%	1.87	32%	38%	1.70
NA	01%	01%	4.09	01%	01%	3.02

Occasion:					
Meal	31%	21%	1.02	31%	22%	1.01
Party	33%	43%	1.96	33%	42%	1.82
Other	35%	34%	1.47	33%	33%	1.41
NA	01%	02%	1.68	02%	03%	2.01

Food:					
Full meal	35%	33%	1.39	36%	34%	1.35
Snacks	21%	23%	1.68	20%	22%	1.60
No Food	43%	42%	1.47	43%	43%	1.41
NA	01%	02%	3.14	01%	01%	2.26

Relation to Others Present:					
Related	52%	43%	1.22	51%	42%	1.18
Unrelated	36%	45%	1.87	35%	43%	1.75
Both	11%	10%	1.47	11%	12%	1.50
NA	01%	02%	3.04	03%	03%	1.77

Number of Others Present:					
≤2	56%	49%	1.29	56%	49%	1.26
≥3	43%	50%	1.75	43%	50%	1.64
NA	01%	01%	6.20	01%	01%	3.28

*NA = Not Ascertained; Source: See Note 41.

Intoxicated people also pose less of a power threat, especially when increasing frequency of drunkenness leads to a loss of control over the management of household or business affairs. Roman, for example, described how alcoholic executives have been manipulated by colleagues seeking power and control.[42]

People are also incited to drink to intoxication so they will manifest the sexuality or aggressiveness which sometimes accompanies intoxication.

Others may have more "noble" reasons for encouraging their companions to drink more than intended. For example, excessive drinking may be promoted to help a friend "prove himself a man." These misguided individuals have been influenced by the frontier image of drinking where "holding one's liquor" was an accomplishment to be desired. Nowadays more constructive and socially desirable behaviors are hallmarks of manliness.

Another motivation for encouraging a friend to overindulge is to help him become less inhibited, to relax, and to be more sociable and likeable. Unfortunately, intoxication leads some people to become aggressive, ineffectual, and generally obnoxious. For this and other reasons, encouraging drinking for this motivation is undesirable.

The mere fact that individuals have gotten drunk together sometimes creates a unique bond between them even when they have nothing else in common. Some of these groups maintain themselves solely by continuing to get drunk together. Other groups explore their members' activities, exchange interests, and develop a new basis for friendship. Sometimes, however, the getting drunk together is symbolic or satisfies some unexpressed need. The most common need is for acceptance. Military men, for instance, tell of situations in which subordinates who previously were unable to cooperate with them or to work well together suddenly become a smoothly functioning group after an all-night drunk together.

Who Are the Heavy Drinkers?

The majority of people who can control their own drinking wonder what it is about heavy drinkers that allows them to continue drinking excessively despite pleas from loved ones, loss of job, and hazards to their health.

The heavy drinkers studied tend to be alienated from society, more unhappy with their present lives, and pessimistic about their futures. They give many reasons for their drinking, but differ from other drinkers in that they find drinking more helpful in relieving depression.

Age of heavy drinking appears to differ for men and women. Studies by Cahalan and others found that more problems with drinking were reported for men in their twenties. Women, on the other hand, were more likely to be problem drinkers when in their thirties and forties.[43] With the increasing proportion of the national population in the older age groups and the accompanying changing lifestyles for senior citizens, however, there may well be an upsurge of problem drinkers among men and women in their later years. Studies of drinking among residents of retirement villages, for example, may contribute much to our knowledge of this phenomenon.

Heavy drinkers may be found among all socioeconomic classes and may be men or women, young or old, tool-and-die maker, farmer, lawyer, judge, soldier, minister, business man, or doctor. Although the stereotype is that alcoholics are homeless, skid-row types, the truth is that only about 5 percent of the alcoholics are derelicts. Indeed, studies have shown that not even all of the skid-row inhabitants are alcoholics.[44] Maurer suggested that alcoholism is more of a problem in the executive suite than on skid row.[45]

Alcoholism may go undetected in middle- or upper-class persons because of the social stigma attached to alcoholism which leads patients to minimize their drinking to their physicians. The doctors, in turn, are reluctant to suggest the possibility of a drinking problem, especially in the early stages of the condition.[46] In the later stages where there are severe medical problems, the patient may be acknowledged as having alcohol problems. The prognosis, however, is not as good as it might have been if diagnosed earlier.

The courage of public figures like talented actors and actresses, noted congressmen, and professional athletes to publicly admit that they are alcoholics has helped the growing acceptance of problem drinking as a condition to be treated rather than stigmatized. The changing social climate has also helped more women to admit their drinking problems and seek treatment early.[47]

Epidemiological or sociological studies have found certain groups to be at "high risk" for developing alcohol problems. These groups include certain ethnic groups or nationalities in which drinking to excess is either encouraged or widely tolerated. Children from unfortunate home situations, especially those involving an alcoholic parent, are also at high risk because of their difficulties in being able to learn ways of coping with troubles in life. A study of the effect of the father's drinking on their children found that children of both abstainers and heavy drinkers had high levels of stress. The ways the children of heavy drinkers used to deal with their anxiety and depression, however, were less adaptive.[48]

People in general who find themselves in stressful situations may be at high risk of becoming heavy drinkers regardless of their age, ethnic group, or sex. Such circumstances include divorce, separation, adverse job changes, or the death of a loved one. In addition, drinkers who find themselves relocated to unfamiliar places without friends tend to increase their drinking. Those moving from small towns or rural areas into large cities are especially vulnerable.

It is important to deal with excessive drinking as soon as it is recognized. Excessive drinking and/or drinking to escape personal problems lead to an increase in the man's or woman's risk of becoming alcoholic. Many times the drinker's own awareness of his or her use of alcohol to deal with loneliness or personal difficulties is enough to remedy the drinking problem. Often, however, professional help is needed.

Can the Problem Drinker Be Helped?

Yes! There are a variety of treatment approaches and sources of help available today, some of which were discussed in chapter 6. The heritage of prohibition and the long history of moral and religious controversy about drinking have contributed to the mixed attitudes of laymen and professionals toward persons with drinking problems. The person who abuses alcohol has been viewed in various ways: as a patient, as a victim, and as a criminal. The beliefs that problem drinking is a self-inflicted condition and that the inability to control drinking is a sign of moral weakness have hindered both the seeking and the application of treatment. This coupled with difficulties in treatment due to often unrealistic or inappropriate goals have led many to feel pessimistic concerning helping problem drinkers. However, by matching the patient with the appropriate treatment facility and therapeutic method and by determining realistic outcome goals, the treatment of the problem drinker can be maximized.[49]

Not only are there alcoholic rehabilitation centers to provide help but a variety of agencies such as social services, community mental health centers, and health departments now include alcoholism counselors on their staff. Industries are also becoming increasingly interested in helping their workers who are having problems with drinking, and a variety of work organizations are providing medical services, counseling, and encouragement.[50] Moreover, the military services have instituted alcohol and drug treatment programs on military bases throughout the world.[51]

In addition to Alcoholics Anonymous,[52] Al-Anon, and Recovery, various other self-help groups exist. Blacks, Indians, and Spanish-speaking people have organized their own groups to help with problem drinking. Examples of such special groups include the National Black Caucus on Alcoholism, the National Indian Board on Alcoholism and Drug Abuse, and the National Spanish-speaking Commission on Alcoholism.

American Indians have recently become active in the planning and management of alcohol education treatment and rehabilitation programs for their people.[53] Such programs with total American Indian involvement include the Inter-Tribal Alcoholism Treatment Center in Sheridan, Wyoming, and the Chemawa Indian School Alcoholism Prevention Program near Salem, Oregon, where student volunteers help classmates who are intoxicated. In Alaska, efforts to find constructive alternatives to drinking were initiated by about 160 isolated native Alaskan villages with the aid of grants from the National Institute on Alcohol Abuse and Alcoholism (NIAAA). Some of the alternative activities provided have included educational programs, employment training, recreational activities, and competitive sports events.

Spanish-speaking people wishing alcoholism information can obtain a special package developed by the NIAAA. It includes some pamphlets in Spanish and may be obtained from the NIAAA National Clearinghouse for Alcohol Information in Washington, D.C.

Anyone can obtain complete information about sources for help that are immediately available in his community from a local affiliate of the National Council on Alcoholism or from the alcoholism treatment facility listed in the telephone directory.

The most important ingredient for successful treatment is to seek help as soon as problem drinking is recognized! The earlier the treatment, the more successful the outcome.

Is the Proportion of
Heavy Drinkers Increasing?

While the United States may not be in the top fifteen alcohol consuming nations among developed countries, the per capita consumption rate is increasing here as in most other parts of the world. The 1970 per capita consumption in the United States represented a 24 percent increase over the rate of drinking ten years earlier.

The increase in drinking in that decade, however, was much greater in many other countries. The Netherlands had the greatest increase — 104 percent. Others with marked increases in per capita consumption included Finland which increased 64 percent, West Germany 58 percent, Yugoslavia 53 percent, Republic of Ireland 48 percent, Spain 42 percent, and Russia 40 percent. Portugal had the smallest rate of increase, 3 percent, and France was the only country with a decrease. The French rate represented a 12 percent decrease over that of 1960.[54]

Information on distilled spirits at least indicates that the trend toward increased per capita consumption in the United States is continuing. According to data published by the Distilled Spirits Industry, the apparent per capita consumption of distilled spirits in America was 1.82 wine gallons in 1970, 1.88 in 1972, and 1.96 in 1974.[55] The estimate is called apparent consumption because it is based on the census population and not on the actual number of drinkers. Surveys of drinkers also indicate that there is an increase in the number of drinkers in the population. There are, for example, more women who are drinking now than in previous years.

An increase in the number of drinkers in a society, according to the research by Popham, Schmidt, and de Lint, will lead to an *increase* in the number of alcoholics or problem drinkers. Their thesis, with supporting data and a discussion of some consequences of this position, is presented in chapter 14. Their conclusions have important implications for education, legislation, and other efforts to reduce alcohol problems. Because of its importance, this "constant proportion" thesis has been subjected to scrutiny by others[56] and will be discussed again later in this chapter. This theory is among the positions examinded by Robin Room in chapter 15.

The opposite viewpoint, however, has also been espoused. This position, also examined by Room, advocates greater acceptance of drinking to inoculate society against its harmful effects. According to the "inoculation" theory, an increase in the number of drinkers will lead to a *decrease* in alcohol problems. Plaut and others supporting this position base their recommendations on alcohol studies of both nonliterate and literate societies as well as on surveys of various ethnic groups within the United States.[57] They found that the groups which were characterized by widespread drinking but minimal alcohol problems had integrated their drinking with a variety of activities. Popham and his colleagues, however, contend that as drinking becomes an incidental part of many activities, the excessive drinker simply becomes less noticeable.

Many cross-cultural studies of alcohol use, however, involve comparisons of homogeneous groups. Whether greater acceptance of drinking in our heterogeneous society will lead to an increase or a decrease in problem drinkers is still open to debate and requires further, rigorous research to resolve.

This question is of more than academic interest. In order to prevent or reduce alcohol problems in our society, those agreeing with the constant proportion thesis would try to reduce alcohol consumption in the total population. Proponents of other viewpoints, such as the inoculation theory, would direct their efforts primarily toward those subgroups in society that are considered a high risk for developing alcohol problems.

Nevertheless, proposals to reduce the number of problem drinkers should also include preventive and intervention measures not generally regarded as directly related to alcohol consumption. These include improving the general life experiences of the members of our society. Indeed, Blum from his review of alcohol research and his own cross-cultural studies of drinking concluded:

> [problem drinking would likely] be reduced by educational endeavors, by socioeconomic reforms which reduce misery, deprivation and anxiety, by child-rearing procedures which foster mental health, by nutritional and hygienic regimens fostering good physical health and by social controls which limit drinking and the variety of behavior allowed under the influence of alcohol.[58]

These measures, however, are not within the immediate and direct control of individuals; they require group action. Yet the individual is not without influence. He can begin by evaluating his own drinking and the role he plays in the drinking behavior of others.

Should I Be Concerned About My Own Drinking?

The thoughtful drinker who asks himself this question may not have the obvious problems with drinking: quarrels with friends or family about drinking, frequent intoxication, a drunk driving incident, or physiological signs of withdrawal such as shakes, delirium tremens (DT's), or blackouts. These are the symptoms which make a drinking problem obvious to observers and which readily identify the friend, relative, or coworker with a drinking problem.

Yet, there are warning signs for the drinker who has never or very seldom ever gotten intoxicated. Some of these indications that alcohol may be assuming undue control over one's life include a tendency to refuse invitations to events where alcohol will not be served, a growing preference for associating with people who drink excessively, a feeling of impatience when waiting for one's drink to be served, and unsuccessful attempts to reduce the amount of alcohol drunk at a sitting. Sometimes the warning is no more than an anxious feeling that there won't be enough to drink at a party;

this may be accompanied by taking a drink or two before leaving, "to be on the safe side."

Several myths about drinking give excessive drinkers a false sense of security about their drinking. One is that only "hard liquor" leads to problems and that one doesn't become an alcoholic from drinking "just beer."[59] De Lint and Schmidt in a review of the data from twenty-one countries found that the purpose and patterns of drinking were more important indicators of problem drinking than the type of beverage.[60] The overall amount of alcohol consumed may not be the best indicator either; a man or woman alcoholic may drink little the entire year but once or twice go on drinking binges.[61]

The other myth concerns being able to drink large amounts without feeling the effects. To be able to hold one's liquor may itself be a sign of problem drinking, as strange as that may seem. The average sized man who consumes large amounts of alcohol often, such as eight or nine quarts of beer or a fifth of whiskey, has a drinking problem whether or not he shows behavioral signs of intoxication. Chronic damage to a drinker's health is not as conspicuous as the social consequences of heavy drinking, but it is just as important.[62] See chapters 4, 5, and 8 of this book.

Each drinker needs to evaluate the amount of alcohol consumed, the importance of drinking in his life, and its effect on his social and physical functioning. Both chapters 6 and 12 help the individual examine the use and meaning of alcohol in his own life.

Whether or not we personally drink, alcohol affects us all in some way. In order to both understand and deal effectively and appropriately with these consequences we need to be aware of the use and meaning of alcohol in our society.

A Conceptual Model of the Influences and Consequences of Drinking Behavior

Since alcohol is such an integral part of our society, it may be helpful to conceptualize drinking behavior as part of a system. Figure 18-1 shows a model proposed by Rouse which includes both the influences and the consequences of drinking behavior.

Various attributes of this system should be noted. First,

although health considerations are an important aspect of life, the public health/medical sector is not represented separately. It, like education and other societal institutions, is subsumed under various components such as sociocultural factors or communications—depending upon the institutional activity of interest. The physician's handling of a drinking patient, for example, is subsumed under "Feelings/Reactions to Drinking."

Second, the arrows indicate the direction of influence and many components in the system are involved in reciprocal exchanges of influence. For illustrative purposes, consider the relationship between legal and sociocultural factors. One function of the sociocultural sphere is to determine which aspects of drinking behavior are to be legalized. Public drunkenness is an example of a drinking behavior that is considered illegal. The law enforcement and judicial personnel, however, are becoming increasingly unable to perform their other functions due to the workload imposed by public drunkenness cases. As a consequence, increasing pressures from the legal sector are being exerted on social attitudes to make public drunkenness not a criminal matter but one of public health.

Sometimes the feedback from one aspect of the system to another is mutually reinforcing. As an example, consider the assumption that alcoholism is a problem of the lower class and the derelict. The legal profession, recognizing this assumption, finds it easy to reduce drunk driving charges for those who can afford a lawyer; the police officers are less willing to make public drunkenness arrests of well-dressed individuals or those known to be members of good standing in the community; and judges are less likely to suggest that such individuals be required to participate in alcohol rehabilitation or drunk driving education programs.

The relationship between the legal sphere and the alcoholic beverage industries is also reciprocal. For example, legislation regulates the manufacture of various alcoholic beverages. Yet, lobbies from the different industries can affect such regulations, including the tax rate for the beverages. Therefore, the alcoholic beverage industries and the legal factors affect each other and are also represented in Figure 18-1 as having a feedback loop.

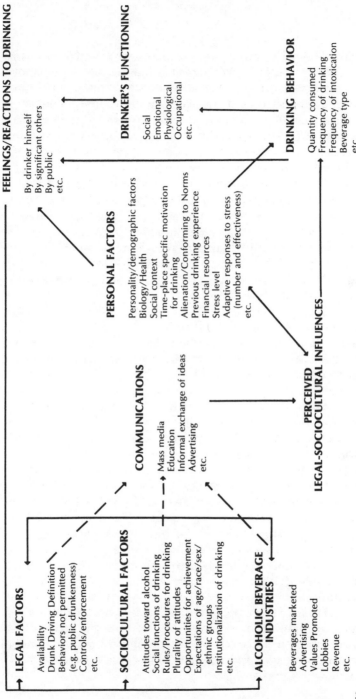

Figure 18-1. Conceptual model of influences and consequences of drinking behavior.

FEELINGS/REACTIONS TO DRINKING

By drinker himself
By significant others
By public
etc.

DRINKER'S FUNCTIONING

Social
Emotional
Physiological
Occupational
etc.

DRINKING BEHAVIOR

Quantity consumed
Frequency of drinking
Frequency of intoxication
Beverage type
etc.

PERSONAL FACTORS

Personality/demographic factors
Biology/Health
Social context
Time-place specific motivation
  for drinking
Alienation/Conforming to Norms
Previous drinking experience
Financial resources
Stress level
Adaptive responses to stress
  (number and effectiveness)
etc.

COMMUNICATIONS

Mass media
Education
Informal exchange of ideas
Advertising
etc.

PERCEIVED
LEGAL-SOCIOCULTURAL INFLUENCES

LEGAL FACTORS

Availability
Drunk Driving Definition
Behaviors not permitted
  (e.g. public drunkenness)
Controls/enforcement
etc.

SOCIOCULTURAL FACTORS

Attitudes toward alcohol
Social functions of drinking
Rules/Procedures for drinking
Plurality of attitudes
Opportunities for achievement
Expectations of age/race/sex/
  ethnic groups
Institutionalization of drinking
etc.

ALCOHOLIC BEVERAGE
INDUSTRIES

Beverages marketed
Advertising
Values Promoted
Lobbies
Revenue
etc.

367

Another reciprocal relationship is that between the drinker's functioning and the reactions of others to his drinking. While the pharmacological properties of the ethanol a drinker consumes have their effect on the drinker,[63] the significance to others of his act of drinking also is influential.

Third, the system illustrates not only that drinking behavior may be affected by a variety of factors but also that these influences may be either direct or indirect. For example, personal factors such as the need to appear sociable at a cocktail party or to drink in order to relieve feelings of anxiety and stress operate directly in producing certain kinds of drinking behaviors. Sociocultural attitudes regarding the social function or stress relief function of drinking, on the other hand, are influential only as they are communicated and perceived, that is, they operate indirectly. The effects of a specific influence also may be either inflated or suppressed by other factors in the system.

Fourth, both the drinker's behavior and his functioning are affected by an accumulation of the previous processes. The legal sociocultural, and economic factors regarding alcoholic beverages, in turn, are affected by the drinker's behavior and functioning, but by way of the reactions of others to the drinking.

Fifth, the system contains counteracting forces. For example, the alcoholic beverage industry communicates messages encouraging drinking while school alcohol programs generally advocate abstinence.

Sixth, the system should be conceived of as dynamic and constantly undergoing changes. The time lag between a change in one factor resulting in changes in another, however, varies. The time between a social policy being proposed, legislated, and implemented, for instance, is greater than that between the drinker's reactions to his own alcohol consumption. In addition, the time between the effect of intoxication on motor coordination is less than that on impairment of liver functioning.

Finally, each age-sex-ethnic subgroup in the population may have its own perception of the legal sociocultural factors and may place different emphasis on the importance of the various factors. Indeed, most of the past research has been conducted with white males and may not be totally applicable to other race-sex groups. Wilsnack, for example, found that while drinking may satisfy power needs in men; it enhanced more "feminine" feelings in women.[64]

Such a model is complex but it reflects the interrelation of alcohol with so many aspects of society and of the individual. With theoretical advancements in simulation and analytic techniques and the increasing sophistication and availability of computer programming, the use and evaluation of such a model becomes increasingly possible.[65]

Such a complex network of relationships suggests some of the problems inherent in alcohol research, the importance of a multidisciplinary approach and some of the difficulties faced by intervention and prevention programs.

Why Should There Be Any Laws Concerning Drinking?

There are many and varied motivations for regulations regarding drinking practices; these motivations involve economic, religious, and humanitarian interests. Alcohol laws in general have operated to raise revenue, to promote temperance, and to prevent harm from drinking. The social, medical, and psychiatric complications of alcohol abuse were presented in Part II.

Fallon and Lesesne, in chapter 4, reviewed a variety of medical, neurological, and gastrointestinal complications of drinking. Cancer of the larynx, pharynx, and esophagus, alcoholism, pneumonia, Laennec's cirrhosis of the liver, and cardiomyopathy have all been associated with chronic excessive drinking. Further study is needed, however, to determine the incidence and consequences of alcohol damage as well as to elucidate the mechanisms involved.

Hudson, a chief medical examiner, delineated in chapter 5 the various ways alcohol may be related to the causes of death. Alcohol may be a direct cause of death, as in acute alcohol poisoning, or it may be a contributing factor. Alcohol can contribute to a person's death by aggravating an already existing condition, by increasing the individual's susceptibility to fatal diseases, or by obscuring the underlying condition so that adequate lifesaving treatment is prevented.

The social and psychiatric complications of drinking
were discussed by Ewing in chapter 6. In addition, self-
medication drinking behavior was described; this involves
attempts by the drinker to treat his anxiety, depression, and/or
poor social or work relationships by inappropriate or excessive
alcohol intake. The effects of excessive drinking on the spouse
and family were also considered.

Waller, in chapter 7, reviewed scientific studies of the
role of alcohol in highway crashes and pedestrian deaths. She
pointed out that there is a steep increase in the relative
probability of an accident when young inexperienced drivers
have been drinking and when older people drive with blood
alcohol levels over .08 percent. This level of blood alcohol can
be achieved with seemingly little alcohol depending on the
person involved. A man weighing 160 pounds reaches a blood
alcohol level of .08 percent after drinking four ounces of 86
proof whiskey. A 100 pound woman reaches this after drinking
two and one-half ounces of 86 proof whiskey. In both instances, the calculations are based on the alcohol being consumed
in a relatively short period of time. Table 1-3 and Table 5-1
both help the reader to allow for the time factor.

Chapter 8 examined the risks associated with moderate
levels of drinking and found little evidence of harm, but
further research is needed. In addition to the medical complications, however, other conditions such as suicide, homicide, and
accidental deaths are highly associated with excessive
drinking.

Even if there were no harmful effects associated with its
abuse, alcohol would probably still be regulated simply
because it is a commodity. Historically, as with economic
goods in general, legislation regarding alcohol has tried to
regulate its manufacture, distribution, and sale.[66] Alcohol has
also been used as a source of tax revenue.

Table 18-3 shows the actual amount of revenue in
millions of dollars that federal, state, and local governments
received from alcoholic beverages in 1974 as well as the per
capita contribution to these sources of revenue.[67] The revenue
received from alcohol is also compared with that from tobacco
products.

Alcoholic beverages and tobacco products each contrib-

Table 18-3
Comparison of Public Revenue from Alcoholic Beverages
and Tobacco Products with Total General Revenue
and Total Sales Tax for 1975

(Millions of Dollars) Per Capita

	All Governments	Federal	State and Local	All Governments
Total General Revenue	383,831	218,426	207,730	$1,815.75
Total Sales/Gross Receipts	66,632	20,534	46,098	$ 315.21
Alcoholic Beverages Taxes	7,338	5,339	1,999	$ 34.71
Tobacco Products Taxes	5,804	2,437	3,367	$ 27.45

(Source: U.S. Bureau of the Census, Governmental Finances in 1973-74 Series GF74-No.5, U.S. Government Printing Office, Washington, D.C. 1975.)

uted about 2 percent of the total general revenue for all governments combined. They were not comparable, however, in their contributions to total sales and gross receipts for the various governments. For all governments combined, 11 percent of the total sales/gross receipts came from alcoholic beverages and 9 percent from tobacco products. When the governments' total sales/gross receipts are examined separately, it is obvious that alcohol contributes more than tobacco to the federal government. Twenty-six percent of the federal government's total sales/gross receipts came from alcoholic beverages, 12 percent from tobacco products. Four percent of the state and local governments combined sales/gross receipts came from alcoholic beverages and 7 percent from tobacco products.

Of the estimated $1,815.75 paid per capita to all governments, each person paid approximately $34.71 in taxes on alcoholic beverages.

Alcohol, however, is a special commodity. As pointed out in chapter 1, alcohol functions as a food, as a drug, and as a poison. Although only a third of the sample in a national survey considered it such,[68] alcohol is indeed a drug and, like any other drug, it has an effective dose, a toxic dose, and a lethal dose. Because it is able to influence a drinker's behavior by altering his mood, perceptions, or other mental states, alcohol may be considered a psychoactive drug. As a drug, alcohol can also interact adversely with other drugs.[69] Using alcohol and barbiturates in combination is particularly dangerous.

Why Is Alcohol Available Legally?

Given the documented hazards of drinking, why is alcohol, a legal drug, available without a prescription? One reason proposed is that it satisfies the personal needs of people in developed countries. As a society grows more complex and becomes more specialized, industrialized, and competitive, the tensions of its members increase in both intensity and frequency. Accordingly, the need also increases for a substance that will help suppress frustration and that will provide individuals relief from tension and anxiety. Alcohol is one drug that appears to meet these needs.[70]

In addition to its pharmacological effects, alcohol also performs some important societal functions. Without commenting on the desirability of the situation, we find that alcohol performs magic, certifies status and power, and pays for things that money cannot. One of the magical things alcohol does is to transform people, places, and events; for example, individuals from vastly different economic or social levels become equals when drinking together. Special occasions like promotions, buying a new house, or marriage are toasted with champagne or some other alcoholic beverage and thereby are considered official. Furthermore, an alcoholic beverage can be used to repay a friend or neighbor for his help when giving money would have been considered an insult.

In a model which puts drug use in a social and cultural context, Edwards suggested that those drugs like alcohol which result in highly plastic behavior are more likely to be legalized in any society. By "plastic" Edwards meant that the behavior under the influence of the drug is only partly determined by its pharmacological effects; more importantly it is highly influenced by extraneous factors, such as personality or the environment. Therefore, he concluded: "a drug problem is as likely to be the manifestation of inept social responses or an impoverished culture as the properties of the drug itself or the supposed 'deviance' of the individual."[71]

But why is alcohol the drug that is accepted socially and legally? The long tradition of alcohol use in our society and other countries, as described in chapter 2, and the relatively low amount of alcohol abuse are probably the most compelling reasons. Drinking is so integrated in our culture that both its assets and liabilities are found in our music, paintings, films, and literature. Despite its long tradition, however, if alcohol did not continue to satisfy basic needs of the society or support its goals then it would probably not continue to be legalized.

The role of vested interests in the alcoholic beverage industry, however, should not be overlooked. The alcoholic beverage industry itself not only produces the product but also cultivates a demand for it. The advertising industry also benefits. In 1972, for example, about $311 million were spent to advertise alcoholic beverages in magazines, newspapers, television, radio, and outdoor billboards.[72] While this represents about 5 percent of the total advertising expenditures for all industries, alcoholic beverage advertising represents about a fourth of the total of all advertising on outdoor billboards.

Other interests include over 77,800 employees in the production and immediately related activities of the alcoholic beverage industry[73] and those persons who want to retain this source of revenue.

Regulation of the alcoholic beverage industry, therefore, is a complex matter entailing not only the product itself and its use but also the relationships between the various interest groups involved.

What Is the Law Regarding Alcohol?

Some of the current alcohol regulations in the United States were presented in chapters 13 and 17. As Womer pointed out in chapter 16, an adequate understanding of the present attitudes and legislation, as well as the current political problems regarding alcohol use and abuse, requires a knowledge of their historical roots. Accordingly, the alcohol regulations in ancient and European cultures were described by Tongue in chapter 2, and the foundations of American alcohol legislation were outlined in chapter 1.

In chapter 17, Grad discussed the various modern legislative attempts to regulate drinking but concluded that the criminal law offers no solution to the problem of excessive drinking. Recent legislative attempts to substitute treatment for criminal prosecution of public drunkenness offenders were also described, including federal legislation which recognizes alcoholism as a public health problem. Unfortunately, as of 1976 few states had adopted the Uniform Alcoholism and Intoxication Treatment Act.[74]

How Does Alcohol Legislation Affect Drinking Behavior?

It is difficult to determine the effectiveness of legislation regarding drinking. One attempt to evaluate the effect of laws on drinking is presented in chapter 13. Using data on only distilled spirits (hard liquor), Loeb looked at the apparent per capita consumption of various states representing the major geographical regions in the United States and the different kinds of alcoholic beverage control laws. He noted that the per capita consumption in the United States has been steadily increasing since prohibition. Moreover, since 1965, there has been no state which completely prohibits the sale of alcoholic beverages. Looking at the data, Loeb concluded that control states (those with government owned liquor stores) generally have lower per capita consumption than license states (those with privately owned liquor stores that are licensed by the state).

Room, in chapter 15, presented and evaluated the evidence for three hypotheses regarding the effect of laws on drinking behavior. The first was the null hypothesis, that laws have no effect on drinking behavior. Next, he considered the "constant proportion" hypothesis which suggests that the number of excessive drinkers in a society depends on the amount of drinking done in the entire general population. This viewpoint was advocated by Popham, Schmidt, and de Lint in chapter 14. The final hypothesis which Room examined concerned the "inoculation" theory. This theory suggests that society can reduce the number of social disruptions and other adverse effects of drinking by providing adequate models of drinking.

Actually little is known about the overall effects of control measures on the total population and much less information is available about the detailed effects of any control measure on different subgroups. The data presently available are inadequate to evaluate the impact of laws on drinking behavior. A fully controlled study is needed to establish the nature of the relationship between legislative measures of drinking and the prevalence of alcohol use and abuse.

A scientific assessment of the relative contribution of prevailing social attitudes and laws is also needed. However, as both Loeb and Grad indicated, it is difficult to assess whether the laws determine social attitudes or reflect them. To what extent is change in the legislated behavior due to the law and to what extent to the general social or religious attitudes toward drinking?

A further complication to evaluating the effects of law on drinking behavior is the fact that laws vary from state to state. Even laws within the same state may be contradictory.

Why Are the Alcohol Laws
Not More Uniform and Consistent?

The historical perspective gives some insight into the present patchwork of alcohol laws. Over time, changes in alcohol legislation have occurred that are inconsistent with the original purposes or statutes or that are irrelevant to the present. The historical perspective suggests that the present patchwork resulted from a process of experimenting with various regulatory schemes to fit new social conditions.

A case study showing the evolution of different concepts of liquor control in one particular state was presented in chapter 16. There Womer discussed the various public attitudes which motivated the changing regulations concerning alcohol since 1789 in Virginia.

An additional explanation for the lack of consistent policies, even within a single state, is that given by Globetti in chapter 10. He characterized alcohol legislation as the "result of compromises, special concessions, exceptions, and arbitrary decisions." Attempts to solve the liquor problem in North Carolina, for example, have resulted in a series of laws that changed from the unrestricted sale of alcoholic beverages to complete prohibition and then to restricted sale under state supervision. The final change resulted in customs like brown-bagging which was described in chapters 1 and 11. These laws are the result of fierce competitive pressures from various interest groups. The situation had been summarized by Albert Coates, founder of the UNC Institute of Government: "For more than two centuries in North Carolina, liquor has been a fighting issue and every inch of North Carolina soil has been a battleground."[75]

Each state has its own traditions, attitudes, and political pressures regarding alcohol which interfere with the acceptance of uniform legislation. The politicians' dilemma regarding alcohol regulation reflects the public's own difficulty in reconciling the positive and negative aspects of drinking. The politicians' position may be exemplified by the following, perhaps apocryphal, letter written by a congressman to a constituent who wanted to know the congressman's stand on liquor:

If when you say "whiskey" you mean the devil's brew, the poison scourge, the bloody monster that defiles innocence, dethrones reason, destroys the home, creates misery, and poverty, yea, literally takes the bread from the mouths of little children; if you mean the evil drink that topples Christian men and women from the pinnacles of righteous, gracious living into the bottomless pit of degradation and despair, shame and helplessness and hopelessness—then certainly I am against it with all of my power.

But if, when you say "whiskey" you mean the oil of conversation, the philosophic wine, the ale that is consumed when good fellows get together, that puts a song in their hearts, and laughter on their lips and the warm glow of contentment in their eyes; if you mean the drink that enables a man to magnify his joy and his happiness and to forget, if only for a little while, life's great tragedies, heartbreaks, and sorrows; if you mean that drink, the sale of which pours into our treasuries untold millions of dollars to provide tender care for our little crippled children, our blind, our deaf, our dumb, our aged and infirm, and to build highways, hospitals, and schools—then certainly I am in favor of it.

This is my stand, and I will not compromise.[76]

What Should Be Our Social Policy Concerning Alcohol?

Some people think that the way to prevent drinking problems is to eliminate alcohol. They favor total prohibition, that is, a system of laws and coercive controls making it illegal to manufacture, distribute, or consume alcoholic beverages. This approach has been tried in several forms for varying periods of time with limited success. Aztec society, ancient China, feudal Japan, the Polynesian Islands, Iceland, Finland, Norway, Sweden, Russia, and Canada as well as the United States have all tried prohibition.[77]

The large variety of foods which can be converted into alcohol, the demand for alcoholic beverages, and the ease and cheapness of its production and distribution inevitably lead to bootlegging, smuggling, and home manufacturing. A modern example of this occurred in Finland as the result of a strike among the retail liquor stores belonging to the State Alcohol Monopoly of Finland. In describing the situation, Mäkelä concluded: "Alcohol controls cannot be tightened to extremes for when the legal distribution channels are blocked, they are replaced by illicit ones."[78]

Prohibition may reduce the total number of drinkers, but those who do drink are exposed to increased health hazards. The available alcoholic beverages during prohibition are usually of higher and therefore more hazardous concentration of absolute alcohol because these are more profitable and easier to transport than the bulky 4 percent beer. In addition, illicit alcohol may contain toxic ingredients such as lead.

The primary unfortunate effect of prohibition on the American general public was the resulting reduced respect for the law. The mistaken belief that merely passing a law would prevent drinking and solve the alcohol problems ignores the fact that legal and social controls are more effective in relatively homogeneous populations than in a society as pluralistic as the United States.

A more moderate approach is to have legal control over the alcohol industry and drinking behavior. This includes legal regulations of the kinds of alcohol consumed, its costs, methods of distribution, time and place of drinking, and its availability to drinkers according to age, sex, or other socioeconomic characteristic. The underlying assumption is that drinking is a privilege, like driving, and if abused the privilege can be withdrawn from the individual. This approach depends heavily on public opinion and cooperation. Effective law enforcement, surveillance, and the certain possibility of violations being detected and convicted are extremely important.

A major consideration regarding alcohol legislation is who is being legislated and who are the proper targets of such control measures. Alcohol legislation can result in inconvenience or penalties for the majority of people due to the alcohol abuses of a few. Some studies indicate that the heavy consumption of alcohol is concentrated in a small proportion of the population, that is, a small number of drinkers are accounting for a large amount of the alcohol consumed.[79] This viewpoint suggests that there is a group of drinkers who are distinctly different from the others and who should be the proper target of legislative and therapeutic efforts.

Popham, Schmidt, and de Lint, on the other hand, believe that alcohol consumption is distributed throughout the population in such a way that a reduction in the amount the entire society drinks is necessary to reduce the numbers of problem drinkers. In chapter 14, these researchers presented epidemiological research related to legislative attempts by various countries to control alcohol use and abuse. They suggested that economic conditions rather than laws are the more important factors in influencing the sales of alcoholic beverages. They therefore proposed economic measures, such as a high relative price of alcohol, to reduce the overall consumption of alcohol and the incidence of alcoholism. A high relative price of alcohol is the cost of the absolute amount of alcohol in a beverage in relationship to one's personal disposable income.

Legislative measures cannot create behaviors *de novo* as Lemert pointed out, but the law "can strengthen existing tendencies by articulating unspoken values and by organizing unorganized dissidents in a population. Further, it can define programs of action in a way to minimize resistance or gain the support of otherwise opposed or indifferent groups."[80]

Society cannot deal with drinking and problems of intoxication and alcoholism through legislation alone. Education and informal controls, such as those discussed by Cisin, are also needed. The informal control found in religious, educational, family, and peer influences is more potent than the law in its impact on various aspects of drinking behavior. Legislation can reinforce educational efforts and societal attitudes, but whether it can substitute for them is doubtful.

Providing information concerning the consequences of drinking and alcohol abuse can be effective when the family and group values support those of the formal educational programs. Research is needed to evaluate such programs and to determine the appropriate educational techniques when the values of the didactic program conflict with those of the immediate peer group. Not all educational programs suggesting the dangers of a particular behavior are effective deterrents; some may actually induce the undesired behavior.

Closely allied with the educational approach is that of finding substitute behaviors for drinking. These functional equivalents may include hobbies, work or family activities. The idea is that the time, money, and interests devoted to drinking be redirected to sports, travel, hobbies, and similar diversions. The assumption is that the values and satisfactions achieved from drinking can be fulfilled by other activities. Lemert suggests that this approach might be effective in isolated outposts, logging camps, long-term construction projects in sparsely settled areas, technical research teams, diplomatic corps in foreign countries, or military installations. These kinds of sites would also prove useful as research locations where changes in amounts and forms of drinking could be documented. Lemert concluded that "In certain kinds of internally controlled or isolated community situations where boredom and apathy or social isolation have reached critical proportions, diversionary activities may well decrease the extent of drunkenness."[81]

This approach may also be effective with young people who have never learned to rely on alcohol and are learning other ways to cope with their problems and their environment. It may also be useful in therapeutic programs for pathological drinkers who have discovered that drunkenness is not an effective problem solver.

The chief purpose of the above approaches is primary

prevention, that is, precluding drunkenness and alcoholism ever developing. Secondary prevention is also needed; it is important to either terminate or reverse the process of problem drinking in those people at high risk. Treatment to prevent disability in those already having problems with their drinking is the final stage of prevention.

The medical and health professionals are deeply involved in tertiary prevention efforts, but must increase their involvement in secondary prevention. Training to help physicians, nurses, and paraprofessionals recognize the patient's need for help with his drinking is essential. Coordination of the various public, industrial, and voluntary agencies as well as an effective referral system can insure more adequate treatment.

Some researchers have suggested that society's goal should not be the prevention but rather the minimization of alcohol damage.[82] The 1970 liquor law of Finland, for example, stated that minimization of alcohol damage was the primary goal of their alcohol policies. Areas of damage included health, life span, crime rate, public order, work performance, family life, and traffic safety.[83]

Summary

This chapter has attempted to give only a highly compressed survey of drinking behaviors and social policies regarding alcohol. A conceptual model of both the influences and the consequences of drinking presented in this chapter illustrates the importance of a multidisciplinary approach to the study of drinking behavior.[84]

A full range of social and legal responses is also needed to prevent or minimize alcohol problems. Alcohol education, for example, is more effective when considered as part of an educational program regarding effective living and responsible decision making. The public can play an important role by providing models of responsible drinking, by accepting abstainers, and by creating an atmosphere conducive to promoting early identification and early treatment for problem drinkers.

Advocates of various social policies need to consider the costs as well as the benefits of trying to enforce particular legal sanctions. Since any program may have adverse consequences which are unintended, careful consideration and evaluation of various programs are necessary. Controlled studies are also needed to determine the best educational approaches as well as to evaluate the effects of legislative and informal social controls on drinking behavior.

Notes

Chapter 1

1. Brown-bagging is a custom permitted in some areas where drinks are not sold in restaurants. The customer may bring in his own bottle hidden in a paper bag. For more details see chapter 11.
2. D. Guthrie, *A History of Medicine* (London: Nelson and Sons, 1945), p. 324.
3. A Lichine, *Encyclopedia of Wines and Spirits* (New York: Alfred A. Knopf, 1968), p. xi.
4. See note 3, p. 1.
5. L. W. Morrison, *Wines and Spirits* (Baltimore: Penguin Books, 1968), p. 207.
6. Cf. Latin *aqua vitae* and French *eau de vie*. See D. Daiches, *Scotch Whisky: Its Past and Present* (London: Andre Deutsch, 1970), p. 3.
7. See note 3, p. 553. "Corn" here is used in the American sense meaning "maize."
8. R. Wilkinson, *The Prevention of Drinking Problems* (New York: Oxford University Press, 1970), pp. 56-57.
9. K. Bruun, "Legislation and Alcoholism," in *Alcohol and Alcoholism*, ed. R. E. Popham (Toronto: University of Toronto Press, 1970), p. 357.
10. J.A. Ewing, B.A. Rouse, and R.A. Mueller, "Alcohol Susceptibility and Plasma Dopamine β-hydroxylase Activity," *Research*

Communications in Chemical Pathology and Pharmacology 8, no. 3 (July 1974): 551-54.

11. Delirium tremens represents a medical emergency since it has a significant mortality rate. Typically it follows prolonged intake of large amounts of alcohol, such as twelve to thirty-six ounces of whiskey daily for several weeks. When the condition is fully developed the patient is tremulous, irritable, and fearful or terrified. He is in a state of clouded consciousness and may experience hallucinations, typically visual, which must be the origin of the "pink elephant" stories. He may also hear and feel things which are not there, and sleep is usually impossible.

12. P. M. Roman, "The Future Professor: Functions and Patterns of Drinking Among Graduate Students," in *The Domesticated Drug: Drinking Among Collegians*, ed. G. L. Maddox (New Haven: College and University Press, 1970).

13. M. L. Barnett, "Alcoholism in the Cantonese of New York City: An Anthropological Study," in *Etiology of Chronic Alcoholism*, ed. O. Diethelm (Springfield: C.C. Thomas, 1955).

14. P. H. Wolff, "Ethnic Differences in Alcohol Sensitivity," *Science* 175(1972):449-50.

15. J. A. Ewing, B. A. Rouse, and E. D. Pellizzari, "Alcohol Sensitivity and Ethnic Background," *American Journal of Psychiatry* 131 (1974):206-210.

16. M. Keller and J. R. Seeley, *The Alcohol Language*, Brookside Monograph No. 2 (Toronto: University of Toronto Press, 1958).

17. O. Irgens-Jensen, "Use of Alcohol in an Isolated Area of Northern Norway," *British Journal of Addiction* 65 (1970): 181-85.

18. C. MacAndrew and R. B. Edgerton, *Drunken Comportment: A Social Explanation* (Chicago: Aldine Publishing Company, 1969).

19. D. Fenna, L. Mix, O. Schaefer, and J.A.L. Gilbert, "Ethanol Metabolism in Various Racial Groups," *Canadian Medical Association Journal* 105 (1971): 472-75.

20. C. R. Snyder, *Alcohol and the Jews* (Glencoe, Ill.: Free Press, 1958).

21. G. Lolli, E. Serionni, G. Golder, C. Balboni, and A. Mariani, "Further Observations in the Use of Wine and Other Alcoholic Beverages by Italians and Americans of Italian Extraction," *Quarterly Journal of Studies on Alcohol* 14 (1953):395-405.

22. E. G. Baird, "The Alcohol Problem and the Law: I.The Ancient Laws and Customs," *Quarterly Journal of Studies on Alcohol* 4 (1944): 535-56.

23. E. S. Turner, "The Proud and Awful Annals of the Peerless

British Pub" in *Pub: A Celebration,* ed. A. McGill (London: Longmans, Green and Co., 1969).

24. E. G. Baird, "The Alcohol Problem and the Law: II.The Common Law Bases of Modern Liquor Controls," *Quarterly Journal of Studies on Alcohol* 5 (1944): 126-61.

25. See note 24, p. 141.

26. O. T. Binkley, "Attitudes of the Churches," in *Drinking and Intoxication,* ed. R. G. McCarthy (New Haven: College and University Press, 1959), pp. 325-30.

27. See note 9, p. 356.

28. R. G. McCarthy, "Part V: Controls," *Drinking and Intoxication* (New Haven: College and University Press, 1959), pp. 345-429.

29. M. E. Chafetz, "Alcoholism," in *Comprehensive Textbook of Psychiatry,* ed. A. M. Freedman and H.I. Kaplan (Baltimore: Williams and Wilkins, 1967).

30. Prabhudas Balubhai Patwari, "Total Prohibition," paper presented at 31st International Congress on Alcoholism and Drug Dependence, Bangkok, Thailand, Feb. 25, 1975.

31. This 68 percent figure was found in the studies by Cahalan, Cisin, and Crossley which are reported in *American Drinking Practices,* Rutgers Center of Alcohol Studies, New Haven: College and University Press, 1969.

Interestingly, an identical percentage is reported by Dr. George Gallup from a 1974 survey *(Raleigh News and Observer,* June 9, 1974). Gallup reports 4 percentage points increase since his 1969 measurement, continuing a general upward trend since 1958. Such surveys show that 95 million Americans aged eighteen or older presently use alcoholic beverages, at least occasionally. More drinking is associated with more income and more education and significant regional differences are demonstrable. Gallup found that nearly one-fourth of drinkers admit to sometimes drinking to excess. Twelve percent report that liquor has been a cause of trouble in the family—a figure which, when projected, represents 17 million adults each of whom must have had family problems involving at least another 17 million persons, and probably many more than that.

32. Additional readings include:

B. Lockhard, Sir R., *Scotch: The Whisky of Scotland in Fact and Story* (London: Putnam and Co., 1971).

L. W. Marrison, *Wines and Spirits* (Baltimore: Penguin Books, 1968).

D. J. Opperman, ed., *Spirit of the Vine* (Cape Town: Human and Rousseau, 1968).

A. Sichel, *The Penguin Book of Wines* (Baltimore: Penguin Books, 1966).

Chapter 2

1. A. Maurizio, *Geschichte der gegorenen Getranke* (Berlin: Verlagsbuchhandlung Paul Parey, 1933).
2. M. Hoffman, *5000 Jahre Bier* (Berlin: Alfred Meztner Verlag, Frankfurt am Main, 1956).
3. F. A. King, *Beer Has a History* (New York: Hutchinson's Scientific and Technical Publications, 1947).
4. R.G. McCarthy, ed., *Drinking and Intoxication* (New Haven: Yale Center of Alcohol Studies, 1959).
5. C. E. G. Catlin. *Liquor Control* (New York: Henry Holt and Co., 1931).
6. Th. v.Liebenau, *Das Gasthof—und Wirtshauswesen dr Schweiz in alterer Zeit* (Zurich: Verlag von J.A. Preuss, 1891).
7. See note 6.
8. S. and B. Webb, *The History of Liquor Licensing in England Principally from 1700 to 1830* (New York: Longmans, Green and Co., 1903).
9. C. Seltman, *Wine in the Ancient World* (London: Routledge and Kegan Paul, 1957).
10. See note 4.
11. See note 4.
12. C. Washburne, *Primitive Drinking* (New Haven: College and University Press, 1961).
13. B. Roueche, *The Neutral Spirit* (Boston: Little, Brown and Co., 1960).
14. N. Duka, Pociatky statneho intervencionizmu v. teorii a praxi osvietenskej doby na Slovensku, *Proti Alkoholicky Obzor* 3, no. 1 (1968): 23-26.
15. Additional readings include:

     H.W. Allen, *A History of Wine* (London: Faber and Faber, 1961).

     N. Latronico, *I Vini Medicinali* (Milano: Editore Ulrico Hoepli, 1947).

     S.P. Lucia, *A History of Wine as Therapy* (Philadelphia: J.B. Lippincott Co., 1963).

     C. MacAndrew, and R.B. Edgerton, *Drunken Comportment, A Social Explanation* (Ontario, Canada: Nelson, Don Mills, 1970).

     C.R. Snyder, *Alcohol and the Jews* (New Haven: Yale Center of Alcohol Studies, 1958).

Chapter 3

1. B. Rush, "Inquiry into the Effects of Ardent Spirits upon the Human Mind and Body," *Aspects of Alcoholism* (Philadelphia, Pa.: J.B. Lippincott Company, 1966), p. 41.
2. T. Trotter, "Essay, Medical, Philosophical and Chemical on Drunkenness," in M. Mann, *Primer on Alcoholism* (New York: Holt, Rinehart and Winston, 1950), p.6.
3. D. Anderson, "Alcohol and Public Opinion," *Quarterly Journal of Studies on Alcohol* 3(1942):378.
4. D. J. Pittman, *World Health Organizations Committee of Experts in Alcoholism* (New York: Harper and Row, 1967), p.4
5. M. Mann, *Primer on Alcoholism* (New York: Holt, Rinehart and Winston Co., Inc., 1958), p.1.
6. H. M. Trice, *Alcoholism in America* (New York: McGraw-Hill Book Co., 1966), pp.30-42.
7. J. R. Seeley, "Alcoholism Is a Disease," *Society, Culture, and Drinking Patterns,* ed. D. J. Pittman and C. R. Snyder (New York: Wiley and Sons, 1962), p.586.
8. T. Edwards, *The New Dictionary of Thoughts* (New York: Standard Book Co., 1955), pp. 144-45, 300-301.
9. S. P. Lucia, *Alcohol and Civilization* (New York: McGraw-Hill Book Co., 1960).
10. J. A. Krout, *The Origins of Prohibition* (New York: Alfred A. Knopf, 1924), pp.1-25.
11. E. H. Cherrington, *The Evolution of Prohibition in the United States of America* (Westerville, Ohio: American Issue Press, 1920), p.39.
12. J. R. Gusfield, *Symbolic Crusade: Status Politics and the American Temperance Movement* (Urbana: University of Illinois Press, 1963).
13. See note 1.
14. H. Asbury, *The Great Illusion* (New York: Greenwood Press, 1950), p. 13.
15. See note 2.
16. See note 1.
17. See note 12, p.39.
18. See note 11, p.78.
19. See note 5, p.6.
20. D. Dorchester, *The Liquor Problem in All Ages* (New York: Phillips and Hunt, 1884), pp.290-310.
21. C. E. Palmer, *Inebriety; Its Source, Prevention and Cure* (Philadelphia: Union Press, 1912), p.21.

22. See note 12, p.30.
23. See note 11, pp. 154-55.
24. C. D. Leigh, *Prohibition in the United States: A History of the Prohibition Party and of the Prohibition Movement* (New York: George H. Doran, Co., 1926), p.266.
25. J. S. Billings, *The Liquor Problem* (Boston: Houghton, Mifflin and Co., 1905), p. 41.
26. See note 21, p. 21.
27. See note 21, p. 41.
28. See note 21, p. 47.
29. D. Pickett, *Alcohol and the New Age* (New York: Methodist Book Concern, 1926).
30. E. H. Cherrington, *Standard Encyclopedia of the Alcohol Problem* (Westerville, Ohio: American Issue Publishing Co., 1925), vol. 1.
31. See note 21, p.27.
32. See note 12, p. 125.
33. E. M. Jellinek, "Recent Trends in Alcoholism and in Alcohol Consumption," *Quarterly Journal of Studies on Alcohol* 7(1948):1-42.
34. See note 21, p. 147.
35. See note 14, p. 147.
36. See note 12, p. 9.
37. E. J. Lee, "Alcoholism from an Allergic and Mental Viewpoint," *Medical Record* 138(1938):208-10.
38. C. H. Durfee, *To Drink or Not to Drink* (New York: Longmans and Green, 1937).
39. A. Myerson, "Alcohol: A Study of Social Ambivalence," *Quarterly Journal of Studies on Alcohol* 1(1940):13-20.
40. J. Hall, "Drunkenness as a Criminal Offense," *Quarterly Journal of Studies on Alcohol* 1(1941):751-66.
41. L. Kolb, "Alcoholism and Public Health," *Quarterly Journal of Studies on Alcohol* 1(1941):605-21.
42. See note 3, pp. 376-92.
43. A. S. Linsky, "Theories of Behavior and the Image of the Alcoholic in Popular Magazines," *The Public Opinion Quarterly* 34(1970-71):573-81.
44. H. W. Pfautz, "The Image of Alcohol in Popular Fiction 1900-1904," *Quarterly Journal of Studies on Alcohol* 18(1966):49-71.
45. *Alcoholism: A Source Book for the Priest*, National Clergy Conference on Alcoholism, 1960, Indianapolis, private printing, p. 7.

46. J. C. Ford, *Man Takes a Drink* (New York: P. J. Kennedy and Sons, 1955).

Chapter 4

1. P. M. Dreyfus, "The Wernicke-Korsakoff Syndrome," *Textbook of Medicine,* ed. Beeson and McDermott (Philadelphia: W. B. Saunders Co., 1971), pp. 246-47.
2. G. T. Perkoff, M. M. Dioso, V. Bleisch, and G. Klinkerfuss, "A Spectrum of Myopathy Associated with Alcoholism," *Annals of Internal Medicine* 67 (1967): 481-510.
3. C. S. Alexander, "Alcoholic Cardiomyopathy," *Postgraduate Medicine* 58 (1975):127-31.
4. B. M. Parker, "The Effects of Ethyl Alcohol on the Heart," *Journal of American Medical Association* 228 (1974):741-42.
5. H. D. Janowitz and M. Boyer, "Alcohol and Pancreatitis," *Annals of Internal Medicine* 74 (1971):444.
6. D. H. Cowan and J. D. Hines, "Thrombocytopenia of Severe Alcoholism," *Annals of Internal Medicine* 74(1971):37-43.
7. E. J. Fredericks and M. Z. Lazor, "Recurrent Hypoglycemia Associated with Acute Alcoholism," *Annals of Internal Medicine* 59 (1963):90-94.
8. D. W. Jenkins, R. E. Eckel, and J. W. Craig, "Alcoholic Ketoacidosis," *Journal of American Medical Association* 217(1971):177-83.
9. M. S. Tenbrinck and S. Y. Buchin, "Fetal Alcohol Syndrome," *Journal of American Medical Association* 232 (1975):1144-47.
10. H. R. Lesesne and H. J. Fallon, "Alcoholic Liver Disease," *Postgraduate Medicine* 53 (1973): 101-106.
11. E. Rubin and C. S. Lieber, "Alcohol-induced Hepatic Injury in Nonalcoholic Volunteers," *New England Journal of Medicine* 278 (1968):869-76.
12. W. J. Powell, Jr. and G. Klatskin, "Duration of Survival in Patients with Laennec's Cirrhosis," *American Journal of Medicine* 44 (1968):406-20.
13. R. A. Helman, M. H. Temko, S. W. Nye, and H. J. Fallon, "Alcoholic Hepatitis: Natural History and Evaluation of Prednisolone Therapy," *Annals of Internal Medicine* 74 (1971):311-21.

Chapter 5

1. "The Relationship of Alcohol to Acute Abdominal Catastrophes," *Medico-legal Bulletin* 16(1967):1-4 (Published by Office

of the Chief Medical Examiner, Commonwealth of Virginia, Richmond.)

2. R. G. Brayton, P. E. Stokes, M. S. Schwartz, and D. B. Louria, "Effect of Alcohol on Leukocyte Mobilization Phagocytosis and Intracellular Bacterial Killing," *New England Journal of Medicine* 282(1970):123-28.

3. G. E. Burch and A. Ansari, "Chronic Alcoholism and Carcinoma of the Pancreas," *Archives of Internal Medicine* 122(1968):273-75.

4. A. D. Weiss, M. Victor, J. H. Mendelson, and J. LaDou, "Critical Flicker Fusion Studies," *Quarterly Journal of Studies on Alcohol,* Supplement no. 2 (May 1964): 89-95. "Effect of Alcohol on Driving Ability," *Alcohol and the Impaired Driver,* Committee on Medico-legal Problems, American Medical Association, 1970.

5. Editorial: "Rum Fits and DT's," *Journal of American Medical Association* 212(1970):2112-13; N. Freinkel, "Alcohol Hypoglycemia. I. Carbohydrate Metabolism of Patients with Clinical Alcohol Hypoglycemia and Experimental Reproduction of Syndrome with Pure Ethanol," *Journal of Clinical Investigation* 42(1963):1112-13; D. W. Henkins, R. E. Eckel, and J. W. Craig, "Alcoholic Ketoacidosis," *Journal of American Medical Association* 217(1971):177-83.

Chapter 6

1. D. Cahalan, I. H. Cisin, and H. M. Crossley, *American Drinking Practices,* monographs of the Rutgers Center of Alcohol Studies, no. 6 (New Haven: College and University Press, 1969).

2. J. A. Ewing and B. A. Rouse, "Measuring Alcohol Consumption: The 'Alcohol Quotient.'" Presented at 30th International Congress on Alcoholism and Drug Dependence, Amsterdam, Sept. 4-8, 1972.

3. Both Beaubrun's and our categorization are discussed in chapter 11.

4. *Alcohol and Health.* U.S. Dept. of Health, Education and Welfare, Second Special Report to the U.S. Congress (Publication No. HSM-72-9099), Washington, D.C., 1974, p. 104.

5. A useful book for anyone who has doubts about whether or not he is drinking safely is: *The Safe Way to Drink; How to Prevent Alcohol Problems Before They Start,* by William B. Terhune, M.D. Published 1969 by Pocketbooks, a Division of Simon and Schuster. A shorter source of useful suggestions is *The Alcoholic American.* Published by the National Association of Blue Shield Plans, 1970.

6. M. E. Chafetz, in *Comprehensive Textbook of Psychiatry*, ed. A. M. Freedman and H. I. Kaplan (Baltimore: Williams and Wilkins, 1967), p. 1012.
7. See note 1, p. 164 et seq.
8. Al-Anon and Alateen are organizations for the spouses and children of alcoholics. Even if an alcoholic refuses to participate in Alcoholics Anonymous the involvement of family in these organizations helps to restore their morale and sometimes can have major therapeutic effect upon the alcoholic. Write for information to: Al-Anon Family Group Headquarters, Inc., P.O. Box 182, Madison Square Station, New York, N.Y. 10010.
9. D. L. Davies, "Normal Drinking in Recovered Alcohol Addicts," *Quarterly Journal of Studies on Alcohol* 23 (1962):94-104. See also comments on article listed above by thirteen writers in the same journal, 24 (1962):109-21, 321-32.
10. For brief reviews of an extensive literature see, for example, M.E. Chafetz and H. W. Demone, Jr., *Alcoholism and Society* (New York: Oxford University Press, 1962), p. 76 and D. J. Pittman, "Drinking and Alcoholism in American Society," *Alcoholism: The Total Treatment Approach*, ed. R. J. Catanzaro (Springfield: Charles C. Thomas, 1968).
11. G. E. McClearn and D. A. Rodgers, "Differences in Alcohol Preference among Inbred Strains of Mice," *Quarterly Journal of Studies on Alcohol* 20(1959):691-95; K. Eriksson, "Alcohol Consumption and Blood Alcohol in Rat Strains Selected for Their Behavior Towards Alcohol," *Biological Aspects of Alcohol Consumption*, ed. K. Eriksson and O. Forsander (Helsinki: Finnish Foundation for Alcohol Studies, 1972), vol. 20.
12. R. Cruz-Coke and A. Varela, "Inheritance of Alcoholism: Its Association with Color Blindness," *Lancet* 2 (1966): 1282-84.
13. J. W. Smith and G. A. Brinton, "Color-Vision Defects in Alcoholism," *Quarterly Journal of Studies on Alcohol* 32 (1971):41-44.
14. A. Varela, L. Rivera, J. Mardones, and R. Cruz-Coke, "Color Vision Defects in Non-alcoholic Relatives of Alcoholic Patients," *British Journal of Addiction* 64 (1969):67-70.
15. D. W. Goodwin, "Is Alcoholism Hereditary? A Review and Critique," *Archives of General Psychiatry* 25 (1971):545-49.
16. J. Partanen, K. Bruun, and T. Markkanen, *Inheritance of Drinking Behavior* (Helsinki: Finnish Foundation for Alcohol Studies, 1966).
17. M.A. Schuckit, D. A. Goodwin, and G. Winokur, "A Study of Alcoholism in Half Siblings," *American Journal of Psychiatry* 128 (1972):1132-36.

18. D. W. Goodwin, F. Schulsinger, L. Hermansen, S. B. Guze, and G. Winokur, "Alcohol Problems in Adoptees Raised Apart from Alcoholic Biological Parents," *Archives of General Psychiatry* 28 (1973):238-43.

19. D. W. Goodwin, "Drinking Problems in Adopted and Non-adopted Sons of Alcoholics," *Arch. Gen. Psychiat.* 31(1974):164-169.

20. G. Winokur, T. Reich, J. Rimmer, and F. N. Pitts, "Alcoholism III: Diagnosis and Familial Psychiatric Illness in 259 Alcoholic Probands," *Archives of General Psychiatry* 23 (1970):104-11.

21. This work largely stems from the pioneering efforts of Dr. Jack H. Mendelson. He and his colleagues have published many papers. An excellent review is: N.K. Mello, "Behavioral Studies of Alcoholism," *The Biology of Alcoholism*, ed. B. Kissin and H. Begleiter (New York: Plenum Press, 1972), vol. 2. Dr. Mello provides a fully documented picture of studies done by herself, Dr. Mendelson, and many others.

22. D. G. Mayfield and D. Montgomery, "Alcoholism, Alcohol Intoxication, and Suicide Attempts," *Archives of General Psychiatry* 27 (1972):349-53. H. Wallgren and H. Barry III, *Actions of Alcohol* (New York: Elsevier, 1970), 2:725.

23. See for example, J. A. Ewing, "How to Help the Chronic Alcoholic," *American Family Physician* 6(1972):90-97. J.A. Ewing and R.E. Fox, "Family Therapy of Alcoholism," *Current Psychiatric Therapies*, ed. J.H. Masserman (New York: Grune and Stratton, 1968), 8:86–91. J.A. Ewing, "How to Help the Alcoholic Marriage," *Marital and Sexual Counseling in Medical Practice*, ed. D.W. Abse, E.M. Nash and L.M.R. Louden, 2nd edition, (Hagerstown: Harper and Row, 1974), chap. 13.

24. R.W. Jones and A.R. Helrich, "Treatment of Alcoholism by Physicians in Private Practice," *Quarterly Journal of Studies on Alcohol* 33(1972):117-31.

25. J.A. Ewing, T. Dukes, and C. Sugg, "Physician Care of Alcoholics," *North Carolina Medical Journal* 33(1972):859-61.

26. Professional Training on Alcoholism (Report of National Council on Alcoholism meeting) *Annals of New York Academy of Science*, 178, 1971. John A. Ewing, Stumbling Blocks in Alcoholism Education, paper presented at American Medical Society on Alcoholism, San Francisco, December 11, 1974.

27. John L Norris, The 1974 Membership Survey of Alcoholics Anonymous, paper presented at North American Congress on Alcohol and Drug Problems, San Francisco, December 18, 1974.

28. J.W. Riley and C.F. Marden. "The Medical Profession and the

Problem of Alcoholism," *Quarterly Journal of Studies on Alcohol* 7(1946):240-70. N.H. Rathod. "An Enquiry into General Practitioners' Opinions About Alcoholism," *British Journal of Addiction* 62(1967):103-11.

29. M.B. Sobell, H.H. Schaefer, and K.C. Mills, "Differences in Baseline Drinking Behavior Between Alcoholics and Normal Drinkers," *Behavioral Research* 10(1972):257-67.

30. I arranged the symposium "Behavioral Approaches to the Treatment of Alcoholism" as part of the 30th International Congress on Alcoholism and Drug Dependence, held in Amsterdam in September 1972. Seven papers discussed attempts at training controlled drinking and the entire symposium proceedings are published as: *Alcoholism: Journal on Alcoholism and Related Addictions*, vol. 9, no. 2, Zagreb, Yugoslavia, 1973. See also J.A. Ewing, "Behavioral Approaches and Problems with Alcohol," *International Journal of Addictions* 9(1974)369; J.A. Ewing, "Some Recent Attempts to Inculcate Controlled Drinking in Patients Resistant to Alcoholics Anonymous" in *The Person with Alcoholism*, ed. F.A. Seixas, R. Cadoret, and S. Eggleston, *Annals of New York Academy of Sciences* 233(1974):147-54, and J.A. Ewing and B.A. Rouse, "Failure of an Experimental Program to Inculcate Controlled Drinking in Alcoholics," *British Journal of Addiction* 71(1976):123-134.

31. For a fuller discussion of the need to match treatment and patient see, J.A. Ewing, "Is There a Relationship Between Type of Alcoholism and Prognosis?" *Journal of Alcoholism* 8(1974):133-54 and J. A. Ewing, "Matching Therapy and Patients—The Cafeteria Plan," presented at 31st International Congress on Alcoholism and Drug Dependence, Bangkok, Thailand, February 23-28, 1975, *British Journal of Addictions* 72(1977):13-18.

32. *Alcohol Problems: A Report to the Nation* by the Cooperative Commission on the Study of Alcoholism, prepared by T.F.A. Plaut (New York: Oxford University Press, 1967).

33. T. Wilkinson, *The Prevention of Drinking Problems: Alcohol Control and Cultural Influences* (New York: Oxford University Press, 1970).

34. See chapter 11 for more details of this legal phenomenon.

Chapter 7

1. U.S. Department of Transportation, *The 1968 Alcohol and Highway Safety Report* (Washington, D.C.: U.S. Government Printing Office, 1968), pp.xx-xxi.

2. National Safety Council, Statistics Division, *Motor Vehicle*

Deaths and Changes (Chicago: National Safety Council, 1974).

3. R.F. Borkenstein, R.F. Crawther, R.P. Shumate, W. B. Ziel, and R. Zylman, *The Role of the Drinking Driver in Traffic Accidents* (Bloomington: Indiana University Department of Police Administration, 1964).

4. See note 3, page 120.

5. For further discussion of this phenomenon, see P.M. Hurst, "Epidemiological Aspects of Alcohol in Driver Crashes and Citations," *Journal of Safety Research* 5(1973):130-48.

6. See note 3, page 166.

7. M.W. Perrine, J.A. Waller, and L.S. Harris, *Alcohol and Highway Safety: Behavioral and Medical Aspects* (Washington, D.C.: U.S. Department of Transportation NHTSA Technical Report, 1971).

8. See note 1.

9. L. Shapiro and R. G. Mortimer, *Literature Review and Bibliography of Research and Practice in Pedestrian Safety* (Ann Arbor: University of Michigan Highway Safety Research Institute, 1969).

10. W. Haddon, Jr., P. Valien, J. R. McCarroll, and C. J. Umberger, "A Controlled Investigation of Adult Pedestrians Fatally Injured by Motor Vehicles in Manhattan," *Journal of Chronic Diseases* 14(1961):655-78.

11. See D. F. Huelke and R. A. Davis, *Pedestrian Fatalities* (Ann Arbor: University of Michigan Highway Safety Research Institute, 1969), and see also note 9.

12. S.B. White and C.A. Clayton, "Some Effects of Alcohol, Age of Driver, and Estimated Speed on the Likelihood of Driver Injury," *Accident Analysis and Prevention* 4(1972):59-66.

13. R.G. Smart, "Are Alcoholics' Accidents Due Solely to Heavy Drinking?" *Journal of Safety Research* 1(1969):170-73.

14. J. A. Waller, "Impaired Driving and Alcoholism: Personality or Pharmacologic Effect?" *Journal of Safety Research* 1(1969):174-77.

15. See J. B. Haskins, "Effects of Safety Communication Campaigns: A Review of the Research Evidence," *Journal of Safety Research* 1(1969):58-66. J. B. Haskins, "Evaluative Research on the Effects of Mass Communication Safety Campaigns: A Methodological Critique," *Journal of Safety Research* 2(1970):86-96.

16. See note 7.

17. See note 7, page 196.

18. J.A. Waller, "Identification of Problem Drinking among Drunken Drivers," *Journal of the American Medical Association* 200 (1967):134-37.

19. S. Pollack, O.R. Didenko, A.W. McEachern, and R.M. Berger,

Drinking Driver and Traffic Safety Project: Final Report, vol. 1 (Washington, D.C.: U.S. Department of Transportation NHTSA Technical Report, 1972). p. 9.
20. See notes 13 and 14.
21. See note 5.
22. See note 5, p. 135.
23. See note 1.
24. See P. Zador, *Statistical Evaluation of the Effectiveness of "Alcohol Safety Action Programs"* (Washington, D.C.: Insurance Institute for Highway Safety, 1974).
25. G.J. Driessen and J.A. Bryk, "Alcohol Countermeasures: Solid Rock and Shifting Sands." *Journal of Safety Research* 5(1973): 108-28. Over 100 countermeasures are listed.
26. M. Blumenthal and H. Ross, "Two Experimental Studies of Traffic Law," *The Effect of Legal Sanctions on DUI Offenders* (Washington, D.C.: U.S. Department of Transportation NHTSA Technical Report, 1973), vol. 1.
27. See Insurance Institute for Highway Safety, *Status Report* 9, No. 7 (April 9, 1974); and R. Zylman, "When It Became Legal to Drink at 18 in Michigan: What Happened?" *Journal of Traffic Safety Education* 21(1974):15.
28. T.R. Johns and E.A. Pascarella, *An Assessment of the Limited Driving License Amendment to the North Carolina Statutes Relating to Drunk Driving* (Chapel Hill: University of North Carolina Highway Safety Research Center, 1971).
29. H. L. Ross, "Law, Science, and Accidents: The British Road Safety Act of 1967," *The Journal of Legal Studies* 2, No. 1(1973):1-78.
30. K. W. Herrick, "Alcohol and Auto Accidents in Europe," *Report on Alcohol* 31(1973):3-31.
31. B.J. Campbell and D. Levine, "Accident Proneness and Driver License Programs" (paper read at the First International Conference on Driver Behavior, October 8-12, 1973, in Zurich, Switzerland.)
32. D. T. Campbell, "Reforms as Experiments," *American Psychologist* 24(1969): 409-29.

Chapter 8

1. Second Special Report to the U. S. Congress on *Alcohol and Health—New Knowledge.* U. S. Dept. of Health, Education and Welfare, National Institute on Alcohol Abuse and Alcoholism, DHEW Publication No. (ADM) 74-123, 1974.
2. W. O. Menge, "Mortality Experience among Cases Involving

Alcoholic Habits," *Proceedings of the Home Office Life Underwriters Association* 31 (1950):70-93.
3. See note 1, pp. 105-109.
4. P. Nicholls, G. Edwards, and E. Kyle, "Alcoholics Admitted to Four Hospitals in England: II General and Cause-specific Mortality," *Quarterly Journal of Studies on Alcohol* 35 (1974):841-55.
5. M. A. Schuckit and E. K. Gunderson, "Deaths among Young Alcoholics in the U. S. Naval Service," *Quarterly Journal of Studies on Alcohol* 35(1974):856-62.
6. D. Shurtleff, "Some Characteristics Related to the Incidence of Cardiovascular Disease and Death," in *The Framingham Study*, ed. W. B. Kannel and T. Gordon (Washington, D.C.: U.S. Govt. Printing Office, 1970).
7. N. Belloc, "Relationship of Health Practices and Mortality," *Journal of Preventive Medicine* 2 (1973):67-81.
8. See note 1, pp. 110-19.
9. R. Pearl, *Alcohol and Longevity* (New York: Alfred A. Knopf, 1926).
10. See note 1, pp. 69-90.
11. See note 1, pp. 91-97.
12. See note 1, p. 121.
13. Anstie's Limit is described in chapter 6.
14. J. A. Ewing, "Is There a Relationship between Type of Alcoholism and Prognosis?" *Journal of Alcoholism* 8 (1973):133-54.
15. B. A. Rouse, P. F. Waller, and J. A. Ewing, "Adolescents' Stress Levels, Coping Activities and Father's Drinking Behavior," paper presented at 81st Annual Meeting of the American Psychological Association, Montreal, Aug. 27-31, 1973.

Chapter 9

1. D. Cahalan, I.H. Cisin, A.D. Kirsch, and C.H. Newcomb, "Behavior and Attitudes Related to Drinking in a Medium-sized Urban Community in New England," Social Research Project, rep. no. 2 (Washington, D.C.: George Washington University, 1965); D. Cahalan, I.H. Cisin, and H. Crossley, "American Drinking Practices: a National Survey of Behavior and Attitudes Related to Alcoholic Beverages," Social Research Group, rep. no. 3 (Washington, D.C.: George Washington University, 1967); I.H. Cisin, "Community Studies of Drinking Behavior," *Annals of New York Academy of Sciences* 107(1963):607-12; G. Knupfer, R. Fink, W.B. Clark, and A.S. Goffman, "Factors Related to Amount of Drinking in an Urban Community," California Drinking Practices Study, rep. no. 6 (Berkeley: Division of Alcoholic Reha-

bilitation, California State Department of Public Health, 1963), and G. Knupfer and R. Room, "Age, Sex and Social Class as Factors in Amount of Drinking in a Metropolitan Community," *Social Problems* 12 (1064):224-40.

2. D. Cahalan, I.H. Cisin, and H.M. Crossley, *American Drinking Practices* (New Brunswick, N.J.: Rutgers Center of Alcohol Studies, 1969).

3. R. Zylman, "Are Drinking-Driving Laws Enforced?" *The Police Chief* (September 1970): 48-53.

Chapter 10

1. For a general discussion of the various models of alcohol control proposed or established in the United States see E. M. Lemert, *Human Deviance, Social Problems, and Social Control* (Englewood Cliffs, N. J.: Prentice Hall, 1967).

2. H. H. Nowlis, "Marijuana: Its Place among Drugs and Moves for Legalization," paper presented at the 24th National Conference on Higher Education, American Association for Higher Education, Chicago, Illinois, March 4, 1968.

3. The study from which these data are taken was supported by Public Health Research Grant MH14956 from the National Institute of Mental Health.

4. D. J. Pittman, "International Overview: Social and Cultural Factors in Drinking Patterns, Pathological and Nonpathological," in D. J. Pittman, ed., *Alcoholism* (New York: Harper and Row, 1967), pp. 3-20.

5. R. H. Zucker, "Adolescent Drinking: A Problem of Situations or of Personality?" paper presented at the 4th Annual Institute for Health Education for Health Sciences, Hunter College, New York, 1965.

6. Pittman, see note 4, pp. 5-12.

7. H. M. Trice, *Alcoholism* (New York: McGraw-Hill, 1966), pp.22-23.

8. About 90 percent of the students identified with Protestant churches condemn any alcohol use on moral grounds. There are few ethnic groups in the state which approve of moderate alcohol intake. For a discussion of the definition of the role of beverage alcohol in the community studied see G. Globetti and G. Pomeroy, "Characteristics of Community Residents Who Are Favorable Toward Alcohol Education," *Mental Hygiene* 54 (July 1970), pp. 411-15.

9. For a comprehensive summary of research on teenage drinking see G. L. Maddox, "Adolescence and Alcohol," in R. G. McCarthy

(ed.) *Alcohol Education For Classroom and Community* (New York: McGraw-Hill, 1964), pp. 32-47.

10. A. Myerson, "Alcohol: A Study of Social Ambivalance," *Quarterly Journal of Studies on Alcohol* 1 (January 1940), pp. 13-20. The work of Cahalan and Cisin, while it focused on adults rather than young people, is relevant on this point. They found a lower percentage of users in the less urbanized East-South-Central states but an above average proportion of heavy and escape drinkers among those who drank. See D. Cahalan and I. H. Cisin, "American Drinking Practices: Summary of Findings From a National Probability Sample," *Quarterly Journal of Studies on Alcohol* 29 (March 1968), pp. 130-151.

11. This factor was measured by the Straus-Bacon Scale of Social Complications. R. Straus and S. D. Bacon, *Drinking in College* (New Haven: Yale University Press, 1953).

12. C. S. Deschin et al. *Teenagers and Venereal Disease* (Atlanta: U.S. Public Health Service, 1961).

13. R. R. Dynes, A. C. Clark, and S. Dinitz, "Levels of Occupational Aspirations: Some Aspects of Family Experience as a Variable," *American Sociological Review* 21 (April 1956), pp. 212-15.

14. See B. Stacey and J. Davis, "Drinking Behaviour in Childhood and Adolescence: An Evaluative Review," *British Journal of Addiction,* 65 (1970): 203-12. The authors reviewed studies from Finland, Sweden, Great Britain, and the United States (of which the Mississippi data were included) and concluded that "existing regulatory systems are of limited effectiveness in reducing problem drinking or any of their real imputed correlates." Several studies I conducted seem to support this statement, see especially, Gerald Globetti, "The Drinking Patterns of Negro and White High School Students in Two Mississippi Communities," *Journal of Negro Education* (Winter 1970): 60-69; Gerald Globetti and Gerald O. Windham, "The Social Adjustment of High School Students and the Use of Beverage Alcohol," *Sociology and Social Research* 51 (January 1967): 148-157.

15. J. H. Skolnick, "Religious Affiliation and Drinking Behavior," *Quarterly Journal of Studies on Alcohol,* 19 (March 1958): 452-70.

16. See note 14, Stacey and Davis, p. 206.

17. G. Globetti, "What Young People and Adults Think About Alcohol Education," paper read at the 29th International Congress on Alcoholism and Drug Dependence, Sydney, Australia, February 1-14, 1970.

18. R. G. McCarthy, "Introduction," in *Alcohol Education For Classroom and Community* (New York: McGraw-Hill Book Co., 1964) p. 7.

19. R. D. Russell, "Education About Alcohol. . .For Real American Youth," *Journal of Alcohol Education* 14(Spring 1969):1-4.
20. R. R. Robinson, "The Prospect of Adequate Education about Alcohol and Alcoholism," *Journal of Alcohol Education* 14 (Winter 1969): 15-18.

Chapter 11

1. From *The Scottish Students' Songbook* (London: Bayley and Ferguson, 1891). This song is translated from the German, *Kindleben's Studentenliedern, 1781.*
2. D. E. Smith, ed. *The New Social Drug: Cultural, Medical and Legal Perspectives on Marijuana* (Englewood Cliffs, N.J.: Prentice-Hall, Inc., 1970). For the most recent comprehensive examination of college drinking see: G.L. Maddox, ed. *The Domesticated Drug: Drinking Among Collegians* (New Haven, Connecticut: College and University Press, 1970).
3. L. Johnston, *Drugs and American Youth*, a report from the "Youth In Transition" project (Ann Arbor, Mich.: Institute for Social Research, 1973).
4. W. E. Groves, P. H. Rossi, and D. Grafstein, *Study of Life Styles and Campus Communities: Preliminary Report* (Baltimore: Johns Hopkins Univ., 1970); B. A. Rouse, "Johns Hopkins University National Survey of College Drug Use," *Drinking and Drug Practices Surveyor*, ed. R. Room (Berkeley, Calif.: University of California, 1971). No. 4, pp. 6-7; W. E. Groves, "Patterns of College Student Drug Use and Lifestyles" in *Drug Use: Epidemiological and Sociological Approaches*. E. Josephson and E.E. Carroll eds. (New York: John Wiley and Sons, 1974).
5. D. H. Milman and W. H. Su, "Patterns of Drug Usage among University Students: Part V. Heavy use of Marihuana and Alcohol by Undergraduates," *American Journal of College Health Association* 21(1973):181-87.
6. See note 5, p. 185.
7. A dramatic increase in both marijuana and hallucinogen use was reported by a series of Gallup surveys of college populations summarized in the following: "Latest Findings on Marijuana," *U. S. News and World Report*, 1 Feb. 1971; "Gallup Finds a Continued Rise in the Use of Marijuana and LSD on Campuses," *New York Times*, 10 February 1972; and "Poll Finds Surge in Marijuana Use," *New York Times* 26 March 1972. In the Spring of 1967 the percent of students surveyed who had ever used marijuana was 5 percent; two years later it was 22 percent and in December of 1971, it was 51 percent.

8. J. V. Toohey, "An Analysis of Drug Use Behavior at Five American Universities," *Journal of School Health* 41(1971):464-68.

9. D. I. Manheimer and G. D. Mellinger, "Marijuana Use among Urban Adults," *Science* 166(1969):1544-45; A. E. Slaby, J. Lieb, and A. H. Schwartz, "Comparative Study of the Psychosocial Correlates of Drug Use Among Medical and Law Students," *Journal of Medical Education* 47(1972):717-23; M. Blumenfield, A. E. Riester, A. C. Serrano, and R. L. Adams, "Marijuana Use in High School Students," *Diseases of the Nervous System* 33 (1972): 603-10; and M. Lipp, J. Tinklenberg, S. Benson, F. Melges, and Z. Taintor, "Medical Student Use of Marijuana, Alcohol, and Cigarettes: A Study of Four Schools," *International Journal of Addictions* 7(1972):141-52.

10. J. W. Goldstein, T. C. Gleason, and J. H. Korn, "Whither the Epidemic? Psychoactive Drug Use Career Patterns of College Students," Carnegie-Mellon University Report No. 74-2, 1973.

11. W. A. Glenn and L. G. Richards, *Recent Surveys of Nonmedical Drug Use: A Compendium of Abstracts*, National Institute on Drug Abuse, 1974.

12. D. Cahalan, I. H. Cisin, and H. M. Crossley, *American Drinking Practices* (New Brunswick, New Jersey: Rutgers Center of Alcohol Studies, 1969).

13. For a summary of the Gallup poll results and for further information on the South see: J. S. Reed, *The Enduring South* (Chapel Hill, N.C.: University of North Carolina Press, 1975).

14. *Alcoholic Beverage Control Laws of North Carolina* (North Carolina State Board of Alcoholic Control, 1967).

15. North Carolina General Statutes 18A-30.

16. North Carolina General Statutes 18A-26.

17. North Carolina General Statutes 18A-21.

18. North Carolina General Statutes 18A-2.

19. B. A. Rouse, "Preliminary Results of Alamance and Caswell Counties Survey: Respondents' Position on Sales of Alcoholic Beverages" (Chapel Hill: University of North Carolina, Center for Alcohol Studies, 1972).

20. North Carolina General Statutes 18-30.

21. J. A. Ewing, B. A. Rouse, and W. E. Bakewell, "Alcohol Use in a Student Population," paper presented at the 29th International Congress on Alcoholism and Drug Dependence, Sydney, Australia, February, 1970; and J. A. Ewing, B. A. Rouse, M. H. Keeler and W. E. Bakewell, "Why Students Turn On," *British Journal of Social Psychiatry* 4(1970):255-65.

22. M. H. Beaubrun, "Alcohol and Drinking Practices in a Jamaican Suburb," paper presented as a Herman Goldman International Lecture, New York City Medical College, June 9, 1967.

23. A. B. Hollingshead, *Two Factor Index of Social Position*, mimeograph, New Haven, Conn., 1957.

24. J. R. Penn, "College Student Life-Style and Frequency of Alcohol Usage," *Journal of American College Health Association* 22(1974):220-22.

25. E. Campbell, "The Internalization of Moral Norms," *Sociometry* 27(1964): 391-412.

26. M. K. Gergen, K. G. Gergen, and S. J. Morse, "Correlates of Marijuana Use among College Students," *Journal of Applied Social Psychology* 2(1972):1-16.

27. For a description of the study and other results see: B. A. Rouse and J. A. Ewing, "Marijuana and Other Drug Use by Women College Students," *American Journal of Psychiatry* 130(1973):486-90.

28. For a description of the study and other results see: B. A. Rouse and J. A. Ewing, "Marijuana and Other Drug Use by Graduate and Professional Students," *American Journal of Psychiatry* 129(1972):415-20.

29. For a description of the study and the results on the association between drug use and risks, driving, and alienation, see: B. A. Rouse and J. A. Ewing, "Student Drug Use, Risk-Taking, and Alienation," *Journal of American College Health Association* 22(1974):226-30.

30. L. Srole, "Social Integration and Certain Corollaries: An Exploratory Study," *American Sociological Review* 21(1956):709-16.

31. See note 29.

32. N.Q. Brill, E. Crumpton, and H.M. Grayson, "Personality Factors in Marijuana Use," *Archives of General Psychiatry* 24(1971):163-65.

33. See note 29.

34. S.R. Schroeder, J.A. Ewing, B.A. Rouse, et al., "Synergistic Effects of Alcohol, Methapyriline and Chlordiazepoxide on Drivers' Eye Movements and Tracking Errors in Simulated Dangerous Situations." UNC Highway Safety Research Center, 1972; W. Haddon, Jr., E.A. Suchman, and D. Klein, *Accident Research, Methods and Approaches.* (New York: Harper and Row Publishers, 1964); and also see chapter 7 by Waller in this book.

35. A.W. Klein, J.A. Davis, and B.D. Blackbourne, "Marijuana and Automobile Crashes," *Journal of Drug Issues* 1(1971): 18-26.

36. M.C. Jones, "Personality Correlates and Antecedents of Drinking

Patterns in Adult Males," *Journal of Consulting and Clinical Psychology* 32(1968):2-12; M.C. Jones, "Personality Antecedents and Correlates of Drinking Patterns in Women," *Journal of Consulting and Clinical Psychology* 36(1971):61-69; W. McCord, J. McCord, and J. Gudeman, *Origins of Alcoholism* (Stanford, Cal.: Stanford University Press, 1960); and L.N. Robins, *Deviant Children Grow Up: A Sociological and Psychiatric Study of Sociopathic Personality* (Baltimore: Williams and Wilkins, 1966).

37. H. Kleber, "Student Use of Hallucinogens," *Journal of American College Health Association* 14(1965):109-17; R. Blum and Associates, *Student and Drugs* (San Francisco: Jossey-Bass, 1969); and D. Hartmann, "A Study of Drug-taking Adolescents," *Psychoanalytic Study of the Child* 24(1969):384-430.

38. E. Lipinski, and B. Lipinski, "Motivational Factors in Psychedelic Drug Use by Male College Students," *Journal of American College Health Association* 19(1967): 145-49; E. Suchman, "The 'Hang-loose' Ethic and the Spirit of Drug Use," *Journal of Health and Social Behavior* 9(1968): 146-55; and also see notes 39, 40 and 41.

39. H.S. Becker, *Outsiders: Studies in the Sociology of Deviance* (New York: Free Press, 1963).

40. B.D. Johnson, *Marihuana Users and Drug Subcultures* (New York: John Wiley and Sons, 1973).

41. K. Keniston, *Youth and Dissent, The Rise of a New Opposition* (New York: Harcourt Brace Jovanovich, 1971); and K. Keniston, "The Psychology of the Alienated Student," paper presented at the American Psychological Association, New York, September, 1966.

42. C.W. Hobart, "Types of Alienation: Etiology and Interrelationships," *Canadian Review of Sociology and Anthropology* 2(1965):92-107.

43. M. Brown, "The Risk of Being Hip," *Risk Taking Behavior*, ed. R. E. Carney, (Springfield, Illinois: Charles C. Thomas Publisher, 1971), p. 87.

44. S.L. Halleck, "Psychiatric Treatment of the Alienated College Student," *American Journal of Psychiatry* 24(1967):642-50.

45. Paul A. Walters, Jr., G.W. Goethals, and H.G. Pope, Jr., "Drug Use and Life Style Among 500 College Undergraduates," *Archives of General Psychiatry* 26(1972):92-96; and Richard E. Horman, "Alienation and Student Drug Use," *The International Journal of the Addictions* 8(1973): 325-331.

46. See note 29.

47. See note 30.

48. See note 43, p. 87.

49. G.L. Maddox, "Role-Making: Negotiations in Emergent Drink-

ing Careers," *Social Science Quarterly* 49 (1968):331-349.

50. See note 49, p. 343.

51. See note 29.

52. M.W. Sterne, "Drinking Patterns and Alcoholism Among American Negroes," *Alcoholism*, ed. D. J. Pittman (New York: Harper and Row, 1967), pp.66-99.

53. G.L. Maddox and E. Borinski, "Drinking Behavior of Negro Collegians: A Study of Selected Men," *Quarterly Journal of Studies on Alcohol* 25 (1964): 651-668; G.L. Maddox and J.R. Williams, "Drinking Behavior of Negro Collegians," *Quarterly Journal of Studies on Alcohol* 29 (1968): 117-129; L.N. Robins, G.E. Murphy and M.B. Breckenridge, "Drinking Behavior of Young Urban Negro Men," *Quarterly Journal of Studies on Alcohol* 29(1968):657-686 and G.L. Maddox, "Drinking Among Negroes: Inferences From the Drinking Patterns of Selected Negro Male Collegians," *Journal of Health and Social Behavior* 9 (1968): 114-120.

54. R. Straus and S.D. Bacon, *Drinking in College* (New Haven, Connecticut: Yale University Press, 1953).

55. G.L. Maddox and B. Allen, "A Comparative Study of Social Definitions of Alcohol and Its Uses Among Selected Negro and White Undergraduates," *Quarterly Journal of Studies on Alcohol* 22 (1961):418-427.

56. K.C. Powell, *The Drinking Patterns (of Alcohol) Among a Group of Black North Carolina Collegians* (Chapel Hill, North Carolina: M. A. thesis, 1974); and see also note 49.

57. Suggested background readings for those interested in either conducting or interpreting studies of black people include: M. L. Goldschmid, ed. *Black Americans and White Racism: Theory and Research* (New York: Holt, Rinehart and Winston, 1970); W. H. Grier and P. M. Cobbs, *Black Rage* (New York: Bantam Books, 1969); R. L. Jones, ed. *Black Psychology* (New York: Harper and Row, 1972); W. Ryan, *Blaming the Victim* (New York: Vintage Books, 1972); and C. W. Thomas and S. Sillen, *Racism and Psychiatry* (Secaucus, New Jersey: Citadel Press, 1974).

58. K. M. Fillmore, "Drinking and Problem Drinking in Early Adulthood and Middle Age," *Quarterly Journal of Studies on Alcohol* 35(1974):819-40.

59. See note 54.

60. Cooperative Commission on the Study of Alcoholism, *Alcohol Problems: A Report to the Nation*, prepared by T. F. A. Plaut (New York: Oxford University Press, 1967); and D. Cahalan, *Problem Drinkers: A National Survey* (San Francisco, California: Jossey-Bass, 1970).

61. See note 58, p. 839.

62. H. M. Trice and J. A. Belasco, "The Aging Collegian: Drinking Pathologies Among Executive and Professional Alumni," *The Domesticated Drug*, ed. G. L. Maddox (New Haven, Connecticut: College and University Press, 1970), pp.218-33.
63. W. V. Grant and C. G. Lind, *Digest of Educational Statistics, 1974 Edition* U. S. Department of Health, Education and Welfare, Education Division, Washington, D.C., 1975.
64. J. V. Rachal, J. R. Williams, M. L. Brehm, B. Cavanaugh, R. P. Moore, and W. C. Eckerman, *A National Study of Adolescent Drinking Behavior, Attitudes and Correlates*, Mimeograph (Research Triangle Institute Project No. 234-891, April, 1975).

Chapter 12

1. W. C. Fields, *Never Trust a Man Who Doesn't Drink*, compiled by Paul Mason (New York: Stonyan Books, 1971).
2. D. Cahalan and I. H. Cisin, "American Drinking Practices: Summary of Findings From a National Probability Sample. I. Extent of Drinking by Population Subgroups," *Quarterly Journal of Studies on Alcohol* 29(1968a):130-51; "II. Measurement of Massed Versus Spaced Drinking," *Quarterly Journal of Studies Alcohol* 29(1968b): 642-56; and M. B. Sobell, H. H. Schaefer and K. C. Mills, "Differences in Baseline Drinking Behavior between Alcoholic and Normal Drinkers," *Behavioral Research and Therapy* 10(1972):257-77.
3. R. Room, "Governing Images and the Prevention of Alcohol Problems," *Preventive Medicine* 3(1974):11-23.
4. J. J. Conger, "Alcoholism: Theory, Problem and Challenge. II. Reinforcement Theory and the Dynamics of Alcoholism," *Quarterly Journal of Studies on Alcohol* 17(1956):291-324; J. D. Keehn, "Psychological Paradigms of Dependence," *The International Journal of the Addictions* 4, no. 4(1969):499-506; N. K. Mello, "Behavioral Studies of Alcoholism," in *The Biology of Alcoholism vol. 2: Physiology and Behavior*, ed. B. Kissin and H. Begleiter (New York: Plenum Press, 1972); P. E. Nathan, "Alcoholism," in *Handbook of Behavior Modification*, ed. H. Leitenberg (New York: Appleton Century Crofts, 1974); and P. M. Miller and D. H. Barlow, "Behavioral Approaches to the Treatment of Alcoholism," *Journal of Nervous and Mental Disease* 157, no. 1(1973):10-20.
5. D. L. Dudley, D. K. Roszell, J. E. Mules, and W. H. Hague, "Heroin vs. Alcohol Addiction—Quantifiable Psychosocial Similarities and Differences," *Journal of Psychosomatic Research* 18(1974):327-35; F. W. Ellis and J. R. Pick, "Experimentally

Induced Ethanol Dependence in Rhesus Monkeys," *Journal of Pharmacology and Experimental Therapeutics* 175(1970):88-93; D. Lester, "Self-Selection of Alcohol by Animals, Human Variation, and the Etiology of Alcoholism," *Quarterly Journal of Studies on Alcohol* 27(1966):395-438; and J. R. Weeks, "Experimental Narcotic Addiction," *Scientific American* 210(1964):46-52.

6. J. A. Ewing, B. A. Rouse, and E. D. Pellizzari, "Alcohol Sensitivity and Ethnic Background," *American Journal of Psychiatry* 131(1974):206-10; and N. K. Mello, "Some Aspects of the Behavioral Pharmacology of Alcohol," *Psychopharmacology—A Review of Progress,* ed. O. H. Efron et al. (Washington, D. C.: U. S. Government Printing Office, 1967), PHS Publ.#1836.

7. R. D. Martorano, "Mood and Social Perception in Four Alcoholics," *Quarterly Journal of Studies on Alcohol* 35(1974):445-57; and P. E. Nathan, N. A. Titler, L. M. Lowenstein, P. Solomon, and A. M. Rossi, "Behavioral Analysis of Chronic Alcoholism; Interaction of Alcohol and Human Contact," *Archives of General Psychiatry* 22(1970):418-30.

8. C. MacAndrew and R. B. Edgerton, *Drunken Comportment* (Chicago: Aldine Publishing Co., 1969).

9. R. D. Belleville, "Control of Behavior by Drug-produced Internal Stimuli," *Psychopharmacologia* 5(1964):95-105; D. A. Overton, "State Dependent Learning Produced by Depressant and Atropinelike Drugs," *Psychopharmacologia* 10(1966):6-31; D. A. Overton, "Discriminative Control of Behavior by Drug States," in *Stimulus Properties of Drugs,* ed. T. Thompson and R. Pickens (New York: Appleton-Century-Crofts, 1971), pp.87-110; and C. R. Schuster and R. L. Balster, "The Discriminative Stimulus Properties of Drugs," *Advances in Behavioral Pharmacology No. 1,* ed. T. Thompson and P. B. Dews (New York: Academic Press, 1974).

10. D. S. Blough, "Definitions and Measurement in Generalization Research," *Stimulus Generalization,* ed. D. I. Mostofsky (Stanford, California: Stanford University Press, 1965); S. A. Mednick and J. L. Freedman, "Stimulus Generalization," *Psychological Bulletin* 57 no. 3(1960):169-200; and H. S. Terrace, "Stimulus Control," in *Operant Behavior: Areas of Research and Application,* ed. W. K. Honig (New York: Appleton-Century-Crofts, 1966).

11. N. Guttman and H. I. Kalish, "Discriminability and Stimulus Generalization," *Journal of Experimental Psychology* 51(1956):79-88.

12. P. M. Miller, M. Hersen, R. M. Eisler, and G. Hilsman, "Effects of Social Stress on Operant Drinking of Alcoholics and Social Drinkers," *Behavior Research and Therapy* 12(1974):67-72; and K.

C. Mills, J. W. Bean and J. S. Hutcheson, "Shock Induced Ethanol Consumption in Rats," *Pharmacology, Biochemistry and Behavior* 6(1977):107–15.

Chapter 13

1. Reprinted with permission from *Popular Government,* UNC Institute of Government, 38(1971):11-19.
2. Retail Outlets For the Sale of Distilled Spirits, Distilled Spirits Institute (1970).
3. Alaska (1970) § 04.10.040.
4. Alaska (1970) § 04.10.100.
5. Alaska (1970) § 04.10.070.
6. Alaska (1970) § 04.10.430, .440.
7. Alaska (1970) § 04.15.010.
8. Alaska (1970) § 04.15.020.
9. N.J. Stat. Ann. § 33 1-12.
10. N.J. Stat. Ann. § 33: 1-77, -81.2, -81.6.
11. N.J. Stat. Ann. § 33: 1-40.
12. N.J. Stat. Ann. § 33: 1-47, -47.1.
13. N.J. Stat. Ann. § 33: 1-12.14.
14. Ill. Annot. Stat. 43 § 115 (d).
15. Ill. Annot. Stat. 43 § 95.23, .24, .25.
16. Ill. Annot. Stat. 43 § 166.
17. Ill. Annot. Stat. 43 § 129.
18. Ill. Annot. Stat. 43 § 131.
19. Ill. Annot. Stat. 95 ½ § 11-502.
20. Colo. Rev. Stat. § 75-2-16.
21. Colo. Rev. Stat. § 75-2-4(12), (13).
22. Colo. Rev. Stat. § 75-2-22.
23. Colo. Rev. Stat. § 75-2-23.
24. Colo. Rev. Stat. § 75-2-30.
25. Colo. Rev. Stat. § 75-2-3(3), (4).
26. Colo. Rev. Stat. § 75-2-3(2).
27. Colo. Rev. Stat. § 75-2-3.
28. Annual Statistical Review of the Distilled Spirits Institute (1970), p. 42.
29. Ariz. Rev. Stat. § 4-205.02.
30. Ariz. Rev. Stat. § 4-205.01.
31. Ariz. Rev. Stat. § 4-205.
32. Ariz. Rev. Stat. § 4-101(10).
33. Ariz. Rev. Stat. § 4-101(11).
34. Ariz. Rev. Stat. § 4-206.

35. Summary of State Laws and Regulations Relating to Distilled Spirits, Distilled Spirits Institute (1969), p. 28.
36. Ariz. Rev. Stat. § 4-241.
37. Summary of State Laws and Regulations Relating to Distilled Spirits, Distilled Spirits Institute (1969).
38. Ariz. Rev. Stat. § 4-244.
39. Ariz. Rev. Stat. § 4-242.
40. Ore. Rev. Stat. § 472.110(2).
41. Ore. Rev. Stat. § 472.110 (3-5).
42. Ore. Rev. Stat. § 472.410-.500.
43. Summary of State Laws and Regulations Relating to Distilled Spirits, Distilled Spirits Institute (1969), pp. 10-13.
44. Ore. Rev. Stat. § 471.750.
45. Ore. Rev. Stat. § 471.750.
46. Summary of State Laws and Regulations Relating to Distilled Spirits, Distilled Spirits Institute (1969), pp. 2-17.
47. Ore. Rev. Stat. § 472.310.
48. Ore. Rev. Stat. § 479.990.
49. N.C. Gen. Stat. § 18-45.
50. N.C. Gen. Stat. § 18-61.
51. N.C. Gen. Stat. § 18-51.
52. N.C. Gen. Stat. § 18-45(5), (6).
53. N.C. Gen. Stat. § 18-51(1).
54. N.C. Gen. Stat. § 18-46.
55. Iowa Code Ann. § 123.16(2).
56. Iowa Code Ann. § 123-25.
57. Iowa Code Ann. § 123.27(6).
58. Iowa Code Ann. § 123.27(7).
59. Iowa Code Ann. § 123.46(2)(b).
60. Iowa Code Ann. § 123.43.
61. Iowa Code Ann. § 123.42.
62. Iowa Code Ann. § 123.95.
63. Iowa Code Ann. § 123.96.
64. Annual Statistical Review of the Distilled Spirits Institute (1970), p. 43.

Chapter 14

1. E. M. Jellinek, "Recent Trends in Alcoholism and in Alcohol Consumption," *Quarterly Journal of Studies on Alcohol* 8(1947):1-42.
2. J. Bronetto and J. Moreau, "Statistics on Alcohol Sales and Liver Cirrhosis Mortality for Canada, U.S.A., Various European and Other Countries," (Toronto: Addiction Research Foundation,

1969), and R. E. Popham and W. Schmidt, *Statistics of Alcohol Use and Alcoholism in Canada 1871-1956* (Toronto: University of Toronto Press, 1958).

3. Expert Committee on Mental Health, "Report on the First Session of the Alcoholism Subcommittee," (Geneva: World Health Org., Tech. Rept. Series No. 42, 1951).

4. R. E. Popham, "Indirect Methods of Alcoholism Prevalence Estimation: A Critical Evaluation," in *Alcohol and Alcoholism*, ed. R. E. Popham (Toronto: University of Toronto Press, 1970), pp.294-306.

5. J. de Lint and W. Schmidt, "The Epidemiology of Alcoholism," in *Biological Basis of Alcoholism*, ed. Y. Israel and J. Mardones (New York: Wiley, 1971), pp.423-42.

6. J. R. Seeley, "The Ecology of Alcoholism: A Beginning," in *Society, Culture, and Drinking Patterns*, ed. D. J. Pittman and C. R. Snyder (New York: Wiley, 1962), pp. 330-44.

7. R. E. Popham, "The Jellinek Alcoholism Estimation Formula and Its Application to Canadian Data," *Quarterly Journal of Studies on Alcohol* 17(1956):559-93 and R.E. Popham and W. Schmidt, *A Decade of Alcoholism Research* (Toronto: University of Toronto Press, Brookside Monograph No. 3, 1962).

8. J. L. Simon, "The Economic Effects of State Monopoly of Packaged-Liquor Retailing," *Journal of Political Economics* 74(1966):188-94.

9. See note 1, p. 16.

10. T. W. Barker, "The States in the Liquor Business," *Quarterly Journal of Studies on Alcohol* 18(1957):492-502; B. Y. Landis, "Economic Aspects of State Alcoholic Beverage Monopoly Enterprises, 1937-1946," *Quarterly Journal of Studies on Alcohol* 9(1948):259-69; and see note 8.

11. N. Christie, "Scandinavian Experience in Legislation and Control," in *National Conference on Legal Issues in Alcoholism and Alcohol Usage* (Boston: Boston University Law-Medicine Institute, 1965), pp. 101-22.

12. R. E. Popham, "The Urban Tavern: Some Preliminary Remarks," *Addictions* 9, no.2(1962):16-28.

13. A. Shadwell, *Drink in 1914-1922: A Lesson in Control* (London: Longmans Green, 1923), p. 150.

14. R. E. Popham, "Study of the Urban Tavern," (Toronto: Addiction Research Foundation, 1956); see note 2, Popham and Schmidt, *Statistics;* and note 12.

15. Mass Observation, *The Pub and the People* (London: Gollancz, 1943).

16. S. Ahlström–Laakso, "Arrests for Drunkenness—Two Capital

Cities Compared," *Scandinavian Studies on Criminology* 3(1971):89-105.

17. C. W. Bryant, "Effects of Sale of Liquor by the Drink in the State of Washington," *Quarterly Journal of Studies on Alcohol* 15(1954):320-24.

18. A. D. Entine, *The Relationship between the Number of Sales Outlets and the Consumption of Alcoholic Beverages in New York and Other States* (Albany: New York State Moreland Commission of the Alcoholic Beverage Control Law, Study Paper No. 2, 1963).

19. See note 8, p. 193.

20. P. Kuusi, *Alcohol Sales Experiment in Rural Finland* (Helsinki: The Finnish Foundation for Alcohol Studies, 1957).

21. *Canada Facts, Report of Results of a Study of Attitudes of the Ontario Public Towards the Distribution of Alcoholic Beverages* (Toronto: Canada Facts Ltd., 1946), and C. Wolch, "How Ontario Clergy Look at Alcoholism," *Alcoholism Research* 4, no. 4(1957):1-7.

22. See for example: D. Isaksson, "Forslag till progressivt Beskattningssystem för alkoholhaltiga Drycker, baserat pa Dryckernas relativa Intoxikationseffekt," *Alkoholfrågan* 51(1957):72-80. J. Nielsen and E. Strömgren,"Über die Abhängigkeit des Alkoholkonsums und der Alkoholkrankheiten vom Preis alkoholisscher Getränke," *Akt. Fragen Psychiat. Neurol.* 9(1969):165-70; Seeley, "Death by Liver Cirrhosis and the Price of Beverage Alcohol," *Canadian Medical Association Journal* 83(1960):1361-66. and M. Tolkan, "Polityka cen a Wzrost Spozycia Alkoholu," *Problemy Alkoholizmu* 4, no. 1(1969):7-10.

23. A. Nyberg, *Alkoholijuomien kulutus ja Hinnat* (Helsinki: The Finnish Foundation for Alcohol Studies, 1967); and J. L. Simon, "The Price Elasticity of Liquor in the U.S. and a Simple Method of Determination," *Economet,* 34(1966):193-205.

24. See note 22, Seeley 1960. An objection to the relative price index has been that it obscures the separate effects of price and income. However, a significant price effect independent of income has been adequately demonstrated. (See the recent review of H. H. Lau, "Cost of Alcoholic Beverages as a Determinant of Alcohol Consumption," in *Research Advances in Alcohol and Drug Problems,* ed. Y. Israel et al. (New York: Wiley, 1975). The relative price index remains of value from the standpoint of policy development and implementation. Thus, it draws attention to the fact that increases in taxation may not have the intended effects on economic accessibility unless concurrent changes in income level are taken into account when the amount of increase is determined.

25. J. Bronetto, *Alcohol Price, Alcohol Consumption and Death by Liver Cirrhosis* (Toronto: Addiction Research Foundation, Substudies 1 - 8 - 60 to 1.7 - 8 - 63, 1960-63).

26. M. Terris, "Epidemiology of Cirrhosis of the Liver: National Mortality Data," *American Journal of Public Health* 57 (1967):2076-88 and see note 4.

27. N. Jolliffe and E. M. Jellinek, "Vitamin Deficiencies in Alcoholism, Part VII: Cirrhosis of the Liver," *Quarterly Journal of Studies on Alcohol* 2(1941):544-83.

28. K. Bruun, E. Koura, R. E. Popham, and J. R. Seeley, *Liver Cirrhosis Mortality as a Means to Measure the Prevalence of Alcoholism* (Helsinki: The Finnish Foundation for Alcohol Studies, 1960); S. C. Ledermann, *Alcool, Alcoolisme, Alcoolisation; Données Scientifiques de Caractère Physiologique, Economique et Social* (Paris: Institut National d'Etudes Démographique, Trav. et Doc., Cah. No. 29, 1956); and see note 4.

29. See note 26, p. 2078.

30. E. M. Jellinek, *Government Programs on Alcoholism: A Review of the Activities in Some Foreign Countries* (Ottawa: Department of National Health and Welfare, Mental Health Division Report Series, Memo. No. 6, 1963); H. Wallgren, Alkoholism och Alkoholförbrukning, *Alkoholpolitik* 23:146-149, 1960; and see note 22, Nielsen and Strömgren 1969.

31. J. de Lint and J. Bronetto, "Konsumtion av destillerade Alkoholdrycker och Dödligheten i Levercirrhos," *Alkoholpolitik* 29(1966):62-64, and see note 5.

32. P. Wilkinson, J. N. Santamaria, J. G. Rankin, and D. Martin, "Epidemiology of Alcoholism: Social Data and Drinking Patterns of a Sample of Australian Alcoholics," *Medical Journal of Australia* 1(1969):1020-25.

33. J. Skala, "Some Characteristic Signs of Alcoholism in Czechoslovakia" (Selected papers presented at the 12th International Institute for the Prevention and Treatment of Alcoholism, Lausanne: Internat. Council Alc. Alcsm., vol. 1, pp. 21-34, 1967).

34. S. C. Ledermann, *Alcool, Alcoolisme, Alcoolisation; Mortalité, Morbidité, Accidents du Travail.* (Paris: Institut National d'Etudes Démographique, Trav. et Doc., Cah. No.41, 1964); and W. K. Lelbach, "Zur leberschädigenden Wirkung verschiedener Alkoholika," *Deutsche Medizinische Wochenschrift* 92(1967): 233-38.

35. J. de Lint, The Distribution of Alcohol Consumption in Male and Female Alcoholic Samples, Toronto: Addiction Research Foundation, Substudy 16 - 10 - 64, 1964; and W. Schmidt and R. E. Popham, *Study of an Out-patient Clinical Population in*

Toronto. Mimeographed (Toronto: Addiction Research Foundation 1965).

36. See for example: C. S. Alexander, "Idiopathic Heart Disease, I: Analysis of 100 Cases with Special Reference to Chronic Alcoholism," *American Journal of Medicine* 41(1966):213-14; "Heart Disease and Beer Drinking," *Pub. Hlth. Reports* 83(1968):1998; H. Frank, W. Heil, and I. Leodolter, "Leber und Bierkonsum; Vergleichende Untersuchungen an 450 Arbeitern," *Munchener Medizinische Wochenschrift* 109(1967):892-97; P. H. McDermott, R. L. Delaney, J. D. Egan, and J. F. Sullivan, "Myocardosis and Cardiac Failure in Men," *Journal of American Medical Association* 198(1966):253-65; C. Sjoberg, "Olutalkoholismi lisaantyy Ruotsissa," *Alkoholikysymys* 3(1967):81-84; and see note 34, Lelbach, 1967.

37. H. Wallgren, *On the Relationship of the Consumption of Alcoholic Beverages to the Genesis of Alcoholic Disorders* (Helsinki: Alkon Keskuslaboratorio, Report 7378, 1970), and W. K. Lelbach, "Organic Pathology Related to Volume and Pattern of Alcohol Use," in *Research Advances in Alcohol and Drug Problems*, ed. R. J. Gibbins et al. (New York: Wiley, 1974), pp. 93-198.

38. C. Reuss, *History of Beer Consumption in Belgium 1900-1957* (Louvain: Institut de Recherche Economizue et Sociale, Universitaire de Louvain, 1959); and see note 22, Nielson and Stromgren, 1969.

39. See note 22, Isaksson, 1957.

40. Alcoholic Beverage Study Committee, *Beer, Wine and Spirits: Beverage Differences and Public Policy in Canada* (Ottawa: Brewers Association of Canada, 1973).

41. H. Kalant, A. E. LeBlanc, and A. Wilson, Sensorimotor and Physiological Effects of Various Alcoholic Beverages (paper presented at the 6th International Conference on Alcohol, Drugs and Traffic Safety, Toronto, 1974).

42. R. F. Borkenstein, E. F. Crowther, R. P. Shumate, W. B. Ziel, and R. Zylman, *The Role of the Drinking Driver in Traffic Accidents* (Bloomington, Ind.: Report of the Department of Police Administration, Indiana University, 1964).

43. P. Devrient and G. Lolli, "Choice of Alcoholic Beverage among 240 Alcoholics in Switzerland," *Quarterly Journal of Studies on Alcohol* 23(1962):459-67; G. Lolli, G. M. Golder, E. Serianni, G. Bonfiglio, and C. Balboni, "Choice of Alcoholic Beverage among 178 Alcoholics in Italy," *Quarterly Journal of Studies on Alcohol* 19(1958): 303-308; G. Lolli, E. Schesler, and G. M. Golder, "Choice of Alcoholic Beverage among 105 Alcoholics in New York," *Quarterly Journal of Studies on Alcohol* 21(1960):475-82;

D. Parreiras, G. Lolli, and G. M. Golder, "Choice of Alcoholic Beverages among 500 Alcoholics in Brazil," *Quarterly Journal of Studies on Alcohol* 17(1956):629-32; R. Sadoun and G. Lolli, "Choice of Alcoholic Beverages among 120 Alcoholics in France," *Quarterly Journal of Studies on Alcohol* 23(1962):449-58; and J. Terry, G. Lolli, and G. M. Golder, "Choice of Alcoholic Beverage among 531 Alcoholics in California," *Quarterly Journal of Studies on Alcohol* 18(1957):417-28.

44. W. Schmidt and J. Bronetto, "Death from Liver Cirrhosis and Specific Alcoholic Beverage Consumption: An Ecological Study," *American Journal of Public Health* 52(1962):1473-82.

45. J. de Lint, "Pathological Wine Consumption in Toronto: A Study of Its Definition for Sociological Analysis," (M.A. thesis, University of Toronto, 1962); and J. de Lint, W. Schmidt, and F. Jorge, *Statistics of Alcohol Buying in Toronto*, mimeographed (Toronto: Addiction Research Foundation, 1967).

46. In Ontario as of May 1973, the cheapest alcohol obtainable through a distilled liquor cost 55 percent more than the cheapest in wine. The cost of alcohol in beer fell between these two.

47. E. M. Jellinek, *The Disease Concept of Alcoholism* (New Haven: Hillhouse Press, 1960).

48. For an enlightening statement of the ramifications of the "disease concept" see Powell v. Texas, Supreme Court of the United States, No. 405, October Term, 1967.

49. J. de Lint and W. Schmidt, "The Distribution of Alcohol Consumption in Ontario," *Quarterly Journal of Studies on Alcohol* 29(1968):968-73.

50. R. G. Smart and W. Schmidt. "Blood Alcohol Levels in Drivers Not Involved in Accidents," *Quarterly Journal of Studies on Alcohol* 31(1970):968-71.

51. See note 28, Ledermann 1956.

52. The validity of this contention is more fully discussed in our paper, "The Effects of Legal Restraint on Drinking," in *Biology of Alcoholism*, vol. 4: *Social Biology*, ed. B. Kissin and H. Begleiter (New York: Plenum, 1975).

53. W. K. Lelbach, "Leberschäden bei chronischen Alkoholismus," *Acta Helato-Splenologica* 13(1966):321-49; G. Péquignot, "Enquête par Interrogatoire sur les Circonstances Diététiques de la Cirrhose Alcoolique en France," *Bulletin Institute of National Hygiene* 13(1958):719-39; and see notes 32 and 35, Popham and Schmidt 1965.

54. W. Schmidt and J. de Lint, "Estimating the Prevalence of Alcoholism from Alcohol Consumption and Mortality Data," *Quarterly Journal of Studies on Alcohol* 31(1970):957-64.

55. See note 53, Pequinot 1958.

56. R. E. Popham, "Some Social and Cultural Aspects of Alcoholism," *Canadian Psychiatric Association Journal* 4(1959):222-29; and see notes 6 and 47.

57. I. Gadourek, "Riskante Gewoonten en Zorg voor eigen Welzijn" (Groningen: Wolters, 1963), and see note 47.

58. R. F. Bales, "Cultural Differences in Rates of Alcoholism," *Quarterly Journal of Studies on Alcohol* 6(1946):480-99; R. Blaney, "The Prevalence of Alcoholism in Northern Ireland," *Ulster Medical Journal* 36(1967):33-43; and R. Lynn and S. Hampson, "Alcoholism and Alcohol Consumption in Ireland," *Journal of Irish Medical Association* 63(1970): 39-42.

59. See note 47.

60. See note 58, Bales, 1946.

61. G. Bonfiglio, "Alcoholism in Italy," *British Journal of Addictions* 59(1963):3-10; and see note 28, Ledermann, 1956.

62. See note 28, Bruun et al., 1960.

63. P. Kuusi, *Suomen Viinapulma: Gallup Tutkimuksen Valossa* (Helsinki: Otava, 1948.)

64. S. Sariola, *Drinking Patterns in Finnish Lapland* (Helsinki: Finnish Foundation for Alcohol Studies, 1956), and see note 20.

65. W. Schmidt, R. G. Smart, and R. E. Popham, "The Role of Alcoholism in Motor Vehicle Accidents," *Traffic Safety Research Reviews* 6 no.4(1962):21-27.

66. In Ontario as of May 1973, this would mean an increase in the price of the cheapest fortified wines of sixty-five cents per 26 ounce bottle, and of about five cents per 12 ounce bottle of most beers.

67. C. Warburton, *The Economic Results of Prohibition* (New York: Columbia University, Studies in History, Economics and Public Law No. 379, 1932); and see note 7, Popham 1956; and note 27.

68. For an excellent discussion of the cost-benefit issue with respect to the control of alcohol and other drug use, see H. and O. J. Kalant, *Drugs, Society and Personal Choice* (Toronto: General Publishing, 1971).

69. J. D. Armstrong, "The Search for the Alcoholic Personality," in *Understanding Alcoholism*, ed. S.D. Bacon (Philadelphia: Annals American Academy Political and Social Science, 1958) 315:46-47; D. Lester, "Self-selection of Alcohol by Animals, Human Variation and the Etiology of Alcoholism: A Critical Review," *Quarterly Journal of Studies on Alcohol* 27(1966):395-438; E. Lisansky, "The Etiology of Alcoholism: The Role of Psychological Predisposition," *Quarterly Journal of Studies on Alcohol* 21(1960): 314-43; and see note 56, Popham, 1959.

70. M. Keller, "The Oddities of Alcoholics," *Quarterly Journal of Studies on Alcohol* 33(1972):1147-48.

71. E. M. Jellinek, " Alcoholism, a Genus and Some of Its Species," *Canadian Medical Association Journal* 83(1960):1341-45.
72. D. L. Davies, "Normal Drinking in Recovered Alcohol Addicts," *Quarterly Journal of Studies on Alcohol* 23(1962):94-104; and E. M. Pattison, E. B. Headley, G. C. Gleser, and L. A. Gottschalk, "Abstinence and Normal Drinking: An Assessment of Changes in Drinking Patterns in Alcoholics after Treatment," *Quarterly Journal of Studies on Alcohol* 29(1968):610-33.
73. R. J. Gibbins, H. Kalant, A. E. LeBlanc, and J. W. Clark, "The Effects of Chronic Administration of Ethanol on Startle Thresholds in Rats," *Psychopharmacologia* 19(1971): 95-104; H. Kalant, A. E. LeBlanc, and R. J. Gibbins, "Tolerance to, and Dependence on, Some Non-Opiate Psychotropic Drugs," *Pharmacological Reviews* 23(1971):135-91; A. E. LeBlanc, H. Kalant, R. J. Gibbins, and N. D. Berman, "Acquisition and Loss of Tolerance to Ethanol in the Rat," *Journal of Pharmacology and Experimental Therapeutics* 168(1969):244-50; and A. E. LeBlanc, R. J. Gibbins, and H. Kalant, "Behavioral Augmentation of Tolerance to Ethanol in the Rat," *Psychopharmacologia* 30(1973):117-22.
74. G. Bigelow and I. Liebson, "Cost Factors Controlling Alcoholic Drinking," *The Psychological Record* 22(1972):305-14; G. M. Hunt and N. H. Azrin, "A Community-reinforcement Approach to Alcoholism," *Behaviour Research and Therapy* 11(1973):91-104; and J. D. Keehn, "Translating Behavioral Research into Practical Terms for Alcoholism," *The Canadian Psychological Association Journal* 10(1969):438-46.
75. W. Schmidt and J. de Lint, "Mortality Experience of Male and Female Alcoholic Patients," *Quarterly Journal of Studies on Alcohol* 30(1969):112-18; and W. Schmidt and J. de Lint, "Causes of Death of Alcoholics," *Quarterly Journal of Studies on Alcohol* 33(1972):171-85.
76. Registrar-General's Decennial Supplement, England and Wales, 1951, *Occupational Mortality* (London: H. M. Stationery Office, PT. II, Vol. 1, 1958).

Chapter 15

1. R. Wilkinson, *The Prevention of Drinking Problems: Alcohol Control And Cultural Influences* (New York: Oxford University Press, 1970).
2. R. Room, "Assumptions and Implications of Disease Concepts of Alcoholism," paper presented at the 29th International Congress on Alcoholism and Drug Dependence, Sydney, Australia, 1970.
3. J. Gusfield, *Symbolic Crusade: Status Politics and the American*

Temperance Movement (Urbana, Ill.: University of Illinois Press, 1963; reprinted 1966).

4. There is a large unorganized reservoir of ambivalence toward drinking even in the wetter states. This has recently been reemphasized in discussions of the legal status of eighteen-year-olds, who are often cast in the role of moral surrogates in such situations. Thus the former governor of California commented that "having an eighteen-year-old, I still feel I should have enough parental control that I don't want her to go into a bar and buy a drink . . . . I guess we'd all be better off if we didn't have a drink" (*San Francisco Chronicle*, 24 March 1971, p. 24). In a poll of adults in the same state on the extension of adult rights to eighteen-year-olds, there was 59 percent approval for voting, 59 percent for incurring debts and legal responsibility for them, 37 percent for gambling at state race tracks, but only 31 percent for purchasing liquor (*San Francisco Chronicle*, 9 March 1971, p. 8).

5. K. E. Lanu, *Control of Deviating Drinking Behavior: An Experimental Study of Formal Control over Drinking Behavior* (Helsinki: Finnish Foundation for Alcohol Studies, reprint from the English Summary in the Publication No. 2, 1956).

6. I have found two other published studies which bear some relation to the formal design as described. One is a before-and-after study, but with no control community, of the effects in a rural Saskatchewan community of changing the local "beer parlor" limited to men to a "license beverage room" serving also wine and open to both sexes [R. Dewar and R. Sommer, *The Consumption of Alcohol in a Saskatchewan Community Before and After the Opening of a New Liquor Outlet* (Regina, Saskatchewan: Bureau on Alcoholism, Department of Social Welfare and Rehabilitation, 1962)]. As might be expected, the study did not show any great changes in patterns of drinking. The other was a fully controlled study of "the preventive effect of fines for drunkenness" in middle-sized Finnish towns, in which the proportion of those arrested for drunkenness who were sentenced to a fine rather than being released the next morning was systematically reduced without any public announcement. This study concluded that the addition of a fine to the fact of arrest had no preventive effects: the arrestees did not even recognize that the policy had changed [P. Tornudd, "The Preventive Effect of Fines for Drunkenness: A Controlled Experiment," *Scandinavian Studies in Criminology* 2(1968):109-24]. Other Scandinavian studies are apparently in progress, but no report, at least in English, has yet appeared. There are by now a few well-designed studies of the effects of changes in drunk-driving laws.

7. P. Kuusi, *Alcohol Sales Experiment in Rural Finland* (Helsinki: Finnish Foundation for Alcohol Studies, 1957), vol. 3a.

8. N. Christie and K. Bruun, "Alcohol Problems: The Conceptual Framework," ed. M. Keller and T. Coffey, *Proceedings of the 28th International Congress on Alcohol and Alcoholism* (Highland Park, N. J.: Hillhouse Press, 1969), 2:65-73.

9. New York State Moreland Commission on the Alcoholic Beverage Control Law, *The Licensing and Regulation of Retail Package Liquor Stores*, New York, N.Y., Report and Recommendations no. 1, January 3, 1964, p. 26.

10. S.D. Bacon, "American Experiences in Legislation and Control Dealing with the Use of Beverage Alcohol," in *National Conference on Legal Issues in Alcoholism and Alcohol Usage* (Boston: Boston University Law-Medicine Institute, 1965), pp. 123-41.

11. S. Bacon, Abstract of "The Role of Law in Meeting Problems of Alcohol and Drug Use and Abuse," *29th International Congress on Alcoholism and Drug Dependence: Abstracts* (Sydney, Australia: 1970), p. 3.

12. C. Warburton, *The Economic Results of Prohibition* (New York: Columbia University Studies in History, Economics and Public Law, Columbia University, No. 379, 1932; reprinted 1968).

13. New York State Moreland Commission on the Alcoholic Beverage Control Law, *The Relationship of the Alcoholic Beverage Control Law and the Problems of Alcohol*, New York, N.Y., Study Paper no. 1, October 18, 1963, p. 54.

14. R. Room, "Interrelations of State Policies, Consumption, and Alcohol Problems in the United States," in *Law and Drinking Behavior*, ed. J. A. Ewing and B. A. Rouse (Chapel Hill, N.C.: University of North Carolina Center for Alcohol Studies, 1971), pp. 56-78.

15. R. Room, "Drinking in the Rural South: Some Comparisons in a National Sample," in *Law and Drinking Behavior*, ed. J. A. Ewing and B. A. Rouse (Chapel Hill, N.C.: University of North Carolina Center for Alcohol Studies, 1971), pp. 79-108.

16. N. Christie, "Scandinavian Experience in Legislation and Control," *National Conference on Legal Issues in Alcoholism and Alcohol Usage* (Boston: Boston University Law-Medicine Institute, 1965), pp. 101-22.

17. See notes 14 and 15.

18. K. Bruun, "Implications of Legislation Relating to Alcoholism and Drug Dependence: Government Policies," ed. L. G. Kiloh and D. S. Bell, *Proceedings 29th International Congress on Alcoholism and Drug Dependence, Sydney, Australia*, February 1970, pp. 173-81.

19. Some anecdotal evidence of this can be found in notes 1, 9, and 40.
20. See references in paper cited in note 14.
21. See note 7.
22. T. Coffey, "Beer Street: Gin Lane. Some Views of 18th Century Drinking," *Quarterly Journal of Studies on Alcohol* 27(1966):669-92.
23. H. Carter, *The Control of the Drink Trade in Britain* (London: Longmans, Green, and Company, 1919), and A. Shadwell, *Drink in 1914-1922: A Lesson in Control* (London: Longmans, Green, and Company, 1923).
24. See also other evidence in note 1.
25. Addiction Research Foundation of Ontario, "Summary with Comments on the Interim Report of the Commission of Inquiry into the Non-Medical Use of Drugs," *Addictions*, 17(Fall 1970):7-46.
26. L. Curtis, *The Million Dollar Report: An Exposé: A Self-Indictment* (Dallas: Tane Press, 1968).
27. J. de Lint and W. Schmidt, "The Distribution of Alcohol Consumption in Ontario," *Quarterly Journal of Studies on Alcohol*, 29(December 1968):968-73 and S. Ledermann, "Can One Reduce Alcoholism Without Changing Total Alcohol Consumption in a Population?" *Selected Papers Presented at the 27th International Congress on Alcohol and Alcoholism* (Frankfurt-am-Main, West Germany, 1964), 2:1-90.
28. J. de Lint and W. Schmidt, "The Distribution of Consumption," paper presented at the 28th International Congress on Alcohol and Alcoholism, Washington, D. C., 1968.
29. D. Cahalan, I. Cisin, and H. Crossley, *American Drinking Practices* (New Brunswick, N. J.: Publications Divisions, Rutgers Center of Alcohol Studies, Monograph No.6,1969).
30. M. Keller, "The Definition of Alcoholism and the Estimation of Its Prevalence," in ed. D. Pittman and C. Snyder *Society, Culture, and Drinking Patterns* (New York and London: Wiley, 1962), pp.310-29.
31. R. Room, "Concentration of Consumption: The U.S.," *Drinking and Drug Practices Surveyor* 2(Summer 1970):1.
32. F. H. Allport, "The J-Curve Hypothesis of Conforming Behavior," *Journal of Social Psychology* 5(May 1934):141-83. I am indebted to Don Cahalan and Ira Cisin for drawing this to my attention and for the benefit of our discussion in this area.
33. See note 1, pp. 229-232 and item 6 on p. 246; see note 12, pp. 74-86, also see K. Bruun, E. Koura, R. Popham, and J. Seeley, *Liver Cirrhosis Mortality as a Means to Measure the Prevalence of Alcoholism* (Helsinki: Finnish Foundation for Alcohol Studies,

1960, Vol. 8; J. Seeley, "Death by Liver Cirrhosis and the Price of Beverage Alcohol," *Canadian Medical Association Journal* 83 (December 24, 1960):1361-66; M. Terris, "Epidemiology of Cirrhosis of the Liver: National Mortality Data," *American Journal of Public Health* 57 (December 1967):2076-88; R. E. Popham, "Indirect Methods of Alcoholism Prevalence Estimation: A Critical Evaluation," in *Alcohol and Alcoholism*, ed. R. E. Popham (Toronto: University of Toronto Press, 1970), pp. 294-306; A contrary case, for a relatively limited span of years when there seem to have been considerable changes in the distribution of drinking in the population, can be found in note 30, p. 324. Popham found relatively high correlations in 15 time series, but one of them—for Britain—was highly negative.

34. See note 33, Terris p. 2086.

35. T. Plaut, *Alcohol Problems: A Report to the Nation* (London, Oxford, and New York: Oxford University Press, 1967) p. 125 and see note 1.

36. M. Chafetz, "Alcoholism Prevention and Reality," *Quarterly Journal of Studies on Alcohol* 28(June 1967):345-50. See also the discussions in the same and succeeding issues of the *Quarterly Journal of Studies on Alcohol*.

37. S. Hiltner, "Alcohol Prevention and Reality: Comment on the Article by M. E. Chafetz," *Quarterly Journal of Studies on Alcohol* 28(June 1967):348-49.

38. See note 14.

39. See note 23, Shadwell pp. 149-50, 152.

40. New York State Moreland Commission on the Alcoholic Beverage Control Law, *Mandatory Resale Price Maintenance*, New York, N.Y., Report and Recommendations No. 3, January 21, 1964.

41. R. E. Popham, W. Schmidt, and J. de Lint, "Epidemiological Research Bearing on Legislative Attempts to Control Alcohol Consumption and Alcohol Problems," *Law and Drinking Behavior*, ed. J. A. Ewing and B. A. Rouse (Chapel Hill, N.C.: University of North Carolina, Center for Alcohol Studies, 1971), pp.4-16.

42. See note 33, Seeley; New York State Moreland Commission on the Alcoholic Beverage Control Law, *Resale Price Maintenance in the Liquor Industry*, New York, N. Y., Study Paper no. 5, October 28, 1963, pp.52-54; J. Simon, "The Price Elasticity of Liquor in the U. S. and a Simple Method of Determination," *Econometrica* 34(January 1966):195-205; H. S. Houthakker and L. D. Taylor, *Consumer Demand in the United States: Analyses and Projections*, Second and Enlarged Edition (Cambridge, Mass.: Harvard University Press, 1970); B. Walsh and D. Walsh, "Economic Aspects of Alcohol Consumption in the Republic of Ireland,"

Economic and Social Review 2(1970):115-38.
43. See note 42, Houthakker and Taylor p. 145.
44. See note 12, pp. 235, 240.
45. See note 29, p. 167.
46. D. Cahalan, I. Cisin, and H. Crossley, *American Drinking Practices: A National Survey of Behavior and Attitudes Related to Alcoholic Beverages* (Washington, D.C.: George Washington University Social Research Group, 1967), Report no. 3, p.224.
47. See note 33, Terris p. 2086.
48. See note 7, p. 173.
49. W. Schmidt and J. Bronetto, "Death from Liver Cirrhosis and Specific Alcohol Consumption: An Ecological Study," *American Journal of Public Health* 52(September 1962): 1473-82.
50. This work was partly supported by grants from the National Institute on Alcohol Abuse and Alcoholism (AA000275). A version of this paper was presented at the annual meeting of the Society for the Study of Social Problems, Denver, Colorado, August, 1971.

Chapter 16

1. Act of October, 1779 (Virginia General Assembly) 10 *Hening's Statutes at Large.*
2. Act of February 25, 1890 (Virginia General Assembly), c.118.
3. Temperance meant total abstinence in the language of the League. Alan Burton Clarke, *Seventeen Years in the Desert: A History of Prohibition in Virginia,* typescript (Richmond, 1933), p.18.
4. *Liquor Control:* Report of the Committee appointed under authority of an act approved August 29, 1933, Senate Document No. 5.
5. The Virginia Alcohol Beverage Control Board, Annual Reports.
6. Refer to table 3.
7. I am indebted to the Bureau of Public Administration of the University of Virginia which presented a study of the Virginia Alcohol Beverage Control Board from the period of 1789 to September 1946, conducted by Dr. H. Wesley Ward. This study provides the people of Virginia, and interested persons in other states with a carefully drawn descriptive and analytical study of the more significant institutions of state and local government and administration in Virginia. Dr. Rowland Egger, Director of the Bureau of Public Administration, in his introduction to this document writes, "On the whole, however, the problem of the administration of alcoholic beverage control seems to be mainly

that of tightening up, speeding up, and gearing in operations inside the organization, rather than anything that can be solved by legislative tinkering with the fundamental structure of the control mechanism."
Other sources include:
Report of the Committee (Act of 1933, Senate Document #5);
Department of Welfare and Institutions, Commonwealth of Virginia;
Alcoholic Beverage Control Board of Virginia;
Governor's Highway Safety Commission of Virginia;
Division of Motor Vehicles of Commonwealth of Virginia.

Chapter 17

1. *Cf.* MODEL PENAL CODE, Sec. 1,02. Purposes: Principles of Construction.
2. U.S. Dept HEW, Public Health Service, ALCOHOL AND HEALTH—NEW KNOWLEDGE (2nd Special Report to the U.S. Congress, June 1974). (Hereinafter cited as ALCOHOL AND HEALTH—NEW KNOWLEDGE).
3. See chapters 13, 14, 15, and 16 of this book.
4. PLAUT, ALCOHOL PROBLEMS: A REPORT TO THE NATION, Cooperative Commission on the Study of Alcoholism 132 (1967).
5. See note 4 pp. 136-152. The Commission proposes that only "harmful types of drinking and harmful attitudes toward drinking" (p. 136) be discouraged—not *all* drinking, since some drinking has socially acceptable and beneficial functions. See also ALCOHOLISM AND HEALTH—NEW KNOWLEDGE.
6. See note 4 p. 131.
7. See note 2 pp. 201-207.
8. See note 4.
9. All of the laws that prohibit public intoxication, drunk and disorderly conduct, drinking in public, or being a vagrant by reason of habitual drunkenness are part of the states' respective penal codes. *See* GRAD, GOLDBERG and SHAPIRO, ALCOHOLISM AND THE LAW, Appendix A, Criminal Prohibitions against Drunkenness and Public Drinking, 217-31 (1971).
10. See, e.g., *Powell v. Texas*, 392 U.S. 514, 528 (1968) where the majority opinion speaks of "helpless, sometimes dangerous and frequently unsanitary inebriates" in the streets.
11. There have been some statistical correlations between violent crimes and intoxication, e.g., GLASER and O'LEARY, THE

ALCOHOLIC OFFENDER 11-12 (1966); PRESIDENT'S COM-
MITTEE ON LAW ENFORCEMENT AND ADMINISTRA-
TION OF JUSTICE, TASK FORCE REPORT; DRUNKEN-
NESS 40 (1967). These statistical correlations fail, however, to
establish any causal connection between intoxication and crime.
12. *E.g.*, Alabama, Arkansas, Iowa, Kentucky, Maine, Michigan,
Missouri, Montana, Nebraska, New Jersey, Oklahoma, South
Carolina, Utah, West Virginia. *See* GRAD., GOLDBERG and
SHAPIRO, *supra* note 9, Appendix A, Chart II, 228-231 (1971).
13. GA. CODE ANN. Sec. 58-605 (1965); S.C. CODE ANN. Sec. 16-
557 (1962).
14. UTAH CODE ANN. Sec. 32-7-13.
15. MINN. STAT. ANN. Sec. 254A.01 *et seq.* (Supp. 1974). In all
other respects, Minnesota has decriminalized public drunkenness.
16. MD. ANN. CODE art. 27, Sec. 123(b)(1957); N.J. REV. STAT.
Sec. 2A:170-25.3 (1953).
17. In Maryland this is no longer a violation, if, upon warning, the
offender promptly discontinues.
18. E.g., MO. STAT. ANN. Sec. 562.260 (Supp. 1967).
19. Finch v. State, 101 Ga. App. 73, 112 S.E.2d 824 (1960); Duluth v.
Oberg, 210 Minn. 262, 297 N.W. 712 (1941) (interpreting a city
ordinance); Boydstun v. State, 152 Tex. Crim. 273, 213 S.W.2d 825
(1948); Clark v. State, 53 Tex. Crim. 529, 111 S.W. 659 (1908).
20. E.g., Berry v. Springdale, 238 Ark. 328, 381 S.W.2d 745 (1964);
State v. Heller, 4 Conn. 174, 228 A.2d 815 (1966); Dryden v. State,
81 Ga. App. 177, 58 S.E.2d 519 (1950).
21. ALA. CODE tit. 14, Sec. 120 (1958).
22. E.g., VT. STAT. A,,. tit. 7, Sec. 562 (1959). *See* GRAD, GOLD-
BERG, SHAPIRO, supra note 9, Appendix A, Chart I, 219-226.
23. See, e.g., ALA. CODE tit. 14, Sec. 120 (1966) ($5.00 to $100); MO.
ANN STAT. Sec. 562, 260 (Supp. 1967) (maximum $1,000);
TENN. CODE. ANN. Sec. 39-2518 (1955) (maximum $1,000).
24. See, e.g., ARK. STAT. ANN. Sec. 48-943 (1964) (5 to 30 days); MO.
ANN. STAT. Sec. 562.260 (1 year).
25. See, e.g., MISS. CODE. ANN. Sec. 2291 ($100); see note 9 p. 219 *et.
seq.*, Appendix A, Chart I.
26. ALA. CODE tit. 14, § 120 (1958).
27. Ford v. State, 10 Ga. App. 442, 73 S.E. 605 (1912).
28. Cf. K. C. DAVIS, DISCRETIONARY JUSTICE 80-96 (1969).
29. E.g., ALA. CODE tit. 14, § 437 (1958); IOWA CODE
ANN. § 746.1 (Supp. 1969).
30. Pappachristo v. City of Jacksonville, 405 U.S. 156 (1972); Lazarus
v. Faircloth, 301 F.Supp. 266 (1969); Broughton v. Brewer, 298
F.Supp. 260 (1969). See also cases cited in note 32.

31. Perkins, The Vagrancy Concept, 9 HAST. L. J. 237, 250-253 (1958).
32. In re Newbern, 53 Cal.2d 786, 350 P.2d 116, 3 Cal. Rptr. 364 (1960); also see Prince v. State, 36 Ala. App. 529, 59 So.2d 878 (1952).
33. There are about 2 million arrests annually for drunkenness offenses (excluding drunken driving), a number which represents more than one-third of all criminal arrests. See note 11. Task Force Report, p. 7.
34. *E.g.,* D. PITTMAN & W. GORDON, REVOLVING DOOR, A STUDY OF THE CHRONIC POLICE CASE INEBRIATE (1958); TASK FORCE REPORT: DRUNKENNESS, *supra* note 11 at 73.
35. See notes 34, 40 and 46.
36. *Infra,* text at note 51.
37. Sixteen persons arrested for intoxication died while in police custody in 1964-65. PRESIDENT'S COMMISSION ON CRIME IN THE DISTRICT OF COLUMBIA, REPORT 476 (1966).
38. 370 U.S. 660 (1962).
39. 356 F.2d 761 (4th Cir. 1966).
40. 361 F.2d 50 (D.C. Cir. 1966).
41. *E.g.,* Fultz v. United States, 365 F.2d 404 (6th Cir. 1966); Dobs v. State, 2 Md. App. 524, 235 A.2d 764 (1967); Prather v. Warden, Maryland State Penitentiary, 1 Md. App. 478, 231 A.2d 726 (1967); State v. Freiberg, 35 Wisc.2d 480, 151 N.W.2d. 1 (1967).
42. MD. ANN. CODE art. 2c (Supp. 1970) and art. 27, § 122, 123 (Supp. 1970).
43. D. C. CODE ANN. §§ 24-521 - 535 (Supp. II, 1969).
44. HAWAII REV. STAT. §§ 334-1 - 334-86 (1968).
45. N.D. CENT. CODE §§ 5-01—05.1, 5-01—05.2 (Supp. 1969).
46. 392 U.S. 514 (1968).
47. See note 46 p.517. The opinion by Mr. Justice Marshall was joined in by Justices Warren, Black, and Harlan.
48. See note 46 p. 548, by Mr. Justice White.
49. See note 46 p. 537, by Mr. Justice Black joined in by Mr. Justice Harlan.
50. See note 46 p. 554, dissenting opinion by Mr. Justice Fortas, joined in by Justices Douglas, Brennan and Stewart.
51. See note 46 p. 528.
52. See note 49.
53. MD. ANN. CODE art. 2c (Supp. 1970) and art. 27, §§ 122, 123, (Supp. 1970).
54. D. C. CODE ANN. §§ 24-521—535 (Supp. II, 1969).
55. N.D. CENT. CODE §§ 5-01—05.1, 5-01—05.2 (Supp. 1969).

56. Pub. L. No. 90-574, 82 Stat. 1006 (1968), 42 U.S.C.A. 299a.
57. Pub. L. No. 91-211, 84 Stat. 54, 57-59 (1970).
58. Pub. L. No. 91-616, 84 Stat. 1848, 42 U.S.C.A. § 45½1 *et seq.* (1970).
59. Pub. L. No. 93-282, 88 Stat. 125 (1974).
60. Pub. L. No. 93-282, § 107 adding new Section 304.
61. The Act is reprinted in THE COUNCIL OF STATE GOVERN-MENTS, 1973 SUGGESTED STATE LEGISLATION, at 225-248.
62. Model Alcoholism and Intoxication Treatment Act, in GRAD, GOLDBERG, SHAPIRO, note 9 *supra,* at 170 *et seq.*
63. ALASKA STAT. § 47.37.010 *et seq.* (Supp. 1973).
64. S.D. CODE § 34-20A-1 *et seq.* (Supp. 1974).
65. WASH. REV. CODE ANN. § 70.96A *et seq.* (1974).
66. Ariz., Calif., Fla., Ind., Kans., Mass., Minn., N.H., R.I., Tenn.
67. Maine
68. S.C.
69. *See, e.g.,* COLO. REV. STAT. ANN. § 66-36-1 *et seq.* (Supp. 1970-71); IOWA CODE ANN. § 123B.1 *et seq.* (Supp. 1974-5); UTAH CODE ANN. § 63-43-1 *et seq.* (Supp. 1973).
70. *See, e.g.,* ORE. REV. STAT. § 430.260 *et seq.* (1973).
71. *See, e.g.,* WIS. STAT. ANN. § 51.09 *et seq.* (Supp. 1974-5).
72. N.M. STAT. ANN. § 46-14-23 (Supp. 1973).
73. CAL. PENAL CODE § 647(f)-(ff)(West Supp. 1974).
74. MD. ANN. CODE art. 2c § 201 (Supp. 1973).
75. D.C. CODE ANN. §§ 24-524 (Supp. 1972).
76. DEL. CODE ANN. tit 11 § 612(c)(Supp. 1971-2).
77. CONN. GEN. STAT. ANN. § 53a-184(6)(1972).
78. ME. REV. STAT. ANN. tit. 22 § 7118 (Supp. 1973-4).
79. GA. CODE ANN § 88-405.4 (1971).
80. IND. ANN. STAT. § 22-1516 (Supp. 1973).
81. N.C. GEN. STAT. § 14-335.1 (1974).
82. *E.g.,* Arkansas, Oklahoma.
83. *E.g.,* D. PITTMANN & W. GORDON, REVOLVING DOOR, A STUDY OF THE CHRONIC POLICE INEBRIATE (1958); D. GLASER & U. O'LEARY, THE ALCOHOLIC OFFENDER (1961); Pinardi, *The Chronic Drunkenness Offender: What one City is Doing About the Revolving Door,* 12 CRIME & DELIN-QUENCY 339 (1966); E. Rubington, *The Chronic Drunkenness Offender,* 315 ANNALS 66 (1950).
84. *See,* generally, Felix v. Hall-Brooke Sanitarium, 140 Conn. 496, 101 A.2d 500 (1953) (30-day emergency confinement); Belger v. Arnot, 183 N.E.2d 866 (Mass. 1962) (10 days); Warner v. State, 297 N.Y. 395, 79 N.E.2d 459 (1948) (2 weeks).

85. See, generally KITTRIE, *Compulsory Mental Treatment and the Requirements of the "Due Process"*, 21 OHIO S.L.J. 28 (1960); Note, *Civil Commitment of Narcotics Addicts*, 76 YALE L.J. 1160 (1967).

86. Note 61 supra at Sec. 12(d). See also Model Alcoholism and Intoxication Treatment Act Sct. 10(d), in GRAD, GOLDBERG & SHAPIRO, *supra* note 9 at 178.

87. D.C. CODE ANN. Sec. 24-524 *et seq.* (Supp. II, 1969).

88. E.g., In re Estate of Brooks, 32 Ill.2d 361, 205 N.E.2d 435, cert.den., 382 U.S. 945. *But see* Application of Georgetown College, 331 F.2d 1000 (D.C. Cir.) cert.den., 377 U.S. 978 (1964) where the court granted an order to permit a transfusion against a patient's religious objections in order to protect the interest of her children. See Ross, *Commitment of the Mentally Ill: Problems of Law & Policy*, 57 MICH.L.REV. 945 (1959).

89. For a particularly outspoken comment on subject, see Szasz, *Alcoholism: A Socio-Ethical Perspective*, 6 WASH.L.J. 255, 268 (1967).

90. E.g., Rouse v. Cameron, 373 F.2d 451 (D.C. Cir. 1966); Nason v. Superintendent of Bridgewater State Hosp., Mass., 233 N.E.2d 908 (1968), holding that a person committed for treatment has an enforceable right to be treated, or else his detention violates statutory or constitutional protections.

91. This is the position of the Model Alcoholism and Intoxication Treatment Act, *supra* note 86, Sec. 13(a) at 180. The section requires allegation and proof that the alcoholic "has threatened, attempted or actually inflicted physical harm on others, and that unless committed he is likely to inflict physical harm on others . . . ."

92. E.g., ARK. STAT. ANN. Sections 83-703—717 (Supp. 1967); KAN. GEN. STAT. Sec. 65-4028(3) (1972); MISS. CODE ANN. Sections 435-01—12 (1956).

93. E.g., KAN. GEN. STAT. ANN. Sec. 65-4028(3)1972).

94. A number of states have very lengthy maximum terms of commitment, e.g., TENN. CODE. ANN. Section 33-810 (Supp. 1968) (1 yr.). *See infra* note 95.

95. See GRAD, GOLDBERG & SHAPIRO, *supra* note 9, at Appendix C. *Compare* Chart V, 300, regarding duration of involuntary commitments to inpatient facilities with Chart II, 250, setting forth statutory provisions for involuntary commitment. The actual length of commitment varies from 2 weeks to six months, with most releases after 1-2 months.

96. E.g., KAN. GEN. STAT. ANN. Sec. 65-4028(3)(1972); WIS. STAT. ANN. Sec. 51.09 (1955).

97. For alcoholism commitments to a state *agency, see, e.g.*, ARK. STAT. ANN. Sec. 83-709 (Supp. 1967); CONN. GEN. STAT. ANN. Sec. 17-155(e)(Supp.1969); TEX. REV.CIV.STAT.ANN. Art. 5561c, Sec. 9(d)(Supp. 1968). *See also* notes 63, 64, 65, *supra.* Uniform Alcoholism and Intoxication Treatment Act, Sec. 14, *supra* note 61. Model Alcoholism and Intoxication Treatment Act, Sec. 13 *supra* note 86; MODEL PENAL CODE Sec. 304.1.
98. See note 4, p. 166 *et seq.*

Chapter 18

1. Also see L.A. Greenberg, ed., "Studies of Congeners in Alcoholic Beverages," *Quarterly Journal of Studies on Alcohol,* Supplement No. 5 (May 1970).
2. W. P. Rohan, "Drinking Behavior and 'Alcoholism'," *Journal of Studies on Alcohol* 36(1975):908-16.
3. E. M. Jellinek, "Phases of Alcohol Addiction," *Quarterly Journal of Studies on Alcohol* 13(1952):673-84.
4. National Council on Alcoholism, Criteria Committee, "Criteria for the Diagnosis of Alcoholism," *American Journal of Psychiatry* 129(1972):127-35. Also in *Annals of Internal Medicine* 77(1972):249-58. Copies may be obtained from Publications Division, NCA, Inc., 2 Park Avenue, New York, New York 10016.
5. See for example: M. Galanter, "Models of Drug Abuse: The Intoxication State of Consciousness," paper presented at the 128th Annual Meeting of the American Psychiatric Association, May 6, 1975, Anaheim, California. M. Siegler, H. Osmond & S. Newell, "Models of Alcoholism," *Quarterly Journal of Studies on Alcohol* 29(1968):571–591.
6. J. de Lint, "Current Trends in the Prevalence of Excessive Alcohol Use and Alcohol Related Health Damage," *British Journal of Addiction* 70(1975):3-13.
7. G. R. Stewart, *American Ways of Life* (New York: Doubleday, 1954), p. 124.
8. C. Rainwater, *Statement on Soft Drink Industry,* Appendix II, Hearings before the Subcommittee on Antitrust and Monopoly of the Senate Committee of the Judiciary (Washington, D. C.: U. S. Government Printing Office, 1973).
9. U. S. Bureau of the Census, *Statistical Abstract of the United States* (Washington, D.C.: U. S. Government Printing Office, 1974) p. 376.
10. D. Cahalan, I. H. Cisin, and H. M. Crossley, *American Drinking Practices: A National Study of Drinking Behavior and Attitudes*

(New Brunswick, New Jersey: Rutgers Center of Alcohol Studies, Publications Division, 1969).

11. See note 6.

12. Previous books which examined the sociocultural aspects of alcohol use include C. H. Patrick, *Alcohol, Culture, and Society* (Durham, North Carolina: Duke University Press, 1952); R. G. McCarthy, *Drinking and Intoxication* (Glencoe, Illinois: Free Press, 1959); D. J. Pittman and C. R. Snyder, *Society, Culture, and Drinking Patterns* (New York: John Wiley and Sons, 1962); R. G. McCarthy, *Alcohol Education for Classroom and Community* (New York: McGraw-Hill Book Company, 1964); and D. J. Pittman, *Alcoholism* (New York: Harper and Row Publishers, 1967). Up-to-date research results may be obtained from a number of newsletters and journals on alcohol. Brief descriptions of many of these publications have been compiled by Andrea Mitchell, *The Drinking and Drug Practices Surveyor*, No. 8, pp. 22-24, August, 1973.

13. See note 10.

14. J. L. Haer, "Drinking Patterns and the Influence of Friends and Family," *Quarterly Journal of Studies on Alcohol* 16(1955):178-85.

15. C. L. Randall and D. Lester, "Social Modification of Alcohol Consumption in Inbred Mice," *Science* (July 11, 1975): 149-51.

16. H. Cappell and C. P. Herman, "Alcohol and Tension Reduction," *Quarterly Journal of Studies on Alcohol* 33(1972):33-64.

17. W. Madsen, *The American Alcoholic: The Nature-Nurture Controversy in Alcoholic Research and Therapy* (Springfield, Illinois: Charles C. Thomas, 1974).

18. J. S. Brown and C. R. Crowell, "Alcohol and Conflict Resolution," *Quarterly Journal of Studies on Alcohol* 35(1974):66-85.

19. A. L. Myrsten, "Effects of Alcohol on Psychological Functions, Experimental Studies on Non-alcoholic Subjects" *(Reports from the Psychological Laboratories, The University of Stockholm Supplement Series #7*, May, 1971).

20. J. A. Ewing, B. A. Rouse, and E. D. Pellizzari, "Alcohol Sensitivity and Ethnic Background," *American Journal of Psychiatry* 131(1974):206-10; P. H. Wolff, "Ethnic Differences in Alcohol Sensitivity," *Science* 175(1972):449-50; P. H. Wolff, "Vasomotor Sensitivity to Alcohol in Diverse Mongoloid Populations," *American Journal of Human Genetics* 25(1973):193-99; and D. Fenna, L. Mix, O. Schaefer, and J. A. L. Gilbert, "Ethanol Metabolism in Various Racial Groups," *Canadian Medical Association Journal* 105(1971):472-75.

21. E. Brecher and the Editors of Consumer Reports, eds., *Licit and Illicit Drugs* (Boston: Little, Brown and Co., 1972).

22. G. L. Maddox and B. C. McCall, *Drinking Among Teen-agers: A Sociological Interpretation of Alcohol Use by High School Students* (New Brunswick, New Jersey: Rutgers Center of Alcohol Studies Publications Division, 1964).

23. M. Bacon and M. B. Jones, *Teenage Drinking* (New York: Crowell, 1968). Also see note 22.

24. J. D. Preston, "Community Norms and Adolescent Drinking Behavior: A Comparative Study," *Social Science Quarterly* 49(1968):350-59.

25. J. R. MacKay, D. L. Phillips, and F. O. Bryce, "Drinking Behavior Among Teen-agers: A Comparison of Institutionalized and Non-Institutionalized Youth," *Journal of Health and Social Behavior* 8(1967):46-54.

26. R. Jessor and S. L. Jessor, "Adolescent Development and the Onset of Drinking: A Longitudinal Study," *Journal of Studies on Alcohol* 36(1975):27-51.

27. For cross-cultural studies of alcohol use see M. Bacon, H. Barry, and E. Child, "A Cross-cultural Study of Drinking," *Quarterly Journal of Studies on Alcohol* Supp. #3, 1965; M. K. Bacon, "The Dependency-Conflict Hypothesis and the Frequency of Drunkenness: Further Evidence from a Cross-cultural Study," *Quarterly Journal of Studies on Alcohol* 35(1974):863-76; R. F. Bales, "Cultural Differences in Rates in Alcoholism," *Quarterly Journal of Studies on Alcohol* 6(1946):448-99; P. B. Field, "A New Cross-cultural Study of Drunkenness," *Society, Culture and Drinking Patterns*, ed. D. J. Pittman and C. R. Snyder (New York: Wiley and Sons, 1962); and D. Horton, "The Function of Alcohol in Primitive Societies: A Cross-cultural Study," *Quarterly Journal of Studies on Alcohol* 4(1943):199-320.

28. R. Straus and S. D. Bacon, *Drinking in College* (New Haven, Conn.: Yale University Press, 1953).

29. M. Clinard, "The Public Drinking House and Society," *Society, Culture and Drinking Patterns*, ed. D. J. Pittman and C. P. Snyder (New York: Wiley and Sons, 1962), pp.270-92.

30. S. Cavan, *Liquor License: An Ethnography of Bar Behavior* (Chicago: Aldine Pub. Co., 1966).

31. Those interested in scientifically studying public drinking places see M. Kessler and C. Gomberg, "Observations of Barroom Drinking: Methodology and Preliminary Results," *Quarterly Journal of Studies on Alcohol* 35 (1974): 1392-96.

32. J. S. Tamerin, S. Weiner, and J. H. Mendelson, "Alcoholics' Expectancies and Recall of Experiences during Intoxication," *American Journal of Psychiatry* 126(1970):1697-1704.

33. Also see R. E. Reinert, "The Concept of Alcoholism as a Bad Habit," *Bulletin of the Menninger Clinic* 32 (1968): 35-46.

34. D. C. McClelland, W. N. Davis, R. Kalin, and E. Wanner, *The Drinking Man* (New York: Free Press, 1972); and D. C. McClelland, "The Power of Positive Drinking," *Psychology Today* (January, 1971): 40-41, 78-79.
35. A. A. Sorensen, "Need for Power Among Alcoholic and Nonalcoholic Clergy," *Journal of Scientific Study of Religion* 12(1973):101-108.
36. H. T. Blane, *The Personality of the Alcoholic: Guises of Dependency* (New York: Harper and Row, 1968); W. McCord and J. McCord, *Origins of Alcoholism* (Stanford, California: Stanford University Press, 1960); and V. Tahka, *The Alcoholic Personality* (Helsinki, Finland: Finnish Foundation for Alcohol Studies, 1966).
37. See for example H.A.Skinner, D. N. Jackson and H. Hoffmann, "Alcoholic Personality Types: Identification and Correlates," *Journal of Abnormal Psychology* 83 (1974): 658-666; and G. K. Litman, "Psychological Aspects of Alcoholism: Theory and Treatment," *Journal of Alcoholism, London* 9 (1974):48-49.
38. S. L. Gorad, W. F. McCourt, and J. C. Cobb, "A Communications Approach to Alcoholism," *Quarterly Journal of Studies on Alcohol* 32(1971):651-68.
39. C. Steiner, *Games Alcoholics Play: The Analysis of Life Scripts* (New York: Grove Press, 1971).
40. R. Straus, *Escape From Custody: A Study of Alcoholism and Institutional Dependency as Reflected in the Life Record of a Homeless Man* (New York: Harper and Row, 1974).
41. E.K. Gerstel, R.E. Mason, P.V. Piserchia, and P.L. Kristiansen, *A Pilot Study of the Social Contexts of Drinking and Correlates* (Research Triangle Park, N.C.: Research Triangle Institute, August, 1975).
42. P. Roman, "Successful Deviance: the Dynamics of Deviant Drinking Among Executives," *Deviant Behavior: Occupational and Organizational Bases*, ed. C. D. Bryant (Chicago: Rand McNally, 1972).
43. D. Cahalan, *Problem Drinkers* (San Francisco: Jossey-Bass, 1970). Also see D. Cahalan and R. Room, *Problem Drinking Among American Men* Monograph No. 7 (New Brunswick, N. J.: Publication Division, Rutgers Center of Alcohol Studies, 1974).
44. L. Blumberg, T. E. Shipley, and I. W. Shandler, *Skid Row and Its Alternatives* (Philadelphia: Temple University Press, 1973); H. M. Bahr *Skid Row: An Introduction to Disaffiliation* (New York: Oxford University Press, 1973); and D. Levinson, "The Etiology of Skid Rows in the United States," *International Journal of Social Psychiatry* 20(1974):25-33.

45. H. Maurer, "The Beginning of Wisdom about Alcoholism," *Fortune*, May (1968): 176-178, 211-215.

46. E. T. Lisansky, "Alcoholism: The Avoided Diagnosis," *Bulletin American College of Physicians* 15(1974):18-24. Also in *Maryland State Medical Journal* 23(1974):26-31.

47. For further information regarding problem drinking or alcoholism in women see L. J. Beckman, "Women Alcoholics: A Review of Social and Psychological Studies," *Journal of Studies on Alcohol*, 36(1975):797-24; M. C. Jones, "Personality Antecedents and Correlates of Drinking Patterns in Women," *Journal of Consulting and Clinical Psychology* 36(1971):61-69; B. A. Kinsey, *The Female Alcoholic: A Social Psychological Study* (Springfield, Ill.: Charles C. Thomas, 1966); V. L. Lindbeck, "The Woman Alcoholic: A Review of the Literature," *International Journal of the Addictions* 7 (1972): 567-580; J.S. Tamerin, C.P. Neumann, and M. H. Marshall, "The Upper-class Alcoholic: A Syndrome in Itself," *Psychosomatics* 12(1971):200-204; S. C. Wilsnack, "Sex Role Identity in Female Alcoholism," *Journal of Abnormal Psychology* 82 (1973):253-261; "The Effects of Social Drinking on Women's Fantasy," *Journal of Personality* 42 (1974):43-61; and S. C. Wilsmack "The Impact of Sex Roles: Women's Alcohol Use and Abuse," in *Alcoholism Problems in Women and Children*, eds. M. Greenblatt and M. A. Schuckit (New York: Grune & Stratton, 1977).

48. B. A. Rouse, P. F. Waller, and J. A. Ewing, "Adolescents' Stress Levels, Coping Activities and Father's Drinking," *Proceedings, 81st Annual Meeting of the American Psychological Association*, pp.683-84, Montreal, Aug. 1973. Also in *Research Previews*, Institute for Research in Social Sciences, University of North Carolina, Chapel Hill, April, 1974, pp. 35-40.

49. E. M. Pattison, R. Coe, and R. J. Rhodes, "Evaluation of Alcoholism Treatment," *Archives of General Psychiatry* 20(1969):478-88; and F. A. Seixas, R. Cadoret, and S. Eggleston, "The Person with Alcoholism," *Annals of the New York Academy of Sciences*, 233(1974):1-177.

50. C. Holden, "Alcoholism: On-the-job Referrals Mean Early Detection and Treatment," *Science* 179(1973): 363-65, 413-15; M. Sadler and J. F. Horst, "Company/Union Programs for Alcoholics," *Harvard Business Review* 50(1972):22-34, 152-56; and J. R. Tucker, "A Worker-oriented Alcoholism and 'Troubled Employee' Program: a Union Approach," *Industrial Gerontology* (Fall 1974):20-24.

51. A. Frances, "A Comprehensive Military Drug and Alcohol Program," *International Journal of Addictions* 9(1974):137-44; G. S.

Glass, "The Alcohol Rehabilitation Unit, National Naval Medical Center, Bethesda," *Military Medicine* 141(1974):468-88; H. L. Ruben, "A Review of the First Year's Experience in the U.S. Army Alcohol and Drug Abuse Program," *American Journal of Public Health* 64(1974):999-1001; and H. L. Ruben, "Rehabilitation of Drug and Alcohol Abusers in the U. S. Army," *International Journal of Addictions* 9(1974):41-55.

52. *Alcoholics Anonymous Comes of Age: A Brief History of A. A.* (New York: Alcoholics Anonymous World Services, 1967); and *Twelve Steps and Twelve Traditions* (New York: Alcoholics Anonymous Publishing Co., 1952).

53. "Self-Help Programs: Indians and Native Alaskans," *Alcohol Health and Research World* (Summer 1974):11-16.

54. See note 6.

55. *Distilled Spirits Industry Annual Statistical Review* (Washington, D.C.: Division of Research and Statistics, Distilled Spirits Institute, 1976), p. 43.

56. G. H. Miller and N. Agnew, "The Ledermann Model of Alcohol Consumption," *Quarterly Journal of Studies on Alcohol* 35(1974):877-98.

57. T. F. A. Plaut, *Alcohol Problems: A Report to the Nation by the Cooperative Commission on the Study of Alcoholism* (New York: Oxford University Press, 1967).

58. R. H. Blum and Associates, *Society and Drugs* (San Francisco: Jossey-Bass, 1970), p. 39.

59. R. Zylman, "Debunking the 'Just Beer' Myth," *Traffic Safety* 74(1974):18-19.

60. J. de Lint and W. Schmidt, "Consumption Averages and Alcoholism Prevalence: A Brief Review of Epidemiological Investigations," *British Journal of Addiction* 66(1971):97-107.

61. M. A. Schuckit, J. Rimmer, T. Reich, and G. Winokur, "The Bender Alcoholic," *British Journal of Psychiatry* 119(1971):183-84.

62. S. Pell and C. A. D'Alonzo, "The Prevalence of Chronic Disease Among Problem Drinkers," *Archives of Environmental Health* 16(1968):679-84; S. Pell and C. A. D'Alonzo, "Sickness Absenteeism of Alcoholics," *Journal of Occupational Medicine* 12 (1970): 198-210; F. A. Seixas, K. Williams, and S. Eggleston, eds., "Medical Consequences of Alcoholism," *Annals of the New York Academy of Sciences* 252(1975): 1-399.

63. A variety of excellent books deal with the biochemical and biological effects of alcohol. Some of these include Y. Israel and J. Mardones, *Biological Basis of Alcoholism* (New York: Wiley and Sons, 1971); B. Kissin and H. Begleiter, *The Biology of Alcoho-*

lism, Vol. I: Biochemistry (New York: Plenum Press, 1971); *Vol. II: Physiology and Behavior* (New York: Plenum Press, 1972); R. E: Popham, ed., *Alcohol and Alcoholism* (Toronto, Canada: University of Toronto Press, 1970); M. K. Roach, W. M. McIsaac, and P. J. Creaven, eds., *Biological Aspects of Alcohol* (Austin, Texas: University of Texas Press, 1971); H. Wallgren and H. Barry, *Actions of Alcohol, Vol. I: Biochemical, Physiological and Psychological Aspects; Vol. II: Chronic and Clinical Aspects* (New York: Elsevier Publishing Co., 1970).

For information on the metabolism of alcohol see: R. M. Myerson, "Metabolic Aspects of Alcohol and Their Biological Significance," ed. J. Katz and D. Kae, *Medical Clinics of North America: Symposium on Changing Concepts of Disease* (Philadelphia, Pa.: W. B. Saunders Co., 1973); and R. G. Thurman, T. Yonetani, J. R. Williamson, and B. Chance, eds., *Alcohol and Aldehyde Metabolizing Systems* (New York: Academic Press, 1974).

64. See note 47.

65. D. R. Heise, *Causal Analysis* (New York: Wiley InterScience, 1975); J. W. Forrester, *World Dynamics.* (Cambridge, Massachusetts: Wright Allen Press, 1974); and G. E. Whitehouse, *Systems Analysis and Design Using Network Techniques* (Englewood, N.J.: Prentice-Hall, 1973).

66. G. Thomann, *Colonial Liquor Laws,* Part II of *Liquor Laws of the United States; Their Spirit and Effect* (New York: The United States Brewers' Association, 1887); and A. H. Martin, Jr. and E. E. McCleish, *State Liquor Legislation,* vol. 4: *The Marketing Laws Survey Series* (Washington, D. C.: U. S. Dept. of Commerce, 1941).

67. For public revenues by beverage type see: Distilled Spirits Council of the United States, Inc., *1973 Public Revenue from Alcohol Beverages* (Washington, D. C., 1974): 5; United States Brewers Association, Inc., *The Brewing Industry in the United States Almanac, 1974* (Washington, D.C.): 110.

68. *Drug Use in America: Problem in Perspective,* 2nd Report of the National Commission on Marijuana and Drug Abuse (Washington, D.C.: U.S. Government Printing Office, March, 1973).

69. D. Bailey, "Some Undesirable Drug-Alcohol Interactions," *Journal of Alcoholism, London* 9(1974):62-68; and R. B. Forney and F. W. Hughes, *Combined Effects of Alcohol and Other Drugs* (Springfield, Ill.: Charles C. Thomas, 1968).

70. S. D. Bacon, "Alcohol and Complex Society," in *Society, Culture, and Drinking Patterns,* D. J. Pittman and C. R. Snyder, eds., (New York: John Wiley and Sons, 1962), pp.78-100.

71. G. Edwards, "Drugs, Drug Dependence, and the Concept of Plasticity," *Quarterly Journal of Studies on Alcohol* 35(1974):176-95.

72. *National Advertising Investments*, 25, No. 2 (January—December 1973): 10; *Expenditures of National Advertisers in Newspapers, 1972.* Compiled by Media Records, Inc. for Newspaper Advertising Bureau, Inc. 485 Lexington Avenue, New York, N.Y. 10017; and U.S. Bureau of the Census, *Statistical Abstracts of the United States, 1974* (Washington, D.C., 1974): 732.

73. U.S. Bureau of the Census, Annual Survey of Manufacturers: *General Statistics for Industry Groups and Industries, 1973*, Report No. M73 (AS)-1 (U.S. Government Printing Office, Washington, D.C., 1975).

74. A copy of the model legislation may be found in F. Grad, A. Goldberg, and B. Shapiro, *Alcoholism and the Law* (New York: Oceans Publications, 1971).

75. A. Coates, "Liquor and the Law in North Carolina, 1795-1937," *Popular Government* 4(1937):1-3, 16-18.

76. The original source is unknown. It has been repeated several times and attributed to politicians from several states. The only written citation known to us is the following report of a speech by an ex-governor of North Carolina, *Inventory* 19, No.2 (1969): 16-17.

77. E. M. Lemert, "Alcohol, Values, and Social Control," *Society, Culture and Drinking Patterns*, ed. D. J. Pittman and C. R. Snyder (New York: John Wiley and Sons, 1962), pp.553-71.

78. K. Makelä, "Types of Alcohol Restrictions, Types of Drinkers and Types of Alcohol Damages: The Case of the Personnel Strike in the Stores of the Finnish Alcohol Monopoly," paper presented at the 20th International Institute on the Prevention and Treatment of Alcoholism, Manchester, England, June 1974.

79. R. Room, "Marketing Research Data on the Distribution of Consumption in the United States," *The Drinking and Drug Practices Surveyor* No. 3 (1971): 14.

80. See note 77, p.569.

81. See note 77, p. 567.

82. R. Room, "Minimizing Alcohol Problems," *Alcohol, Health and Research World* (Fall 1974): 12-17.

83. K. Bruun, "The Minimization of Alcohol Damage," *Drinking and Drug Practices Surveyor*, 8(1973):15, 47.

84. Also see M. Keller, "Multidisciplinary Perspectives on Alcoholism and the Need for Integration: An Historical and Prospective Note," *Journal of Studies on Alcohol* 36(1975):133-47.

Index

Abstinence, 35, 95, 141, 176, 349
Accidents
  drinking motorists, 77–78, 117–29, 262
  drinking pedestrians, 123–24
  drownings and other violent deaths, 79–80
Addiction Research Foundation (Ontario), 239, 276, 277, 279
Adolescents, *See* Students, Teenagers
Adult drinking by college graduates, 197–200
Advertising, expenditures for alcoholic beverages, 373
Aelfric, Archbishop of Canterbury, canons of, 33
Age alcohol and, 153, 354, 359
Ainu, taboo on drinking among the, 36
Akron, Ohio, founding of Alcoholics Anonymous in, 57
Alaska, 328
  alcohol consumption in, 220–25
  alcoholism treatment in, 361

Alcohol
  abuse of, 28–29, 31–32
  as a drug, 16, 207, 211–13, 371
  as a food, 15–16
  as a poison, 16–17, 80–86
  availability and distribution of, 257–61
  caloric value, 15
  cause of death, 73–89
  content of beverages, 14
  cultural approval of, 213–14
  cultural patterns of use, 2
  effects of drinking, 17–20
  functions of, 206, 372
  history of drinking, 31–38
  legal availability of, 372–73
  making of, 6–9
  medical complications from, 63–69
  metabolism, 19
  national trends in consumption of, 236–38

Alcohol continued

Alcohol continued
    occasions for drinking, 353-55
    origin of the term, 10
    per capita consumption 219-22,
        236, 242, 249-61, 303, 341-42,
        362
    poisoning, 81, 82-83, 91
    properties 13-17, 342
    psychological dependence on,
        203-16
    reasons for drinking, by adults,
        345-47
    reasons for studies on, 344
    social policy concerning, 377-80
"Alcohol and Health," 139
"Alcoholed," getting, 208-10
"Alcohol Quotient" (AQ), 95-96
Alcohol Safety Action Projects
    (ASAP), 130-31, 304
Alcoholic, meaning of the term, 205
Alcoholic Beverage Control Board
    (Virginia), 298-300, 301, 302,
    304
Alcoholic Beverage Industry, 366,
    373
"Alcoholic heart disease," 87
Alcoholic myopathies, 6
Alcoholics
    autopsy studies on, 71-91
    treatment for, 360-62
    who are the, 358-60
Alcoholics Anonymous, 46, 57,
    105-10, 257, 269, 361
Alcoholism
    as a biopsycho-social disease, 101
    as a disease, 39-40
    as a health problem, 28
    definitions of, 40-42, 97-98, 205,
        341
    detection, 359
    family tendencies toward, 101-5
    history of, in the u.S., 42-53
    long-term treatment of, 330-36
    mortality rates, 138-40
    prevalence, 53, 244-45, 344
    prevention of, 111-14, 377-80
    rejected by supreme Court as a
        disease, 318-19
    return to disease concept of,
        50-51, 53-54
    studies on, 53-57
    treatment of, 105-129
Alcoholism Rehabilitation Act of
    1968, 324
Ale house laws, early English, 24
Alexei, tsar of Russia, 33
Alienation, drinking and, 190-93
Allen, B., 196
Allport, F. H., 278
America
    colonial legislation on drinking
        in, 25
    history of drinking in, 39-60
    lack of uniformity in drinking
        habits in, 5
American College of Physicians, 48
American drinking Practices, 113
American Indians, alcoholism
    treatment among, 361
American Medical Association, 58
American Medical Society on
    Alcoholism, 106
American Plains Indians, 22
American Temperance Society,
    founding of, 45
"Anstie's Limit," 96-97
Anti-Saloon League, 49, 295
Antisepsis, discovery of, 7
Arizona, alcohol consumption in,
    230-31
Australia, 252, 259, 268
Australian versus American beers, 8
Auto accidents, alcohol-related,
    77-78, 117-36
Autopsy studies on alcoholism,
    71-92
Aztecs, attitudes toward alcohol
    among, 35

BAC See Blood Alcohol
    Concentration
Bacon, Selden, 167, 198
    on liquor control, 167, 198, 273,
        274
Baird, E. G., on drunkenness, 26
Bars, See Drinking places
Beaubrun, M. H., 96, 181
Beer, 8, 341
Behavior
    drinking model of influences,
        265-69

drinking, and legislation, 374-75
effects of law on, 267-89
legal attempts to control, 307-16
modification by alcohol, 204-5,
211-13
Belasco, J. A., 199
Belgium, 253-54
Belloc, N. 140
Beverages
alcohol, revenue from 370-71
alcohol, variety of, 13-15
non-alcohol per capita
consumption, 342-43
Bible, references to drinking, 6, 26
"Binge" drinking, 97, 140
Binghamton, N.Y., asylum for
inebriates at, 48
Binkley, O. T., on abstinence, 26-37
Black college students, drinking
habits of, 194-97
Blood alcohol concentrations, (BAC)
estimating, 18-19, 78, 370
levels in medical examiner cases,
79
levels in traffic accidents, 77,
119-34
Blum, R. H., on problem drinking,
364
Bone marrow function, affected by
alcohol, 66
Bootlegging, 12-14, 162, 167, 178-79
Borkenstein, R. F., 118, 255
Boston, Mass., drinking survey in,
354-55
Bourbon County, Kentucky, 12
Bourbon whiskey, nature of, 12
Brandy, origin of, 11
Brewing, history of, 6-9
Brill, N. Q., 190
British Road Safety Act of 1967, 133
Brocatius, Johannes, 37
Bronetto, J., 289
Brown, M.,
on alienation, 191
on risk-taking, 193
Brown, S. D., 195
Brown-bagging, 177
Bruun, Kettil, 272, 275
Bryant, C. W., 245
Buddhism, prohibition of alcohol
in, 34

Buthypoglycemia, 67

"Cafe coronary," 88
Cahalan, Don, 95, 99, 152, 218, 359
California, 328
Calvin, John, 26
Campbell, B. J., 135
Campbell, D. T., 136
Cannon, Jr., James, on temperance
laws, 295
Canons Regular of St. Gilbert, 36
Cappell, H., 346
Catholic Church, role of, in treating
alcoholism, 56
Cavan, Sherri, on drinking places,
350-51
Center for Alcohol Studies, North
Carolina, 180
Center of Alcohol Studies, Yale
University, 54
Central Control Board, British, 276
Central nervous system,
degeneration of, 87
Chafetz, Morris E.
on alcoholism, 97-99
on education, 281
Charlemagne, 33, 36
Chemawa Indian Alcoholism
Prevention Program, 361
Cherrington, E. H., 51
Children
control of liquor sale to, 148
effect of drinking patterns on, 99
and use of alcohol, 154
China
drinking laws in, 32
prohibition in ancient, 35
Chinese cultural patterns, alcohol
and, 21
Christian churches, attitudes about
drinking, of, 26, 48, 178-79
Christie, N., 272
on liquor laws, 275
Chronic alcoholis, 86-88
Chung K'iang, Emperor of China,
36
Cirrhosis of the liver, 68-69, 252
Cisin, Ira, 93, 95, 143, 379
Civil Service Commission, 325
Civil War, effect of, on the
temperance movement, 47-48

Class bias and drunkenness legislation, 329-30
Clergy, intemperance among the, 35-36
Clinard, Marshall, 350
Clinical studies of drinking, 138
Closing laws, medieval, 33-35
Coates, Albert, 376
Cocaine use, 188
Coincidental death from alcohol, 74-75
College drinking, 171-202
Colorado, alcohol consumption in, 228-29
Color blindness, alcohol and, 104
Committee for a National Alcohol Policy, 112
Committee of Fifty to Investigate the Liquor Problem, 270
Community Mental Health Center Amendments (1970), 324
Community studies on drinking, 138-40
Comprehensive Alcohol Abuse and Alcoholism Prevention, Treatment, and Rehabilitation Act (1970), 320-25, 326
Congeners, 14
Connecticut, 329
Connecticut State Medical Society, report on alcoholis, 45
"Constant proportion" theory, 276-80
Consumer expenditures
   alcoholic beverages and tobacco products, 343
Controls on drinking, 145-58. See also Laws; Legal controls
Cooperative Commission on the Study of Alcoholis, 1967, 277, 281, 309
   study by, 111
Corn whiskey (white lightning), 12
Coroners. See Medical examiners
Crime, birth of organized, 52
Criminal law, drinking and the, 312-16
Crossley, H. M., 95
Crumpton, E., 190
Cultural patterns of drinking, 20-24

Czechoslovakia, 252

Davies, D. L., on social drinking, 100
Davis, J., 166
Deaths
   accidental, 77
   from alcohol, 74-89
Decriminalization of intoxication, 328-29
Delaware, 329
de Lint, Jan, 96, 218, 284, 286, 363, 365, 374, 378
Delinquency and drinking, 349-50
Delirium tremens, 20, 89
Denmark, alcohol studies in, 103-4, 254
Denver, Colorado, study on penalties for drunk drivers, 131-32
Department of Transportation, 150
   1968 report on alcohol and highway safety, 122
Depression and drinking, 186-87
Deschin, C. S., 165
Disease
   aggravation of existing, 75-76
   alcoholism as a, 39-40
   arising from drinking, 369
Distilling, 10-11
   history of, 6-9
District of Columbia Alcoholic Rehabilitation Act (1967), 324, 331, 332, 333
Domitian, Emperor, 35
Domitius Ulpinus, commentaries on law by, 37
Drinking
   behavior types, 339-41
   classification systems, 95, 340
   controls over, 145-58, 307-36
   drunkenness and alcoholism compared, 339-41
   effect of laws on, 267-89
   ethnic differences, 5, 21, 24, 194-97
   excessive, 344, 355-60
   family factors, 99, 153-54, 165, 182, 340, 345, 360
   functional equivalents, 379

hazards of, 239-66
increase in heavy, 362-64
informal controls, 146-47
medical complications, 63-70
occasions for, 353-55
places for, 350-51
prevalence in U.S., 95
psychological dependence and,
203-16
risks of, 137, 150-51
safe versus dangerous, 94-97,
215-16
social contexts, 353-57
social goals of, 151-52
social pressures, 24, 345
state laws on, 219-38
warning signs about, 364-65
*Drinking and Drug Practices
Surveyor* (ed. Room), 218
Drinking drivers, 125-29, 190
Driver v. *Hunt* (1965), ruling on
public intoxication, 317, 318
Driving
and drug use, 190
drinking and, 77-78, 117-36
Drowning deaths, alcohol-related,
78-79
Drugs
alcohol and other, 86
college students' use of, 171-202
Drunken Comportment (MacAndrew
& Edgerton), 209
Drunken driving, penalties for,
131-35, 157-58
Drunkenness
increase of, during Revolutionary
War era, 42-44
legislation on, and class bias,
329-30
as a moral flaw, 44-49
public, offenders, 316-26, 304
reasons for, 351-53
Drunken state, behavior while in a,
22-23
DUI (driving under the influence),
132, 133, 305
Dunstan, Archbishop of Canterbury,
33
Durfee, C. H., on alcoholism as
sickness, 54

DWI (driving while intoxicated),
122-29, 157

Easter v. *District of Columbia*
(1966), ruling on public
intoxication, 317, 318
Edgar, king of England, 33
Edgerton, Robert B., 22, 209
Education, 378-81
Edwards, G., on drug problems, 372
Egypt, prohibition in early, 35
Eighteenth Amendment (1919), 50,
53, 58, 297
Eighth Amendment, court rulings
on the, 317, 318
England
drinking laws in early, 33
medieval regulation of alcohol in,
34
penalties for drunken driving in,
133-34
Entine, A. D., 246
"Escape" drinking, 99
Eskimo, metabolic rates, 23
"Essay, Medical, Philosophical and
Chemical on Drunkenness"
(Trotter), 44
Ethyl alcohol, *See* Alcohol, Ethanol
Ethanol (grain alcohol), 6, 340
Ethnic differences, alcohol and, 21,
153-54, 194-97
Ewing, John A., 1, 370
Excise tax, illegal whiskey-making
and the, 12-13

Fairfax County, Virginia, 304
Fallon, Harold J., 61, 369
Family life, alcohol and, 154
Federal alcohol regulations, 112-13
Federal Highway Safety Act (1966),
130
Federal treatment legislation, 324-26
Fermentation, bottle, 10
"Fetal alcohol syndrome," 67
Fields, W. C., quoted, 203
Filmore, K. M., study on adult
drinking, 197-99
Finland, 258, 259, 269, 275, 362
1970 liquor law in, 380
Ford, J. C., 56

Framingham, Mass., study on
    drinking, 139
France, 258, 259, 262, 362
  penalties for drunk driving in,
    136
  per capita alcohol consumption
    in, 342
Frederick III of Germany, 37

Games alcoholics play, 352-53
Gandhi, Indira, 28
Gastrointestinal complications of
    drinking, 65-66
Generalization, the process of,
    210-11
George Washington University, 152
Georgia, 329
Germany, 252, 259, 362
Gerstel, Eva, 354
Globetti, Gerald, 143, 348, 375
Goodwin, 103-4
Grad, Frank, 218, 373, 375
Graduate students, drinking habits
    of, 185-87
Grain alcohol. See Ethanol
Grand Rapids, Michigan,
    alcoholism study in, 118-22,
    124, 125, 128, 157
Grayson, H. M., 190
Greece, drinking regulations in, 35
Gunderson, E. K., 138
Gusfield, J. R., 43

Habit formation, 286-87
Haddon, W., 124
Hall, J., 55
Halleck, S. L., 191
Hammurabi, code of, 24, 32, 33
Harford, Thomas C., 354
Health regulations, 36-37
Heart failure in alcoholics, 87
Heidelberg, Germany, 38
Hepatitis, 69, 77
Herman, C. P., 436
Heroin use, 188
Herrick, K. W., 134
HEW (Department of Health,
    Education, and Welfare), 325,
    326
Highway safety and rinking, 117-36
Hiltner, S., on cultural attitudes

toward drinking, 281-82
Hollingshead, A. B., 182
Holson Joint Resolution for
    Prohibition (1914), 49
Homicide, alcohol as a factor in, 80
Houthakker, H. S., 285-87
Howland, Joe W., 2
Howland, Richard W., 3
Hudson, Page, 61, 369
Hurst, P. M., 128
Huszty, Zacharius T., 37
"Hyperosmolar syndrome," 67
Hypertriglyceridemia, alcohol as a
    cause of, 67
Hypoglycemia, alcoholic, 66-67

Ikaalinen, Finland, 272
Illinois, alcohol consumption in,
    227-28
India, success of prohibition, in, 28
Indiana, 329
Indians, 22-23, 361
Industry, alcohol programs, 361
Ine, king of Wessex, 32
Injury, alcohol obscuring, 76
"Inoculation theory," 280-82, 363
Insurance company studies on
    drinking, 137-38
Inter-Tribal Alcoholism Treatment
    Center (Sheridan, Wyo.), 361
Intoxication, 17, 195-96, 262, 340
Iowa, alcohol consumption in,
    234-35
Ireland, 362
  making of whiskey in, 11-12
Islam, prohibition of alcohol in, 34
Isopropyl alcohol poisoning, 83
Italians, low rate of heavy drinking
    among, 156
Italy, 262

James I, king of Aragon, 37
"J-curve hypothesis of comforming
    behavior," Allport's, 278-79
Jellinek, E. M., 41, 54, 240, 242, 249,
    262, 264, 341
  quoted on liquor laws, 291
Jessor, R., 349
Jessor, S. L., 349
Jews
  attitude on alcohol among, 24

low rate of heavy drinking
among, 156
Job performance, alcohol and, 36,
200
Joint Committee of the States to
Study Alcoholic Beverage Laws,
275
Jolliffe, N., 250

Kalant, H., 255
Keller, M., 264
Ketoacidosis, 67
Kieft, William, 42
Klatskin, G., 68
Klein, A. W., 190
Knupfer, Genevieve, 152
Kolb, L., 55
Kosice, Slovakia, temperance
movement in, 37
Kublai Khan, 35
Kuusi, Pekka, 246, 262

Laennec's cirrhosis, 68-69
Law, function of, in society, 156-57
Laws regulating alcohol and
drinking, 24-30, 32-36, 112-13,
267-69, 369-76
Layman Act (Virginia) of 1924,
297-98
LeBlanc, A. E., 255
Ledermann curve, 258
Lee, E. J., 54
Legal controls, on alcohol
consumption, 148-49, 239-66,
369-76
Legal penalties for drunken driving,
131-35, 157-58
Legal restrictions on teenage
drinking, failure of, 167-69
Lelbach, W. K., 252
Lemert, E. M., 378, 379
Lesesne, Henry, 61, 369
Lester, D., 345
Levine, D., 135
Licensing system, of alcohol, 32-33,
223-24
Lichine, Alexis, 11
Lieber, C. S., 68
Linsky, A. S., on mass media, 55
Liquor
control of sale and distribution of,

308-11
illegal liquor seizures, 13, 178-79
intoxicating liquors definition,
340
military services
nervous system effects of alcohol,
20, 87
neurological disorders, alcohol
related, 64
per capita consumption, 219-38
Liquor-by-the drink, 179-80, 220,
231-34, 300-3, 310-11
Liquor Control Act (Virginia) of
1792, 292-94
Liquor Control Board of Ontario,
Third report (1929), 247
Lister, Joseph, discovery of
antisepsis by, 7
Litchfield, Conn., founding of first
temperance organization in, 46
Liver disease, 67-69; effects on, of
alcohol, 19, 88-89
Loeb, Jr., Ben F., 217, 374, 375
London (England) closing laws, 33
LSD, use of, 186, 18
Lucerne, Switzerland, 34
Luther, Martin, 26

MacAndrew, Craig, 22, 209
Macbeth, quoted, 150-51
McCall, B. C., on reasons for
drinking, 347
McClelland, D. C., 351, 352
Maddox, G. L., 196
on reasons for drinking, 347
Maine, 329
Maine Law of 1851, 27
Manitoba, 244, 245
Mann, M., on alcoholism, 40-41
Mann Law (Virginia), 295
Man Takes a Drink (Ford), 56
Mapp Act (Virginia) of 1916 ("One
Quart Law"), 296-97
Marijuana, college students' use of,
174-75, 182-94 passim
Marine Corps alcoholics, 138
Marshall, Thurgood, 318
Maryland, 328, 331
Maryland treatment law of 1968,
321-23
Maurer, H., 359

Medical examiners
  contributions of, 90
  duties of, 72-73
Medical Research Institute (Palo
  Alto), 152
Menge, W. O., 138, 140
Metabolic changes dues to alcohol,
  66-67
Methodism, attitude of, toward
  alcohol, 26
Methodist Episcopal Church,
  General Assembly of the, 45
Mice, drinking experiments on,
  345-46
Middle Ages, tavern regulation in
  the, 33-35
Military services, 358, 361
Mills, Kenneth C., 143
Mississippi, study of teenage
  drinking in, 161-64
Monopoly system of liquor sales,
  240-46
Moonshine, 12-13, 180
Morality, failure of laws to control,
  28
Murray Thematic Apperception
  Test, 196
Myerson, A., 55

Nash, Ogden, quoted, 151
National Black Caucus on
  Alcoholism, 361
National Center on Alcoholism, 112
National Clearinhouse for Alcohol
  Information, 358
National Clergy Conference on
  Alcoholism (NCCA), 56
National Council on Alcoholism,
  106, 341, 362
National Indian Board on
  Alcoholism and Drug Abuse,
  361
National Institute of Mental Health,
  325, 326, 327
  studies on drinking, 152, 156
National Institute on Alcohol Abuse
  and Alcoholism (NIAAA), 96,
  281, 325, 326, 354, 361, 362
National Prohibition Act, 297
National Spanish-speaking

Commission on Alcoholism,
  361
National Survey of Drinking
  Practices, 94-95
Navy alcoholics, 138
Netherlands, 261
New Jersey, alcohol consumption
  in, 225-27
New Mexico, 328
New York State Moreland
  Commission, 273
Nonalcholic beverages, American
  drinking of, 342-43
North American Indians, alleged
  incapacity to handle alcohol, 23
North Carolina, 329
  alcohol consumption in, 233-34
  alcohol-related auto accidents in,
  77-78
  case study of drinking in,
  177-80
  drinking laws, 114
  prohibition of liquor-by-the-drink
  in, 238
North Dakota treatment law of
  1969, 324
Norway, drinking regulations in,
  33, 34
Null hypothesis on liquor control
  laws, 272-76
Nuremburg Council of 1496, 34

Oklahoma, prohibition of liquor-
  by-the-drink in, 238
Olaf Kyrre, King of Norway, 33
"On Icebreakers" (Nash), 151
Ontario, 243, 245, 247, 248, 249, 259,
  262, 263, 279
Opium use, 188
Order of St. Christopher, 37-38
Oregon, alcohol consumption in,
  231-32
Orientals, reaction to alcohol
  among, 21

Palmer, C. E.,
  on temperance, 47
  on inebriates, 51
Pancreas, cancer of the, 77
Pancreatic fibrosis, 66

Pancreatitis, 66
Pasteur, Louis, influence of, on winemaking, 7
Pearl, Raymond, 139-40
Pedestrian deaths, 123-24
Pequignot, G., 259
Perrine, M. W., 120, 127
Pfautz, H. W., 56
Physicians, recognition of alcoholism by, 105-6
Pickett, D., 51
Plato, 36, 37
Plaut, T. F. A., 363
"Plaut Report" (Alcohol Problems), 111-12
Plutarch, 24
Pneumonia, 77
Pollack, S., on drinking drivers, 128
Popham, Robert E., 96, 217, 284, 286, 363, 374, 378
Portugal, 362
Positional asphyxia, 88
Powell, Leroy, 318, 319, 320
Powell, W. J., 68
Powell v. *Texas* (1968), history of the ruling on intoxication, 317-20
Pregnancy, effects of alcohol on, 67
Presbyterian Church, General Assembly of the, 45
Price variation, control of consumption by, 246-52, 284-89
Problem drinking
age of, 359
definition, 99, 198
motivations for, 351-53, 355-58
prevention, 111-14, 363-64
rusk factors, 360
student, 199
symptoms, 364-65
treatment, 360-62
Problem Drinking Among American Men (Cahalan & Room), 218
Professional students, drinking habits of, 185-87
Prohibition difficulties with, 377
achievements of, 49-53
as a goal of temperance societies, 47

early attempts at, 35, 295
U.S. experiment with, 27
in Virginia, 296-98
other countries and societies, 377
Prohibition Act, defeat of 1880, 49
"Proof" meaning of the term, 14-15
Psychological Abstracts, 54
Public Health Bureau, 55
Public opinion, shift in attitudes on alcohol of, 55-57

Quarterly Journal of Inebriety, on auto accidents, 117-18
Quarterly Journal of Studies on Alcohol, 54
"Quebec beer-drinker's heart," 87

Randall, C. L., 345
Reader's Guide to Periodical Literature, 55
Rechabites, prohibition of alcohol among the, 36
Reformation, 26
Religion and drinking, 26-27, 36, 153-54, 176, 179, 181
Respiratory tract, disease of the, 87-88
Revenues, alcoholic beverages, 371
Revolutionary War era, change in drinking habits in the, 43
Risks of drinking and other drug use, 188-90
Robinson v. *California* (1962), ruling on addiction, 316-19
Rogers, Will, 27
Roman, P. M., 21
Rome, drinking by women in early, 35
Room, Robin, 218, 363, 374
Ross, H. L., 133, 134
Rouse, Beatrice, A., 2, 109, 350, 365
Rubin, E., 68
Rush, Benjamin, 37, 39
on alcoholism, 43
Russia, 33, 362
Rutgers Center of Alcohol Studies, 157
Saint Boniface, 36
Saint Gall, Switzerland, 34

Saint Louis, Missouri, family studies in, 104
Saint Pachomius of Egypt, Order of, 36
Scale of Anomie, Srole's, 187, 192
Schmidt, Wolfgang, 96, 217, 284, 286, 289, 363, 365, 374, 378
Schuckit, M. A., 138
Schwan, Theodore, experiments on yeast by, 7
Scotch whisky, origins of, 11-12
Scotland, Act of 1436 in, 33
Seeley, J. R., 247, 248
Sex norms, alcoholism and, 153
Shakespeare, William, 37
Shurtleff, D., 139
Sigismund of Dietrichstein, 37
Simon, J. L., 242, 246
Skid Row, 359
Smart, R. G., 128
Society, functions of alcohol in, 153-56, 372
Social controls of liquor, 145-58
Social pressures, alcohol and, 24, 345
Social status, alcohol and, 154, 347, 359
South Carolina, prohibition of liquor-by-the-drink in, 238
South Dakota, 328
Southern California study on drinking drivers, 128
Spain, 362
Srole, L., 187, 192
Stacey, B., 166
State control of liquor outlets, 240-46
State laws on drinking, 219-38
State treatment systems, 326-30
Steiner, C., 352
Stewart, G. R., on U.S. drinking habits, 342
Straus, Robert, 167, 195, 198, 352
Stress, 191, 360
Students, drinking
attitudes toward, 171-72
blacks, 194-97
changes in patterns, 199-200
college vs. non college, 172
ethnic differences, 194-97

fraternal affiliation, 182
graduate and professional, 185-87
highschool, 159-70, 349
influences on, 175-77
junior high school, 349-50
marijuana use and, 174, 181-94
stresses, 191
undergraduate, 173, 180-84
women, 166-85, 195
Suicide, alcohol and, 78-80, 193-94
Susceptibility to alcohol, 76-80
Sweden, 258
penalties for drunken driving in, 134-35
Switzerland, closing laws in, 34

Tacitus, on Germanic drinking habits, 22
Taxation of alcohol, 247, 252-57, 370-71
Taylor, L. D., 285, 286, 287
Tci-Tsung, emperor of China, 32
Teenagers
drinking habits of, 159-73
reasons for drinking, 347-50
Temperance Manual (1836), quoted, 46
Temperance societies, 37-38, 44-49
Terris, M., on cirrhosis, 249, 288
Tongue, Archer, 2, 373
Total Abstination Union (Catholic), 48
Traffic, See Auto accidents, driving
Treatment
for problem drinkers, 360-62
recent state legislation for, 320-24
voluntary versus compulsory, 330-36
Trice, H. M., 199
Trotter, Thomas, 39
on drunkenness, 44
Tuberculosis, 77
Twenty-First Amendment, 298
Twins, rates of alcoholism in, 102
Two-Factor Index, Hollingshead's, 182
Undergraduate men, drinking habits of, 180-84
Undergraduate women, drinking habits of, 184-85

"Unexpected-death-with-fatty-liver-
syndrome," 88-89
Uniform Alcoholism and
Intoxication Treatment Act
(1972), 326, 327, 328, 331, 332,
374
United States
history of drinking in the, 39-60
per capita alcohol consumption
in the, 341-42, 362

University of North Carolina School
of Medicine, 69

Vermont study on alcohol and
highway safety, 120-22, 124.
125, 126, 128
Virginia, history of liquor
legislation in, 291-305
Vitamin B-6, absorption of, 66
Volume-variability index of

drinkers, 95

Waller, J. A., 127-28
Waller, Patricia, 62, 370
Wallgren, H., 252
Warburton, C. on liquor
consumption, 273, 274
War Prohibition Law (1919), 50
Washington state of, 328
Washington, D. C., 328, 331
Wernicke's disease, 82, 87
Wesley, John, 26
Whiskey, discovery of, 11-12
"Whiskey Rebellion" (1794), 12
White, Byron, 319
"White lightning," 12
Wilkinson, T., 112, 113
Willard, Frances, 48
Wilsnack, S. C., 369
Wilson, Woodrow, 43
Wine, 9-10

EDITORS:

John A. Ewing, M.D. is presently the director of
the Center for Alcohol Studies and professor in
the Department of Psychiatry, at the University
of North Carolina at Chapel Hill. He has published over 100 scientific papers in the medical
and psychiatric literature with many of them
focusing on alcohol and other drugs. Beatrice A.
Rouse is a research associate at the Center for
Alcohol Studies with a joint appointment in the
Department of Psychiatry at the University of
North Carolina at Chapel Hill. She has published
articles on alcohol and other drugs in such
periodicals as the *American Journal of
Psychiatry* and the *British Journal of Social
Psychiatry*.